INDIE**FONTS**

A Compendium of Digital Type from Independent Foundries

Richard Kegler
James Grieshaber
Tamye Riggs
Editors

GLOUCESTER MASSACHUSETTS

ROCKPORT PUBLISHERS

Library of Congress Control Number: 2002107002

ISBN: 1-59253-123-7

Published by
Rockport Publishers, Inc.
33 Commercial Street
Gloucester, MA 01930-5089
Phone: 978.282.9590
Fax: 978.283.2742
www.rockpub.com

Printed in China

Contents

Introduction

From the time of Johannes Gutenberg until around the mid-twentieth century, a "type foundry" was literally that: a shop that poured a molten mixture of lead, tin and antimony to cast individual letters for use by printers. This historically precise term has been retained in the digital age. Type foundry is still used to signify a maker of type—with no molten metal in sight.

Indie Fonts is a collection of over 2000 fonts from 18 of the most innovative and active independent type foundries in the field. This compilation is intended as a unique resource for graphic designers, type users and typophiles. An easy-to-use reference, this book features many hard-to-find fonts, as well as fresh type designs that haven't been over-exposed to the public. Assembling this number of typefaces in a single resource makes it truly useful for designers seeking typographic inspiration and practical information.

Each foundry has carefully chosen a selection of fonts to show from their type libraries, producing their own sections from a flexible series of pre-determined design outlines. The result is a type specimen book created with the end user in mind, and one that showcases the personality of each foundry. *Indie Fonts* will also delight those who simply appreciate type and its importance in language and communications.

The CD-ROM included with *Indie Fonts* features 33 fonts licensed for use by you, the owner of this book. The individual foundries with fonts on the CD-ROM spell out the exact terms of their respective license agreements. As with all licensed software, the re-distribution, or "sharing" of these fonts is discouraged—it is ultimately not beneficial to the designers of the typefaces. We encourage you to abide by the terms of use set forth by each foundry represented in this publication, and the rest of the talented type makers hard at work throughout the world. Support these artisans so that they may continue in their efforts to provide us with those essential tools of creativity and communications— new typefaces.

Please design safely.

The Editors

Foreword

What would knowledge and culture itself be, without the alphabet? Think, for a moment, of a world identical to the one we live in, but operating solely on the basis of verbal communication...

Adapted from a four-part editorial by Rubén Fontana, editor of *tipoGráfica* magazine, Buenos Aires, Argentina.

Writing and its formal expression, typography, drive the elementary functions of society. Like air, like water, like knowledge and ideas, typography is a social asset that equalizes opportunities among people— a real heritage of humankind.

Thus expressed, as a supreme legacy, we must bear in mind that this vital asset's only protection lies in the hands of those who take on the task of optimizing the structural details of letters: the type designer. He works on the intimacy of characters, aspects of which have been explored by so many typographers before him. He searches for the alchemy, the secret of the form, which, through the vehicle of letters, will retell man's discourse.

Although its worth first lies in how and for what it was conceived, and the reasons that contributed to its generation, in the final instance, the value of typography lies in its form. But its worth also lies in how it is used.

Linked to the chain of responsibilities entrusted to those who persevere to achieve the optimum quality of a text is the participation of other actors. The actions and intent of those who employ typefaces in their daily work, who choose the letterforms that will convey their messages, take on immeasurable importance.

It is there that the qualitative leap is needed. When knowledge of typography becomes widespread, a significant advance in design and in the quality of the message will have taken place. Knowledge, acquired and universal, creates a heritage that will undoubtedly reinterpret the medium and the culture of each environment.

It does not seem apropos in this case to call on the over-hyped "globalization." What we are talking about is the preservation of cultural habits as a fundamental means to interpret messages—to understand. Nevertheless, we do propose the socialization of this vast and historic knowledge; a search for variations of what we know, and, through learning, a discovery of what we do not know.

With letters, we learn to read; then we can understand what we read. The correct use of letters follows naturally from the primary goal: achieving literacy. In this dialogue between content and form, the letter is the vehicle that will socialize the message, and help us enhance the function of the word.

We must advance in our knowledge of typography. The optimization of the use of letters is a tool that will enable a seldom-measured level of development, that of human communications and the dissemination of information.

As members of a society perpetually in a state of crisis, it is essential that we broaden our field of knowledge. We must learn better.

- Rubén Fontana

Font Style Index

- Serif
- Sans Serif
- Script
- Display
- Non-Latin
- Ornaments

Page	Font	Page	Font	Page	Font
339	*Jillican Ultra Light Italic*	292	Maetl Light	145	MERCURY SC
339	Jillican Extra Light	292	*Maetl Light Oblique*	145	**Mercury Bold**
339	*Jillican Extra Light Italic*	292	Maetl Regular	145	**Mercury Alt. Bold**
339	Jillican Light	292	*Maetl Oblique*	145	***Mercury Bold Italic***
339	*Jillican Light Italic*	292	**Maetl Bold**	145	***Mercury Alt. Bold Italic***
339	Jillican Regular	292	***Maetl Bold Oblique***	145	**MERCURY BOLD SC**
339	*Jillican Italic*	292	**Maetl Extra Bold**	95	**Mingler Nipsy**
339	**Jillican Bold**	292	***Maetl Extra Bold Ob***	95	**Mingler Ritzy**
339	***Jillican Bold Italic***	141	Malmö Sans Regular	332	Modern Grotesque Thin
339	**Jillican Heavy**	141	*Malmö Sans Oblique*	332	*Modern Grotesque Thin*
209	Johnston Underground Reg	141	tjastckeactty Malmö Sans Ligatures & Alterna	332	MODERN GROTESQUE THIN
209	**JOHNSTON UNDERGROU**	141	MALMÖ SANS SC	332	*MODERN GROTESQUE THIN*
291	**Jute Regular**	141	**Malmö Sans Bold**	333	Modern Grotesque Ligh
291	**Jute Semi Bold**	141	***Malmö Sans Bold Oblique***	333	*Modern Grotesque Ligh*
291	**Jute Bold**	141	**MALMÖ SANS HEADLINE**	333	MODERN GROTESQUE LIGH
150	**Ketchupa Regular**	314	**TX Manifesto**	333	*MODERN GROTESQUE LIGH*
150	***Ketchupa Oblique***	314	***TX Manifesto Slant***	334	Modern Grotesque Reg
150	**KETCHUPA SC**	315	**TX Manifesto Stout**	334	*Modern Grotesque Reg*
246	**Leyden Black Sans**	292	mechanical light	334	MODERN GROTESQUE REG
114	Lionel Text Steam	292	*mechanical light obliq*	334	*MODERN GROTESQUE REG*
114	Lionel Text Genuine	292	mechanical regular	335	Modern Grotesque Bold
114	**Lionel Text Diesel**	292	*mechanical oblique*	335	*Modern Grotesque Bold*
94	**Liquorstore**	292	**mechanical bold**	335	MODERN GROTESQUE BOL
94	**LIQUORSTORE Jazz**	292	***mechanical bold obliq***	335	*MODERN GROTESQUE BOL*
304	TX Lithium Light Roman	292	**mechanical extra bo**	167	Modus Light
304	*TX Lithium Light Italic*	292	***mechanical bold obliq***	167	Modus Regular
304	**TX Lithium Regular**	292	**mechanical black**	167	Modus Semibold
304	***TX Lithium Italic***	292	***mechanical black obl***	167	**Modus Bold**
304	**TX Lithium Bold**	145	Mercury Regular	167	**Modus Extra Bold**
304	***TX Lithium Bold Italic***	145	Mercury Alternative	150	**Mustardo Regular**
291	Lunarmod Regular	145	*Mercury Italic*	150	***Mustardo Oblique***
291	Lunarmod *Oblique*	145	*Mercury Alt. Italic*	150	**MUSTARDO SC**

14

Script

114	Al's Motor-Inn
106	Beer Wip
222	Calligraphica Regular
222	Calligraphica Italic
222	Calligraphica Regular SX
222	Calligraphica Italic SX
222	Calligraphica Regular LX
222	Calligraphica Italic LX
200	Cezanne Regular
88	Chunder
108	Continental Railway
202	Da Vinci Forward
202	Da Vinci Backward
223	Dearest Script
223	Dearest Swash
112	Doggie Bag Script
116	El Ranchero
240	Escorial Script Classic
240	Escorial Script Concise
240	Escorial Minuscule Swash Alts : a
208	Hopper Edward
208	Hopper Josephine
117	International Palr
245	Karolin Fraktur
245	KAROLIN VERSA
210	kells round
112	Kitchenette
224	LaDanse
117	Lamplighter Script
117	Lamplighter Script Marquee
118	Leisure Script

118	Leisure Script Marquee
224	Mercator Regular
224	MERCATOR SWASH
211	Michelangelo Regular
119	Mister Television
167	Mockingbird
211	Monet Impressionist
211	Monet Regular
113	Motorcar Atlas
167	Naomi
310	TX NineVolt
310	TX NineBolt
107	Permanent Waves
107	Permanent Waves Exp
115	Refreshment Stand
295	Retron Regular
295	Retron Oblique
211	Rodin Regular
110	Singlesville Script
98	Sister Frisky
115	Starlight Hotel
111	stiletto
218	Vincent Regular

Display

285	6x7oct Extra Light
285	6x7oct Extra Light Al
285	6x7oct Light
285	6x7oct Light Alterna
285	6x7oct Regular
285	6x7oct Alternate
285	6x7oct Bold
285	6x7oct Bold Alternat

285	6x7oct Extra Bold
285	6x7oct Extra Bold Alt
285	6x7oct Black
285	6x7oct Black Alterna
159	3C79 QUEEN
33	Acolyte [Æ]
195	ACROPOLIS NOW
159	Adore Light M
159	Adore Light C
159	ADORE LIGHT C
159	Adore Light M
159	Adore Normal
159	Adore Normal
159	ADORE NORMAL
159	Adore Normal
159	Adore Bold Mc
159	Adore Bold Ob
159	Adore BOLD Mi
221	Akebono Regular
221	Akebono Italic
221	Akebono Alternate
195	Albers 1
195	Albers 2
195	Albers 3
51	Alien Argonaut AOE
285	amber angled
285	amber round
285	amber square
221	AMBIENT
110	AMERICAN CHEESE
114	AMERICAN HIGHWA
159	AMP LIGHT

119	Starburst Lanes Twinkle
64	Stingwire AOE
113	Stovetop
297	subito extra light
297	subito extra light oblique
297	subito light
297	subito light oblique
297	subito regular
297	subito oblique
297	subito bold
297	subito bold oblique
297	subito extra bold
297	subito extra bold oblique
297	subito black
297	subito black oblique
171	Sucubus evil
171	Sucubus out.
353	Sui Generis Deluxe Outl
99	Sunshine
152	Super Normal
152	Super duper
152	Super Sonic
171	Swashbuckler
111	SWINGER!
64	Synchronous AOE - Reg
64	Synchronous AOE - Obl
99	Tabitha
64	TANNARIN AOE - REGOL
64	TANNARIN AOE - OBLIQU
64	TAPEHEAD AOE
107	TAYLORS
340	Telidon Condensed Regular

340	Telidon Condensed Regular Itali
340	Telidon Condensed Bold
340	Telidon Condensed Bold Italic
340	Telidon Condensed Heavy
340	Telidon Condensed Heavy Italic
340	Telidon Regular
340	Telidon Regular Italic
340	Telidon Bold
340	Telidon Bold Italic
340	Telidon Heavy
340	Telidon Heavy Italic
340	Telidon Ex
340	Telidon Ex
340	Telidon Ex
340	Telidon Ex
340	Telidon Ex
340	Telidon Ex
341	Telidon Ink Condensed Regular
341	Telidon Ink Condensed Regular I
341	Telidon Ink Condensed Bold
341	Telidon Ink Condensed Bold Ital
341	Telidon Ink Condensed Heavy
341	Telidon Ink Condensed Heavy Ita
341	Telidon Ink Regular
341	Telidon Ink Regular Ital
341	Telidon Ink Bold
341	Telidon Ink Bold Italic
341	Telidon Ink Heavy
341	Telidon Ink Heavy Italic
340	Telidon Inl
340	Telidon Inl
340	Telidon Inl

340	Telidon Inl
341	Telidon Inl
341	Telidon Inl
205	FLLW TERRACOTTA REGULAR
205	FLLW TERRACOTTA ALTERNATES
146	THEODOR REGULAR
146	THEODOR OBLITALIQUE
171	thomas light
171	thomas light Oblique
171	thomas Extra Black
171	thomas Extra Black I
307	TX Tiny Tin Gimpy
307	TX Tiny Tin Stout
172	tooth 31 medium
172	tooth 31 shadow
216	Toy Box Regular
216	TOYBOX BLOCKS
216	TOYBOX BLOCKS
216	TOYBOX BLOCKS
216	TOYBOX BLOCKS
263	TRILLIUM ROTA
263	TRILLIUM ROTA
263	TRILLIUM ROTA
263	TRILLIUM ROTA
297	Trisect Thin
297	Trisect extra light
297	Trisect light
297	Trisect regular
297	Trisect semi bold
297	Trisect bold
297	Trisect extra bold
297	Trisect black

263	TRIUMPHALIS CAPS	65	Uglystick AOE	38	Verve Multiple Master [FE]
280	Trumen	148	Ultura Light	172	Vestige Regular
280	Trumen Italic	148	Ultura Light Italic	172	Vestige Oblique
280	Trumen Outl	148	Ultura Medium	217	VICTORIAN GOTHI
280	Trumen Outl	148	Ultura Medium Italic	217	Victorian Swash
280	Trumen Outl	148	Ultura Heavy	227	Vidro
280	Trumen Outl	148	Ultura Heavy Italic	217	VIENNA REGULAR
172	TRUTH OF Angel	99	Uncle Stinky	217	VIENNA ROUND
172	TRUTH OF STARS	99	Uncle Stinky Bold	217	ViENNA BLACK
297	Tryptomene Light	172	Underscore	173	Virtual
297	Tryptomene Light Oblique	172	Usher 1 Light	134	Viscosity Interior
297	Tryptomene Regular	172	Usher 1 Bold	134	Viscosity Regular
297	Tryptomene Oblique	172	Usher 2 Ultra Dingbats	134	Viscosity Inline
297	Tryptomene Bold	172	Usher 2 Ultra	263	VM74 Regular
297	Tryptomene Bold Oblique	172	Usher 2 Versal	263	VM74 Irregular
297	Tryptomene Extra Bold	65	Vanguard III AOE - Regula	115	VOLCANO KING
297	Tryptomene Extra Bold Ol	65	Vanguard III AOE - Italic	298	Vortex Light
297	Tryptomene Black	65	Vanguard III AOE - Bold	298	Vortex Light Obliquo
297	Tryptomene Black Obliq	65	Vanguard III AOE - Bold It	298	Vortex Regular
297	Twincities Light	119	VEGAS CARAVAN	298	Vortex Obliquo
297	Twincities Light Oblique	38	Verve Extralight [FE]	298	Vortex Bold
297	Twincities Regular	38	Verve Extralight Alt [FE]	298	Vortex Bold Obliquo
297	Twincities Oblique	39	Verve Light [FE]	298	Vortex Extra Bold
297	Twincities Bold	39	Verve Light Alt [FE]	298	Vortex Extra Bold Obli
297	Twincities Bold Oblique	39	Verve Regular [FE]	298	Vortex Black
297	Twincities Extra Bold	39	Verve Regular Alt [FE]	298	Vortex Extra Bold Obli
297	Twincities Extra Bold Obliq	40	Verve Semibold [FE]	173	Vreehend
281	Two Beers Free	40	Verve Semibold Alt [FE]	173	WACKELKONTAKT
155	UDO REGULAR	40	Verve Bold [FE]	218	Way out West Regular
155	udo leaned	40	Verve Bold Alt [FE]	218	Way out West Slim
155	UDO WIDE	41	Verve Black [FE]	173	Wet
155	UDO WIDE Leaned	41	Verve Black Alt [FE]	152	whatnot regular

152	whotnot mix
152	whotnot wide
152	whotnot wide mix
136	Whiplash Regular
136	Whiplash Regular Mon
136	Whiplash Lineola
173	Wild Toxia Regular
173	Wild Toxia Italic
173	Wild Toxia Bold
173	Wild Toxia Bold Italic
218	WOODCUT
299	xerxes Light
299	xerxes Light alternate
299	xerxes Light oblique
299	xerxes Light alternate ob
299	xerxes Regular Low
299	xerxes Regular Low obli
299	xerxes Regular mid
299	xerxes Regular mid obli
299	xerxes Regular High
299	xerxes Regular High obl
107	Yarn Sale
299	Yeti Light
299	Yeti Light Oblique
299	Yeti Regular
299	Yeti Oblique
299	Yeti Bold
299	Yeti Bold Oblique
299	Yeti Extra Bold
299	Yeti Extra Bold Oblique
299	Yeti Black
299	Yeti Black Oblique

65	Youngitch AOE
173	Zatrulla
299	ZEBRAFLESH REGULAR
299	ZEBRAFLESH BOLD
350	Zekton Deluxe Light Condensed
350	Zekton Deluxe Light Condensed Italic
350	Zekton Deluxe Regular Condensed
350	Zekton Deluxe Regular Condensed Italic
350	Zekton Deluxe Bold Condensed
350	Zekton Deluxe Bold Condensed Italic
350	Zekton Deluxe Heavy Condensed
350	Zekton Deluxe Heavy Condensed Italic
350	Zekton Deluxe Light
350	Zekton Deluxe Light Italic
350	Zekton Deluxe Regular
350	Zekton Deluxe Regular Italic
350	Zekton Deluxe Bold
350	Zekton Deluxe Bold Italic
350	Zekton Deluxe Heavy
350	Zekton Deluxe Heavy Italic
350	Zekton Deluxe Lig
350	Zekton Deluxe Light
350	Zekton Deluxe Re
350	Zekton Deluxe Regu
350	Zekton Deluxe Bol
350	Zekton Deluxe Bold
350	Zekton Deluxe Hea
350	Zekton Deluxe Heav
350	Zekton Delu
350	Zekton Delux
350	Zekton Delu
350	Zekton Delux

350	Zekton Delu
350	Zekton Delux
350	Zekton Delu
350	Zekton Delux
350	Zekton Deluxe Ink
350	Zekton Deluxe Video
350	Zekton Deluxe Wave
350	Zekton Deluxe Outline
65	ZenoPotion AOE
227	Zephyr Regular
227	Zephyr Openface
111	ZIG ZAP
113	¡WARNING!

Non-latin

195	Acropolis Then	ΑΨΡΟΠΟΛΙΣ THEN
201	Constructivist Cyrillic	ЦОНСТРУЦТИВИ
142	Filt Greek	ΔΩΠΕΠΙΔΩΠΕΠ
207	Hieroglyphics Phonetic	
207	Hieroglyphics Decorative	
207	Hieroglyphics Cartouche	
82	Wilson Greek Ligatures	Φιλσον Γρεεκ Γκεθσ
82	Wilson Greek	Φιλσον Γρεεκ Γκεθσ Λιγατι

Ornaments

195	Acropolis Extras	
33	American Spirit Æ	
234	Aquamarine Titling Cameo	
196	Art Deco Extras	
197	Art Nouveau Extras	
198	Arts and Crafts Ornaments	
198	Arts and Crafts Ornaments 2	
160	Astound Dings	
199	Atomica	

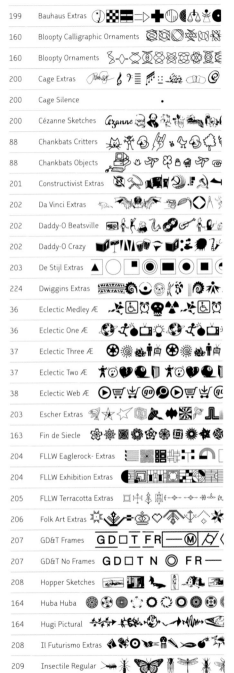

199	Bauhaus Extras	209	Insectile Solid	132	RoarShock One
160	Bloopty Calligraphic Ornaments	209	Johnston Underground Extras	132	RoarShock Two
160	Bloopty Ornaments	210	Kells Extras	132	RoarShock Three
200	Cage Extras	210	Koch Signs 1	132	RoarShock Four
200	Cage Silence	210	Koch Signs 2	132	RoarShock Five
200	Cézanne Sketches	210	Koch Signs 3	132	RoarShock Six
88	Chankbats Critters	210	Koch Signs 4	144	Robotron Dingbats
88	Chankbats Objects	210	Koch Signs 5	211	Rodin Extras
201	Constructivist Extras	177	LettError Rules	190	Salmiak Catchwords
202	Da Vinci Extras	166	Martian Telex Grid	171	Storyboard One
202	Daddy-O Beatsville	166	Martian Telex Things	171	Storyboard Two
202	Daddy-O Crazy	151	Mayo DingBorders	226	Telegdi Dings
203	De Stijl Extras	151	Mayo Dingbats One	191	ThePrintedWord
224	Dwiggins Extras	151	Mayo Dingbats Two	191	TheWrittenWord
36	Eclectic Medley Æ	166	Media Icons	303	Toolshop
36	Eclectic One Æ	211	Michelangelo Extras	216	Toy Box Animals
37	Eclectic Three Æ	154	Mini-Dingbats	172	Usher 2 Dingbats
37	Eclectic Two Æ	211	Monet Sketches	217	Victorian Ornaments One
38	Eclectic Web Æ	212	Morris Ornaments	217	Victorian Ornaments Two
203	Escher Extras	213	Parrish Extras	217	Vienna Extras
163	Fin de Siecle	213	Petroglyphs African	218	Vincent Extras
204	FLLW Eaglerock- Extras	213	Petroglyphs Australian	218	Way out West Critters
204	FLLW Exhibition Extras	213	Petroglyphs European		
205	FLLW Terracotta Extras	213	Petroglyphs North American		
206	Folk Art Extras	214	Pop Art Extras		
207	GD&T Frames	215	Posada Extras		
207	GD&T No Frames	214	Prehistoric Pals		
208	Hopper Sketches	215	Preissig Extras		
164	Huba Huba	294	Pyrotechnics1 Icons1		
164	Hugi Pictural	294	Pyrotechnics1 Icons2		
208	Il Futurismo Extras	169	Ravine- Millharrow Knob		
209	Insectile Regular	169	Renfield's Lunch		

A NEW NAME FROM AN OLD FRIEND. FONTS EXCLUSIVELY
DESIGNED BY BRIAN SOOY, WITH THE BEST YET TO COME.
FONTS THAT PROVIDE SOLUTIONS TO DESIGN PROBLEMS.
ORIGINAL DESIGNS, EXQUISITELY KERNED AND SPACED.
MULTIPLE MASTERS, DINGBAT, TEXT AND DISPLAY FONTS.

Altered Ego Fonts

PREVIEW ONLINE AT WWW.ALTEREDEGOFONTS.COM
CALL US FOR TYPOGRAPHIC COMMISSIONS AND CONSULTING.

Mac | PC
Type One | TrueType | OpenType
Adobe Standard with €

http://www.alteredegofonts.com
info@alteredegofonts.com
440.322.5142 Telephone
1.877.HEY.SOOY Toll-Free

AaBbCcDdEeFfGgHhIiJjKkLlMmNnOoPpQqRrSsTtUuUu
WwXxYyZz[0123456789]£¥¢£ßñ¶ß§?ÆæŒœ
ÄäÅåÃāÃãÃãÃãÅåÉéÈèËëĒēÙùÚúÜüŪūÌìÍíÏïĪīŸÿ
ÒòÓóÖöŌōθθ«"#&*''¿?!¡:;{|}@‡†¢£"»Æ
Ʒ

Tiger, Tiger, burning bright, in the forests of the night, what immortal
hand or eye could frame thy fearful symmetry? (William Blake)
To see a world in a grain of sand, and a heaven in a wildflower,
to hold infinity in the palm of your hand, and eternity in an hour.

Acolyte™ Æ [STF]

Brian Sooy
1998

An elegantly refined typeface with a subtle wedge serif, the character shapes of Acolyte set a rhythm of light and dark like windows in a cathedral. Acolyte will illuminate your designs with a display typeface reminiscent of European twentieth-century letterforms. Its distinctive letterforms are slightly chiseled and angular with curves in just the right places.

Mac | PC
Type One | TrueType | OpenType
Adobe Standard with €

American Spirit™ STF [Æ]

Brian Sooy
2001

American Spirit™ STF is a glorious collection of contemporary patriotic symbols: US Flags (traditional and contemporary), a variety of stars, eagles, torches, and combinations of them all. Designed for print and web, this collection is useful for embellishing your designs with a subtle (or not-so-subtle) patriotic touch.

The flags have been designed for easy ungrouping in a drawing program, in order to colorize the union and stripes. And as a special feature, American Spirit™ splits the flags into two characters (the union and the stripes) that can be separately colored and will kern together based on the character chosen.

Suggestions for doing this are included in every package. This versatile collection also contains a special contemporary version of the US Flag, with rounded corners on the union and stripes, and a five-pointed asterisk-like shape as the stars. (This allows the stars to appear as stars at smaller sizes.)

Mac | PC
Type One | TrueType | OpenType

Arkeo™ Æ C

Brian Sooy
2002

Arkeo has been designed specifically as a 10-point bitmap font in three widths. Highly legible both on-screen and in print applications, it is ideal for many uses. It contains a hand-edited 10-point bitmap, and matching outline for use in all applications.

Onscreen this font should be used in 10-point size increments to avoid antialiasing.

Arkeo C is the most condensed version of the series, with a distinctive bitmap look. The semi-serif nature of the design is distinctive and aids in its legibility.

Mac | PC
Arkeo C-M-X Family
Type One | TrueType | OpenType
Adobe Standard with €

AaBbCcDdEeFfGgHhIiJjKkLlMmNnOoPpQ
qRrSsTtUuVvWwXxYyZz[01234567890]€¥¢
£fifl¶¶ß§?ÆæŒœÄäÅåÀàÃãÂâÁáÉéÈèËëÊê
êÙùÚúÜüÛûÎîÌìÍíÏïÎîŸŷÒòÓóÖöÔôØøø«''#§×''
¿?!¡:;{|}@†‡¢£''» Æ

Tiger, Tiger, burning bright, in the forests of the night,
what immortal hand or eye could frame thy fearful symmetry?
To see a world in a grain of sand, and a heaven in a wildflower,
to hold infinity in the palm of your hand, and eternity in an hour.

(William Blake)

Arkeo™ Æ M

Brian Sooy
2002

Arkeo has been designed specifically as a 10-point bitmap font in three widths. Highly legible both on-screen and in print applications, it is ideal for many uses. It contains a hand-edited 10-point bitmap, and matching outline for use in all applications.

Onscreen this font should be used in 10-point size increments to avoid antialiasing.

Arkeo M is the normal width version of the series, with a distinctive bitmap look. The semi-serif nature of the design is distinctive and aids in its legibility.

Mac | PC
Arkeo C-M-X Family
Type One | TrueType | OpenType
Adobe Standard with €

AaBbCcDdEeFfGgHhIiJjKkLlMmNnOoP
pQqRrSsTtUuVvWwXxYyZz[01234567
890]€¥¢£fifl¶¶ß§?ÆæŒœÄäÅåÀàÃãÂâ
ÁáÉéÈèËëÊêÙùÚúÜüÛûÎîÌìÍíÏïŸŷÒòÓó
ÖöÔôØøø«''#§×''¿?!¡:;{|}@†‡¢£''» Æ

Tiger, Tiger, burning bright, in the forests of the night,
what immortal hand or eye could frame thy fearful symmetry?
To see a world in a grain of sand, and a heaven in a wildflower,
to hold infinity in the palm of your hand, and eternity in an hour.

(William Blake)

34   info@alteredegofonts.com

AaBbCcDdEeFfGgHhIiJjKkLlMm
NnOoPpQqRrSsTtUuVvWwXxYy
Zz[01234567890]€¥¢£fifl¶ß§?Æ
æŒœÄäÅåÀàÃãÂâÁáÉéÈèËëÊ
ŸÿØø«"#§*"'¿?!¡:;[]@‡†¢£"'» Æ

Tiger, Tiger, burning bright, in the forests of the night,
what immortal hand or eye could frame thy fearful symmetry?
To see a world in a grain of sand, and a heaven in a wildflower,
to hold infinity in the palm of your hand, and eternity in an hour.

Arkeo™ ÆX

Brian Sooy
2002

Arkeo has been designed specifically
as a 10-point bitmap font in three
widths. Highly legible both on-screen
and in print applications, it is ideal for
many uses. It contains a hand-edited
10-point bitmap, and matching outline
for use in all applications.

Onscreen this font should be used in
10-point size increments to avoid
antialiasing.

Arkeo X is the widest version of the
series, with a distinctive bitmap look.
The semi-serif nature of the design is
distinctive and aids in its legibility.

Mac | PC
Arkeo C-M-X Family
Type One | TrueType | OpenType
Adobe Standard with €

Altered Ego

AaBbCcDdEeFfGgHhIiJjKkLlMmNnOoPpQqRrSsT
tUuVvWwXxYyZz[01234567890]€¥¢£fifl¶ß§?Ææ
ŒœÄäÅåÀàÃãÂâÁáÉéÈèËëÊêÙùÚúÜüÛûÌìÍíÏïÎîŸÿ
ÔôÓóÖöÕõÔôØø«"#§*''¿!¡:;{|}@‡†¢£"'» Æ

Tiger, Tiger, burning bright, in the forests of the night, what immortal hand or eye could frame thy fearful symmetry?
To see a world in a grain of sand, and a heaven in a wildflower,
to hold infinity in the palm of your hand, and eternity in an hour. [William Blake]

Chevron™ STF [Æ]

Brian Sooy
1993

For that tight fit, STF Chevron is perfect. An ultra-condensed display font,
with a complete character set. The
name? The shapes of the serifs reflect
the chevron serif shape. With some art
deco overtones, try Chevron in places
that you might want a simple art deco
typeface. How should you use it? It's
perfect for posters, packaging and
advertising, CD covers and publications. Exquisitely kerned, Chevron will
be one of your favorite faces for tall
copy that needs to get noticed. It's
really ideal for calendars, when you
want big numbers without losing space
for writing in the date fields.

Mac | PC
Type One | TrueType | OpenType
Adobe Standard with €

Eclectic Medley STF [Æ]

Brian Sooy
1996

STF Eclectic Medley is the budget-conscious answer to your dingbat blues! This "best of" collection from the Eclectic One, Two and Three fonts is the ultimate grab-bag dingbat resource.

The Eclectic family is legendary, with a cult-like following among the initiated. You'll find yourself using Eclectic Medley almost daily to add spice to your otherwise sans-serif typographic existence.

This font is essentially a soap opera of typographic image elements, created for projects when I couldn't find the "thingbat" I needed. More of a collection of illustrations, there are many characters that connect to form patterns, and of course, it's like a utility knife for the creative community.

Mac | PC
Type One | TrueType | OpenType

Eclectic Medley Features "combs" that allow for easy creation of forms and registration cards:

Name:
Name:
Name:
Name:
Name:

Eclectic One™ STF [Æ]

Brian Sooy
1994

STF Eclectic One is a visual cornucopia of symbols, like the junk drawer in your kitchen. Stuff you'll need someday for a graphic element, bullet or dingbat application. Perfect for website icons! The Eclectic family is legendary, with a cult-like following among the initiated. As one of the first dingbat fonts available on the web, it gained popularly after its design in the early 1990s. With more than 150 characters in the complete set, you'll find yourself using Eclectic One almost daily to add spice to your otherwise sans-serif typographic existence.

One reviewer proclaims "for whatever you do, Eclectic One is an excellent dingbat source."

Mac | PC
Type One | TrueType | OpenType

Eclectic Two STF [Æ]

Brian Sooy
1995

STF Eclectic Two contains more of the useful and the sublime. Alarm clock time icons and many characters that connect add extra usefulness to this dingbat font. Stuff you'll need someday for a graphic element, bullet or dingbat application. Perfect for website icons!

Mac | PC
Type One | TrueType | OpenType

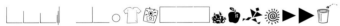

Eclectic Three STF [Æ]

Brian Sooy
1996

Eclectic Three contains dingbats and a special set of glyphs that make it simple and easy to create registration and fill-in forms for print materials. Create rules with hash lines, fill-in boxes and many other variations. Also includes handicapped, recycled and arrow right/left symbols.

The Eclectic family is legendary, with a cult-like following among the initiated. With more than 100 characters in the complete set, you'll find yourself using Eclectic Three almost daily to add spice to your otherwise sans-serif typographic existence.

Mac | PC
Type One | TrueType | OpenType

Eclectic Web STF [Æ]

Brian Sooy
1998

STF Eclectic Web is the ultimate web design dingbat tool—with 80 icons designed for creating ecommerce, navigation and interface designs.

Use it as a starting point in your favorite vector program, or use the icons as is—they are optimized for sizes down to 20 point and antialias beautifully in all of the major applications (any smaller than that and you're on your own).

Shopping carts, directional arrows, buttons galore! It's like a piñata in font format, surprises for everyone! This font includes: a new button, order, buy, and close buttons, home, security, email, search and a host of other icons and image to make designing your next website a breeze!

Mac | PC
Type One | TrueType | OpenType

The toolkit for the new economy.ˢᴹ

Verve™ XLight STF [Æ]

Brian Sooy
1998

Called by some the "Archetype of the millennium," Verve is a seven-weight typeface family. It features a complete Adobe character set with kerning and fit to match. The alternate characters offer some variations on s, f, h, j, k, S, T, Y and others, plus this font has the Euro symbol. Verve is the fourth in an ongoing series of condensed typefaces that I've been designing since 1989. My concept was to create an elegant condensed typeface that would be a "typeface for the millennium" in style and functionality.

There's the challenge of creating a rich and interesting typeface with an austerity of line and elegance of form. I'm a minimalist by nature, but I wanted Verve to have a sensuous feel in certain respects, yet have that sensuality balanced by the uniformity of the uniform character widths. Perfect for book covers, CD packaging, club flyers, retail packaging (especially bottles!), identity design and multimedia.

Mac | PC
Multiple Master
7-weight Family
Type One | TrueType | OpenType
Adobe Standard with €

AaBbCcDdEeffFGgHhIiJjKkLlMmNnOoPpQqRrSsTtUuVvWwXxYyZz[0123456789]€¥¢£Çfifl¶ßS§&*?!:;@¢£ Æ

AaBbCcDdEeffFGgHhIiJjKkLlMmNnOoPpQqRrSsTtUuVvWwXxYyZz[0123456789]€¥¢£Çfifl¶ßS§&*?!:;@¢£ Æ Alternate

Tiger, Tiger, burning bright, in the forests of the night,

what immortal hand or eye could frame thy fearful symmetry?

To see a world in a grain of sand, and a heaven in a wildflower,

to hold infinity in the palm of your hand, and eternity in an hour.

info@alteredegofonts.com

AaBbCcDdEeffGgHhliJjKkLlMmNnOoPpQqRrSsTtUuUuWwXxY
yZz[0123456789]€¥¢£fifl¶ß$&*?!:;@¢£ Æ

AaBbCcDdEeffGgHhliJjKkLlMmNnOoPpQqRrSsTtUuUuWwXx
YyZz[0123456789]€¥¢£fifl¶ß$&*?!:;@¢£ Æ Alternate

Tiger, Tiger, burning bright, in the forests of the night,

what immortal hand or eye could frame thy fearful symmetry?

To see a world in a grain of sand, and a heaven in a wildflower,

to hold infinity in the palm of your hand, and eternity in an hour.

AaBbCcDdEeffGgHhliJjKkLlMmNnOoPpQqRrSsTtUuUuWw
XxYyZz[0123456789]€¥¢£fifl¶ß$&*?!:;@¢£ Æ

AaBbCcDdEeffGgHhliJjKkLlMmNnOoPpQqRrSsTtUuUuWw
XxYyZz€¥¢£fifl¶ß$&*?!:;@¢£ Æ Alternate

Tiger, Tiger, burning bright, in the forests of the night,

what immortal hand or eye could frame thy fearful symmetry?

To see a world in a grain of sand, and a heaven in a wildflower,

to hold infinity in the palm of your hand, and eternity in an hour.

Verve™ Light STF [Æ]

Brian Sooy
1998

Called by some the "Archetype of the millennium," Verve is a seven-weight typeface family. It features a complete Adobe character set with kerning and fit to match. The alternate characters offer some variations on s, f, h, j, k, S, T, Y and others, plus this font has the Euro symbol. Verve is the fourth in an ongoing series of condensed typefaces that I've been designing since 1989. My concept was to create an elegant condensed typeface that would be a "typeface for the millennium" in style and functionality.

There's the challenge of creating a rich and interesting typeface with an austerity of line and elegance of form. I'm a minimalist by nature, but I wanted Verve to have a sensuous feel in certain respects, yet have that sensuality balanced by the uniformity of the uniform character widths. Perfect for book covers, CD packaging, club flyers, retail packaging (especially bottles!), identity design and multimedia.

Mac | PC
Multiple Master
7-weight Family
Type One | TrueType | OpenType
Adobe Standard with €

Verve™ Regular STF [Æ]

Brian Sooy
1998

Mac | PC
Multiple Master
7-weight Family
Type One | TrueType | OpenType
Adobe Standard with €

Brian Sooy
1998

Called by some the "Archetype of the millennium," Verve is a seven-weight typeface family. It features a complete Adobe character set with kerning and fit to match. The alternate characters offer some variations on s, f, h, j, k, S, T, Y and others, plus this font has the Euro symbol. Verve is the fourth in an ongoing series of condensed typefaces that I've been designing since 1989. My concept was to create an elegant condensed typeface that would be a "typeface for the millennium" in style and functionality.

There's the challenge of creating a rich and interesting typeface with an austerity of line and elegance of form. I'm a minimalist by nature, but I wanted Verve to have a sensuous feel in certain respects, yet have that sensuality balanced by the uniformity of the uniform character widths. Perfect for book covers, CD packaging, club flyers, retail packaging (especially bottles!), identity design and multimedia.

Mac | PC
Multiple Master
7-weight Family
Type One | TrueType | OpenType
Adobe Standard with €

AaBbCcDdEeffGgHhIiJjKkLlMmNnOoPpQqRrSsTtUuUvW wXxYyZz[0123456789]€¥¢£fifl¶ß§&*?!:;@¢£ Æ

AaBbCcDdEeffGgHhIiJjKkLlMmNnOoPpQqRrSsTtUuUv WwXxYyZz€¥¢£fifl¶ß§&*?!:;@¢£ Æ Alternate

Tiger, Tiger, burning bright, in the forests of the night,

what immortal hand or eye could frame thy fearful symmetry?

To see a world in a grain of sand, and a heaven in a wildflower,

to hold infinity in the palm of your hand, and eternity in an hour.

Brian Sooy
1998

Mac | PC
Multiple Master
7-weight Family
Type One | TrueType | OpenType
Adobe Standard with €

AaBbCcDdEeffGgHhIiJjKkLlMmNnOoPpQqRrSsTtUuU vWwXxYyZz[0123456789]€¥¢£fifl§&*?!@ Æ

AaBbCcDdEeffGgHhIiJjKkLlMmNnOoPpQqRrSsTtUu UvWwXxYyZz€¥¢£fifl¶ß@¢£ Æ Alternate

Tiger, Tiger, burning bright, in the forests of the night,

what immortal hand or eye could frame thy fearful symmetry?

To see a world in a grain of sand, and a heaven in a wildflower,

to hold infinity in the palm of your hand, and eternity in an hour.

info@alteredegofonts.com

AaBbCcDdEeffGgHhIiJjKkLIMmNnOoPpQqRrSsTtU
uUuWwXxYyZz[01234567890]€¥¢£&*$45.00US
AaBbCcDdEeffGgHhIiJjKkLIMmNnOoPpQqRrSsTtU
uUuWwXxYyZzε¥¢£fifl¶ß$&*@¢£ Æ Alternate

Tiger, Tiger, burning bright, in the forests of the night,

what immortal hand or eye could frame thy fearful symmetry?

To see a world in a grain of sand, and a heaven in a wildflower,

to hold infinity in the palm of your hand, and eternity in an hour.

AaBbCcDdEeffGgHhIiJjKkLIMmNnOoPpQqRrSsTt
UuUuWwXxYyZz[01234567890]€¥¢£!$45.00US
AaBbCcDdEeffGgHhIiJjKkLIMmNnOoPpQqRrSsT
tUuUuWwXxYyZzε¥¢£fifl¶ß Æ Alternate

Tiger, Tiger, burning bright, in the forests of the night,

what immortal hand or eye could frame thy fearful symmetry?

To see a world in a grain of sand, and a heaven in a wildflower,

to hold infinity in the palm of your hand, and eternity in an hour.

Verve™ Black STF [Æ]

Brian Sooy
1998

Called by some the "Archetype of the millennium," Verve is a seven-weight typeface family. It features a complete Adobe character set with kerning and fit to match. The alternate characters offer some variations on s, f, h, j, k, S, T, Y and others, plus this font has the Euro symbol. Verve is the fourth in an ongoing series of condensed typefaces that I've been designing since 1989. My concept was to create an elegant condensed typeface that would be a "typeface for the millennium" in style and functionality.

There's the challenge of creating a rich and interesting typeface with an austerity of line and elegance of form. I'm a minimalist by nature, but I wanted Verve to have a sensuous feel in certain respects, yet have that sensuality balanced by the uniformity of the uniform character widths. Perfect for book covers, CD packaging, club flyers, retail packaging (especially bottles!), identity design and multimedia.

Mac | PC
Multiple Master
7-weight Family
Type One | TrueType | OpenType
Adobe Standard with €

Verve™ ExtraBlack STF

Brian Sooy
1998

Mac | PC
Multiple Master
7-weight Family
Type One | TrueType | OpenType
Adobe Standard with €

Altered Ego

Veritas™ STF [Æ]

Brian Sooy
1995

STF Veritas is a four-weight serif text family. It is a narrow-width typeface, with a taller x-height than Times Roman for added legibility, but maintains a similar character count in text. It is a typeface designed for book, publication, newspaper (anywhere where narrow columns are necessary) and identity design. It is exquisitely spaced and kerned, even in European characters.

Mac | PC
4-weight Family
Veritas One (Roman, Italic, Bold, BoldItalic)
Veritas Two (Semibold, SB Italic, Black, Black Italic)
Unimaster | Multiple Master
Type One | TrueType | OpenType
Adobe Standard with €

AaBbCcDdEeFfGgHhIiJjKkLlMmNnOoPpQqRrSs
TtUuVvWwXxYyZz[01234567890]€¥¢£fifl¶ß§?Æ
æŒœÄäÅåÀàÃãÂâÁáÉéÈèËëÊêÙùÚúÜüÛûÌìÍíÏïÎî
ŸÿÒòÓóÖöÔôØø«"#&*"¿?!i:;{ǀ}@‡†¢£"»

Tiger, Tiger, burning bright,
in the forests of the night,
what immortal hand or eye could
frame thy fearful symmetry?

The *Digital Type Review* says of Veritas: "…I find Veritas to be highly legible and just stylish enough to be a pleasure to read. What's more, the heavier weights retain the legibility and elegance of the regular weight.

The italic just gets better, and both the roman and italic are carefully spaced… Veritas is one of the most important contributions (and one of the only multiple master families) from any independent foundry. It is sturdy and incredibly useful…"

Veritas™ Italic STF [Æ]

Brian Sooy
1995

Originally conceived of for use in Bibles, Veritas is Latin for *Truth*.

Mac | PC
4-weight Family
Veritas One (Roman, Italic, Bold, BoldItalic)
Veritas Two (Semibold, SB Italic, Black, Black Italic)
Unimaster | Multiple Master
Type One | TrueType | OpenType
Adobe Standard with €

*AaBbCcDdEeFfGgHhIiJjKkLlMmNnOoPpQqRrSsTtU
uVvWwXxYyZz[01234567890]€¥¢£fifl¶ß§?ÆæŒœÄ
äÅåÀàÃãÂâÁáÉéÈèËëÊêÙùÚúÜüÛûÌìÍíÏïÎîŸÿÒòÓóÖ
öÔôØø«"#&*"¿?!i:;{ǀ}@‡†¢£"»*

*To see a world in a grain of sand, and
a heaven in a wildflower,
to hold infinity in the palm of your
hand, and eternity in an hour.*

The Digital Type Review *says of Veritas: "…I find Veritas to be highly legible and just stylish enough to be a pleasure to read. What's more, the heavier weights retain the legibility and elegance of the regular weight.*

The italic just gets better, and both the roman and italic are carefully spaced… Veritas is one of the most important contributions (and one of the only multiple master families) from any independent foundry. It is sturdy and incredibly useful…"

info@alteredegofonts.com

AaBbCcDdEeFfGgHhIiJjKkLlMmNnOoPpQqRrSsTtUuVvWwXxYyZz[01234567890]€¥¢£fifl¶ß§?ÆæŒœÄäÅåÀàÃãÂâÁáÉéÈèËëÊêÙùÚúÜüÛûÌìÍíÏïÎîŸÿÒòÓóÖöÔôØø«"#&*"¿?!i:;{|}@‡†¢£"»

Veritas™ SB STF [Æ]

Brian Sooy
1995

STF Veritas is a four-weight serif text family. It is a narrow-width typeface, with a taller x-height than Times Roman for added legibility, but maintains a similar character count in text. It is a typeface designed for book, publication, newspaper (anywhere where narrow columns are necessary) and identity design. It is exquisitely spaced and kerned, even in European characters.

Mac | PC
4-weight Family
Veritas One (Roman, Italic, Bold, BoldItalic)
Veritas Two (Semibold, SB Italic, Black, Black Italic)
Unimaster | Multiple Master
Type One | TrueType | OpenType
Adobe Standard with €

Altered Ego

Tiger, Tiger, burning bright,
in the forests of the night,
what immortal hand or eye could
frame thy fearful symmetry?

The *Digital Type Review* says of Veritas: "...I find Veritas to be highly legible and just stylish enough to be a pleasure to read. What's more, the heavier weights retain the legibility and elegance of the regular weight.

The italic just gets better, and both the roman and italic are carefully spaced... Veritas is one of the most important contributions (and one of the only multiple master families) from any independent foundry. It is sturdy and incredibly useful..."

AaBbCcDdEeFfGgHhIiJjKkLlMmNnOoPpQqRrSsTtUuVvWwXxYyZz[01234567890]€¥¢£fifl¶ß§?ÆæŒœÄäÅåÀàÃãÂâÁáÉéÈèËëÊêÙùÚúÜüÛûÌìÍíÏïÎîŸÿÒòÓóÖöÔôØø«"#&"¿?!i:;{|}@‡†¢£"»*

Veritas™ SB Italic STF [Æ]

Brian Sooy
1995

Originally conceived of and subsequently used in Bibles, Veritas is Latin for *Truth*.

Mac | PC
4-weight Family
Veritas One (Roman, Italic, Bold, BoldItalic)
Veritas Two (Semibold, SB Italic, Black, Black Italic)
Unimaster | Multiple Master
Type One | TrueType | OpenType
Adobe Standard with €

To see a world in a grain of sand,
and a heaven in a wildflower,
to hold infinity in the palm of your
hand, and eternity in an hour.

The Digital Type Review *says of Veritas:* "...I find Veritas to be highly legible and just stylish enough to be a pleasure to read. What's more, the heavier weights retain the legibility and elegance of the regular weight.

The italic just gets better, and both the roman and italic are carefully spaced... Veritas is one of the most important contributions (and one of the only multiple master families) from any independent foundry. It is sturdy and incredibly useful..."

Brian Sooy
1995

STF Veritas is a four-weight serif text family. It is a narrow-width typeface, with a taller x-height than Times Roman for added legibility, but maintains a similar character count in text. It is a typeface designed for book, publication, newspaper (anywhere where narrow columns are necessary) and identity design. It is exquisitely spaced and kerned, even in European characters.

Mac | PC
4-weight Family
Veritas One (Roman, Italic, Bold, BoldItalic)
Veritas Two (Semibold, SB Italic, Black, Black Italic)
Unimaster | Multiple Master
Type One | TrueType | OpenType
Adobe Standard with €

AaBbCcDdEeFfGgHhIiJjKkLlMmNnOoPpQqRr SsTtUuVvWwXxYyZz[01234567890]€¥¢£fifl¶ß §?ÆæŒœÄäÅåÀàÃãÂâÁáÉéÈèËëÊêÙùÚúÜüÛûÌ ìÍíÏïÎîŸÿÒòÓóÖöÔôØø«"#&*''¿?!ı:;{|}@‡†¢£"»

Tiger, Tiger, burning bright, in the forests of the night, what immortal hand or eye could frame thy fearful symmetry?

The *Digital Type Review* says of Veritas: "...I find Veritas to be highly legible and just stylish enough to be a pleasure to read. What's more, the heavier weights retain the legibility and elegance of the regular weight.

The italic just gets better, and both the roman and italic are carefully spaced... Veritas is one of the most important contributions (and one of the only multiple master families) from any independent foundry. It is sturdy and incredibly useful..."

Brian Sooy
1995

Originally conceived of for use in Bibles, Veritas is Latin for *Truth*.

Mac | PC
4-weight Family
Veritas One (Roman, Italic, Bold, BoldItalic)
Veritas Two (Semibold, SB Italic, Black, Black Italic)
Unimaster | Multiple Master
Type One | TrueType | OpenType
Adobe Standard with €

AaBbCcDdEeFfGgHhIiJjKkLlMmNnOoPpQqRrS sTtUuVvWwXxYyZz[01234567890]€¥¢£fifl¶ß§? ÆæŒœÄäÅåÀàÃãÂâÁáÉéÈèËëÊêÙùÚúÜüÛûÌìÍí ÏïÎîŸÿÒòÓóÖöÔôØø«"#&''¿?!ı:;{|}@‡†¢£"»*

To see a world in a grain of sand, and a heaven in a wildflower, to hold infinity in the palm of your hand, and eternity in an hour.

The Digital Type Review *says of* Veritas: "...I find Veritas to be highly legible and just stylish enough to be a pleasure to read. What's more, the heavier weights retain the legibility and elegance of the regular weight.

The italic just gets better, and both the roman and italic are carefully spaced... Veritas is one of the most important contributions (and one of the only multiple master families) from any independent foundry. It is sturdy and incredibly useful..."

info@alteredegofonts.com

AaBbCcDdEeFfGgHhIiJjKkLlMmNnOoPpQq
RrSsTtUuVvWwXxYyZz[01234567890]€¥¢£fi
fl¶ß§?ÆæŒœÄäÅåÀàÃãÂâÁáÉéÈèËëÊêÙùÚúÜ
üÛûÌìÍíÏïÎîŸÿÒòÓóÖöÔôØø«"#&*"¿?!i@‡†¢£"»

Veritas™ Black STF [Æ]

Brian Sooy
1995

STF Veritas is a four-weight serif text family. It is a narrow-width typeface, with a taller x-height than Times Roman for added legibility, but maintains a similar character count in text. It is a typeface designed for book, publication, newspaper (any-where where narrow columns are necessary) and identity design. It is exquisitely spaced and kerned, even in European characters.

Mac | PC
4-weight Family
Veritas One (Roman, Italic, Bold, BoldItalic)
Veritas Two (Semibold, SB Italic, Black, Black Italic)
Unimaster | Multiple Master
Type One | TrueType | OpenType
Adobe Standard with €

Altered Ego

Tıger, Tıger, burning bright, in the forests of the night, what immortal hand or eye could frame thy fearful symmetry?

The *Digital Type Review* says of Veritas: "...I find Veritas to be highly legible and just stylish enough to be a pleasure to read. What's more, the heavier weights retain the legibility and elegance of the regular weight.

The italic just gets better, and both the roman and italic are carefully spaced... Veritas is one of the most important contributions (and one of the only multiple master families) from any independent foundry. It is sturdy and incredibly useful..."

AaBbCcDdEeFfGgHhIiJjKkLlMmNnOoPpQqR
rSsTtUuVvWwXxYyZz[01234567890]€¥¢£fifl¶ß
§?ÆæŒœÄäÅåÀàÃãÂâÁáÉéÈèËëÊêÙùÚúÜüÛ
ûÌìÍíÏïÎîŸÿÒòÓóÖöÔôØø«"#&"¿?!i:;{|}@‡†¢£"»*

Veritas™ Black Italic STF

Brian Sooy
1995

Originally conceived of for use in Bibles, Veritas is Latin for *Truth.*

Mac | PC
4-weight Family
Veritas One (Roman, Italic, Bold, BoldItalic)
Veritas Two (Semibold, SB Italic, Black, Black Italic)
Unimaster | Multiple Master
Type One | TrueType | OpenType
Adobe Standard with €

To see a world in a grain of sand, and a heaven in a wildflower, to hold infinity in the palm of your hand, and eternity in an hour.

The Digital Type Review says of Veritas: "...I find Veritas to be highly legible and just stylish enough to be a pleasure to read. What's more, the heavier weights retain the legibility and elegance of the regular weight.

The italic just gets better, and both the roman and italic are carefully spaced... Veritas is one of the most important contributions (and one of the only multiple master families) from any independent foundry. It is sturdy and incredibly useful..."

Brian Sooy
1995

The two families shown on this page
make up Veritas One, a subset of the
Veritas family.

Mac | PC
Veritas One
(Roman, Italic, Bold, Bold Italic)

Unimaster | Multiple Master
Type One | TrueType | OpenType
Adobe Standard with €

The *Digital Type Review* says of Veritas: "What's more, the heavier weights retain the legibility and elegance of the regular weight. The italic just gets better, and both the roman and italic are carefully spaced... Veritas is one of the most important contributions (and one of the only multiple master families) from any independent foundry..." set 9'/12'

The *Digital Type Review* says of Veritas: "What's more, the heavier weights retain the legibility and elegance of the regular weight. The italic just gets better, and both the roman and italic are carefully spaced... Veritas is one of the most important contributions (and one of the only multiple master families) from any independent foundry..." set 8'/12'

The *Digital Type Review* says of Veritas: "What's more, the heavier weights retain the legibility and elegance of the regular weight. The italic just gets better, and both the roman and italic are carefully spaced... Veritas is one of the most important contributions (and one of the only multiple master families) from any independent foundry..." set 7'/12'

The Digital Type Review *says of Veritas: "What's more, the heavier weights retain the legibility and elegance of the regular weight. The italic just gets better, and both the roman and italic are carefully spaced... Veritas is one of the most important contributions (and one of the only multiple master families) from any independent foundry..."* set 9'/12'

The Digital Type Review *says of Veritas: "What's more, the heavier weights retain the legibility and elegance of the regular weight. The italic just gets better, and both the roman and italic are carefully spaced... Veritas is one of the most important contributions (and one of the only multiple master families) from any independent foundry..."* set 8'/12'

The Digital Type Review *says of Veritas: "What's more, the heavier weights retain the legibility and elegance of the regular weight. The italic just gets better, and both the roman and italic are carefully spaced... Veritas is one of the most important contributions (and one of the only multiple master families) from any independent foundry..."* set 7'/12'

Brian Sooy
1995

The two families shown on this page
make up Veritas One, a subset of the
Veritas family.

Mac | PC
Veritas One
(Roman, Italic, Bold, Bold Italic)

Unimaster | Multiple Master
Type One | TrueType | OpenType
Adobe Standard with €

The *Digital Type Review* says of Veritas: "What's more, the heavier weights retain the legibility and elegance of the regular weight. The italic just gets better, and both the roman and italic are carefully spaced... Veritas is one of the most important contributions (and one of the only multiple master families) from any independent foundry..."

The *Digital Type Review* says of Veritas: "What's more, the heavier weights retain the legibility and elegance of the regular weight. The italic just gets better, and both the roman and italic are carefully spaced... Veritas is one of the most important contributions (and one of the only multiple master families) from any independent foundry..." set 8'/12'

The *Digital Type Review* says of Veritas: "What's more, the heavier weights retain the legibility and elegance of the regular weight. The italic just gets better, and both the roman and italic are carefully spaced... Veritas is one of the most important contributions (and one of the only multiple master families) from any independent foundry..." set 7'/12'

The* Digital Type Review *says of Veritas: "What's more, the heavier weights retain the legibility and elegance of the regular weight. The italic just gets better, and both the roman and italic are carefully spaced... Veritas is one of the most important contributions (and one of the only multiple master families)

The* Digital Type Review *says of Veritas: "What's more, the heavier weights retain the legibility and elegance of the regular weight. The italic just gets better, and both the roman and italic are carefully spaced... Veritas is one of the most important contributions (and one of the only multiple master families) from any independent foundry..." set 8'/12'

The* Digital Type Review *says of Veritas: "What's more, the heavier weights retain the legibility and elegance of the regular weight. The italic just gets better, and both the roman and italic are carefully spaced... Veritas is one of the most important contributions (and one of the only multiple master families) from any independent foundry..." set 7'/12'

info@alteredegofonts.com

Veritas™ SB STF [Æ]

Brian Sooy
1995

The two families shown on this page make up Veritas Two subset of the Veritas family.

Mac | PC
Veritas Two
(Semibold, SB Italic, Black and Black Italic)

Unimaster | Multiple Master
Type One | TrueType | OpenType
Adobe Standard with €

The *Digital Type Review* says of Veritas: "What's more, the heavier weights retain the legibility and elegance of the regular weight. The italic just gets better, and both the roman and italic are carefully spaced... Veritas is one of the most important contributions (and one of the only multiple master families) from any independent

The *Digital Type Review* says of Veritas: "What's more, the heavier weights retain the legibility and elegance of the regular weight. The italic just gets better, and both the roman and italic are carefully spaced... Veritas is one of the most important contributions (and one of the only multiple master families) from any independent foundry..." set 8'/12'

The *Digital Type Review* says of Veritas: "What's more, the heavier weights retain the legibility and elegance of the regular weight. The italic just gets better, and both the roman and italic are carefully spaced... Veritas is one of the most important contributions (and one of the only multiple master families) from any independent foundry..." set 7'/12'

The Digital Type Review *says of Veritas: "What's more, the heavier weights retain the legibility and elegance of the regular weight. The italic just gets better, and both the roman and italic are carefully spaced... Veritas is one of the most important contributions (and one of the only multiple master families) from any independent foundry..." set 9'/12'*

The Digital Type Review *says of Veritas: "What's more, the heavier weights retain the legibility and elegance of the regular weight. The italic just gets better, and both the roman and italic are carefully spaced... Veritas is one of the most important contributions (and one of the only multiple master families) from any independent foundry..." set 8'/12'*

The Digital Type Review *says of Veritas: "What's more, the heavier weights retain the legibility and elegance of the regular weight. The italic just gets better, and both the roman and italic are carefully spaced... Veritas is one of the most important contributions (and one of the only multiple master families) from any independent foundry..." set 7'/12'*

Veritas™ Black STF [Æ]

Brian Sooy
1995

Originally conceived of and subsequently used in Bibles, Veritas is Latin for Truth.

Mac | PC
Veritas One
(Roman, Italic, Bold, BoldItalic)
Veritas Two
(Semibold, SB Italic, Black and Black Italic)
Unimaster | Multiple Master
Type One | TrueType | OpenType
Adobe Standard with €

The *Digital Type Review* says of Veritas: "What's more, the heavier weights retain the legibility and elegance of the regular weight. The italic just gets better, and both the roman and italic are carefully spaced... Veritas is one of the most important contributions (and one of the only multiple master families) from any independent

The *Digital Type Review* says of Veritas: "What's more, the heavier weights retain the legibility and elegance of the regular weight. The italic just gets better, and both the roman and italic are carefully spaced... Veritas is one of the most important contributions (and one of the only multiple master families) from any independent foundry..." set 8'/12'

The *Digital Type Review* says of Veritas: "What's more, the heavier weights retain the legibility and elegance of the regular weight. The italic just gets better, and both the roman and italic are carefully spaced... Veritas is one of the most important contributions (and one of the only multiple master families) from any independent foundry..." set 7'/12'

The* Digital Type Review *says of Veritas: "What's more, the heavier weights retain the legibility and elegance of the regular weight. The italic just gets better, and both the roman and italic are carefully spaced... Veritas is one of the most important contributions (and one

The* Digital Type Review *says of Veritas: "What's more, the heavier weights retain the legibility and elegance of the regular weight. The italic just gets better, and both the roman and italic are carefully spaced... Veritas is one of the most important contributions (and one of the only multiple master families) from any independent foundry..." set 8'/12'

The* Digital Type Review *says of Veritas: "What's more, the heavier weights retain the legibility and elegance of the regular weight. The italic just gets better, and both the roman and italic are carefully spaced... Veritas is one of the most important contributions (and one of the only multiple master families) from any independent foundry..." set 7'/12'

A.STIGMATIC

ONE EYE TYPOGRAPHIC INSTITUTE

One score and seven years ago on a bitter Winter evening, Ezra and Madeleine Bonislav, exhausted from a long voyage across the Atlantic, stepped foot on American soil to begin their new life together.

Ezra was a studious man with an acutely irritating propensity for mathematics and sciences came from a noble family in Warsaw, Poland. His father William "Goodie" Bonislav was the original creator and patent holder of the first plastic hair pick and other personal grooming devices.

Ezra's brother, Grey, went on to bring America London's finest teas. So prolific was his nature, he was the first to introduce the concept of serving teas cold, or "iced" as he referred to them. While the trend never caught on in the United Kingdom, for his contributions to the Queens royal beverage coalition, he was appointed Earl of Teas. (from thus came Earl Grey)

Madeleine was the daughter of Munich's brightest soap making empire, the Hazenfabulpopinziegus Family. Her father, Rudolph, worked relentlessly to build the Hazenfabulpopinziegus Soap empire to it's height until his unfortunate demise in 1892 when he suffered a severe stoke after consuming 13 lbs. of wienerschnitzle.

Madeleine's mother, Connie, was left to raise the children on her own and maintain the Hazenfabulpopinziegus Soap empire. By then, most of the children in the family were old enough to help run the business, with the exception of Manny Hazenfabulpopinziegus, who became a drunkard and a scallywag and was disowned from the family. His whereabouts were never discovered.

In 1904 Ezra and Madeleine met, fell in love, and began a new life together in Egypt. Madeleine studied new soap making techniques while Ezra accompanied many archaeological digs there in on the nearby Isles of Greece. It was not long until Ezra's methods were deemed unorthodox and he was asked to leave Egypt.

Five years later, with only 15 Francs to their name, Madeleine acquired a loan from her sister, Dorathia Hazenfabulpopinziegus, to cover the passage overseas to New York City in the United States of America.

Shortly after their arrival in America, they were blessed with a son, Brian J. Bonislawsky, the new legal name in the states. He was a bright boy, and so fascinated was he by the alphabet, that he pretended to read just so he could stare at the letters in the books of his parents.

He went on to study at the Ivy League Brown University, RISD, and a stint abroad where he earned his doctorate in the typographical sciences. While in England, he was notorious for examining typographic specimens at such length that he developed an acute straining of his left eye and a minor astigmatism.

When word of his condition spread, he was known to his colleagues as One Eye, or "Stiggy" as he'd been jokingly referred. He was not ashamed, but instead honored to be revered throughout Europe as "the" typographic authority.

Upon his return to New York, he began the Astigmatic One Eye Typographic Institute in Rochester, later relocating to Miami, a more tourist attracting area, dedicated to bringing fantastic typographic specimens to the public. Often Professor Bonislawsky would lead many dangerous typographic expeditions throughout South America and Asia, yielding many exciting and rarely seen specimens.

We invite you to examine each wing of our glorious 265,000 square foot facility and look forward to your enjoyment of our fine quality collection.

Professor Brian J. Bonislawsky

FLUIDIC

abcdefghijklmnopqrstuvwxyzABCDEFGHIJK
LMNOPQRSTUVWXYZ-$1234567890("',;'!*?:)

Alien Argonaut AOE

Brian J. Bonislawsky
1998

OXYGEN VOID

Anoxia AOE

Brian J. Bonislawsky
1998

Anoxia AOE - Thin

abcdefghijklmnopqrstuvwxyzABCDEFGHIJKLMNOPQRSTUUVWXYZ-$12
34567890("',;'!*?:)&fifILß-äïöüåçèîñóœøœÄÖÜÅÇÆØŒ«»[¶§◆†‡]¡¿

AIR ABSENCE

Anoxia AOE

abcdefghijklmnopqrstuvwxyzABCDEFGHIJKLMNOPQRSTUUVWXY
Z-$1234567890("',;'!*?:)&fifILß-äïöüåçèîñóœøœÄÖÜÅÇÆØŒ

GIVE ME AIR

Anoxia AOE - Bold

abcdefghijklmnopqrstuvwxyzABCDEFGHIJKLMNOPQRSTU
UVWXYZ-$1234567890("',;'!*?:)&fifILß-äïöüåçèîñóœøœÄÖ

Anoxia AOE - Thin Italic

abcdefghijklmnopqrstuvwxyz-ABC
DEFGHIJKLMNOPQRSTUUVWXYZ-$1234

Anoxia AOE - Italic

abcdefghijklmnopqrstuvwxyz-
ABCDEFGHIJKLMNOPQRSTUUVWXYZ

Anoxia AOE - Bold Italic

abcdefghijklmnopqrstuvwxyz
ABCDEFGHIJKLMNOPQRSTUUVWXYZ

ANDRIOD

Automatic AOE

Brian J. Bonislawsky
2000

ABCDEFGHIJKLMNOPQRSTUVWXYZABCDEFGHIJK
LMNOPQRSTUVWXYZ-$1234567890("',;'!*?:)¢

NOTES

BadComp AOE

Brian J. Bonislawsky
1997

abcdefghijklmnopqrstuvwxyzABCD
EFGHIJKLMNOPQRSTUVWXYZ-$123

BigLimbo AOE

BigLimbo AOE

Brian J. Bonislawsky
1998

Typeface styles can overlap for
different effect.

abcdefghijklmnopqrstuvwxyzABCDEFGH
IJKLMNOPQRSTUVWXYZ-$1234567890("

Astigmatic

BigLimbo Outline AOE

abcdefghijklmnopqrstuvwxyzABCDEFGH
IJKLMNOPQRSTUVWXYZ-$1234567890("

Bitrux AOE

Brian J. Bonislawsky
1999

Bitrux AOE

ABCDEFGHIJKLMNOPQRST
UVWXYZ-$1234567890(,.!*?:)

PIXELLATED FOR 7PT USE

Bitrux AOE - Bold

ABCDEFGHIJKLMNO
PQRSTUVWXYZ-$123

AS POSTSCRIPT OR BITMAP

Bound AOE

Brian J. Bonislawsky
1997

abcdefghijklmnopqrstuvwxyzABCDEFG
HIJKLMNOPQRSTUVWXYZ-$1234

KNOTS

Cake & Sodomy AOE

Brian J. Bonislawsky
1997

Cake AOE

abcdefghijklmnopqrstuvwxyzAB
CDEFGHIJKLMNOPQRSTUVWXYZ

TASTY

Sodomy AOE

abcdefghijklmnopqrstuvwxyzABCDEFGHIJKLMNOP
QRSTUVWXYZ-$1234567890(".;'!*?:)&fifß-äöüåçè

TEMPTING

Cavalero AOE

Brian J. Bonislawsky
1999

Typeface styles can overlap
for different effect.

Cavalero AOE

abcdefghijklmnopqrstuv
wxyzABCDEFGHIJKLMNOPQR
STUVWXYZ-$1234567890(",;'!*

ENDURE
PASSION

Cavalero AOE - Italic

abcdefghijklmnopqrstuv
wxyzABCDEFGHIJKLMNOPQR
STUVWXYZ-$1234567890(",;'!*

PROPEL
POWERS

astigma@astigmatic.com

Cavalero Outline AOE

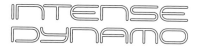

aBCDEFGHIJKLMNOPQRSTUV
WXYZABCDEFGHIJKLMNOPQR
STUVWXYZ-$1234567890("„;)✱

Cavalero Outline AOE - Italic

aBCDEFGHIJKLMNOPQRSTUV
WXYZABCDEFGHIJKLMNOPQR
STUVWXYZ-$1234567890("„;)✱

Celtic Lion AOE

CELTIC

aBCDEFGhIJKLMNOPQRSTUVWXYZABC
DEFGhIJKLMNOPQRSTUVWXYZ-$

Celtic Lion AOE - Italic

DRUID

aBCDEFGhIJKLMNOPQRSTUVWXYZABC
DEFGhIJKLMNOPQRSTUVWXYZ-$

Celtic Lion AOE - Bold

SOLID

aBCDEFGhIJKLMNOPQRSTUVWXYZA
BCDEFGhIJKLMNOPQRSTUVWX

Celtic Lion AOE - Bold Italic

STATE

aBCDEFGhIJKLMNOPQRSTUVWXYZA
BCDEFGhIJKLMNOPQRSTUVWX

Clunker AOE

BREAK'N

ABCDEFGHIJKLMNOPQRSTUVWXYZ-$12
34567890("„:'!*?:)¢FIFLß-ÄÖÜÅÇÈÑÓÆØŒ

Display of Clunker AOE (Red) and Clunker AOE - Bold (Black)

ELECTRIC DANCE

Clunker AOE - Bold

ABCDEFGHIJKLMNO
PQRSTUVWXYZ-$1

Clunker AOE

Brian J. Bonislawsky
1999

Red & Black Display of
Overlap of Type for Graffiti Effect.

Culture Vulture AOE

Brian J. Bonislawsky
1999

ABCDEFGHIJKLMNOPQRSTUVWXYZABCDEFGHIJKLMNOPQRSTUVWX
YZ-$1234567890(".;'!*?:)4FIFLß-ÄÖÜÅÇÊÍÑÓÆØŒÄÖÜÅÇÊÍÑÓÆ

THE REAPER

DarkNight AOE

Brian J. Bonislawsky
1998

abcdefghijklmnopqrstuvwxyzABCDEFGHIJKLM
NOPQRSTUVWXYZ-$1234567890(".;'!*?:)&fiflß-

STALKER

Data Error AOE

Brian J. Bonislawsky
1998

Data Error AOE

abcdefghijklmnopqrstuvwxyzABCDEFGHIJ
KLMNOPQRSTUVWXYZ-$1234567890(",;'!*?:)&

DIGITAL

Data Error AOE - Italic

abcdefghijklmnopqrstuvwxyzABCDEFGHIJ
KLMNOPQRSTUVWXYZ-$1234567890(",;'!*?:)&

SYSOPS

Data Error AOE - Bold

abcdefghijklmnopqrstuvwxyzABCDEFGHIJ
KLMNOPQRSTUVWXYZ-$1234567890(",;'!*?:)&

LOADER

Data Error AOE - Bold Italic

abcdefghijklmnopqrstuvwxyzABCDEFGHIJ
KLMNOPQRSTUVWXYZ-$1234567890(",;'!*?:)&

BOOTUP

Delivery Matrix AOE

Brian J. Bonislawsky
1999

abcdefghijklmnopqrstuvwxyz
ABCDEFGHIJKLMNOPQRSTUVWX
YZ-$1234567890(",;'!*?:)&fiflß-ä

Detour AOE

Brian J. Bonislawsky
1997

abcdefghijklmnopqrstuvwxyzABCDEFGHIJKLM
NOPQRSTUVWXYZ-$1234567890(",;'!*?:)&flflß-

HIGHWAY

VOLTAGE

Digelectric AOE

Digelectric AOE

Brian J. Bonislawsky
1998

abcdefghijklmnopqrstuvwxyzABCDEFGHIJKLM
NOPQRSTUVWXYZ-$1234567890("'.;'**?:)&fiflß-äü

ZAPPED!

Digelectric AOE - Oblique

abcdefghijklmnopqrstuvwxyzABCDEFGHIJKLM
NOPQRSTUVWXYZ-$1234567890("'.;'**?:)&fiflß-äü

MANERO

Digital Disco AOE

Digital Disco AOE

Brian J. Bonislawsky
1998

ABCDEFGHIJKLMNOPQrSTUVWXYZABCDEFG
HIJKLMNOPQRSTUVWXYZ-$1234567890("'

ODYSSEY

Digital Disco AOE - Oblique

ABCDEFGHIJKLMNOPQrSTUVWXYZABCDEFG
HIJKLMNOPQRSTUVWXYZ-$1234567890("'

DYNAMIC

Europa Twin AOE

Europa Twin AOE

Brian J. Bonislawsky
2002

ABCDEFGHIJKLMNOPQRSTUVWXYZABCDEFGHIJKL
MNOPQRSTUVWXYZ-$1234567890("'.;!**?:)fIFL-Ä

T. DOLBYs

Europa Twin AOE - Oblique

ABCDEFGHIJKLMNOPQRSTUVWXYZABCDEFGHIJKL
MNOPQRSTUVWXYZ-$1234567890("'.;!**?:)fIFL-Ä

BRUSHED

Filth AOE

Brian J. Bonislawsky
1998

abcdefghijklmnopqrstuvwxyzABCDEFGHIJKLMNOPQRSTUVW
XYZ-$1234567890("'.;'!*?:)&fiflß-äöüàçèíñó œøæÄÖÜÅ

ALCHEMY

Gargamel AOE

Gargamel AOE

Brian J. Bonislawsky
1997

abcdefghijklmnopqrstuvwxyzABCDEFGHIJ
KLMNOPQRSTUVWXYZ-$1234567890("'.;'!*

Astigmatic

Gargamel AOE - Italic

abcdefghijklmnopqrstuvwxyzABCDEFGHIJ
KLMNOPQRSTUVWXYZ-$1234567890(".;'!*

EVIL MAN

Gargamel Smurf AOE

abcdefghijklmnopqrstuvwxyzABCDEFGHIJ
KLMNOPQRSTUVWXYZ-$1234567890(".;'!*

AMAZING

Gargamel Smurf AOE - Italic

abcdefghijklmnopqrstuvwxyzABCDEFGHIJ
KLMNOPQRSTUVWXYZ-$1234567890(".;'!*

MAGICAL

GateKeeper AOE

Brian J. Bonislawsky
1999

ABCDEFGHIJKLMNOPQRSTUVWXYZABCDEFGHIJKLMNOPQR
STUVWXYZ-$1234567890(".;'!*?:)ᴬᴺᴰFIFLß-äöüåçèñó

HORRIFYING

Geisha Boy AOE

Brian J. Bonislawsky
2001

abcdefghijklmnopqrstuvwxyzABCD
EFGHIJKLMNOPQRSTUVWXYZ-$123

Fiesta

Gobe AOE

Brian J. Bonislawsky
2001

Gobe AOE

abcdefghijklmnopqrstuvwxyzAB
CDEFGHIJKLMNOPQRSTUVWXYZ-$1

PAINT

Gobe AOE - Oblique

abcdefghijklmnopqrstuvwxyzAB
CDEFGHIJKLMNOPQRSTUVWXYZ-$1

Spray

Gobe Compressed AOE

abcdefghijklmnopqrstuvwxyzABCDEFGHIJKLMNOP
QRSTUVWXYZ-$1234567890(".;'!*?:)‡fiflß-äöüåçèñó

GRAFFITI

TAGGING

Gobe Compressed AOE - Oblique

abcdefghijklmnopqrstuvwxyzABCDEFGHIJKLMNOP
QRSTUVWXYZ-$1234567890(",.'!*?:)#fiflß-äöüåçèîñó

Medusa

Gorgon Cocoon AOE

Brian J. Bonislawsky
1997

abcdefghijklmnopqrstuvwxyzABCD
EFGHIJKLMNOPQRSTUVWXYZ-$1

DESERT

Gulag AOE

Brian J. Bonislawsky
1998

Typeface styles can overlap
for different effect.

abcdefghijklmnopqrstuvwxyzABCDEFGHIJ
KLMNOPQRSTUVWXYZ-$1234567890(",.;

TIED UP

Gulag AOE - Italic

abcdefghijklmnopqrstuvwxyzABCDEFGHIJ
KLMNOPQRSTUVWXYZ-$1234567890(",.;

NOMAD

Gulag AOE - Bold

abcdefghijklmnopqrstuvwxyzABCDEFGHIJ
KLMNOPQRSTUVWXYZ-$1234567890(",.;

BARTER

Gulag AOE - Bold Italic

abcdefghijklmnopqrstuvwxyzABCDEFGHIJ
KLMNOPQRSTUVWXYZ-$1234567890(",.;

KILLING

Gulag Outline AOE

abcdefghijklmnopqrstuvwxyzABCDEFGHIJ
KLMNOPQRSTUVWXYZ-$1234567890(",.;

BEASTS

Gulag Outline AOE - Italic

abcdefghijklmnopqrstuvwxyzABCDEFGHIJ
KLMNOPQRSTUVWXYZ-$1234567890(",.;

Astigmatic

Brian J. Bonislawsky
2001

Interchange Habitual Upper & Downer for stepping effect.

Habitual AOE

ABCDEFGHIJKLMNOPQRSTUVWXYZ−$1234567890("·.;
'!*?:)¢FIFLß−ÄÖÜÅÇÈÎÑÓŒØŒ−¡⅀£¢∞§¶•℗©†‡‡¿

CONSUMER

Habitual Downer AOE

MEDICINAL

Habitual Upper AOE

INGESTION

Brian J. Bonislawsky
1998

Red & Black Display of Overlap of Type for Tech Effect.

HAL 9000 AOE

abcdefghijklmnopqrstuvwxyzABCDEFGHI
JKLMNOPQRSTUVWXYZ−$1234567890("·.;'!*

COMPUTE

HAL 9000 AOE - Italic

abcdefghijklmnopqrstuvwxyzABCDEFGHI
JKLMNOPQRSTUVWXYZ−$1234567890("·.;'!*

COMPILE

HAL 9000 AOE - Italic

abcdefghijklmnopq
rstuvwxyzABCDEFG

HAL 9000 AOE - Italic

abcdefghijklmnopq
rstuvwxyzABCDEFG

Display of HAL 9000 AOE (Red) and HAL 9000 AOE - Bold (Black)

PROTECT

Brian J. Bonislawsky
1998

Intruder AOE

abcdefghijklmnopqrstuvwxyzABCDEFGHI
JKLMNOPQRSTUVWXYZ−$1234567890("·.;

ALIENATE

Intrduer AOE - Bold

abcdefghijklmnopqrstuvwxyzABCDEFGHI
JKLMNOPQRSTUVWXYZ−$1234567890("·.;

INVADER

ROOTED

ABCDEFGHIJKLMNOPQRSTUVWXYZ-$1234567890(
".;'!*?:)&FIFLß-ÄÖÜÅÇÈÎÑÓÆØŒ-í™£¢∞§¶♦€¡¿

LOST

ABCDEFGHIJKLMNOPQRSTUV
WXYZ-$1234567890(".;'!*?:)&FIß

FALTER

Jericho AOE

ABCDEFGHIJKLMNOPQRSTUVWXYZ-
$1234567890[.,!?:]+@#?ŒŒ¡¿£¢0

DOMAIN

Jericho AOE - Oblique

ABCDEFGHIJKLMNOPQRSTUVWXYZ-
$1234567890[.,!?:]+@#?ŒŒ¡¿£¢0

IMAGINATION

abcdefghijklmnopqrstuvwxyzABCDEFGHIJKLMNOPQRSTUVWXYZ-$12345
67890(".;'!*?:)&fiflß-äöüåçèîñóæøœÄÖÜÅÇÈÎÑÓÆØŒ-í™£¢∞§¶♦€¡¿

SIRBO TURBO

Krelesanta AOE

abcdefghijklmnopqrstuvwxyzABCDEFGHIJKLMNOPQRSTUVWXYZ-$1234567
890(".;'!*?:)&fiflß-äöüåçèîñóæøœÄÖÜÅÇÈÎÑÓÆØŒ-í™£¢∞§¶□¡¿☉👁

PRIYA & JAN 9

Krelesanta AOE - Bold

abcdefghijklmnopqrstuvwxyzABCDEFGHIJKLMNOPQRSTUVWXYZ-$1234567
890(".;'!*?:)&fiflß-äöüåçèîñóæøœÄÖÜÅÇÈÎÑÓÆØŒ-í™£¢∞§¶□¡¿☉👁

TOUCH-UP

Krylo-Tag AOE

abcdefghijklmnopqrstuvwxyzABCDEFGHIJKLMNOP
QRSTUVWXYZ-$1234567890(.,;'!👹?:)fiflfl-äöüåçèîñóæø

Krylo-Tag Back AOE

abcdefghijklmnopqrstuvwxyzABCDEFGHIJKLMNOP
QRSTUVWXYZ-$1234567890(.,;'!@?:)PR-äöüçàíñóø

Display of Krylo-Tag AOE (Red) and Krylo-Tag Back AOE (Black)

Krylo-Tag Outline AOE

abcdefghijklmnopqrstuvwxyzABCDEFGHIJKLMNOP
QRSTUVWXYZ-$1234567890(.,;'!@?:)PR-äöüçàíñóø

Lavatype AOE

Brian J. Bonislawsky
2000

abcdefghijklmnopqrstuvwxyzABCD
EFGHIJKLMNOPQRSTUVWXYZ-$123

GLOBS

Luna AOE

Brian J. Bonislawsky
1998

Luna 9 AOE

abcdefghijklmnopqrstuvwxyzAB
CDEFGHIJKLMNOPQRSTUVWXYZ-$1

Liquid

Luna 9 AOE - Oblique

abcdefghijklmnopqrstuvwxyzAB
CDEFGHIJKLMNOPQRSTUVWXYZ-$1

ECHOES

Luna 9 SC AOE

ABCDEFGHIJKLMNOPQRSTUVWXYZA
BCDEFGHIJKLMNOPQRSTUVWXYZ-$

LISTEN

Luna 9 SC AOE - Oblique

ABCDEFGHIJKLMNOPQRSTUVWXYZA
BCDEFGHIJKLMNOPQRSTUVWXYZ-$

SEARCH

Luna 10 AOE

abcdefghijklmnopqrstuvwxyzA
BCDEFGHIJKLMNOPQRSTUVWXYZ
-$1234567890<>.,;'!@*?:)PR-äíçàíñóç

GRID

astigma@astigmatic.com

GLOW

Luna 10 AOE - Oblique

cakɔ:cdcz fcghɔjkcl mncɔ ɔɔcɔqrɔr tuʌ ʌɔʌɔacɔ rʌ
BCCDEF-GHIJKL MNΓOFQRƆSTUJJUPSS4EƆ
-S2Lc23345EƆ7E3ɔɔ .;'!***?:ɔFiFl--ȧ̃ə̈ɔ̇ü̃ȧ̧̈ç̈z̈

TURN

Lunokhod AOE

abcdef ghijkl mnopqrstuvwxyz
ABCDEFGHIJKLMNOPQRSTUVWXY
Z-$1234567890◇(.;'!*?:)fi fl-ȧöü

BEND

Lunokhod AOE - Italic

abcdef ghijkl mnopqrstuvwxyz
ABCDEFGHIJKLMNOPQRSTUVWXY
Z-$1234567890◇(.;'!*?:)fi fl-ȧöü

Motherlode AOE

Brian J. Bonislawsky
1998

Typeface styles can overlap
for different effect.

HESTON

Motherlode Loaded AOE

abcdefghijklmnopqrstuvwxyzABCDEFG
HIJKLMNOPQRSTUVWXYZ-$123456789

GOLDEN

Motherlode Loaded AOE - Italic

abcdefghijklmnopqrstuvwxyzABCDEFG
HIJKLMNOPQRSTUVWXYZ-$123456789

THE VEIN

Motherlode Stripped AOE

abcdefghijklmnopqrstuvwxyzABCDEFG
HIJKLMNOPQRSTUVWXYZ-$123456789

BROTHER

Motherlode Stripped AOE - Italic

abcdefghijklmnopqrstuvwxyzABCDEFG
HIJKLMNOPQRSTUVWXYZ-$123456789

Neuntotter AOE

Brian J. Bonislawsky
1998

VAMPIRELLA

Neuntotter AOE

abcdeFghijklmnopqrstuvwxyzABCDEFGHIJKLMNOPQRSTUVWX
YZ-$1234567890(.;'!*?:)FiFl-äöüå̧çéîñóæœ̈ÄÖÜÅ̧ÇÊÎÑÓÆ̈ŒÇ-i

abcdefghijklmnopqrstuvwxyzABCDEFGHIJKLMNOPQRSTUVWX
YZ-$1234567890(.,'!*?:)fifl-äöüåçèîñóæøœÄÖÜÅÇÈÎÑÓŒ-i

NIGHTCRAWL

Penicillin AOE

Brian J. Bonislawsky
2001

abcdefghijklmnopqrstuvwxyzABCDEFGHIJKLMNOPQR
STUVWXYZ-$1234567890(.,'!*?:)fifl-äöüåçèîñóæøœÄ

HEAL ME

Pixel Gantry AOE

Brian J. Bonislawsky
1998

Red & Black Display of Overlap
of Type for Digital effect.

Pixel Gantry AOE

abcdefghijklmnopqrstuvwxyzABCDEFGHIJ
KLMNOPQRSTUVWXYZ-$1234567890(.,'!*?:)£

TYPE IT

Pixel Gantry AOE - Italic

abcdefghijklmnopqrstuvwxyzABCDEFGHIJ
KLMNOPQRSTUVWXYZ-$1234567890(.,'!*?:)£

PLAN-9

Pixel Gantry AOE - Bold

abcdefghijklmnopqrstuvwxyzABCDEFGHIJ
KLMNOPQRSTUVWXYZ-$1234567890(.,'!*?:)£

Load Us

Pixel Gantry AOE - Bold Italic

abcdefghijklmnopqrstuvwxyzABCDEFGHIJ
KLMNOPQRSTUVWXYZ-$1234567890(.,'!*?:)£

Stacks

Pixel Gantry AOE - Heavy

abcdefghijklmnopqrstuvwxyzABCDEFGHIJ
KLMNOPQRSTUVWXYZ-$1234567890(.,'!*?:)£

LAYERS

Pixel Gantry AOE - Heavy Italic

abcdefghijklmnopqrstuvwxyzABCDEFGHIJ
KLMNOPQRSTUVWXYZ-$1234567890(.,'!*?:)£

4 LEVEL

Pixel Gantry Hilite AOE

Gleams

abcdefghi jklmnopqrstuvwxyzABCDEFGHIJ
KLMNOPQRSTUVWXYZ-$1234567890(.;'!*?.:)

Pixel Gantry Hilite AOE - Italic

Shines

abcdefghi jklmnopqrstuvwxyzABCDEFGHIJ
KLMNOPQRSTUVWXYZ-$1234567890(.;'!*?.:)

Pixel Gantry Hilite AOE (Red) & Pixel Gantry AOE - Bold (Black)

EFFECT

Pixel Gantry AOE (Red) & Pixel Gantry AOE - Heavy (Black)

VERSUS

Pixel Gantry AOE (White) & Pixel Gantry Hilite AOE (Red)
& Pixel Gantry AOE - Heavy (Black)

AFFECT

Astigmatic

Quilted AOE

Quilted AOE

COMFY

abcdefghijklmnopqrstuvwxyzABCDE
FGHIJKLMNOPQRSTUVWXYZ-$12345

Brian J. Bonislawsky
1997

Typeface styles can overlap
for different effect.

Quilted AOE - Black

quilted

abcdefghijklmnopqrstuvwxyzABCDE
FGHIJKLMNOPQRSTUVWXYZ-$12345

Saratoga Slim AOE

Saratoga Slim AOE

OLD GUNSLINGER

abcdefghijklmnopqrstuvwxyzABCDEFGHIJKLMNOPQRSTUVWXYZ-$1234
567890(.;'!*?.:)fifl –äöüåçèîñó æœŒÄÖÅÇÈÎÑÓÆØŒ-ì™£{∞§¶•€<>®®

Brian J. Bonislawsky
2001

Screwed AOE

Screwed AOE

BOLT

ABCDEFGHIJKLMNOPQRSTUVWXYZABCD
EFGHIJKLMNOPQRSTUVWXYZ-$1
234567890(.;'!*?.:)FIFL-ÄÖÜÅÇÈÎÑÓ

Brian J. Bonislawsky
1996

Screwed AOE - Oblique

NUTS

ABCDEFGHIJKLMNOPQRSTUVWXYZABCD
EFGHIJKLMNOPQRSTUVWXYZ-$1
234567890(.;'!*?.:)FIFL-ÄÖÜÅÇÈÎÑÓ

Stingwire AOE

Brian J. Bonislawsky
2000

abcdefghijklmnopqrstuvwxyzABCDE
FGHIJKLMNOPQRSTUVWXYZ-$1234

BARBS

Synchronous AOE

Brian J. Bonislawsky
1998

Synchronous AOE

abcdefghijklmnopqrstuvwxyzAB
CDEFGHIJKLMNOPQRSTUVWXYZ-$1

BRICK

Synchronous AOE - Oblique

abcdefghijklmnopqrstuvwxyzAB
CDEFGHIJKLMNOPQRSTUVWXYZ-$1

tense

Tannarin AOE

Brian J. Bonislawsky
1999

Tannarin AOE

ABCDEFGHIJKLMNOPQRSTU
VWXYZ-$1234567890(.;'!*?:)

ELVIN

Tannarin AOE - Oblique

ABCDEFGHIJKLMNOPQRSTU
VWXYZ-$1234567890(.;'!*?:)

SLAY

Tapehead AOE

Brian J. Bonislawsky
2000

Red & Black Display of Overlap
of Type for special effect.

Tapehead AOE

ABCDEFGHIJKLMNOPQRSTUVWXYZABCDE
FGHIJKLMNOPQRSTUVWXYZ-$1234567890

VIDEO

Tapehead Block AOE

Tapehead AOE (Red) & Tapehead Block AOE (Black)

GO SWANKY MODES!

BEATBOX

Uglystick AOE

Brian J. Bonislawsky
1997

abcdefghijklmnopqrstuvwxyzABCDEFGHIJKLMNOPQR
STUVWXYZ-$1234567890(.;'!*?:)fifl-áöüåçèîñóæøœÁ

Vanguard III AOE

Vanguard III AOE

Brian J. Bonislawsky
1998

Red & Black Display of Overlap
of Type for special effect.

abccde_fgthytklmnopqr_stuv-wxyzA
BCDEFGHIJKLMNOPQRSTUVWXYZ-$

Vanguard III AOE - Italic

abccde_fgthytklmnopqr_stuv-wxyzA
BCDEFGHIJKLMNOPQRSTUVWXYZ-$

Vanguard III AOE - Bold

VEGA

abccde_fgthytklmnopqr_stuv-wxyzA
BCDEFGHIJKLMNOPQRSTUVWXYZ-$

Vanguard III AOE - Bold Italic

RILOS

abccde_fgthytklmnopqr_stuv-wxyzA
BCDEFGHIJKLMNOPQRSTUVWXYZ-$

Vanguard III AOE (Black) & Vanguard III AOE - Bold (Red)

ALPHA CENTAURI

ANGST?

YoungItch AOE

Brian J. Bonislawsky
1999

abcdefghijklmnopqrstuvwxyzABCDEFGHIJKLMNOPQR
STUVWXYZ-$1234567890(.;'!*?:)fifl-áöüåçèîñóæøœÄ

BIOLOGICAL

ZenoPotion AOE

Brian J. Bonislawsky
2001

abcdefghijklmnopqrstuvwxyzABCDEFGHIJKLMNOPQRSTUV
WXYZ-$1234567890(.;'!*?:)fifl-áöüåçèîñóæøœÄÖÜÅÇÈÎÑ

Astigmatic

CARTER & CONE TYPE INC.

CARTER & CONE TYPE INC. is a two-person typefoundry that designs original typefaces and makes fonts. It was started in January 1992 by Cherie Cone and Matthew Carter, who still run it.

In addition to the faces shown on the following pages, Carter & Cone have produced types on commission for Apple (Skia), Microsoft (the screen fonts Verdana, Tahoma, Nina and Georgia), *Time, Newsweek, Wired, U.S. News & World Report, Sports Illustrated, The Washington Post, The Boston Globe, The Philadelphia Inquirer, The New York Times, El País* and the Walker Art Center.

Contact Cherie at cecone@earthlink.net, or telephone her at 800 952–2129.

CAPITALS ABCDE FGHIJKLMNOPQRS TUVWXYZ&ÆŒ

lowercase abcdefghij klmnopqrstuvwxyz æffffifjflffiffl µœß

figures 1234567890ᵃᵒ ¼½¾%$£¢¥ƒ§¶*†‡©

points .,:;!?...""""‹›()[]{}—

accents áàâäãåçéèêë íìîïñóòôöõøúùûüÿ &c.

Ionic Number One

Matthew Carter
1999

Set at 36-point.

Carter & Cone

Mantinia®

Matthew Carter
1993

This titling face is meant for use at display sizes. The letters are based on inscriptional forms, inspired by those painted and engraved by the Italian Renaissance artist Andrea Mantegna.

CAPS & SUPERIORS

AᴬBᴮCᶜDᴰEᴱFᶠGᴳHᴴ
IᴵJᴶKᴷLᴸMᴹNᴺOᴼPᴾQ Q
RᴿSˢTᵀUᵁVⱽWXˣ
Yʸ&&ZᶻÆᴁŒŒ

FIGURES 1234567890

SMALL·CAPITALS

ACEHIORSTUWYZ

TALLᴸ ϙ CAPItALˢ I T LY

Mantinia®

Matthew Carter
1993

Mantinia has a number of
"inscriptional" characters not
normally found in type:
16 ligatures, four tall capitals,
13 small capitals, and a complete
alphabet of superior capitals
kerned to combine with the
regular caps. The font also
includes an interpoint and two
leaves. The specimen is set at
36-point.

LIGATURES

TH V CT Æ UP LA TT Œ
TU TW TY ÆE MP MD MB 'E

ALERNATIVES

ᴬ ᴼ T&YRʳQ Q

INERPOINTS ♠ ϙ ▾

Matthew Carter
1994

Big Caslon is a display face intended to be used at large sizes.
The design is based on the largest Romans from the foundry of William Caslon.

CAPITALS ABCD
EFGHIJJKLMNO
PQRSTQUVWXYZ
&ÆŒ& SMALL CAPS
ABCDEFGHIJJKLMNO
PQRSTQUVWXYZ&ÆŒ
& figures 1234567890
symbols = @£$¢€¥ƒ©
→ points .,-–:;·!?"" ‹›()[]{}

1-800-952-2129

lowercase abcdefg
hijklmnopqrstuvwxyz
ßæœ ligatures ctst
fbfffhfifjfkflftffhffiffllfft
fractions $\frac{1}{4}\frac{1}{2}\frac{3}{4}\frac{1}{3}\frac{2}{3}\frac{1}{8}\frac{3}{8}\frac{5}{8}\frac{7}{8}$
sup¹²³⁴⁵⁶⁷⁸⁹⁰/inf₁₂₃₄₅₆₇₈₉₀
reference marks ¶§*†‡
& accents áàâäãåçéèêë
íìîïñóòôöõøúùûüÿ etc.

Big Caslon

Matthew Carter
1994

Big Caslon comes in a set of
four fonts:
Big Caslon
Big Caslon Small Caps
Big Caslon Expert
Big Caslon Alternatives.

Carter & Cone

Matthew Carter
1992

Big Figgins Roman and Italic
are essentially the same
typefaces as the Elephant and
Elephant Italic that were
included in Microsoft's
TrueType Fontpack 2.
Set at 36-point.

☞ **Big Figgins Roman**
ABCDEFGHIJKLMN
OPQRSTUVWXYZ&
abcdefghijklmnopqrstu
vwxyz 1234567890

Big Figgins Italic ☞
ABCDEFGHIJKLM
NOPQRSTUVWXYZ
&abcdefghijklmnopqrs
tuvwxyz 1234567890

BIG FIGGINS OPEN

ABCDEFGHIJKLMc
NOPRSTUVWXYZ&
ÆŒ 1234567890½%
$¢£¥ƒ¶§*†‡@❀ 36-PT.

BIG FIGGINS OPEN CC

ABCDEFGHIJKLMcNOP
RSTUVWXYZ&ÆŒ 1234
567890%$¢£¥ƒ¶§*†‡@.,.;:-
O[]{}""''‹›¡!¿?... ❀ 30-POINT.

Big Figgins Open

Matthew Carter
1998

These display faces are derived from types shown in the specimens of Vincent Figgins of 1815 and 1817.
Big Figgins Open is a titling face with no lowercase.

Carter & Cone

Sammy Roman

Matthew Carter
1996

Sammy Roman is loosely based on the seventeenth-century Romans of Jean Jannon. It was originally designed to accompany kanji and kana types produced by DynaLab, Taiwan.

¶ABCDEFGHIJKLMNOP
QRSTUVWXYZ&ÆŒabc
defghijklmnopqrstuvwxyzæœ
ctstfffifjflffiffllß1234567890 42·

¶ABCDEFGHIJKLMNOPQR
STUVWXYZ&ÆŒabcdefghijkl
mnopqrstuvwxyzæœctstfffifjflffiffl
1234567890$¢£.,:;!?()[]{}... 36-pt.

¶ABCDEFGHIJKLMNOPQRSTUVWXYZ&
ÆŒabcdefghijklmnopqrstuvwxyzæœctstfffifjflffiffl
1234567890$¢£.,:;-!?""""◦()[]{}/|\@©®™ 24-point

❦ AABCDEFFGHIIJKKLMMNOPQRRSTTUVWXXYZ❦

SOPHIA HAS TEN JOINING CHARACTERS

C E F G H L R T T Z

THAT LINK TO OTHER LETTERS TO FORM LIGATURES. FOR EXAMPLE C+A=CA

CA CT EC EE EG EQ ET
FE FO FT GE GG GO HE
HO LA LL LS LZ RÆ ST
TT TV TW TY TZ ZA ZZ

Sophia®

Matthew Carter
1993

The design of Sophia was suggested by hybrid alphabets of capitals, uncials and Greek letterforms from 6th-century Constantinople.
In the specimen the capitals (with alternatives in red) are set at 48-point.

Carter & Cone

Fenway Roman

ABCDEFGHIJKLMNOPQRSTUVWXYZ&ÆŒ
abcdefghijklmnopqrstuvwxyzæœfiflß1234567890

FENWAY SMALL CAPS

ABCDEFGHIJKLMNOPQRSTUVWXYZ&ÆŒ

Fenway Italic

ABCDEFGHIJKLMNOPQRSTUVWXYZ&ÆŒ
abcdefghijklmnopqrstuvwxyzæœfiflß 1234567890

Fenway was commissioned by *Sports Illustrated* to replace Times Roman as the text face of the magazine. It has a stronger color than Times but an equivalent character count, achieved in part by making the capitals more compact. The copy-fitting issue was critical: the writers and editors insisted that the new text face should get as many words on the page as Times had delivered. 14-point.

One important aspect of Fenway was the design of the Roman Small Capitals. These were intended mainly for setting ACRONYMS, very common in the text of the magazine, and were made slightly bigger, therefore, than the small capitals conventionally found in typefaces for books. 12-point.

The figures, which occur very frequently in the magazine as dates, scores, averages and other statistics, are a hybrid between the ranging capital form (too prominent, as in Times) and the old-style lowercase form (too literary). Fenway was introduced in February 1998. 10-point.

ITC Galliard Roman

ABCDEFGHIJKLMNOPQRSTUVWXYZ&Æ
abcdefghijklmnopqrstuvwxyzæœffffiffiflffifflß &
1234567890$¢£€¥ƒ 1234567890 1/8 3/8 5/8 7/8 1/6 5/6 1/5 2/5 3/5 4/5 1/4 3/4 1/2
$¢1234567890,.-/$¢1234567890,.- 1234567890 (abdehilmnorstv)
& Q a ct ct d e h m n r R st t t z

ITC Galliard Small Caps

ABCDEFGHIJKLMNOPQRSTUVWXYZ&ÆŒÇĐŁŠŽÞQ

ITC Galliard Italic

ABCDEFGHIJKLMNOPQRSTUVWXYZ&ÆŒ
abcdefghijklmnopqrstuvwxyzæœffffiffiflffifflfrßij
1234567890$¢£€¥ƒ 1234567890 1/8 3/8 5/8 7/8 1/4 3/4 1/2
$¢1234567890,.-/$¢1234567890,.- (abdehilmnorstv) *@ 20-point*
& Q a ct d e é g k m n nt sp st st t v z

Galliard was designed as a four-weight family for Mergenthaler Linotype in 1978. Three years later it was acquired by the International Typeface Corporation and re-released as ITC Galliard. The Carter & Cone digitization of the regular weight of Roman and Italic, done in 1992, includes the flourished final letters and other peculiars that were part of the original photocomposition fonts. 12-point

ITC Galliard® CC

Matthew Carter
1978

Galliard is a revival of the types of the sixteenth-century French punchcutter Robert Granjon.

There are 11 fonts in the Carter & Cone version of ITC Galliard. Not shown here is a font of Roman old-style figures on uniform width for setting tables.

Miller Display Light *and Light Italic* **Miller Display Roman** *and Italic* Miller Display Roman Small Caps & *Italic Small Caps* Miller Display Semibold *& Semibold Italic* **Miller Display Bold**

1-800-952-2129

Miller Text Roman & *Italic*

ABCDEFGHIJKLMNOPQRSTUVWXYZ&ÆŒ&

ABCDEFGHIJKLMNOPQRSTUVWXYZ&ÆŒ&

abcdefghijklmnopqrstuvwxyzæœfiflß 1234567890

ABCDEFGHIJKLMNOPQRSTUVWXYZ&ÆŒ&

ABCDEFGHIJKLMNOPQRSTUVWXYZ&ÆŒ&

abcdefghijklmnopqrstuvwxyzæœfiflß 1234567890

Miller Text Bold & *Bold Italic*

ABCDEFGHIJKLMNOPQRSTUVWXYZ&ÆŒ&

abcdefghijklmnopqrstuvwxyzæœfiflß 1234567890

ABCDEFGHIJKLMNOPQRSTUVWXYZ&ÆŒ&

abcdefghijklmnopqrstuvwxyzæœfiflß 1234567890

Miller®

Matthew Carter
1997

The Text alphabets are shown at 18-point.

Carter & Cone

MILLER is a 'Scotch Roman,' a style that had its beginnings in the foundries of Alexander Wilson in Glasgow and William Miller in Edinburgh between about 1810 and 1820. It is considered that the punchcutter Richard Austin was responsible for the types of both Scottish foundries—they are certainly difficult to tell apart. 14-pt.

IN 1839 the Dickinson foundry of Boston imported types from Scotland that became extremely popular in the United States (where the 'Scotch' name was first used). Given its former success and its sturdy legibility it's perhaps odd that so few contemporary versions of Scotch Roman have been made. Miller is a revival of the style, but is not based on any one historical model. 12-pt.

Matthew Carter
1995

The design of Wilson Greek is based on a type cut by Alexander Wilson for the Glasgow Homer of 1756.

Wilson Greek is shown here as a font for the GreekKeys layout. It is also available as WilsonGk-Polytonic.
Wilson Greek is compatible with Miller Text in the sense that the capitals common to both Roman and Greek are the same, as are the figures, etc.
A font called Miller-Classical (not shown here) has vowels with macrons for setting Latin. These fonts are available as PostScript for the Macintosh only.

Set at 20-point.

Wilson Gkeys

ΑΒΓΔΕΖΗΘΙΚΛΜΝΞΟΠΡΣΤΥΦΧΨΩ

αβϐγδεζηϑθικλμνξοπρϱϛσϲϲςτυφϕχψω ϡϝϟ

άὰᾶἀἁἂἃἄἅἆἇᾀᾁᾂᾃᾄᾅᾆᾇέὲἐἑἒἓἔἕἠἡἢἣἤἥ

ἦἧἤὴῆἠῃῄῂῇῃῆῃ ιὶῖἰἱἲἳἴἵἶἷῐῑΐ ὀόὸὂὃὄὅ ρῥ ύὺῦὐὑ

ὒὓὔὕῠῡΰ ϋὖ ϋ ὤ ὠὢῶὣὤὥὦὧ ῲ ῴ ῶ ῳῴῷῲῶῷῲῷ

.,·;"—‐˘()[]{}⟦⟧⟨⟩␣/|*† ʽʼ˜᾿῾᾿´`῀῎῍῞῟῝῾ ͺ .

Wilson Gkeys ligatures

αι αί αὶ αῖ ἀι ἀί ἀί ἀῖ ἀι ἀῖ ἀῖ ἀῖ αγ αί ἀπο ἀπο ας ἀς αυ αύ αῦ

αὐ αὐ αὐ αῦ Γ γα γά γὰ Γ γε γέ γι γκ γο γό γν γυ γω

ει εί εὶ εῖ ἐι ἐί ἐί ἐῖ ἐῖ ἐῖ ἐν Θ κα καὶ καὶ κὴ κε κέ κλ κυ

κλ μα μαι με μέ μὲ Θ ᾽

ϖ πε πέ πη πη πι πί πὶ πλ πν πο πγ ππ πῂ πυ πω

σϐ σε ση ση σθ ϑ ϑ σι σκ σμ σο σό σπ ας στ συ χ σφ σω

Τ ται τε τέ τη τή τὴ τῆ τη τι τί τὶ τλ τν το τγ Τ τυ τω τῳ

χα χε χη χθ χ χυ χο χρ χω

Alisal

ABCDEFGHIJKLMNOPQRSTU
VWXYZ&ÆŒ 1234567890
abcdefghijklmnopqrstuvwxyzfifl

Alisal Italic

ABCDEFGHIJKLMNOPQRSTUVW
XYZ&ÆŒ 1234567890
abcdefghijklmnopqrstuvwxyzæœfiflß

Alisal Bold

ABCDEFGHIJKLMNOPQRSTU
VWXYZ&ÆŒ 1234567890
abcdefghijklmnopqrstuvwxyzfi

Alisal®

Matthew Carter
1995

Alisal is available both from Carter & Cone and from fonts.com.

Set at 30-point.

Carter & Cone

Chank

STUDIO CHANK MINNEAPOLIS USA

CHANK FONTS

Mister Chank Diesel
Photo by Chris Sheehan

The Chank Company
P.O. Box 580736
Minneapolis, MN 55458
Phone 612.782.2245
Toll-Free 1.877.GO.CHANK!
www.chank.com
contact@chank.com

The Chank Company operates out of a warehouse studio in the arts community of Northeast Minneapolis. Mister Chank Diesel, president and CEO, began making fonts in 1992 when he worked as creative director of the alternative music magazine, *Cake*.

Chank started selling fonts door-to-door as The Travelling Font Salesman in 1995. His fonts were featured in the Smithsonian's Cooper-Hewitt National Design Museum as a notable example of contemporary typography in 1996, the same year he established **www.chank.com**. In 1997, Chank incorporated the company and he was profiled in *The Wall Street Journal,* complete with etched portrait.

The first font Chank created, Mister Frisky, remains his most popular. Mister Frisky and its companion font Uncle Stinky have enhanced packaging for a vast array of clients, from McDonalds to Taco Bell, from Girl Scouts and Barbie to Howard Stern and Willy Wonka, from Aunt Jemima to Walt Disney, from Coca-Cola to Welch's Grape Soda, from Prince to Wendy's.

The Chank Company also creates custom fonts for companies who want exclusive rights and a specific design for a typeface. Clients who have used Chank's custom font services include Belkin, Bop! Magazine, Church's Chicken, Magnetic Poetry, Medtronic, Mervyn's California, Multitech, Ocean Spray, P. Puff Industries, and 2 Grrrls.

Chank's worldwide fame for the alphabet doesn't end with fonts. Since 1995, the Minneapolis designer has been churning out quirky alphabetic illustrations and paintings – including his interpretation of Gainsborough's Blue Boy – with a hope to beat Picasso's Guinness Book record by creating more than a million pieces in his lifetime. As of May 2002, Chank's pieces number more than 9,300.

Chank's art and fonts are collected by fans around the world, including Sweden, Spain, Germany, Japan, Australia, New Zealand, Canada, and the USA.

Chank has also built an international reputation through mentoring and representing font designers from other countries such as Sweden, New Zealand, Germany, Denmark, Australia, and Canada.

In these pages, you'll find font specimens by Chank, David Buck of New Zealand, Joseph Churchward of New Zealand, Bill Moran of St. Paul, and Martin Fredrikson of Sweden.

Chank fonts are available in Mac and PC, PostScript and True Type. They can be instantly downloaded from www.chank.com or ordered by phone, toll-free, at 1-877-GO-CHANK.

ABRA KEBOB
my powers aren't working

AaBbCcDdEeFfGgHhIiJjKkLlMmNnOoPpQq
RrSsTtUuVvWwXxYyZz 123456789 ?@&$%

Billsville

Chank Diesel
1998

Originally created as a custom font created for Tripod.com, this playful display font is named after the company's hometown of Williamsville, MA.

Billy Regular

AaBbCcDdEeFfGgHhIiJjKkLlMmNnOoPpQqRrSs
TtUuVvWwXxYyZz 123456789 ?@&$%(*)

Billy Bold

AaBbCcDdEeFfGgHhIiJjKkLlMmNnOoPp
QqRrSsTtUuVvWwXxYyZz 123456789

Billy & Billy Bold

David Buck
1998, 2001

The quintessential SparkyType font; a charming, informal, pleasant sans.

Bonehead

AaBbCcDdEeFfGgHhIiJjKkLlMmNn
OoPpQqRrSsTtUuVvWwXxYyZz !123

Brainhead

AaBbCcDdEeFfGgHhIiJjKkLlMmNn
OoPpQqRrSsTtUuVvWwXxYyZz !123

Buckethead

AaBbCcDdEeFfGgHhIiJjKkLlMmNn
OoPpQqRrSsTtUuVvWwXxYyZz !123

B-head Family

Chank Diesel
1994

As an exercise in creating fonts with no curves, Chank designed Buckethead for CAKE magazine.

Chank

Chank Diesel
1998

This industrial display font is inspired by a big neon Grain Belt Beer sign that welcomes visitors into Northeast Minneapolis. It is the unofficial flag of Chank's neighborhood. This simple geometric serif font was featured as the Chank Font of the Month for August 1999.

Notice the bottlecap that dots the lowercase i.

Inspirational Beer

AaBbCcDdEeFfGgHhIiJjKkLlMmNnOoPpQqRr
SsTtUuVvWwXxYyZz 123456789 ?@&$%ø:()

Chankbats

Chank Diesel
2001

A trip to the hospital gave Chank the time to draw all his favorite doodles for these two fonts, Chankbats Critters and Chankbats Objects. Chank's iconic repertoire has been growing over the years, evolving from the simple cat, dog, and spoon sketches to the more advanced chair, tick, and Justin-Timberlake-wearing-Christina-Aguilera's-bandana.

Chankbats Critters

Chankbats Objects

Chunder

Chank Diesel
1996

Sometimes the prettiest faces aren't the most inviting. And sometimes the ugliest faces front a great personality.

Chunder is inspired by the hand-painted cursive signage of urban boutiques where a shopkeeper can't afford to hire a very good sign painter.

Columbia Garden

AaBbCcDdEe FfGgHhIiJjKkLlMmN
nOoPpQqRrSsTtUuVvWwXxYyZz

go make some more coffee!

will nothing stop the shakes?

Nothing pharmaceutical even begins to match the required effect

ESPRESSO TIME

suckle it down, savor the flavor. Relief at last. Thank goodness

simmer down now

Chauncy Family

Chank Diesel & David Buck
1997-2002

Originally released as the free font Chauncy Snowman in the winter of 1996, the playful font of Chank's whimsical handwriting has been continuously updated, now with a complete character set and three new additions to the family arriving in the spring of 2002.

Chauncy Deluxxe

AaBbCcDdEeFfGgHhIiJjKkLlMmNnOoPpQqRrSsTtUu
VvWwXxYyZz 123456789 ?@¢$%¢:(¡™ß☆S☺⊘©Ⓐ)

Chauncy Deluxxe Bold

AaBbCcDdEeFfGgHhIiJjKkLlMmNnOoPpQqRrSsTtUu
VvWwXxYyZz 123456789 ?@¢$%¢:()

Chauncy Decaf

AaBbCcDdEeFfGgHhIiJjKkLlMmNnOoPpQqRrSsTtUuVv
WwXxYyZz 123456789 ?@¢$%¢:()

Chauncy Decaf Bold

AaBbCcDdEeFfGgHhIiJjKkLlMmNnOoPpQqRrSsTtUuVv
WwXxYyZz 123456789 ?@¢$%¢:()

Chank

MINT SHUFFLE

AaBbCcDdEeFfGgHhIiJjKkLlMmNnOoPp
OqRrSsTtUuVvWwXxYyZz 123456789 ?&

In 2001, New Zealand type designer Joseph Churchward partnered with Chank to release *Churchward Type Volume One*, the first collection of Churchward type ever released digitally. Churchward's typefaces had been out of circulation since the 1980s, when typesetting technologies went digital. Churchward's notable type designs of the '70s were distributed by Berthold of Germany and used in photolettering machines.

Churchward's type designs vary from functional to ornamental and traditional to cutting edge. His work is influenced by conventional type techniques, New Zealand native island art, and his rich ethnic heritage in Chinese, Tongan, Scottish, English, and Samoan cultures. His portfolio includes more than 300 original typefaces, created over the past thirty years.

"It wasn't easy choosing merely 15 fonts from such a fruitful collection of exquisite craftsmanship," said Chank. "The fonts we compiled for this initial release come together as a snapshot of the innovation and diversity of Mr. Churchward's talents in typography."

SCREAM

with that much flexibility, you might expect a person to snap

summer women ransom

WINTER MEN, ALL HANDSOME & JACKETED BURLY

security measures seem futile

Hooliganism continues unabated

Churchward Heading Extralight

AaBbCcDdEeFfGgHhIiJjKkLlMmN
nOoPpQqRrSsTtUuVvWwXxYyZz

Churchward Heading Light

AaBbCcDdEeFfGgHhIiJjKkLl
MmNnOoPpQqRrSsTtUuVvW

Churchward Heading Medium

AaBbCcDdEeFfGgHhIiJj
KkLlMmNnOoPpQqRrSs

Churchward Heading Extrabold

AaBbCcDdEeFfGg
HhIiJjKkLlMmNn

Churchward Heading Ultrabold

AaBbCcDdEe
FfGgHhIiJjKk

Churchward Heading Superbold

AaBbCcDd
EeFfGgHhIi

AaBbCcDdEeFfGgHhIiJjKkKlLlMm
NnOoPpQqRrSsTtUuVvWwXxYyZz

OBCDEFGHIJKLMNOPQRSTUVWXYZ
123456789 &*(~)?!LI

Churchward Maori Bold

Joseph Churchward
1998

Churchward Ta-Tiki

Joseph Churchward
1999

Churchward Samoa

Joseph Churchward
2001

Churchward is meticulous about his
type design, working up to 300 hours
to design one font. The process involves
intricate penciling to get the right
shape, then it gets onto board,
penciled again, and then inked and
retouched. Lastly, Churchward sends
quality copies to The Chank Company,
where the designs are scanned, redrawn
digitally, spaced and kerned.

Three generations of type designers
worked on the *Churchward Type Volume
One* project, including Chank, 33;
David Buck, a 24-year-old New
Zealand type designer training with
The Chank Company; and Churchward,
born in 1933.

POLYNESIAN

Sun-soaked beaches & clear blue lagoons brimming with tropical fish.

Prime Vacation Destination

Would you climb that palm tree and fetch me a tasty coconut?

RAPTURE

Churchward Samoa Light

AaBbCcDdEeFfGgHhIiJjKkLlMmNnOoPpQqRr
SsTtUuVvWwXxYyZz 123456789 ?@&$%ø()

Churchward Samoa Regular

AaBbCcDdEeFfGg
HhIiJjKkLlMmNnO
oPpQqRrSsTtUuVv

Churchward Samoa Medium

AaBbCcDdEeFfGg
HhIiJjKkLlMmNnO
oPpQqRrSsTtUuV

Churchward Samoa Bold

AaBbCcDdEeFfG
gHhIiJjKkLlMmNn
OoPpQqRrSsTtU

Churchward Samoa Extrabold

AaBbCcDdEeFfGgHhIiJjKkLlMmNnOo
PpQqRrSsTtUuVvWwXxYyZz 1234567

Chank

Chank Diesel
1997

Corndog is a super chunky handwriting font with teeth. The original art for this font was drawn very, very tiny with an extrafine rollerball pen. Then it was enlarged on a crappy copier, which accounts for the little bits of flotsam and jetsam that adorn this alphabet.

The original Corndog font was tidied up to create the friendlier Corndog Clean.

vaniSHiNg ice cReam

Corndog

AaBBCcDDEeFfGGHHIiJjKKℒLMmNNOOPPQqRRSs
TtUuVvWwXxYyZz 123456789 ?@¿¦§%(*)

Corndog Clean

AaBbCcDDEeFfGGHHIiJjKkℒLMmNNOOPPQqRRSs
TtUuVvWwXxYyZz 123456789 ?@¿¦§%(*)

Chank Diesel
1993

Chank designed Crusti, Crustier, Crustiest, and Crusti Wacky to use in *Cake*, a fanzine that celebrated grunge music.

With a D.I.Y. ethic, inspiration from the likes of Nirvana, and a copier at Kinko's, Chank created his own fonts. Chank made the four different weights of the Crustis by enlarging and reducing repeated copies to get just the right amounts of grit and grime on his grunge alphabet.

"Grunge Typography? I invented it!" claims Chank.

CHUMMING

the bleeding chunks of ground bait tempt all kinds of savory characters

you believe in cod?

I tried it, now I'm hooked

Crusti

AaBbCcDdEeFfGgHhIiJjKkLlMmNnOoPpQqRrSsTt
UuVvWwXxYyZz 123456789 ?@&$%(*)

CrustiEr

AaBbCcDdEeFf
GgHhIiJjKkLl

CrustiEst

AaBbCcDdEeF
fGgHhIiJjKkL

CrustiWacky

AaBbCcDdEeFfG
gHhIiJjKkLlMmN

Napkin Dribblets

AaBbCcDdEeFfGgHhIiJjKkLlMmNnOoPpQqRrSs
TtUuVvWwXxYyZz 123456789 ?¿$%ø:(*)

stallion riders club

aabbccddeeffgghhiijjkkllmmnnooppqqrrss
ttuuvvwwxxyyzz 123456789 ?&$%ø:(*)

Irritated Saddle Rash

AaBbCcDdEeFfGgHhIiJjKkLlMmNnOoPpQqRrSs
TtUuVvWwXxYyZz 123456789 ?&$%ø:(*)

GIDDY-UP HORSEY

AABBCCDDEEFFGGHHIIJJKKLLMMNNOOPPQQR
RSSTTUUVVWWXXYYZZ 123456789 ?&$%ø:()

Gobbler

Chank Diesel
1997

This font was drawn with a leaky pen on a napkin at the Modern Cafe in Northeast Minneapolis while the designer, Mister Chank Diesel, was waiting for his pot roast dinner. "Apple cobbler drippings on the napkin add more character to the strokes of each letter," says Chank.

Gobbler works great for either text or display purposes.

Gideon

Bill Moran
2001

A "significant other" font for the popular Goshen typeface, Gideon was featured as the Chank Font of the Month for August 2001.

As with all Blinc fonts by Bill Moran, it has its roots in letterpress. To keep it real, we left in the crud that can only come from proofing type on a printing press. Wet ink meets vector technology.

Golgotha

Bill Moran & Chank Diesel
2001

Golgotha is a quirky, jerky remix of Goshen's caps with Gideon's lowercase letters.

Goshen

Bill Moran
2000

Goshen was printed from wooden letterpress blocks, and then fontified by handyman Bill Moran at Blinc Studio. The distressed textures of these printed letters mingle with the strong, simple letterforms.

Chank

Created by the famed creator of the *Rolling Stone* logo, this font won a Type Director's Club TDC Award and was featured as the Chank Font of the Month in September 2001.

THE FOGGY CITY

OR POP OVER TO VENICE BEACH TO PEEP THE LADIES. YOU CHOOSE

Keester

ABCDEFFGHIJKLMMNNOPQRSTUV
WWXYZ 123456789 ?@&$%ø:()

Keester Black

ABCDEEFFGHIJKLMMNNOPQRSTUVWW
XYZ 123456789 ?@&$%ø:()

Chank Diesel
1993

One of Chank's famous retro fonts, based on the Lambretta scooter logo.

AaBbCcDdEeFfGgHhIiJjKkLlMmNnOoPpQqRr
SsTtUuVvWwXxYyZz 123456789 ?&$%¿:()

Chank Diesel
1997, 1999

Chank's favorite font ever. When you have a liquor store, you don't have to do anything fancy to get people in there. Just have a big, clear, easy-to-read sign that says LIQUOR and people will come.

Inspired by the *Life* magazine logo and hand-painted liquor store signage in Northeast Minneapolis, Chank created Liquorstore as an exercise in font creation based on simple yet elegant geometric forms.

The regular version came first in 1997; the jazzy small caps arrived in 1999.

OPEN SATURDAY

WILL IMPAIR JUDGEMENT, AND MAKE YOU DANCE LIKE A WHITE MAN SHOULDN'T

Door Charge: $15

Liquorstore

AaBbCcDdEeFfGgHhIiJjKkLlMmNnOoPpQqRrSs
TtUuVvWwXxYyZz 123456789 ?&$%ø:[*]

Liquorstore Jazz

AaBbCcDdEeFfGgHhIiJjKkLlMmNnOoPpQqRrSs
TtUuVvWwXxYyZz 123456789 ?&$%ø:[*]

Overhead Projection Unit

Prices do vary, but honestly, they all do the same thing. Don't be fooled by bells and whistles

AaBbCcDdEeFfGgHhIiJjKkLlMmNnOoPpQqRrSsTtUuVv
WwXxYyZz 123456789 ?@&$%ø:([*])

McKracken

David Buck
1999

McKracken was featured as the Chank Font of the Month in May 2001. Use it real big and you'll see the details. Use it small and it wiggles around a bit.

forklift

OPERATED BEYOND THE MANUFACTURER'S RECOMMENDED SPECIFICATIONS

PLOWING COMPANY

Mingler Family

Chank Diesel
1998, 1999

Chank created the Minglers as alternatives to Futura Condensed Extrabold. The family was first featured as the Chank Font of the Month for January 1998.

Mingler Nipsy is jazzed up with stars instead of dots on the i, j, !, and ? characters. Mingler Ritzy is flashy, with lots of stars and more geometric, stylized letterforms. Mingler Snowy is a frosty sensation, a perfect partner for snow-capped holiday gatherings.

Mingler Nipsy

AaBbCcDdEeFfGgHhIiJjKkLlMmNnOoPpQqRr
SsTtUuVvWwXxYyZz 123456789 ?@&$%(*)

Mingler Ritzy

AaBbCcDdEeFfGgHhIiJjKkLlMmNnOoPpQqRr
SsTtUuVvWwXxYyZz 123456789 ?@&$%(*)

Mingler Snowy

AaBbCcDdEeFfGgHhIiJjKkLlMmNnOoPpQq
RrSsTtUuVvWwXxYyZz 123456789 ?@

Chank

Chank Diesel
1992, 1999

Chank's first font ever is also his most popular. The new standard in holiday joviality, whether it's Christmas, Halloween, or Valentine's Day. Comes with the alternate character set Uncle Stinky and Uncle Stinky Bold.

Since it was created in 1992, Mister Frisky has been used on beverage containers, movie posters, candy boxes, CD covers and other printed matter all over the world.

James' Adventures

touring the world on a humungous summer fruit

wonderment aplenty swiftly ensued

Long live the magician

Generous servings of nachos

Mister Frisky

AaBbCcDdEeFfGgHhIiJjKkLlMmNnOoPpQqRrSsTt
UuVvWwXxYyZz 123456789 ?@&$%ø:([*])

Mister Frisky Bold

AaBbCcDdEeFfGgHhIiJjKkLlMmNnOoPpQqRr
SsTtUuVvWwXxYyZz 123456789 ?@&$%ø(*)

Chank Diesel
1996

Inspired by circles, lines and the future.

Trans-Atlantic

AaBbCcDdEeFfGgHhIiJjKkLlMmNnOoPpQq
RrSsTtUuVvWwXxYyZz 123456789 ?&(*)

Parkway Motel

AaBbCcDdEeFfGgHhIiJjKkLlMmNnOo
PpQqRrSsTtUuVvWwXxYyZz 1234567

Parkway Hotel

AaBbCcDdEeFfGgHhIiJjKkLlMmNnOo
PpQqRrSsTtUuVvWwXxYyZz 1234567

Parkway Resort-o-tel

AaBbCcDdEeFfGgHhIiJjKkLlMmNnOoPpQqRr
SsTtUuVvWwXxYyZz 123456789 ?&$%([*])

SHOELACES
faking the funk

AaBbCcDdEeFfGgHhIiJjKkLlMmNnOo
PpQqRrSsTtUuVvWwXxYyZz 12345678

Vehicular I.D.

AaBbCcDdEeFfGgHhIiJjKkLlMmNnOoPpQqRr
SsTtUuVvWwXxYyZz 123456789 ?&$%([*])

Parkway Family

Chank Diesel
1994

The Parkway font family was inspired by the Parkway Theater marquee in South Minneapolis and the abandoned hotel signage along a strip of U.S. highway running from Tallahassee to Tampa in Florida. A class retro font trio, the Parkways speak of nostalgia and Americana.

Rosemary

Chank Diesel
2000

Chank's ode to Cooper Black. It's a little flashier than Cooper, but it's still a nice, friendly, black font with curves everywhere.

Sauerkrauto

Martin Fredrikson Core
2000

A Swedish type designer's fascination with German license plates led to the creation of this stylish display face.

Chank

Starlit Canoe Fanatic

AaBbCcDdEe FfGgHhIiJjKkLlMmNnOoPpQqRr
SsTtUuVvWwXxYyZz 123456789 ?&$%([*])

That'll Learn Ya

Sodom

AaBbCcDdEeFfGgHhIiJjKkLlMmNnOoPpQqRrSs
TtUuVvWwXxYyZz 123456789 ?&$%ø:(*)

Gomorrah

AaBbCcDdEeFfGgHhIiJjKkLlMmNnOoPpQqRr
SsTtUuVvWwXxYyZz 123456789 ?&$%ø:(*)

Thistle Farmers

Space Toaster

AaBbCcDdEeFfGgHhIiJjKkLlMmNnOoPpQqRrSsTt
UuVvWwXxYyZz 123456789 ?&$%ø:(*)

Space Toaster Bold

AaBbCcDdEeFfGgHhIiJjKkLlMmNnOoPpQqRrSs
TtUuVvWwXxYyZz 123456789 ?&$%ø:(*)

This is a warming

AaBbCcDdEeFfGgHhIiJjKkLlMmNnOoPpQqRr
SsTtUuVvWwXxYyZz 123456789 ?&$%ø:(*)

Sunshine

Chank Diesel
2000

Liquorstore meets Gobbler.
Something entirely different.

RUNAWAY TRAIN

AaBbCcDdEeFfGgHhIiJjKkLlMmNnOoPpQqRrSs
TtUuVvWwXxyyZz 123456789 ?&$%ø:(*)

Tabitha

Chank Diesel
1993

Chank created Tabitha for *Cake* magazine. This font was inspired by cable TV,
urban graffiti and sugary cereals.
Tabitha is proving to be very popular
for toy and cereal packaging.

Jemima's Husband

UNEXPECTED ENTRANCE

Uncle Stinky Family

Chank Diesel
1992, 1999

As Mister Frisky's alternate character
set, use Uncle Stinky to prevent
character repetition.

Uncle Stinky

AaBbCcDdEeFfGgHhIiJjKkLlMmNnOoPpQqRrSs
TtUuVvWwXxYyZz 123456789 ?n'$%ø:(*)

Uncle Stinky Bold

AaBbCcDdEeFfGgHhIiJjKkLlMmNnOoPpQqRr
SsTtUuVvWwXxYyZz 123456789 ?&$%ø:(*)

Chank

Chank Diesel
2001

Venis rhymes with "tennis."

Chank's attempt at a Roman Sans with a Venetian influence, Venis is clean, simple and elegant with nice contrast. Still, it is not the most academically correct font. Chank's creative liberties give Venis some unique qualities in its characters that you'll especially notice in the signature lowercase y.

CLEANSING

Refreshingly Insincere and Feisty

Serenity Gene Pool

Go Back to Square One, Briefly

DISOBEDIENCE

at last the tale can be told

Venis Regular

The Venis family has an interesting family tree. Old grandpa Kraftwek begat his chosen son Liquorstore. Liquorstore hooked up with Gobbler, a saucy lass from the wrong side of the train tracks. Liquor store's rigid geometry danced

Venis Italic

with Gobbler's organic crustiness to create a terrible trio briefly known as the Trainwrecks. But alas, their name was already spoken for, and the three trainwrecks (light, regular and black) got a name change and became what we now know as the

Venis Bold

Shipwreck family. But the Shipwrecks were a vulgar bunch, and their child Sunshine ran off to college to learn refinement. Enhanced contrast showed a new elegance, but the bad complexion was hard to overcome. So

Venis Bold Italic

Sunshine lived a brief but happy lifetime, and eventually had four children of her own, with father unknown. The Venis family is the result of a complete redrawing of the Sunshine skeleton. A sans serif font with Roman contrast, graceful but quirky, kinda like Jenna Elfman. Display sizes make me think of Aveda or Clinique, but the text size is a different critter altogether.

SOPHISTICATED MEANS CORRUPTED

Yearling Lite

AaBbCcDdEeFfGgHhIiJjKkLlMmNnOoPpQqRrSsTt
UuVvWwXxYyZz 123456789 !?&$%ø:(*)

Yearling Lite Oblique

AaBbCcDdEeFfGgHhIiJjKkLlMmNnOoPpQqRrSsTt
UuVvWwXxYyZz 123456789 !?&$%ø:(*)

Yearling Regular

AaBbCcDdEeFfGgHhIiJjKkLlMmNnOoPpQqRr
SsTtUuVvWwXxYyZz 123456789 !?&$

Yearling Regular Oblique

AaBbCcDdEeFfGgHhIiJjKkLlMmNnOoPpQqRr
SsTtUuVvWwXxYyZz 123456789 !?&$

Yearling Bold

AaBbCcDdEeFfGgHhIiJjKkLlMmNnOoPp
QqRrSsTtUuVvWwXxYyZz 123456789?!

Yearling Bold Oblique

AaBbCcDdEeFfGgHhIiJjKkLlMmNnOoPp
QqRrSsTtUuVvWwXxYyZz 123456789?

Yearling Extrabold

AaBbCcDdEeFfGgHhIiJjKkLlMmNnOo
PpQqRrSsTtUuVvWwXxYyZz 123456

Yearling Extrabold Oblique

AaBbCcDdEeFfGgHhIiJjKkLlMmNnOo
PpQqRrSsTtUuVvWwXxYyZz 123456

Yearling Family

Chank Diesel
2000-2001

"After years of using my fonts, Liquorstore had cemented itself as one of my all-time favorite fonts ever. It seemed to work almost anywhere I decided to put it," says Chank.

But Liquorstore was too heavy to be a text face, and one if its most alluring attributes was the fact that the positive space and the negative space carry equal weight. Problem with that is all the blacks and whites share space evenly, like a checkerboard, then it's impossible to change weight without changing the character of the font.

As a text font to complement Liquorstore, Chank created the Yearlings, using Liquorstore as the base. He kept the emphasis on horizontal and vertical strokes (to make for nice faxes!) and the round corners to make things a bit softer, but changed the rhythm so the weights could change.

Crisp and clean, like a chrome toaster.

Chank

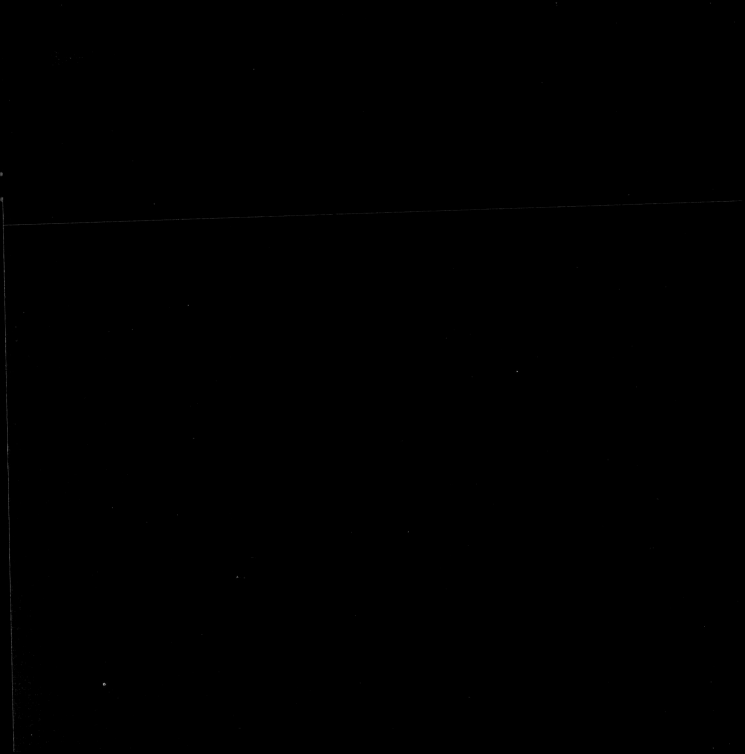

Font Diner

PREMIUM QUALITY RETRO FONTS

Font Diner
PREMIUM QUALITY RETRO FONTS

FONTSETS

Our Deluxe Collections

over 70 GREAT RETRO FONT DINER FONTS are featured in this exclusive collection.
ORDER your FONT DINER FONTS online at http://www.fontdiner.com for fast delivery.
Our postal delivered font orders come complete with a host of swell retro trinkets!

U.S.
INSPECTED
AND PASSED BY
DEPARTMENT OF
RETRO DESIGN

THESE RETRO TYPEFACES HAVE BEEN PREPARED
WITH THE UTMOST QUALITY AND FOCUS ON GENUINE
CUSTOMER SATISFACTION. EACH ITEM HAS BEEN TESTED
AND RETESTED TO ASSURE RELIABILITY AND SATISFACTION

FEATURING
GENUINE QUALITY
FONT DINER
RETRO FONTS

Preparation Instructions

FOR OPTIMUM RESULTS WE RECOMMEND THE FOLLOWING:

1 BOOT UP YOUR PERSONAL COMPUTING DEVICE AND REMEMBER TO MOUSE WITH CARE WHILE YOU ARE WAITING, TAKE THIS TIME TO HUM A SNAPPY TUNE IF YOU LIKE.

2 TAKE A MOMENT TO EXAMINE YOUR BILLFOLD OR PURSE AND DETERMINE WHICH OF YOUR PLASTIC CHARGING OR CREDIT CARDS YOU'D PREFER TO HONOR WITH US.

3 WITH YOUR PERSONAL COMPUTING DEVICE, LAUNCH YOUR FAVORITE INTERNET BROWSING APPLICATION AND HEAD TO HTTP://WWW.FONTDINER.COM

4 SELECT FROM OUR VARIETY OF FONT SETS AND PLACE YOUR ORDER ONLINE FOR FAST DELIVERY! AND REMEMBER, THE MORE FONT SETS PURCHASE, THE MORE YOU SAVE!

Get started here ...

Beer Dip

Stuart Sandler
1997

This font is sold as part of the Doggie Bag Font Set.

Beer Dip 19/14

Wear Good Housekeeping . . . I must say that I am quite disappointed with your latest quiche recipe. My husband was certainly disappointed to come home from a long day at the office to be greeted at the supper table with this unsavory dish. While I fancy myself a decent meal maker, I found four tablespoons of flour is more than adequate. Warmly, Mrs. R.h. Smith

Beer Dip

AaBbCcDdEeFfGgHhIiJjKkLlMmNnOoPpQqRrSsTtUuVv
WwXxYyZz1234567890!@#$%^&*()[]{};:'",.<>/?

Etiquette

Stuart Sandler
1997

This font is sold as part of the Doggie Bag Font Set.

EVEN THE SAVAGE BEAST MUST LEARN PROPER ETIQUETTE
ABCDEFGHIJKLMNOPQRSTUVWXYZ1234567890!@#$%^&*()[]{};:'",.<>/?

Fat Sam

Stuart Sandler
1997

This font is sold as part of the Doggie Bag Font Set.

QUARTER POUNDER WITH EXTRA MAYO
AaBbCcDdEeFfGgHhIiJjKkLlMmNnOoPpQqRrSsTtUuVv
WwXxYyZz1234567890!@#$%^&*()[]{};:'",.<>/?

Finer Diner

Stuart Sandler
1997

These fonts are sold as part of the Doggie Bag Font Set.

Finer Diner Uptown 18/12

UPPER MANHATTAN OFFERS MANY EXCITING AND HISTORICAL LANDMARKS. OFTEN TIMES ONE CAN EASILY FIND A HOT DOG VENDOR ON THEIR WAY TO THE GUGGENHEIM.

Finer Diner Uptown

AABBCCDDEEFFGGHHIIJJKKLLMMNNOoPPQQRRSSTTUUVVVW
WXXYY½¼1234567890!@#$%^+*()[]{};:'",.<>/?

Finer Diner Downtown 23/16

LOWER MANHATTAN OFFERS THE JET SET LIVE JAZZ AND ULTRA COOL MARTINI LOUNGES

Finer Diner Downtown

AABBCCDDEEFFGGHHIIJJKKLLMMNNOoPPQQRRSSTTU
VVVWWXXYY½¼1234567890!@#$%^+*()[]{};:'",.<>/?

Jack Bisio

Stuart Sandler
1997

This font is sold as part of the Doggie Bag Font Set.

Cigarette in one hand, phone number in the other, Jack was the envy of every guy in the bar. W

AaBbCcDdEeFfGgHhIiJjKkLlMmNnOoPpQqRrSsTtUuVvWwXxYyZz1234567890!@#$%^&*()[]{};:'",.<>/?

SALSA & GUACAMOLE CON TORTILLAS
ABCDEEFGHIJKLMNOPQRSTUVWXYZ1234567890!@#$%^&*()[]{}::'"..<>/?

Jumping Bean

Stuart Sandler
1997

This font is sold as part of the Doggie Bag Font Set.

Kentuckyfried 26/28

Finger lickin' chicken, taters, & such taste yummy at the finish of a good days work!

Kentuckyfried

Stuart Sandler
1997

This font is sold as part of the Doggie Bag Font Set.

Kentuckyfried

AaBbCcDdEeFfGgHhIiJjKKLlMmNnOoPpQqRrSsTtUuVvWwXxYZz
1234567890!@#$%^&*()[]{}::'"..<>/?

Permanent Waves 16/18

Airstream travel along the interstate without a radio

Permanent Waves

Stuart Sandler
1997

These fonts are sold as part of the Doggie Bag Font Set.

Permanent Waves

AaBbCcDdEeFfGgHhIiJjKkLlMmNnOoPpQqRrSsTtUu
VvWwXxYyZz1234567890!@#$%^&*()[]{}::'"..<>/?

Permanent Waves Expanded 15/17

Extra wide wiper blades for really big insects

Permanent Waves Expanded

AaBbCcDdEeFfGgHhIiJjKkLlMmNnOoPpQqRrSsTt
UuVvWwXxYyZz1234567890!@#$%^&*()[]{}::'"..<>/?

MILWAUKEE'S FINEST NIGhTSPOT
AABBCCDDEEFfGGHhIiJJKKLLMMNºOPPQₐRRSSTTUUVVWWXXYYZZ1234567890!@#$%^&*()[]{}::'"..<>/?

Taylors

Dan Taylor & Stuart Sandler
1997

This font is sold as part of the Doggie Bag Font Set.

a trip to the local craft show goes horribly awry
aaBbCcDdEeFfGg hIiJjKkLlMmNnOoPpqqRrSsTtUuVvWwXxYyZz1234567890!@#$%^*()[]{}::'"

Yarn Sale

Stuart Sandler
1997

This font is sold as part of the Doggie Bag Font Set.

Font Diner

Lounge peanuts are usually rather satty on the tongue

AaBbCcDdEeFfGgHhIiJjKkLlMmNnOoPpQqRrSsTtUuVvWwXxYyZz1234567890!@No.$%^£*()[]{}::'",.<>/?

Coffee Shop 25 Point

Caffeinated with Cream

Coffee Shop

A a B b C c D d E e F f G g H h I i J j K k L l M m N n O o P p Q q R r S s T t U u V v W w X x Y y Z z

Continental Railway 18/20

Luxury travel with a dime to spare! Impressive I'd say!

Continental Railway

AaBbCcDdEeFfGgHhIiJjKkLlMmNnOoPpQqRrSsTtUuVvWwXxYyZz1234567890!@No.$%^£*()[]{}::'",.<>/?

El Niño 18/19

Winter storms threaten the Florida coast while today in Minnesota another perfect 80° day thanks to our friend El Niño!

El Niño

AaBbCcDdEeFfGgHhIiJjKkLlMmNnOoPpQqRrSsTtUuVvWwXxYyZz1234567890!@#$%^&*()[]{};:'",.<>/?

THE MANAGEMENT KINDLY REQUESTS YOUR DEPARTURE

AaBbCcDdEeFfGgHhIiJjKkLlMmNnOoPpQqRrSsTtUuVvWwXxYyZz1234567890!@#$%^&*()[]

HOW MANY TUESDAYS MUST I WAIT FOR THAT FREELOADIN' WIMPY TO PAY UP?

Hamburger Sandwitch

A B C D E F G H I J K L M N O P Q R S T U V W X Y Z 1 2 3 4 5 6 7 8 9 0
! @ # $ % ^ & * ( ) [ ] { } ; : ' " , . < > / ?

Hamburger Sandwitch

Stuart Sandler
1998

This font is sold as part of the Brown Bag Font Set.

Font Diner

PROPER MAINTENANCE OF THE BAKELITE ENGINE REQUIRES JUST A DROP OF OIL

Lionel Classic

A B C D E F G H I J K L M N O P Q R S T U V W X Y Z 1 2 3 4 5 6 7
8 9 0 ! @ No. $ % ^ & * ( ) [ ] { } ; : ' " , . < > / ?

Lionel Classic

Stuart Sandler
1998

This font is sold as part of the Brown Bag Font Set.

ENJOY BOWLING ALLEYS AND HANDCRAFTED BEER MADE IN THE HEART OF DAIRYLAND

Milwaukee

A B C D E F G H I J K L M N O P Q R S T U V W X Y Z 1 2 3 4 5 6 7 8
9 0 ! @ # $ % ^ & * ( ) [ ] { } ; : ' " , . < > / ?

Milwaukee

Stuart Sandler
1998

This font is sold as part of the Brown Bag Font Set.

GREASY LIKE A '78 TRANNY
ABCDEFGHIJKLMNOPQRSTUVWXYZ1234567890!@No.$%^&*()[]{};:'"..<>/?

Motor Oil

Stuart Sandler
1998

This font is sold as part of the Brown Bag Font Set.

Her sister is nice lookin'...
AaBbCcDdEeFfGgHhIiJjKkLlMmNnOoPpQqRrSsTtUuVvWwXxYyZz

Ophelia

Stuart Sandler
1998

This font is sold as part of the Brown Bag Font Set.

American Cheese

Stuart Sandler
1999

This font is sold as part of the
TV Dinner Font Set.

American Cheese 18/20

DRIVE THRU SERVICE MEANS YOU'LL ALWAYS GET THE FRESHEST BURGERS RIGHT OFF OUR GRILL!

American Cheese

A B C D E F G H I J K L M N O P Q R S T U V W X Y Z 1 2 3 4 5 6 7 8 9 0 ! @ # $ % ^ ↘ * ( ) [ ] { } ; : ' " , . < > / ?

Devilette

Stuart Sandler
1999

This font is sold as part of the
TV Dinner Font Set.

Devilette 31/26

THE HAUNTED MANSION AT THE TOP OF OLD MILLER'S HILL USED TO SCARE THE LIVING CRAP OUT OF ME, NOW IT'S A SHOE STORE!

Devilette

A A B B C C D D E E F F G G H H I I J J K K L L M M N N O O P P Q Q R R S S T T U U V V W W X X Y Y Z Z 1 2 3 4 5 6 7 8 9 0 ! @ # $ % ^ & * ( ) ( ) ( ) ; : ' " , . ◄ ► / ?

Dry Cleaners

Stuart Sandler
1999

This font is sold as part of the
TV Dinner Font Set.

WE ARE NOT RESPONSIBLE FOR LOST SOCKS

ABCDEEFGHIJKLMNOPQRSTUVWXYZ 1 2 3 4 5 6 7 8 9 0 ! @ # $ % ^ & * ( ) [ ] { } ; : ' " , . < > / ?

Rojo Frijoles

Stuart Sandler
1999

This font is sold as part of the
TV Dinner Font Set.

The Special This evening is yesterdays matador!

a a B b c c D d E e f f G g H h r r j j k k l l m n N n o o P p q q R r S s T t u u V v W w x x y y z z 1 2 3 4 5 6 7 8 9 0

Singlesville Script

Stuart Sandler
1999

This font is sold as part of the
TV Dinner Font Set.

Singlesville Script 44/29

Our department store accepts all forms of payment, but if you sign-up for our exclusive credit card, you get an extra 50¢ off today! Wow!

Singlesville Script

A a B b C c D d E e F f G g H h I i J j K k L l M m N n O o P p Q q R n S s T t U u V v W w X x Y y Z z 1 2 3 4 5 6 7 8 9

ORANGE ASTRONAUT DRINK FOR INSTANT VITALITY!

Spaceman

AABBCCDDEEFFGGHHIIJJKkLLMMNNOOPPQQRRSSTTUuVVWW
XxYYZZ IIIIIIVVVIVIIVIIIIXO!@#$%^&*()[]{}:: "',. <>/?

DON'T DOUBLE CROSS OLD BLACK BART THE MEANEST. ROUGHEST DERN TOOTIN' HOMBRE YOU EVER LAID EYE'S ON OR HELL. SEE THAT YOU TAKE A DIRT NAP!

Spaghetti Western

aBCDEFGHIJKLMNOPQRSTUVWXYZ1234567890!@#$%^&*()::"'..<>/?

like a neon silhouette with an attitude
abcdefghijklmnopqrstuvwxyz1234567890!at#$%^&*];:'",.<>/?

IN HIS SOUPED UP DEUCE COUPE HE LIGHTS UP THE TIRES — NOBODY KNEW THE STRANGER WAS REALLY A SQUARE

Swinger!

AABBCCDDEEFFGGHHIIJJKKLLMMNNOOPPQQRRSSTTUUVVWWXXY
YZZI234567890!@#$%^&*()()()::'"..<>/?

AT NIGHTIME THE CITY COMES ALIVE
ABCDEFGHIJKLMNOPQRSTUVWXYZ1234567890!at#$%^&*()()::'".<>/?

Font Diner

Automatic

Stuart Sandler
2000

This font is sold as part of the
Lunch Box Font Set.

STEAMSHIP CARGO SHOULDN'T SQUEAK

ABCDEFGHIJKLMNOPQRSTUVWXYZ1234567890!@№$%^3*()[]{}::'"..<>/?

Chicken King

Stuart Sandler
2000

This font is sold as part of the
Lunch Box Font Set.

Chicken King 28/26

NAT KING COLE WAS A SWINGIN' OLD SOUL WITH A NIGHTLY SHOW & A VELVETY VOICE OF GOLD.

Chicken King

AaBBCCDDEEFFGGHHiiIiJKKLLMMNNOOPPQQRRSSTTuuVV
WWXXYYZZ1234567890!®#$%^&*()[][];:'",.<>/?

Doggie Bag Script

Stuart Sandler
2000

This font is sold as part of the
Lunch Box Font Set.

Once you've enjoyed all you can eat, bring some back for Pete!

AaBbCcDdEeFFGgHhIiJjKkLlMmNnOoPpQqRrSsTtUuVvWwXxYyZz1234567890!@#$%^3*[][][]::'"..<>/?

Johnny Lunchpail

Stuart Sandler
2000

This font is sold as part of the
Lunch Box Font Set.

Johnny Lunchpail 24/26

WHEN THE CLOCK WHISTLE BLOWS, HE DIVES INTO HIS TUNAFISH SANDWICH!

Johnny Lunchpail

aaBBCCDDEEFFGGHHiiJJKKLLMMNNOOPPQQRRSSTTUU
VVWWXXYYZZ1234567890!@#$%^&*()[][];:'",.<>/?

Kitchenette

Stuart Sandler
2000

This font is sold as part of the
Lunch Box Font Set.

Kitchenette 20/17

Kitchen appliances offer the modern hostess conveneince and elegance with simple one-touch button operation!

Kitchenette

AaBbCcDdEeFfGgHhIiJjKkLlMmNnOoPpQq
RrSsTtUuVvWwXxYyZz1234567890!@#$%^3*()()::'"..<>/?

Milwaukee Neon 33/26

DISCOUNT PHARMACY & LIQUOR STORE
CERTAIN TO HAVE A MEDICINE FOR YOU

Milwaukee Neon

ABCDEFGHIJKLMNOPQRSTUVWXYZ 1234567
890!@#$%^&*()[]{};:'",.<>/?

Milwaukee Neon

Stuart Sandler
2000

The family is composed of two fonts, a Shadow version and a Neon version to be combined to create the neon effect.

This font is sold as part of the Lunch Box Font Set.

Frosted Donuts & Hot Coffee

AaBbCcDdEeFfGgHhIiJjKkLlMmNnOoPpQqRrSsTtUu

Motorcar Atlas

Stuart Sandler
2000

This font is sold as part of the Lunch Box Font Set.

ARCHITECTURE PLANS

ABCDEFGHIJKLMNOPQRSTUVWXYZ1234567890!@#$%^&*()||||;:'",.<>//?

Regulator

Stuart Sandler
2000

This font is sold as part of the Lunch Box Font Set.

Stovetop 28/25

My Pop Loves His Chicken flavored
Stuffing With Giblets and Gizzards!

Stovetop

aaBBCCDDEeFfGGHHIiJJKKLLMmNnOoPPQQRRSSTt
UUVVWWXXyyZZ1234567890!@#$%^&*()[][];:'",.<>/?

Stovetop

Stuart Sandler
2000

This font is sold as part of the Lunch Box Font Set.

¡Warning! 18/20

EACH CRATE CONTAINS PLANS AND PARTS
TO ASSEMBLE A HELICOPTER OR TOASTER.

¡Warning!

ABCDEFGHIJKLMNOPQRSTUVWXYZ123456
7890!@#$%^&*()()();:'",.<>/?

¡Warning!

Stuart Sandler
2000

This font is sold as part of the Lunch Box Font Set.

Al's Motor-Inn 31/21

Just south past Exit 82 you'll see the bright orange neon glowing in the distance, look for the rusty sign

Al's Motor-Inn

AaBbCcDdEeFfGgHhIiJjKkLlMmNnOoPpQqRrSsTtUuVv
WwXxYyZz1234567890!@#$%^&*()[]{};:'",.<>/?

AIR CONDITIONED COMFORT
ABCDEEFGHIJHLMNOPQRSTUVWHYZ1234567890!@#$%^&*()[]{};:'",.<>/?

Kiddie Cocktails 30/26

SYRUPY GRENADINE AND LEMON-LIME SODA
GARNISHED WITH A MARASCHINO CHERRY

Kiddie Cocktails

ABCDEFGHIJKLMNOPQRSTUVWXYZ1234567890
!@#$%^&*()[][]:;'",.<>/?

Lionel Text Steam

Brimming with classic style and modern deco accessories

AaBbCcDdEeFfGgHhIiJjKkLlMmNnOoPpQqRrSsTtUuVvWwXxYyZz1234567890!@#$%^&*()[]{};:'",.<>/?

Lionel Text Genuine

the Twentieth Century Limited roars past the New York skyline

AaBbCcDdEeFfGgHhIiJjKkLlMmNnOoPpQqRrSsTtUuVvWwXxYyZz1234567890!@#$%^&*()[]{};:'",.

Lionel Text Diesel

Its bright chrome beauty reflects the Tuesday evening sunset

AaBbCcDdEeFfGgHhIiJjKkLlMmNnOoPpQqRrSsTtUuVvWwXxYyZz1234567890!@#$%^&•()[]{};:'

Mosquito Fiesta 41/25

UP iN CANADA, MOSQUiTOS CONSiDER BUGSPRAY a MARiNADE FOR HUMANS!

Mosquito Fiesta

a B C D E F G H i J K L M N O P Q R S T U V W X Y Z 1 2 3 4 5 6 7 8 9
0 ! @ # $ % ^ & * ( ) [ ] { } : : ' " . . < > / ?

Mosquito Fiesta

Stuart Sandler
2001

This font is sold as part of the In-Flight Meal Font Set.

Motion Discomfort Satchels

AaBbCcDdEeFfGgHhIiJjKkLlMmNnOoPpQqRrSsTtUuVvWwXxYyZz12

New York to Las Vegas

Stuart Sandler
2001

This font is sold as part of the In-Flight Meal Font Set.

Pink Flamingo 36/25

Pardon me sir, but I believe your fountain pen is leaking ink on my polyester slacks.

Pink Flamingo

AaBbCcDdEeFfGgHhIiJjKkLlMmNnOoPpQqRrSsTtUuVvWwXxYyZz
1234567890!@#$%^&*()[]{}:;'",..<>/?

Pink Flamingo

Stuart Sandler
2001

This font is sold as part of the In-Flight Meal Font Set.

Refreshing hot-buttered popcorn and all-meat hot dogs!

AaBbCcDdEeFfGgHhIiJjKkLlMmNnOoPpQqRrSsTtUuVvWwXxYyZz1234567890!@#$%^&*()[]{}:;'",..<>/?

Refreshment Stand

Stuart Sandler
2001

This font is sold as part of the In-Flight Meal Font Set.

Bring some quarters for the magic vibrating mattress

AaBbCcDdEe FfGgHhIiJjKkLlMmNnOoPpQqRrSsTtUuVvWwXxYyZz1234567890!@#$%^&*()[]{}:;'",.<>/?

Starlight Hotel

Stuart Sandler
2001

This font is sold as part of the In-Flight Meal Font Set.

PIÑA COLADAS CALM THE ISLAND GODS

AABBCCDDEEFFGGHHIIJJKKLLMMNNOOPPQQRRSSTTUUVVWWXXYYZZ1234567890!@#$%^&*()[]{}:;'",.<>/?

Volcano King

Stuart Sandler
2001

This font is sold as part of the In-Flight Meal Font Set.

El Ranchero

Brian Bonislawsky and Stuart Sandler
2002

This font is sold as part of the Casino Buffet Font Set.

El Ranchero 34/26

Enjoy all them tasty critters and vittles you can eat at Arizona's Roadkill Café

El Ranchero

AaBbCcDdEeFfGgHhIiJjKkLlMmNnOoPpQqRrSsTtUuVvWwXxYyZz
*1234567890! @#$%^3*O[]{};: '".<>/?*

Hamburger Menu

Brian Bonislawsky and Stuart Sandler
2002

This font is sold as part of the Casino Buffet Font Set.

Hamburger Menu 30/27

LUNCHEON SPECIALS TODAY INCLUDE FREE SODA AND YOUR CHOICE OF COLE SLAW OR CHOWDER

Hamburger Menu

ABCDEFGHIJKLMNOPQRSTUVWXYZ123456789
0!@#$%^&*()[]{};:'",.<>/?

Hamburger Menu

Brian Bonislawsky and Stuart Sandler
2002

The Marquee weight was created for larger viewing applications.

This font is sold as part of the Casino Buffet Font Set.

Hamburger Menu Marquee 26/26

TRY OUR CAJUN GRILLED CATFISH SANDWICH WITH TARTER SAUCE AND BEER-BATTERED HUSH PUPPIES

Hamburger Menu Marquee

ABCDEFGHIJKLMNOPQRSTUVWXYZ1234567
890!@#$%^&*()[]{};:'",.<>/?

Holiday Ranch

Brian Bonislawsky and Stuart Sandler
2002

A complete set of alternate characters are available for every word.

This font is sold as part of the Casino Buffet Font Set.

Holiday Ranch 25/23

COWBOYS BRING YER COWGIRLS AND ENJOY OUR TWILIGHT SQUARE DANCIN' STARTIN' AT 7:00PM

Holiday Ranch

AABBCCDDEEFFGGHHIiJJKKLLMMNNOOPPQQRRSSTTUUV
VWWXXYYZZ1234567890!@#$%^&*()[]{};:'",.<>/?

diner@fontdiner.com

Palm Springs offers luxurious California modern desert living!

International Palms

AaBbCcDdEeFfGgHhIiJjKkLlMmNn
OoPpQqRrSsTtUuVvWwXxYyZz12345

International Palms

Brian Bonislawsky and Stuart Sandler
2002

This font is sold as part of the Casino Buffet Font Set.

Font Diner

Lamplighter Script 34/26

Enjoy the Lamplighter's world famous mouth meltin' Buffalo wings with homemade creamy bleu cheese dressing and sticks of crisp fresh celery.

Lamplighter Script

AaBbCcDdEeFfGgHhIiJjKkLlMmNnOoPpQqRrSsTtUuVvWwXxYyZz
1234567890 ! @ # $ % ^ & * ( ) [ ] { } :: ' " . . < > / ?

Lamplighter Script

Brian Bonislawsky and Stuart Sandler
2002

This font is sold as part of the Casino Buffet Font Set.

Lamplighter Script Marquee 56 Point

Tonight Only! Enchanted B-Movies Under the Stars

Lamplighter Script Marquee

AaBbCcDdEeFfGgHhIiJjKkLlMmNnOoPpQqRrSsTtUuVvWwXxYyZz
1234567890 ! @ # $ % ^ & * ( ) [ ] { } :: ' " . . < > / ?

Lamplighter Script

Brian Bonislawsky and Stuart Sandler
2002

The Marquee weight was created for larger viewing applications.

This font is sold as part of the Casino Buffet Font Set.

Las Vegas to Rome 20/20

ENJOY A ROMAN HOLIDAY IN OUR WORLD FAMOUS SPA COMPLETE WITH MUD BATH AND CLEAN TOWELS

Las Vegas to Rome

A B C D E F G H I J K L M N O P Q R S T U V W X Y Z I II III
IV V VI VII VIII IX ◇ ! ⚛ # $ % ^ ‡ * ( ) [ ] { } ; : ' " , . < > / ?

Las Vegas to Rome

Brian Bonislawsky and Stuart Sandler
2002

This font is sold as part of the Casino Buffet Font Set.

Leisure Script

Brian Bonislawsky and Stuart Sandler
2002

This font is sold as part of the Casino Buffet Font Set.

Leisure Script 41/26

The lucky lounge lizard is a smooth operator with his leisure suit and breath spray... watch out girls. this is the guy your mother warned you about... if you can resist.

Leisure Script

*A a B b C c D d E e F f G g H h I i J j K k L l M m N n O o P p Q q R r S s T t U u V v W w X x Y y Z z 1 2 3 4 5 6 7 8 9 0 ! @ # $ % ^ & * ( ) [ ] { } : ; ' " . . < > / ?*

Leisure Script

Brian Bonislawsky and Stuart Sandler
2002

The Marquee weight was created for larger viewing applications.

This font is sold as part of the Casino Buffet Font Set.

Leisure Script Marquee 62 Point

Finally Sand, Sun, and Luxury can all be yours ... Florida swamps real cheap!

Leisure Script Marquee

*A . B . C . D . E . F . G . H . I . J . K . L . M . N . O . P . Q . R . S . T . U . V . W . X . Y . Z . 1 2 3 4 5 6 7 8 9 0 ! @ # $ % ^ & * ( ) [ ] { } : ; ' " . . < > / ?*

Mirage Bazaar

Brian Bonislawsky and Stuart Sandler
2002

This font is sold as part of the Casino Buffet Font Set.

Mirage Bazaar 36/26

GLORIOUS PERSIAN RUGS BY MARKETPLACE MERCHANTS WHO KNOW YOUR PRICE!

Mirage Bazaar

AaBbCcDdEeFfGgHhIiJjKkLlMmNnOoPpQqRrSsTtUuVv WwXxYyZz1234567890!@#$%^&*()[]{};:'",.<>/?

Mirage Zanzibar

Brian Bonislawsky and Stuart Sandler
2002

This font is sold as part of the Casino Buffet Font Set.

Mirage Zanzibar 32/27

WHEN IN LAS VEGAS, THE WISE BUFFET SULTAN KNOWS TO ONLY GRAB FOR CLEAN PLATES!

Mirage Zanzibar

AaBbCcDdEeFfGgHhIiJjKkLlMmNnOoPpQqRrSsTt UuVvWwXxYyZz1234567890!@#$%^&*()[]{};:'",.<>/?

Every handyman knows for best reception wrap aluminum foil around the television set antennae and aim for the direction of the signal tower.

Mister Television

A a B b C c D d E e F f G g H h I i J j K k L l M m N n O o P p Q q R r S s T t U u V v W w X x Y y Z z 1 2 3 4 5 6 7 8 9 0 ! @ # $ % ^ & * ( ) [ ] { } : ; " ' . . < > / ?

Brian Bonislawsky and Stuart Sandler 2002

This font is sold as part of the Casino Buffet Font Set.

A STEADY HAND AND A CLEAR MIND ARE ESSENTIAL FOR THE PROFESSIONAL KEGLER TO BOWL A PERFECT GAME!

Starburst Lanes

A A B B C C D D E E F F G G H H I I J J K K L L M M N N O O P P Q Q R R S S T T U U V V W W X X Y Y Z Z 1 2 3 4 5 6 7 8 9 0 ! @ # $ % ^ & * ( ) [ ] { } ; : ' " , . < > / ?

Brian Bonislawsky and Stuart Sandler 2002

This font is sold as part of the Casino Buffet Font Set.

STARS COME FROM ALL OVER IN THE EVENING TO LIGHT UP THE LAS VEGAS DESERT SKYLINE BABY!

Starburst Lanes Twinkle

A A B B C C D D E E F F G G H H I I J J K K L L M M N N O O P P Q Q R R S S T T U U V V W W X X Y Y Z Z 1 2 3 4 5 6 7 8 9 0 ! @ # $ % ^ & * ( ) [ ] { } ; : ' " , . < > / ?

Brian Bonislawsky and Stuart Sandler 2002

This font is sold as part of the Casino Buffet Font Set.

ENJOY OUR EVENING ENTERTAINMENT IN THE ZANZIBAR ROOM! THE 'AMAZING' BOB!

Vegas Caravan

A A B B C C D D E E F F G G H H I I J J K K L L M M N N O O P P Q Q R R S S T T U U V V W W X X Y Y Z Z 1 2 3 4 5 6 7 8 9 0 ! @ # $ % ^ & * ( ) [ ] { } ; : ' " , . < > / ?

Brian Bonislawsky and Stuart Sandler 2002

This font is sold as part of the Casino Buffet Font Set.

Font Diner

fontBoy was launched in 1995 to manufacture and distribute fonts designed by Bob Aufuldish and Kathy Warinner.

fontBoy fonts available in Type 1 format for Mac and Windows.

visit our web site at www.fontboy.com, where you can shop and download 24/7 with your credit card on our secure virtual storefront.

text in this section from Mark Bartlett's essay, "Beyond the Margins of the Page." (thank you, Mark). ©1993, Mark Bartlett

contact us at info@fontboy.com

Armature
Baufy
New Clear Era
Punctual
RoarShock
Viscosity
Whiplash

fontBoy

type
you can
read

Imagine a fisherman standing on the shore and casting a line into the ocean. Imagine the immensity of the Pacific and the inconsequential frame of a human being. What an astonishing act; what an absurd image. To expect to catch something under these conditions is **almost pathological. The odds of success are apparently miniscule. The pursuit of meaning is an even more astonishing act as we cast into a vastly greater ocean. It requires a type of faith, because even when communication is appar ently successful, it can never be guaranteed to be so.**

MARK BARTLETT from "Beyond the Margins of the Page"

Aa Bb Cc Dd Ee Ff Gg Hh Ii Jj Kk Ll Mm Nn Oo Pp Qq Rr Ss Tt Uu Vv Ww Xx Yy Zz 0123456789 (<!@#$%^&*+=?>) {©®}

Armature Light

Bob Aufuldish
1992-97

Armature Light dingbat

Armature Light 9/11

The design strategy of an icon, a poster, a book, a sign, is the visual counterpoint to what the writer calls rhetoric. Graphic design is visual rhetoric meant to persuade, to convince, to move, to mobilize, to affect behavior. It manipulates the graphic to focus a message in a shifting field of multiple meanings. Of all forms of language, it is closest to mathematics.

Aa Bb Cc Dd Ee Ff Gg Hh Ii Jj Kk Ll Mm Nn Oo Pp Qq Rr Ss Tt Uu Vv Ww Xx Yy Zz 0123456789 (<!@#$%^&*+=?>) {©®}

Armature Regular

Bob Aufuldish
1992-97

Armature Regular dingbat

Armature Regular 9/11

The design strategy of an icon, a poster, a book, a sign, is the visual counterpoint to what the writer calls rhetoric. Graphic design is visual rhetoric meant to persuade, to convince, to move, to mobilize, to affect behavior. It manipulates the graphic to focus a message in a shifting field of multiple meanings. Of all forms of language, it is closest to mathemat-

Aa Bb Cc Dd Ee Ff Gg Hh Ii Jj Kk Ll Mm Nn Oo Pp Qq Rr Ss Tt Uu Vv Ww Xx Yy Zz 0123456789 (<!@#$%^&*+=?>) {©®}

Armature Bold

Bob Aufuldish
1992-97

Armature Bold dingbat

Armature Bold 9/11

The design strategy of an icon, a poster, a book, a sign, is the visual counterpoint to what the writer calls rhetoric. Graphic design is visual rhetoric meant to persuade, to convince, to move, to mobilize, to affect behavior. It manipulates the graphic to focus a message in a shifting field of multiple meanings. Of all forms of language, it

Aa Bb Cc Dd Ee Ff Gg Hh Ii Jj Kk Ll Mm Nn Oo Pp Qq Rr Ss Tt Uu Vv Ww Xx Yy Zz 0123456789 (<!@#$%^&*+=?>) {©®}

Armature Extra Bold

Bob Aufuldish
1992-97

Armature Extra Bold dingbat

Armature Extra Bold 9/11

The design strategy of an icon, a poster, a book, a sign, is the visual counterpoint to what the writer calls rhetoric. Graphic design is visual rhetoric meant to persuade, to convince, to move, to mobilize, to affect behavior. It manipulates the graphic to focus a message in a shifting field of multiple meanings. Of all forms of language,

fontBoy

When we look into the distance, the horizon appears closer to us than it did to earlier cultures. Space and time are compressed. Around-the-world is no longer far. The moon is near. And beyond that, beyond our solar system, beyond our galaxy are others, so often visited in thought, that they have become familiar. Familiarity itself is now the material of myth-making. The familiar is deepening, revealed not to be, not a surface, but a volume. We ourselves, wedged between near and far, are the objects of myth. We exist, somehow, somewhere, between the infinitesimally small and the infinitely large, and from this place, navigate through conceptual and perceptual waters.

MARK BARTLETT from "Beyond the Margins of the Page"

info@fontboy.com

Aa Bb Cc Dd Ee Ff Gg Hh Ii Jj Kk Ll Mm Nn Oo Pp Qq Rr Ss Tt
Uu Vv Ww Xx Yy Zz 0 1 2 3 4 5 6 7 8 9 (<!@#$%^&*+=?>) {©®}

Baufy Normal

Bob Aufuldish
1994

Baufy Normal dingbat

Baufy Normal 9/10

The design strategy of an icon, a poster, a book, a sign, is the visual counter point to what the writer calls rhetoric. Graphic design is visual rhetoric meant to persuade, to convince, to move, to mobilize, to affect behavior. It manipu all

Aa Bb Cc Dd Ee Ff Gg Hh Ii Jj Kk Ll Mm Nn Oo Pp Qq Rr Ss Tt
Uu Vv Ww Xx Yy Zz 0 1 2 3 4 5 6 7 8 9 (<!@#$%^&*+=?>) {©®}

Baufy Medium

Bob Aufuldish
1994

Baufy Medium dingbat

Baufy Medium 9/10

The design strategy of an icon, a poster, a book, a sign, is the visual counter point to what the writer calls rhetoric. Graphic design is visual rhetoric meant to persuade, to convince, to move, to mobilize, to affect behavior. It manipu all

Aa Bb Cc Dd Ee Ff Gg Hh Ii Jj Kk Ll Mm Nn Oo Pp Qq Rr Ss Tt
Uu Vv Ww Xx Yy Zz 0 1 2 3 4 5 6 7 8 9 (<!@#$%^&*+=?>) {©®}

Baufy Bold

Bob Aufuldish
1994

Baufy Bold dingbat

Baufy Bold 9/10

The design strategy of an icon, a poster, a book, a sign, is the visual counter point to what the writer calls rhetoric. Graphic design is visual rhetoric meant to persuade, to convince, to move, to mobilize, to affect behavior. It manipu all

Aa Bb Cc Dd Ee Ff Gg Hh Ii Jj Kk Ll Mm Nn Oo Pp Qq Rr Ss Tt
Uu Vv Ww Xx Yy Zz 0 1 2 3 4 5 6 7 8 9 (<!@#$%^&*+=?>) {©®}

Baufy Bulky

Bob Aufuldish
1994

Baufy Bulky dingbat

Baufy Bulky 9/10

The design strategy of an icon, a poster, a book, a sign, is the visual counter point to what the writer calls rhetoric. Graphic design is visual rhetoric meant to persuade, to convince, to move, to mobilize, to affect behavior. It manipu all

Aa Bb Cc Dd Ee Ff Gg Hh Ii Jj Kk Ll Mm Nn Oo Pp Qq Rr Ss Tt
Uu Vv Ww Xx Yy Zz 0 1 2 3 4 5 6 7 8 9 (<!@#$%^&*+=?>) {©®}

Baufy Chunky

Bob Aufuldish
1994

Baufy Chunky dingbat

Baufy Chunky 9/10

The design strategy of an icon, a poster, a book, a sign, is the visual counter point to what the writer calls rhetoric. Graphic design is visual rhetoric meant to persuade, to convince, to move, to mobilize, to affect behavior. It manipu all

Wherever we are in the world, we must forge a correspondence between something written and something visual, and from these signals, plot our course. We may choose the type of ter rain we wish to navigate, whether watery or earthly. And we may choose a direct or indirect itinerary. But at each point there is a correspondance bet ween word and image.

THEY FORM EACH OTHER, AND FORM OUR RELATIONSHIP TO WHATEVER IS OTHER THAN US.

MARK BARTLETT from "Beyond the Margins of the Page"

info@fontboy.com

Aa Bb Cc Dd Ee Ff Gg Hh Ii Jj Kk Ll Mm Nn Oo Pp Qq Rr Ss Tt Uu Vv Ww Xx Yy Zz 0123456789 (<!@#$%^&*+=?>) {©®}

New Clear Era Regular

Bob Aufuldish
1995-99

New Clear Era Regular dingbat

New Clear Era Regular 9/11

The design strategy of an icon, a poster, a book, a sign, is the visual counterpoint to what the writer calls rhetoric. Graphic design is visual rhetoric meant to persuade, to convince, to move, to mobilize, to affect behavior. It manipulates the graphic to focus a message in a shifting

Aa Bb Cc Dd Ɛɛ Ff Gg Hh Ii Jj Kk Ll Mm Nn Oo Pp Qq Rr Ss Tt Uu Vv Ww Xx Yy Zz 0123456789 (<!@#$%^&*+=?>) {©®}

New Clear Era Display One

Bob Aufuldish
1995-99

New Clear Era Display One dingbat

New Clear Era Display One 9/11

The design strategy of an icon, a poster, a book, a sign, is the visual counterpoint to what the writer calls rhetoric. Graphic design is visual rhetoric meant to persuade, to convince, to move, to mobilize, to affect behavior. It manipulates the graphic to focus a message in a shifting

Aa Bb Cc Dd Ɛɛ Ff Gg Hh Ii Jj Kk Ll Mm Nn Oo Pp Qq Rr Ss Tt Uu Vv Ww Xx Yy Zz 0123456789 (<!@#$%^&*+=?>) {©®}

New Clear Era Display Two

Bob Aufuldish
1995-99

New Clear Era Display Two dingbat

New Clear Era Display Two 9/11

The design strategy of an icon, a poster, a book, a sign, is the visual counterpoint to what the writer calls rhetoric. Graphic design is visual rhetoric meant to persuade, to convince, to move, to mobilize, to affect behavior. It manipulates the graphic to focus a message in a shifting

AA BB CC DD ƐƐ FF GG HH II JJ KK LL MM NN OO PP QQ RR SS TT UU VV WW XX YY ZZ 0123456789 (<!@#$%^&*?>)

New Clear Era Display Caps

Bob Aufuldish
1995-99

New Clear Era "Mile" monetary symbol

New Clear Era Display Caps 9/11

THE DESIGN STRATEGY OF AN ICON, A POSTER, A BOOK, A SIGN, IS THE VISUAL COUNTERPOINT TO WHAT THE WRITER CALLS RHETORIC. GRAPHIC DESIGN IS VISUAL RHETORIC MEANT TO PERSUADE, TO CONVINCE, TO MOVE, TO MOBI

fontBoy

Though myth-making has retreated from the centers of culture, it is alive and well in the margins, where it plays a vigorous, though often unperceived role. Since science has cornered the market on explanations of the natural world, myth has taken up residence elsewhere. It is ensconced in the narratives, the stories, not of origins, not of our physical place in the cosmos, not of other lives and other worlds beyond this one, but of this one, here, in all its immediacy, its nearness, as it comes into and out of existence before our very eyes.

MARK BARTLETT from "Beyond the Margins of the Page"

info@fontboy.com

Aa Bb Cc Dd Ee Ff Gg Hh Ii Jj Kk Ll Mm Nn Oo Pp Qq Rr Ss
Tt Uu Vv Ww Xx Yy Zz 0123456789 (<!@#$%^&*+=?>) {©®}

Punctual Four dingbat

Punctual Four 9/10

The design strategy of an icon, a poster, a book, a sign, is the visual counter point to what the

---

Aa Bb Cc Dd Ee Ff Gg Hh Ii Jj Kk Ll Mm Nn Oo Pp Qq Rr Ss
Tt Uu Vv Ww Xx Yy Zz 0123456789 (<!@#$%^&*+=?<) {©®}

Punctual Four Inline dingbat

Punctual Four Inline 9/10

The design strategy of an icon, a poster, a book, a sign, is the visual counter point to what the

---

Aa Bb Cc Dd Ee Ff Gg Hh Ii Jj Kk Ll Mm Nn Oo Pp Qq Rr Ss
Tt Uu Vv Ww Xx Yy Zz 0123456789 (<!@#$%^&*+=?<) {©®}

Punctual Four Interior dingbat

Punctual Four Interior 9/10

The design strategy of an icon, a poster, a book, a sign, is the visual counter point to what the

---

Aa Bb CC Dd Ee Ff Gg Hh Ii Jj Kk Ll MM NN OO PP QQ Rr SS
Tt UU VV WW XX YY ZZ 0123456789 (<!@#$%^&*+=?>) {©®}

Punctual Universal Four dingbat

Punctual Universal Four 9/10

The design strategy of an icon, a poster, a book, a sign, is the visual counter point to what the

---

Aa Bb CC Dd Ee Ff Gg Hh Ii Jj Kk Ll MM NN OO PP QQ Rr SS
Tt UU VV WW XX YY ZZ 0123456789 (<!@#$%^&*+=?<) {©®}

Punctual Universal Four Inline dingbat

Punctual Universal Four Inline 9/10

The design strategy of an icon, a poster, a book, a sign, is the visual counter point to what the

---

Aa Bb CC Dd Ee Ff Gg Hh Ii Jj Kk Ll MM NN OO PP QQ Rr SS
Tt UU VV WW XX YY ZZ 0123456789 (<!@#$%^&*+=?<) {©®}

Punctual Universal Four Interior dingbat

Punctual Universal Four Interior 9/10

The design strategy of an icon, a poster, a book, a sign, is the visual counter point to what the

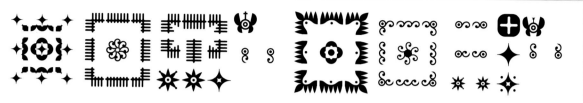

RoarShock One

Bob Aufuldish
1995-97

RoarShock Two

Bob Aufuldish
1995-97

RoarShock Three

Bob Aufuldish
1995-97

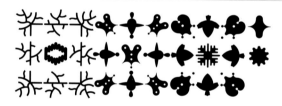

RoarShock Four

Bob Aufuldish
1995-97

RoarShock Five

Bob Aufuldish
1995-97

RoarShock Six

Bob Aufuldish
1995-97

fontBoy

When do we know that an individual or group of individuals has understood the same thing by the same linguistic act? Only when, collectively, they agree that this is so. By coupling word to image the designer may enhance clarity and reduce ambiguity, and thereby lead the audience into the necessary agreement that they have been addressed by (nearly) identical messages.

MARK BARTLETT *from "Beyond the Margins of the Page"*

info@fontboy.com

Aa Bb Cc Dd Ee Ff Gg Hh Ii Jj Kk Ll Mm Nn
Oo Pp Qq Rr Ss Tt Uu Vv Ww Xx Yy Zz
0123456789 (<!@#$%^&*+=?>) {©®}

Viscosity Regular

Kathy Warinner, Bob Aufuldish
199

Viscosity Regular dingbats

Viscosity Regular 9/11

The design strategy of an icon, a poster, a book, a sign, is the visual counterpoint to what the writer calls rhetoric. Graphic design is visual rhetoric meant to persuade, to convince, to move, to mobilize, to affect behavior. It manipulates the graphic to focus a message in a shifting field of multiple meanings. Of all forms of language, it is closest to mathematics. Like mathematics, it does this through the patterning

Aa Bb Cc Dd Ee Ff Gg Hh Ii Jj Kk Ll Mm Nn
Oo Pp Qq Rr Ss Tt Uu Vv Ww Xx Yy Zz
0123456789 (<!@✱$%^&*+=?>) {©®}

Viscosity Inline

Kathy Warinner, Bob Aufuldish
199

Viscosity Inline dingbats

Viscosity Inline 9/11

The design strategy of an icon, a poster, a book, a sign, is the visual counterpoint to what the writer calls rhetoric. Graphic design is visual rhetoric meant to persuade, to convince, to move, to mobilize, to affect behavior. It manipulates the graphic to focus a message in a shifting field of multiple meanings. Of all forms of language, it is closest to mathematics. Like mathematics, it does this through the patterning

Aa Bb Cc Dd Ee Ff Gg Hh Ii Jj Kk Ll Mm Nn
Oo Pp Qq Rr Ss Tt Uu Vv Ww Xx Yy Zz
0123456789 (<!@#$%^&*+=?>) {©®}

Viscosity Interior

Kathy Warinner, Bob Aufuldish
199

Viscosity Interior dingbats

Viscosity Interior 9/11

The design strategy of an icon, a poster, a book, a sign, is the visual counterpoint to what the writer calls rhetoric. Graphic design is visual rhetoric meant to persuade, to convince, to move, to mobilize, to affect behavior. It manipulates the graphic to focus a message in a shifting field of multiple meanings. Of all forms of language, it is closest to mathematics. Like mathematics, it does this through the patterning

fontBoy

Time flows differently along the banks of the Ganges than it does along Madison Avenue. History expands and contracts, varying in density, even in an individual's life time. History might be a line or a circle, a spiral or a turtle, an expanding sphere or a contracting star. Words might be magical, sacred, might be able to conjure demons or predict fate. Words mediate between gods and humans, between the neurotic and the shrink, between the press and politics, between the individual and the public. Every word is an empty vessel, perfectly general, free from all particularity, the perfect projection screen that takes on any degree of specificity.

MARK BARTLETT   from "Beyond the Margins of the Page"

info@fontboy.com

Aa Bb Cc Dd Ee Ff Gg Hh Ii Jj Kk Ll Mm Nn
Oo Pp Qq Rr Ss Tt Uu Vv Ww Xx Yy Zz
0123456789 (<!@#$%^&*+=?>) {©®}

Whiplash Regular dingbat

Whiplash Regular 9/11

The design strategy of an icon, a poster, a book, a sign, is the visual counterpoint to what the writer calls rhetoric. Graphic design is visual rhetoric meant to persuade, to convince, to move, to mobilize, to affect behavior. It manipulates the graphic to focus a message in a shifting field of multiple meanings. Of all forms of language, it is closest to mathematics. Like mathematics, it does this through the patterning of its elements and conventions. To design a graphic means to provide, in visual/verbal form, a demonstration, a proof, or an

---

Aa Bb Cc Dd Ee Ff Gg Hh Ii Jj Kk Ll Mm Nn
Oo Pp Qq Rr Ss Tt Uu Vv Ww Xx Yy Zz
0123456789 (<!@#$%^&*+=?>) {©®}

Whiplash Lineola dingbat

Whiplash Lineola 9/11

The design strategy of an icon, a poster, a book, a sign, is the visual counterpoint to what the writer calls rhetoric. Graphic design is visual rhetoric meant to persuade, to convince, to move, to mobilize, to affect behavior. It manipulates the graphic to focus a message in a shifting field of multiple meanings. Of all forms of language, it is closest to mathematics. Like mathe-

---

Aa Bb Cc Dd Ee Ff Gg Hh Ii Jj Kk Ll Mm Nn
Oo Pp Qq Rr Ss Tt Uu Vv Ww Xx Yy Zz
0123456789 (<!@#$%^&*+=?>) {©®}

Whiplash Mono dingbat

Whiplash Mono 9/11

The design strategy of an icon, a poster, a book, a sign, is the visual counterpoint to what the writer calls rhetoric. Graphic design is visual rhetoric meant to persuade, to convince, to move, to mobilize, to affect behavior. It manipulates the graphic to focus a message in a shifting field of multiple meanings. Of all forms of language, it is closest to mathematics. Like mathe-

FOUNTAIN™

FOUNTAIN IS AN INDEPENDENT AND FRIENDLY DIGITAL TYPE FOUNDRY. OUR AIM IS TO PROVIDE OUR DISCERNING CLIENTS WITH MODERN, WELL-CRAFTED FONTS GUARANTEED TO MEET THE MOST STRENUOUS REQUIREMENTS OF AESTHETICS, LEGIBILITY AND ORIGINALITY.

TO THE CLIENT IN NEED OF A UNIQUE AND DIFFERENT VISUAL IDENTITY WE OFFER CUSTOM TYPEFACE DESIGN, AS WELL AS IMPROVEMENT AND ADAPTATION OF EXISTING TYPEFACES. TO THE INDIVIDUAL DESIGNER LOOKING FOR MINTY-FRESH CONTEMPORARY FONT GOODNESS, WE OFFER A CATALOGUE OF ORIGINAL FONTS AVAILABLE FOR ONLINE PURCHASE.

FOUNTAIN IS BASED IN MALMÖ, SWEDEN, BUT SINCE OUR DESIGNERS COME FROM EVERY PART OF THE WORLD, THERE ARE NO LIMITS TO WHAT YOU MAY FIND IN OUR COLLECTION.

» WWW.FOUNTAIN.NU

» INFO@FOUNTAIN.NU

» FOUNTAIN
KORNETTSGATAN 13 B
SE-211 50 MALMÖ
SWEDEN

Malmö is the City of Parks

Go see Ribban Beach

Lee går ofta själv på Idoff och tjyvar

KOCKUMSKRANEN €2.367

MIDNIGHT AT P-HUSET ANNA

RÖRSJÖSTADEN

Hela vägen från Värnhemstorget

Malmö Sans

Martin Fredrikson Core
2001

Fountain

Regular

ZWEEDSE, EX-VIP, BEHOORLIJK GEK
OP QUANTUMFYSICA. Portez ce vi-
eux whisky au juge blond qui fume.
Five wine experts jokingly quizzed

Oblique

*ZWEEDSE, EX-VIP, BEHOORLIJK GEK
OP QUANTUMFYSICA. Portez ce vi-
eux whisky au juge blond qui fume.
Five wine experts jokingly quizzed*

Small Caps

ZWEEDSE, EX-VIP, BEHOORLIJK GEK
OP QUANTUMFYSICA. PORTEZ CE VI-
EUX WHISKY AU JUGE BLOND QUI FUME.
FIVE WINE EXPERTS JOKINGLY QUIZZED

Bold

ZWEEDSE, EX-VIP, BEHOORLIJK
GEK OP QUANTUMFYSICA. Portez
ce vieux whisky au juge blond
qui fume. Five wine experts joke

Bold Oblique

*ZWEEDSE, EX-VIP, BEHOORLIJK
GEK OP QUANTUMFYSICA. Portez
ce vieux whisky au juge blond
qui fume. Five wine experts joke*

Ligatures & Alternates

Garlic type stutter catched star. Och,
stilla skrockade vid Losjön, satte Lee
sin sista tjuga på loftet.Gaáàâäååçç
e é è ê ë ch ct ck ee ff ft si sj sk st tt ti tj ty

Headline

**ZWEEDSE, BEHOORLIJK GEK OP QUANTUMFYSICA
FIVE WINE EXPERTS JOKINGLY QUIZZED SAMPLE CHABLIS**

Pussy

Peter Bruhn
1997

Regular

behoorlijk gek op quantumfysica

five wine experts jokingly quizzed sample chablis 012345@?

Sloped

zweedse, ex-vip, behoorlijk gek
op quantumfysica. portez qui
vieux whisky au juge blond ee

Extra

zweedse, ex-vip, behoorlijk gek
op quantumfysica. portez qui
vieux whisky au juge blond ee

Extra Sloped

zweedse, ex-vip, behoorlijk gek
op quantumfysica. portez qui
vieux whisky au juge blond ee

Filt

Martin Fredrikson Core
2001

BEHOORLIJK GEK OP QUANTUMFYSICAUG

♥⊡⊡⊙♫⬆⬆⬆⬆**f**✳⬅?!0123456789@♔♔☞➤

Roman

**PORTEZ CE VIEUX WHISKY
AU JUGE BLOND QUI FUME
FIVE WINE EXPERTS SAMP**

Black

**PORTEZ CE VIEUX WHISKY
AU JUGE BLOND QUI FUME
FIVE WINE EXPERTS SAMP**

Greek

**ΠΟΡΤΕΖ ΧΕ ΙΕVΞ ΩΗΙΣΚΨ
ΑΥ ϋΥΓΕ ΒΛΟΝΔ ΘΥΙ ΘΥΜΕ
ΦΙΕ ΩΙΝΕ ΕΞΠΕΡΤΕ ΣΑΜΠ**

Ness

Simon Schmidt
2000

Regular & Italic

Zweedse, ex-VIP, behoorlijk gek op quantumfysica!0123

Five wine experts jokingly quizzed sample chablis. Portez ce vieux whisky

Leash

Peter Bruhn
1996

Zweedse, behoorlijk gek op quantumfysica
Five wine experts jokingly quizzed sample chablis!&

Regular

ZWEEDSE, BEHOORLIJK GEK
OP QUANTUMFYSICA. Portez
ce vieux whisky au juge blond

Fat

ZWEEDSE, BEHOORLIJK GEK
OP QUANTUMFYSICA. Portez
ce vieux whisky au juge blond

XL

ZWEEDSE, BEHOORLIJK GEK
OP QUANTUMFYSICA. Portez
ce vieux whisky au juge blond

UniF

Nina David
2000

Regular & Italic

ORLIJK GEK OP QUANTUMFYSICA

five wine experts jokingly quizzed sample chablis

BEHOORLIJK GEK OP QUANTUMFYSICA
FIVE WINE EXPERTS JOKINGLY QUIZZED SAMPLE CHABLIS

Peter Bruhn
1996

Regular & Straightened

Zweedse, ex-VIP, behoorlijk gek op quantumfysica!012345

Five wine experts jokingly quizzed sample chablis. Portez ce vieux whisky

Bruhn Script
Peter Bruhn
1997

Regular & Italic

Zweedse, ex-VIP, behoorlijk gek op quantumfysica!01234

Five wine experts jokingly quizzed sample chablis. Portez ce vieux

Hybrid
Simon Schmidt
2001

gek op quantumfysica012345
experts jokingly quizzed!¥®¤?6

Nuephoric
Lee Basford/Fluid
1998

Thin

Five wine experts
jokingly quizzed
sample chablis.
Portez ce vieux

Regular

Five wine experts
jokingly quizzed
sample chablis.
Portez ce vieux

Heavy

Five wine experts
jokingly quizzed
sample chablis.
Portez ce vieux

Thin Italic

Five wine experts
jokingly quizzed
sample chablis.
Portez ce vieux

Regular Italic

Five wine experts
jokingly quizzed
sample chablis.
Portez ce vieux

Heavy Italic

Five wine experts
jokingly quizzed
sample chablis.
Portez ce vieux

BEHOORLIJK GEK OP QUANTUMFYSICA!0123
Five wine experts jokingly quizzed sample chablis. Portez ce

Dang
Jay David
1998

Regular & Italicus

Zweedse, behoorlijk gek op quantumfysica!
Five wine experts jokingly quizzed sample chablis. Portez ce vieux whisky

Revival
Peter Bruhn
1996

Fountain

Regular & Stuffed

Zweedse, behoorlijk gek op quantumfysica
Five wine experts jokingly quizzed sample chablis.0123456789

Five wine experts 123
Portez ce vieux whisky au

Thin

Portez ce vi eux whisky au juge blon

Regular

Portez ce vi eux whisky au juge blon

Heavy

Portez ce vi eux whisky au juge blon

Thin Italic

Portez ce vi eux whisky au juge blon

Italic

Portez ce vi eux whisky au juge blon

Heavy Italic

Portez ce vi eux whisky au juge blon

Dingbats

Zweedse, behoorlijk gek op quantumfysica
Five wine experts jokingly quizzed 0123456789!?@€$

Regular

ZWEEDSE, EX-VIP, BEHOORLIJK GEK OP QUANTUMFYSICA. Portez ce vi eux whisky au juge blond qui

Italic

ZWEEDSE, EX-VIP, BEHOORLIJK GEK OP QUANTUMFYSICA. Portez ce vi eux whisky au juge blond qui

Small Caps

ZWEEDSE, EX-VIP, BEHOORLIJK GEK OP QUANTUMFYSICA. PORTEZ CE VI EUX WHISKY AU JUGE BLOND QUI

Bold

ZWEEDSE, EX-VIP, BEHOORLIJK GEK OP QUANTUMFYSICA. Portez ce vi eux whisky au juge blond qui

Bold Italic

ZWEEDSE, EX-VIP, BEHOORLIJK GEK OP QUANTUMFYSICA. Portez ce vi eux whisky au juge blond qui

Bold Small Caps

ZWEEDSE, EX-VIP, BEHOORLIJK GEK OP QUANTUMFYSICA. PORTEZ CE VI EUX WHISKY AU JUGE BLOND QUI

info@fountain.nu

La Pastie de la Bourgoisie

PUT THE QUEEN UNDERNEATH THE SHELF

Pocketbook Angel

the highest quality loans with most economical

A century of Elvis

La Bourgoisie de la Pastie

Mercury

Peter Bruhn
1998

Fountain

Regular

ZWEEDSE, EX-VIP, BEHOORLIJK GEK OP QUANTUMFYSICA
five wine experts jokingly quizzed sample chablis!? 0123456789&%

Italic

ZWEEDSE, EX-VIP, BEHOORLIJK GEK OP QUANTUMFYSICA. Portez ce vieux whisky au juge blond qui fume. Five wine experts jokingly quizzed sample chablis

Alternative Italic

ZWEEDSE, EX-VIP, BEHOORLIJK GEK OP QUANTUMFYSICA. Portez ce vieux whisky au juge blond qui fume. Five wine experts jokingly quizzed sample chablis

Bold

ZWEEDSE, EX-VIP, BEHOORLIJK GEK OP QUANTUMFYSICA. Portez ce vieux whisky au juge blond qui fume. Five wine experts jokingly quizzed sample chablis

Small Caps

ZWEEDSE, EX-VIP, BEHOORLIJK GEK OP QUANTUMFYSICA. PORTEZ CE VIEUX WHISKY AU JUGE BLOND QUI FUME. FIVE WINE EXPERTS JOKINGLY QUIZZED SAMPLE CHABLIS. ZWEI BOX

Alternative Bold

ZWEEDSE, EX-VIP, BEHOORLIJK GEK OP QUANTUMFYSICA. Portez ce vieux whisky au juge blond qui fume. Five wine experts jokingly quizzed sample chablis

Bold Italic

ZWEEDSE, EX-VIP, BEHOORLIJK GEK OP QUANTUMFYSICA. Portez ce vieux whisky au juge blond qui fume. Five wine experts jokingly quizzed sample chablis

Alternative

ZWEEDSE, EX-VIP, BEHOORLIJK GEK OP QUANTUMFYSICA. Portez ce vieux whisky au juge blond qui fume. Five wine experts jokingly quizzed sample chablis

Alternative Bold Italic

ZWEEDSE, EX-VIP, BEHOORLIJK GEK OP QUANTUMFYSICA. Portez ce vieux whisky au juge blond qui fume. Five wine experts jokingly quizzed sample chablis

Small Caps

ZWEEDSE, EX-VIP, BEHOORLIJK GEK OP QUANTUMFYSICA. PORTEZ CE VIEUX WHISKY AU JUGE BLOND QUI FUME. FIVE WINE EXPERTS JOKINGLY QUIZZED SAMPLE CHABLIS. ZWEI BOX

Gas

Peter Bruhn
1997

Regular & Lite

BEHOORLIJK GEK OP QUANTUMFYSICA
FIVE WINE EXPERTS JOKINGLY QUIZZED SAMPLE CHABLIS

Can D

Matthew Chiavelli
1996

Regular & Italic

behoorlijk gek op quantumfysica
five wine experts jokingly quizzed sample chablis

Drunk

Peter Bruhn
1995

Zweedse, behoorlijk gek op quantumfysica! 012
Five wine experts jokingly quizzed sample chablis. Portez ce

Theodor

Peter Bruhn
1996

Regular & Oblitalique

HOORLIJK GEK OP QUANTUMFYSICA
FIVE WINE EXPERTS JOKINGLY QUIZZED SAMPLE CHABLIS 1974

Corpus Gothic

Peter Bruhn
1998

Zweedse, ex-VIP, behoorlijk gek op quantumfysica!01234
Five wine experts jokingly quizzed sample chablis. Portez ce vieux whisky

Regular

ZWEEDSE, EX-VIP, BEHOORLIJK GEK OP QUANTUMFYSICA. Portez ce vieux whisky au juge blond qui fume.

Alternative

ZWEEDSE, EX-VIP, BEHOORLIJK GEK OP QUANTUMFYSICA. Portez ce vieux whisky au juge blond qui fume.

Condensed

ZWEEDSE, EX-VIP, BEHOORLIJK GEK OP QUANTUMFYSICA. Portez ce vieux whisky au juge blond qui fume. Five wine experts

Oblique

ZWEEDSE, EX-VIP, BEHOORLIJK GEK OP QUANTUMFYSICA. Portez ce vieux whisky au juge blond qui fume.

Alternative Italic

ZWEEDSE, EX-VIP, BEHOORLIJK GEK OP QUANTUMFYSICA. Portez ce vieux whisky au juge blond qui fume.

Condensed Oblique

ZWEEDSE, EX-VIP, BEHOORLIJK GEK OP QUANTUMFYSICA. Portez ce vieux whisky au juge blond qui fume. Five wine experts

Small Caps

ZWEEDSE, EX-VIP, BEHOORLIJK GEK OP QUANTUMFYSICA. PORTEZ CE VIEUX WHISKY AU JUGE BLOND QUI

Alternative Small Caps

ZWEEDSE, EX-VIP, BEHOORLIJK GEK OP QUANTUMFYSICA. PORTEZ CE VIEUX WHISKY AU JUGE BLOND QUI

Style comparison

Elliott Straße & Me
Elliott Straße & Me

info@fountain.nu

Delay

Simon Schmidt
2001

korpulente Pauschaltouristen

AIRBUS-A318

jauchzendes Bodenpersonal

CHECK-IN-COUNTER

Piloten im Vollrausch

Grid Italic

BEHOORLIJK GEK op quantumfysica

Grid Italic

FIVE WINE EXPERTS jokingly quizzed

Grid Italic

PORTEZ CE VIEUX whisky au juge

Grid Italic

BOKKÄMPFER JAGEN Eva quer durch

Fountain

www.fountain.nu

147

Baskerville 1757

Lars Bergquist
2002

Also includes extra ligatures for
Regular & Italic.

Zweedse, behoorlijk gek op quantumfysica!

Five wine experts jokingly quizzed sample chablis. Flygande bäcka

Regular

Zweedse, behoorlijk gek op quantumfysica. Portez ce vieux whisky
au juge blond qui fume. A quick

Italic

*Zweedse, behoorlijk gek op quantum-
fysica. Portez ce vieux whisky au juge
blond qui fume. A quick brown fox*

Small Caps

ZWEEDSE, EX-VIPBEHOORLIJK GEK
OP QUANTUMFYSICA. PORTEZ CE VI-
VIEUX WHISKY AU JUGE BLOND QUI

London

Peter Bruhn
1997

BEHOORLIJK GEK OP QUANTUMFYSICA

FIVE WINE EXPERTS JOKINGLY QUIZZED 0123456789!?@$

76

ZWEEDSE, EX-VIP, BEHOORLIJK GEK
OP QUANTUMFYSICA. PORTEZ CE VI
EUX WHISKY AU JUGE BLOND. FIVE

77

ZWEEDSE, EX-VIP, BEHOORLIJK GEK
OP QUANTUMFYSICA. PORTEZ CE VI
EUX WHISKY AU JUGE BLOND. FIVE

78

ZWEEDSE, EX-VIP, BEHOORLIJK GEK
OP QUANTUMFYSICA. PORTEZ CE VI
EUX WHISKY AU JUGE BLOND. FIVE

76 Fall

*ZWEEDSE, EX-VIP, BEHOORLIJK GEK
OP QUANTUMFYSICA. PORTEZ CE VI
EUX WHISKY AU JUGE BLOND. FIVE*

77 Fall

*ZWEEDSE, EX-VIP, BEHOORLIJK GEK
OP QUANTUMFYSICA. PORTEZ CE VI
EUX WHISKY AU JUGE BLOND. FIVE*

78 Fall

*ZWEEDSE, EX-VIP, BEHOORLIJK GEK
OP QUANTUMFYSICA. PORTEZ CE VI
EUX WHISKY AU JUGE BLOND. FIVE*

Ultura

Matthew Chiavelli
1996

ZWEEDSE, EX-VIP, BEHOORLIJK GEK OP QUANTUMFYSICA!?12458

five wine experts jokingly quizzed sample chablis. Portez ce vieux

Light

ZWEEDSE, BEHOORLIJK GEK OP QUANTUM-
FYSICA. Portez ce vieux whisky au juge
blond. five wine experts jokingly quiz

Medium

ZWEEDSE, BEHOORLIJK GEK OP QUANT-
UMFYSICA. Portez ce vieux whisky
au juge blond. five wine experts

Heavy

ZWEEDSE, BEHOORLIJK GEK OP QUANT-
UMFYSICA. Portez ce vieux whisky
au juge blond. five wine experts

Light Italic

*ZWEEDSE, BEHOORLIJK GEK OP QUANTUM-
FYSICA. Portez ce vieux whisky au juge
blond. five wine experts jokingly quiz*

Medium Italic

*ZWEEDSE, BEHOORLIJK GEK OP QUANT-
UMFYSICA. Portez ce vieux whisky
au juge blond. five wine experts*

Heavy Italic

*ZWEEDSE, BEHOORLIJK GEK OP QUANT-
UMFYSICA. Portez ce vieux whisky
au juge blond. five wine experts*

info@fountain.nu

Regular & Italic

BEHOORLIJK gek op quantumfysica
FIVE WINE EXPERTS jokingly quizzed sample chablis

Regular & Italic

Zweedse, behoorlijk gek op quantumfysica
Five wine experts jokingly quizzed sample chablis. Portez ce vieux

Zweedse, behoorlijk gek op quantumfysica!?
FIVE WINE EXPERTS JOKINGLY quizzed sample chablis

Regular & Falling

Zweedse, behoorlijk gek op quantumfysica
Five wine experts jokingly quizzed sample chablis. Portez ce vieux

BEHOORLIJK GEK OP QUANTUMFYSICA
Five wine experts jokingly quizzed sample

Regular & Diet

Zweedse, behoorlijk gek op quantumfysica
Five wine experts jokingly quizzed sample chablis. Portez ce vieux

Zweedse, ex-VIP, behoorlijk gek op quantumfysica
Five wine experts jokingly quizzed sample chablis. Portez ce vieux

Coma01 Medium & Coma02 Bold Oblique

FIVE WINE EXPERTS JOKINGLY quizzed sample chablis
FIVE WINE EXPERTS JOKINGLY quizzed sample chablis

Ketchupa

SMALL TASTY SAUSAGE

Everywhere I go I always bring a roasted chicken

345 West 78th Street

O' SALAD, MY SALAD!

Mustardo

JUNK de LITTÉRATUR

DECORATIVE FIELD INSPECTOR BADGE 2954

Hot Dog Manifesto

hamburgers have feelings too

Ketchupa Regular

ZWEEDSE, EX-VIP, BEHOORLIJK GEK OP QUANTUMFYSICA. Portez ce vieux whisky au juge blond qui fume.

Ketchupa Oblique

ZWEEDSE, EX-VIP, BEHOORLIJK GEK OP QUANTUMFYSICA. Portez ce vieux whisky au juge blond qui fume.

Ketchupa Small Caps

ZWEEDSE, EX-VIP, BEHOORLIJK GEK OP QUANTUMFYSICA. PORTEZ CE VIEUX WHISKY AU JUGE BLOND QUI

Mustardo Regular

ZWEEDSE, EX-VIP, BEHOORLIJK GEK OP QUANTUMFYSICA. Portez ce vieux whisky au juge blond qui fume.

Mustardo Oblique

ZWEEDSE, EX-VIP, BEHOORLIJK GEK OP QUANTUMFYSICA. Portez ce vieux whisky au juge blond qui fume.

Mustardo Small Caps

ZWEEDSE, EX-VIP, BEHOORLIJK GEK OP QUANTUMFYSICA. PORTEZ CE VIEUX WHISKY AU JUGE BLOND QUI

info@fountain.nu

MAYORNAISE

❂ IN TYPE WE TRUST ❂

PINEAPPLE & TOMATOES & ONIONS

FOOD ✳ +POLKA+

✳ GARLIC DANGER ✳

✳ SAUSAGE ✳

⇐ SPANISH PEPPERS ⇒

Dingbats One

ZWEEDSE BEHOORLIJK GEK OP QUANTUMFYSICA

☜ ☞ ⇒ ⇐ → ← → ← → ← 0123456789 #

Dingbats One

♥ ♠ ♦ ♣ ✿ ❀ ♛ ♕ ⊙ ❄ ⊠ ✓ ❉ ✈ ★ ☆ ♀ ♂ BUY ❀ ❄ A NEW NEW NEW
AIR MAIL 0 1 2 3 4 5 6 7 8 9 ⊠ E i ✎ ✿ ♣ ♦ → ← ↓ ↑ ❉ → ←

DingBorders

KINGO & FLAPPY QUANTUMFYSICA ● ✳

Peter Hoffmann
2002

Zweedse, ex-VIP, behoorlijk gek op quantumfysica!

Five wine experts jokingly quizzed sample chablis. Portez ce vieux au

Regular

Zweedse, behoorlijk gek op quan-tumfysica. Portez ce vieux whisky au juge blond. Five wine experts jokingly quizzed sample chablis.

Small Caps

ZWEEDSE, BEHOORLIJK GEK OP QUANTUMFYSICA. PORTEZ CE VIEUX WHISKY AU JUGE BLOND. FIVE WINE EXPERTS JOKINGLY QUIZZED SAMPLE

Bold

Zweedse, behoorlijk gek op quan-tumfysica. Portez ce vieux whisky au juge blond. five wine experts jokingly quizzed sample chablis.

Barbera

Peter Bruhn
1996

BEHOORLIJK GEK OP QUANTUMFYSICA

Five wine experts jokingly quizzed 0123456789!?

Thin

Five wine experts jokingly quizzed sample chablis. Zweedse, behoorlijk gek op quantumfysica. A qui

Regular

Five wine experts jokingly quizzed sample chablis. Zweedse, behoorlijk gek op quantumfysica. A qui

Fat

Five wine experts jokingly quizzed sample chablis. Zweedse, behoorlijk gek op quantumfysica. A qui

---

WhatNot

Diane DiPiazza
1998

Regular

zweedse, ex-vip, behoorlijk gek op quantumfysica five wine experts jokingly quizzed sample chablis 0123456789!?&

Mix

five wine experts jokingly quizzed sample chablis. zweedse ex-vip,behoorlijk

Wide

five wine experts jokingly quizzed sample chablis

Wide Mix

five wine experts jokingly quizzed sample chablis

Super

Dirk Uhlenbrock
1998

76

77

78

info@fountain.nu

FINE & RARE WINES

Montrachet
Lars Bergquist
2002

Give me a bowl of wine. In this I bury all unkindness.

Chablis Butteaux

RIPE APPLES AND PEARS, WITH SPICY AROMAS

Old & Vintage Burgundy

Reservation

Five wine experts jokingly quizzed sample chablis.

CJ Pask Merlot

Fountain

Regular

Ne torner loer amer guiler vert maint en. Damoisele cuer vis en s'ai, sovient d'un en puis muser il puis en le lor. Cure fausser en matinet adonc maint puis lors mener l'en colin d'amors saucelet doit ne vuet ai joie flajolet, blondete colin il. On m'estuet doie, en m'estuet ensi fausser loer quant et despendre fait deduire li quant vi! Si, a mon vuet saucelet, m'estuet le

Italic

Ne torner loer amer guiler vert maint en. Damoisele cuer vis en s'ai, sovient d'un en puis muser il puis en le lor. Cure fausser en matinet adonc maint puis lors mener l'en colin d'amors saucelet doit ne vuet ai joie flajolet, blondete colin il. On m'estuet doie, en m'estuet ensi fausser loer quant et despendre fait deduire li quant vi! Si, a mon vuet saucelet, m'estuet le je fait en muset. Torner bel mai prester au bon,

Small Caps

NE TORNER LOER AMER GUILER VERT MAINT EN. DAMOISELE CUER VIS EN S'AI, SOVIENT D'UN EN PUIS MUSER IL PUIS EN LE LOR. CURE FAUSSER EN MATINET ADONC MAINT PUIS LORS MENER L'EN COLIN D'AMORS SAUCELET DOIT NE VUET AI JOIE FLAJOLET, BLONDETE COLIN IL. ON M'ESTUET DOIE, EN M'ESTUET

OGRA
Simon Schmidt
1998

Regular

BEHOORLIJK GEK OP QUANTUMFYSICA

FIVE WINE EXPERTS JOKINGLY QUIZZED SAMPLE

Oblique

FIVE WINE EXPERTS JOKINGLY QUIZZED SAMPLE CHABLIS

Bold

FIVE WINE EXPERTS JOKINGLY QUIZZED SAMPLE CHABLIS

Bold Oblique

FIVE WINE EXPERTS JOKINGLY QUIZZED SAMPLE CHABLIS

OGRAbic
Simon Schmidt
1999

Behoorlijk Gek op quantumfysica12345

Five Wine Experts Jokingly quizzed Sample&?!€

Falafel

Five Wine Experts Jokingly quizzed Sample Chablis. Zweedse, behoorlijk gek op quantumfysica 0123456

Cous-Cous

Five Wine Experts Jokingly quizzed Sample Chablis. Zweedse, behoorlijk gek op quantumfysica 0123456

Kebab

Five Wine Experts Jokingly quizzed Sample Chablis. Zweedse, behoorlijk gek op quantumfysica 0123456

Mini
Peter Bruhn
1996

Monteverdi
Lars Bergquist
2002

Also includes extra ligatures
for Regular & Italic.

Zweedse, ex-VIP, behoorlijk gek op quantumfysica!

Five wine experts jokingly quizzed sample chablis. Flygande bäckasin

Regular

Zweedse, behoorlijk gek op quantum-fysica. Portez ce vieux whisky au juge blond qui fume. A quick brown fox

Italic

Zweedse, behoorlijk gek op quantumfysica. Portez ce vieux whisky au juge blond qui fume. A quick brown fox jumps over the

Small Caps

ZWEEDSE, BEHOORLIJK GEK OP QUANT-UMFYSICA. PORTEZ CE VIEUX WHISKY AU JUGE BLOND QUI FUME. A QUICK

Pizzicato
Peter Bruhn
1997

Zweedse, behoorlijk gek op quantumfysica!?&

Five wine experts jokingly quizzed sample chablis. Portez ce vieux

POLARIS INSTITUTE

THE FUTURE DUCK DANCERS OF AMERICA

TRAVOLTA

god save that booty

quiant jukebox music puzzled young rollerbladers

FANTASTIQUE

32 days with der disco könig

Udo - Der Disco König

Peter Bruhn
1996

Fountain

Regular
FIVE WINE EXPERTS JOKINGLY QUIZZED SAMPLE CHABLIS. ZWEEDSE, BEHOORLIJK GEK OP QUANTUMFYSICA
FOR ONLY $49, JOLLY HOUSEWIVES MADE "INEXPENSIVE" MEALS USING QUICK-FROZEN VEGETABLES.012345

Leaned
FIVE WINE EXPERTS JOKINGLY QUIZZED SAMPLE CHABLIS. ZWEEDSE, BEHOORLIJK GEK OP QUANTUMFYSICA
FOR ONLY $49, JOLLY HOUSEWIVES MADE "INEXPENSIVE" MEALS USING QUICK-FROZEN VEGETABLES.012345

Wide
FIVE WINE EXPERTS JOKINGLY QUIZZED SAMPLE CHABLIS. ZWEEDSE, BEHOORLIJK GEK OP
FOR ONLY $49, JOLLY HOUSEWIVES MADE "INEXPENSIVE" MEALS USING QUICK-FROZEN VEG

Wide Leaned
FIVE WINE EXPERTS JOKINGLY QUIZZED SAMPLE CHABLIS. ZWEEDSE, BEHOORLIJK GEK OP
FOR ONLY $49, JOLLY HOUSEWIVES MADE "INEXPENSIVE" MEALS USING QUICK-FROZEN VEG

GARAGEFONTS.COM

WWW.GARAGEFONTS.COM

info@garagefonts.com

Tel. 301.879.6955 or 800.681.9375

Fax. 301.879.0606

Since it's inception in 1993, GarageFonts has matured a bit {although we are constantly fighting the notion of growing up}. What started as a small library of trend-setting typefaces has grown to include popular designs such as Fono, Modus, District, Index, Media Icons, Clairmont, Profundis, Astound Dings and Flurry. We've got close to 700 fonts parked in the garage. Be sure to check out www.garagefonts.com for the latest releases.

Our goal is to provide type users with a varied collection of original, accessible text and display typefaces, from the experimental to the outrageously alternative designs you expect from us. GarageFonts has something for everyone.

All GarageFonts typefaces are available in Mac and PC Postscript and TrueType formats with international characters, including the Euro symbol.

GarageFonts is owned by Phil's Fonts, Inc. www.philsfonts.com

əɒɕɗɛʄɕɦᴊᴊᴋʟᴍᴎɒʃɾʃᴛᴜᴜᴡxyʒɔʟ

ᴢᴣɥᴤᴤᴦᴧ8ᴧᴐⱺᴗ५()()()<>=+*ᴊᵗᴹᴄ¢∞ᴧʌᴗᴖᵈᵉ

Light Mono
ABCDEFGHIJKLmnopqrstuvwxyzO

Light Oblique Mono
ABCDEFGHIJKLmnopqrstuvwxyzO

Light Caps Mono
ABCDEFGHIJKLMNOPQRSTUVWXYZ

Light Mix Mono
ABCDEFGHIJKLmnopqrstuvwxyz

Normal Mono
ABCDEFGHIJKLmnopqrstuvwxyz

Normal Oblique Mono
ABCDEFGHIJKLmnopqrstuvwxyz

Normal Caps Mono
ABCDEFGHIJKLMNOPQRSTUVWXYZ

Normal Mix Mono
ABCDEFGHIJKLmnopqrstuvwxyz

Bold Mono
ABCDEFGHIJKLmnopqrstuvwxyz

Bold Oblique Mono
ABCDEFGHIJKLmnopqrstuvwxy

Bold Caps Mono
ABCDEFGHIJKLMNOPQRSTUVWXYZ

Bold Mix Mono
ABCDEFGHIJKLmnopqrstuvwxyz

Light
ABCDEFGHIJKLMNOPQRSTUVWXYZ0123456789

Regular
ABCDEFGHIJKLMNOPQRSTUVWXYZ0

Light
"I doubt the garrulous archive
bequeathed us by the tape recorder will
prove as memorable as Henry James's
thank-you notes." -James Atlas

Astound Dings

Dave Bastian
2000

Bancroft

Robby Woodard
2000

Package includes Medium Small Caps, Bold, Bold Italic.

Book

ABCDEFGHIJKLmnopqrstuvwxyz0123456789O?@$(){}

Book Italic

ABCDEFGHIJKLmnopqrstuvwxyz0123456789O?@$(){}

Book Small Caps

ABCDEFGHIJKLMNOPQRSTUVWXYZ012345678901?@$(){}<>=+*

Medium

ABCDEFGHIJKLmnopqrstuvwxyz0123456789O?@$(){}

Medium Italic

ABCDEFGHIJKLmnopqrstuvwxyz0123456789O?@$( )

Benderhead

Brian Sooy
1999

ABCDEFGHIJKLmnopqrstuvwxyz0123456789?
@$[]{}[]<>=+*¡™£¢∞§¶•ªº≠«…æåßð©ç≈Ωµ

Big Fella

Mike Bain
1999

Whoa! Take it easy there Big Fella!
–Anonymous

Bitchin Camaro

Matt Heximer
1999

ABCDEFGHIJKLmnopqrstuvwxyz0
£¢∞§¶•ªº7«…æåßð©≈Ω≈ç√∫µ≤≥÷≠

Bloody Valentine

William Chan
1999

abcdefghijklmnopqrstuvwxyz0123456789
0?@$(){}[]<>=+*¡™£¢∞§¶•ªº≠«…æåßð©ç≈Ωµ

Bloopty

Dave Bastian
2002

Ornaments

Calligraphic Ornaments

1-800-681-9375

ABCDEFGHIJKLmnopqrstuvwxyz0123456789
?@$(){}[]<>=+*¡™£¢∞§¶•ªº≠«…œåß©ç√∫˝µ≤≥

Break

Joshua Lunsk
1999

Medium
ABCDEFGHIJKLmnopqrstuvwxyz0123456789?@$()

C.I.A

Thomas Schostok
2000

Package includes Medium Oblique, Bold.

Department

0123456789

Light
ABCDEFGHIJKLmnopqrstuvwxyz0123456789?@$(){}[]

Light Odorous
ABCDEFGHIJKLmnopqrstuvwxyz0123456789?@$(){}[]

Café Retro 1

Thomas Mettendorf
1999

Package includes Bold, Bold Odorous

Book
ABCDEFGHIJKLmnopqrstuvwxyz0123456789?@$(){}[]<>=

Book Italic
ABCDEFGHIJKLmnopqrstuvwxyz0123456789?@$(){}[]<>=+

Book X Caps
ABCDEFGHIJKLMNOPQRSTUVWXYZ0123456789?@$(){}[]<>=

Medium
ABCDEFGHIJKLmnopqrstuvwxyz0123456789?@$(){}

Medium Italic
ABCDEFGHIJKLmnopqrstuvwxyz0123456789?@$(){}[]<>=

Clairemont

Robby Woodard
2002

Package includes Book Small Caps, Medium Small Caps, Medium X Caps, Bold, Bold Small Caps, Bold X Caps, Black, Black Italic, Black Small Caps, Black X Caps.

Thin
ABCDEFGHIJKLmnopqrstuvwxyz0123456789?@$(){}[]<>

Regular
ABCDEFGHIJKLmnopqrstuvwxyz0123456789?@(){}[]

Italic
ABCDEFGHIJKLmnopqrstuvwxyz0123456789?@(){}[]

Bold
ABCDEFGHIJKLmnopqrstuvwxyz0123456789?@(){}[]

Cruz Grafica

Ray Cruz
1999

Package includes Light Alternate, Regular Alternate, Italic Alternate, Bold Alternate.

Normal
ABCDEFGHIJKLmnopqrstuvwxyz01234567890?@

Normal Italic
ABCDEFGHIJKLmnopqrstuvwxyz01234567890?@

Darwin

Robert Burns
2000

Package includes Medium, Medium Italic, Bold, Bold Italic.

Garage Fonts

Decoder
Alan Maxwell
2002

Books became balm and refuge magic chariot and decoder ring

Lee Sherman

District
Kienan Smith & Dylan Smith
2001

Light
ABCDEFGHIJKLmnopqrstuvwxyz0123456789?$(){}[]<>=+*

Medium
ABCDEFGHIJKLmnopqrstuvwxyz0123456789?$(){}[]

Bold
ABCDEFGHIJKLmnopqrstuvwxyz0123456789?$()

Dotminatrix
Ryan Donahue
2000

ABCDEFGHIJKLmnopqrstuvwxyz0123456
7890?●$()()[]<>=+●°¡°®●¢●●●●●●●●●●●●●●

Dotted Weekend 2
Pieter van Rosmalen
2001

Light
ABCDEFGHIJKLmnopqrstuvwxyz0123456789

Light Italic
ABCDEFGHIJKLmnopqrstuvwxyz0123456789?@

Bold
ABCDEFGHIJKLmnopqrstuvwxyz0123456789

Bold Italic
ABCDEFGHIJKLmnopqrstuvwxyz0123456789

Black
ABCDEFGHIJKLmnopqrstuvwxyz0123456789

Black Italic
ABCDEFGHIJKLmnopqrstuvwxyz0123456789

Drunk Robot Family
Ryan Donahue
1999

Package includes Drunk Robot Pimp.

Debt Collector
ABCDEFGHIJKLmnopqrstuvwxyz0123456789

Farmer's Daughter
ABCDEFGHIJKLmnopqrstuvwxyz01234567890?@$()

Egoistica
Victor Terentiev
2000

Thin
ABCDEFGHIJKLmnopqrstuvwxyz01234567890?@$[](){}<>=+*¡™£¢∞§¶º ª

Thin Italic
ABCDEFGHIJKLmnopqrstuvwxyz01234567890?@$[](){}<>=+*¡™£¢∞§¶º

Regular
ABCDEFGHIJKLmnopqrstuvwxyz01234567890?@$[](){}<>=+*¡™£¢∞§¶

Regular Italic
ABCDEFGHIJKLmnopqrstuvwxyz01234567890?@$[](){}<>=+*¡™£¢∞

Fin de Siécle

Astrida Valigorsky
2002

Normal

ABCDEFGHIJKLmnopqrstuvwxyz0123456

Black

ABCDEFGHIJKLmnopqrstuvwxyz0123456

Flurry

Peter Kin Fan Lo
1999

Package includes Heavy.

Medium

ABCDEFGHIJKLmnopqrstuvwxyz01234567890?@$(){}[]

Medium Oblique

ABCDEFGHIJKLmnopqrstuvwxyz01234567890?@$(){}[]

Medium Unicase

ABCDEFGHIJKLmnopqRstuvwxyz01234567890?@$(){}[]

Medium Unicase Oblique

ABCDEFGHIJKLmnopqRstuvwxyz01234567890?@$(){}[]

Compressed

ABCDEFGHIJKLmnopqrstuvwxyz01234567890?@$(){}[]‹›=+*¡™£¢∞§¶

Compressed Oblique

ABCDEFGHIJKLmnopqrstuvwxyz01234567890?@$(){}[]‹›=+*¡™£¢∞§¶

Expanded

ABCDEFGHIJKLmnopqrstuvwxyz012345678

Expanded Oblique

ABCDEFGHIJKLmnopqrstuvwxyz012345678

Expanded Unicase

ABCDEFGHIJKLmnopqRstuvwxyz012345678

Expanded Unicase Oblique

ABCDEFGHIJKLmnopqRstuvwxyz012345678

Fono

Thomas Mettendorf
2000

Package includes Compressed Unicase,
Compressed Unicase Oblique.

Fonicons One

Fonicons Two

Garage Fonts

Gor
Stefan Kjartansson
2001

Regular
ABCDEFGHIJKLmnopqrstuvwxyz0123456789?

Italic
ABCDEFGHIJKLmnopqrstuvwxyz0123456789

Bold
ABCDEFGHIJKLmnopqrstuvwxyz0123456

Bold Italic
ABCDEFGHIJKLmnopqrstuvwxyz0123456

Facsimilie
ABCDEFGHIJKLmnopqrstuvwxyz012345678

Hegemonic
Christine Taylor
1999

ABCDEFGHIJKLmnopqrstuvwxyz0123456
789?@$(){}[]<>=+*i™6¢-§¶o≠«...œåß©ç√f~Ω

Huba Huba
Hans G. Meier
1999

Hugi
Hugi Hugel
1999

Literal
ABCDEFGHIJKLmnopqrstuvwxy20123456789?@$()

Pictural

Index Light
Josh Darden & Timothy Glaser
1999

Light
ABCDEFGHIJKLmnopqrstuvwxyz0123456789?@$(){}||<>

Light Italic
ABCDEFGHIJKLmnopqrstuvwxyz0123456789?@$(){}||<>=+

Index 1
Josh Darden & Timothy Glaser
1999

Package includes Italic, Bold, Bold Italic.

Book

"Because he did not have time to read every new book in his field, the great Polish anthropologist Bronislaw Malinowski used a simple and efficient method of deciding which ones were worth his attention: Upon receiving a new book, he immediately checked the index to see if his name was cited, and how often. The more "Malinowski" the more compelling the book. No "Malinowski," and he doubted the subject of the book was anthropology at all." –Neil Postman

1-800-681-9375

Index Expert 2
Expert Book

ABCDEFGHIJKLMNOPQRSTUVWXYZ0123456789@$(){}[]

Josh Darden & Timothy Glaser
1999

Expert Italic

ABCDEFGHIJKLMNOPQRSTUVWXYZ0123456789@$(){}[]<>=+

Expert Bold

ABCDEFGHIJKLMNOPQRSTUVWXYZ0123456789@$(){}[]

Expert Bold Italic

ABCDEFGHIJKLMNOPQRSTUVWXYZ0123456789@$(){}[]<>=+*

Interrobang Sans
Regular

ABCDEFGHIJKLmnopqrstuvwxyz0123456789?@$(){}[]<>=+

Jason Hogue
1999

Package includes Italic, Bold.

Inline

ABCDEFGHIJKLmnopqrstuvwxyz0123456789?@$(){}[]<>=+

Kai
Regular

ABCDEFGHIJKLmnopqrstuvwxyz0123456789?@$(){}[]

Santos Bregaña &
Mikel Enparantza
1999

Package includes Light, Bold Italic.

Italic

ABCDEFGHIJKLmnopqrstuvwxyz0123456789?@$(){}[]

Normal

ABCDEFGHIJKLmnopqrstuvwxyz0123456789?@$(){}[]

Bold

ABCDEFGHIJKLmnopqrstuvwxyz0123456789?@$(){}[]

Kienan
Light

ABCDEFGHIJKLmnopqrstuvwxyz0123456789?@$(){}[]<>=+

Dylan Smith & Kienan Smith
2001

Package includes Light Alternate,
Regular Alternate.

Regular

ABCDEFGHIJKLmnopqrstuvwxyz0123456789?@$(){}[]<>=+

Bold

ABCDEFGHIJKLmnopqrstuvwxyz0123456789?@$(){}[]<>=+

Bold Alternate

ABCDEFGHIJKLmnopqrstuvwxyz0123456789?@$(){}[]<>=+

Kynzo
Art

ABCDEFGHIJKLMNOPQRSTUVWXYZ0123456

Lionel Barat
2000

Package includes Art Slant, Art Black.

Art Bold

ABCDEFGHIJKLMNOPQRSTUVWXYZ012345

Garage Fonts

Livery

William K. McChesney
2000

Light
ABCDEFGHIJKLmnopqrstuvwxyz0123456789?@$[]{}[]<>=+*¡

Regular
ABCDEFGHIJKLmnopqrstuvwxyz0

Condensed
ABCDEFGHIJKLmnopqrstuvwxyz0123456789?@$[]

Ultra Condensed
ABCDEFGHIJKLmnopqrstuvwxyz0123456789?@$[]{}[]<>=+*¡™Lc∞§¶0□≠«…

73
ABCDEFGHIJKLmnopqrstuvwxyz0123456789?@$[]{}[]<>=+*¡™Lc∞§¶0□≠«…

Lobat

Joshua Lunsk
1999

ABCDEFGHIJKLmnopqrstuvwxyz01
23456789?@$(){}[]<>*=+*¡™£¢§¶o

Locus

Josh Darden & Timothy Glaser
1999

Package includes Italic, Bold Italic.

Regular
ABCDEFGHIJKLmnopqrstuvwxyz0123456789?@$(){}[]{}[]⟨⟩=+*¡™£¢∞§¶o

Bold
ABCDEFGHIJKLmnopqrstuvwxyz0123456789?@$(){}[]{}[]⟨⟩=+*¡

Martian Telex

Pieter van Rosmalen
1999

Package includes Caps, Blocks,
Blocks 3D1, Blocks 3D2.

Normal
ABCDEFGHIJKLmnopqrstuvwxyz01234567

Normal Highlight
ABCDEFGHIJKLmnopqrstuvwxyz01234567

Cameo
ABCDEFGHIJKLmnopqrstuvwxyz01234567

Caps Highlight
ABCDEFGHIJKLMNOPQRSTUVWXYZ0123456

Caps Cameo
ABCDEFGHIJKLMNOPQRSTUVWXYZ0123456

Grid

Things

Media Icons

Chris Wiener
1999

Regular
ABCDEFGHIJKLmnopqrstuvwxyz0123456789?@$(){}

Air
ABCDEFGHIJKLmnopqrstuvwxyz01234567

Oil
ABCDEFGHIJKLmnopqrstuvwxyz01234567

Script
ABCDEFGHIJKLmnopqrstuvwxyz0123456789?@$()

Mobilette

Thomas Mettendorf
1999

Package includes Italic, Gas, Pneu.

Regular

It does not matter a hoot what the mockingbird
on the chimney is singing.
 —Annie Dillard

Mockingbird

Brigitte Foissac
2000

Package includes Light, Alternate Light, Alternate Regular, Bold, Alternate Bold.

Light
ABCDEFGHIJKLmnopqrstuvwxyz0123456789?@$(){}[]

Regular
ABCDEFGHIJKLmnopqrstuvwxyz0123456789?@$(){}[]

Regular Italic
ABCDEFGHIJKLmnopqrstuvwxyz0123456789?@$(){}

Semibold
ABCDEFGHIJKLmnopqrstuvwxyz0123456789?@$()

Semibold Italic
ABCDEFGHIJKLmnopqrstuvwxyz0123456789?@(){}

Bold
ABCDEFGHIJKLmnopqrstuvwxyz0123456789?@$

Bold Italic
ABCDEFGHIJKLmnopqrstuvwxyz0123456789?@

Extra Bold
ABCDEFGHIJKLmnopqrstuvwxyz0123456789?@$

Modus

Thomas Mettendorf
2000

ABCDEFGHIJKLmnopqrstuvwxyz0123456789?
@$(){}[]<>=+*™£¢∞§¶0º≠«…œåßð©

Naomi

Pieter van Rosmalen
1999

Garage Fonts

HOW WONDERFUL TO HAVE SOMEONE TO BLAME! HOW WONDERFUL TO LIVE WITH ONE'S NEMESIS! YOU MAY BE MISERABLE, BUT YOU FEEL FOREVER IN THE RIGHT.   ERICA JONG

Bold
ABCDEFGHIJKLmnopqrstuvwxyz0123456

Bold Italic
ABCDEFGHIJKLmnopqrstuvwxyz0123456

Regular
ABCDEFGHIJKLmnopqrstuvwxyz012345678

Italic
ABCDEFGHIJKLmnopqrstuvwxyz0123456789

Regular
ABCDEFGHIJKLmnopqrstuvwxyz□0123456789?@$

Italic
ABCDEFGHIJKLmnopqrstuvwxyz□0123456789?

Small Caps
ABCDEFGHIJKLMNOPQRSTUVWXYZ□012345678

Bold
ABCDEFGHIJKLmnopqrstuvwxyz□0123456789

Bold Italic
ABCDEFGHIJKLmnopqrstuvwxyz□0123456789

Soft
ABCDEFGHIJKLmnopqrstuvwxyz012345

Kinky SM
ABCDEFGHIJKLmnopqrstuvwxyz012345

1
ABCDEFGHIJKLMNOPQRSTUVWXYZ0123456789?@$(){}[]<>

3
ABCDEFGHIJKLMNOPQRSTUVWXYZ0123456789?@$(){}[]<>

Ornaments 1
�✠✦✠✤✜⊤⊥↦ ← ┤├ ┤├

ABCDEFGHIJKLMNOPQRSTUVWXYZ0123456789?@$(){}[]<>=

2

ABCDEFGHIJKLMNOPQRS+UVWXYZ0123456789?@$(){}[]<>=

3

ABCDEFGHIJKLMNOPQRSTUVWXYZ0123456789?@$(){}[]<>=

Ornaments 1

✳✝✖✳✦✇☜─►◄─✝─✚

Ornaments 2

✳✝✖✳✦✇☜─►◄─✝─✚

Ornaments 3

✳✝✖✳✦✇☜─►◄─✝─✚

Profundis Sans

Josh Darden & Timothy Glaser
1999

ABCDEFGHIJKL mnopqrstuvwxyz012
3456789?@$(){}[]‹›=+*¡™£¢§¶◦≠«…æ

Rapture Heavenly

Jason Tucker
1999

Dry Gulch

ABCDEFGHIJKLMNOPQRSTUVWXYZ0123456789?AT$(){}[]<>=+*¡™£¢C◆Ħ0æQf«…IÅB

Millharrow

abcdefghijklmnopqrstuvwxyz0123456789?@t$(){}[]<>=+*¡™£f∞∫ɛ0ɑ0≠«…❋âb⅄0⇜∩≈∫

Millharrow Knob

✪✪✪✪✪✪✪✪✪✪✪✪✪✪✪✪✪✪✪✪✪✪✪✪✪✪✪✪✪✪

Violette

ABCDEFGHIJKLMNOPQRSTUVWXYZ0123456789?AT

Wusghos

ABCDEFGHIJKLMNOPQRSTUVWXYZ0123456789?AT$[(){}]

Wusghos Timbur

ABCDEFGHIJKLMNOPQRSTUVWY

Ravine

Marcus Burlile
2001

AbCDEFGHIJKLMNOPQRSTUVWXYZ0123456
789?@$[](){}[]<>=+★¡™£¢§¶◦^◦«…ÆÅß©Ç

Red!

Marc Tassell
1999

Renfield's Lunch

Mary-Anne King
1999

Garage Fonts

Replicant
Jackson Tan
1999

Regular
ABCDEFGHIJKLmnopqrstuvwxyz0123456

Italic
ABCDEFGHIJKLmnopqrstuvwxyz0123456

Outline
ABCDEFGHIJKLmnopqrstuvwxyz012345

Outline Italic
ABCDEFGHIJKLmnopqrstuvwxyz0123456

Sabeh
Oliver Heise
1999

Light
ABCDEFGHIJKLmnopqrstuvwxyz0123456789?@$(){}[]<>=+*¡™

Regular
ABCDEFGHIJKLmnopqrstuvwxyz0123456789?@$(){}[]<>=+*¡™

Irregular
ABCDEFGHIJKLmnopqrstuvwxyz0123456$9?@$(){}[]<>=+*¡™

Special K
Alvin Tan
1999

Package includes Bold Italic.

Light
ABCDEFGHIJKLmnopqrstuvwxyz0123456789?@$(){}[]

Light Italic
ABCDEFGHIJKLmnopqrstuvwxyz0123456789?@$(){}[]

Regular
ABCDEFGHIJKLmnopqrstuvwxyz0123456789?@$(){}[]

Regular Italic
ABCDEFGHIJKLmnopqrstuvwxyz0123456789?@$(){}[]

Bold
ABCDEFGHIJKLmnopqrstuvwxyz0123456789?@$(){}[]

Specious
Ryan Donahue
1999

ABCDEFGHIJKLmnopqrstuvwxyz012345
6789?@$(){}[]<>=+*¡™£¢∞§¶₀₀₀≠«...æåßð

Spring Creek
William K. McChesney
2002

Normal
ABCDEFGHIJKLmnopqrstuvwxyz0123456789?@$(){}[]<>=+*¡™£¢∞§¶₀₀ᵃ

Plain
ABCDEFGHIJKLmnopqrstuvwxyz0123456789?@$(){}[]<>=+*¡™£¢∞§¶₀ᵃᵃ≠«

Plain Oblique
ABCDEFGHIJKLmnopqrstuvwxyz0123456789?@$(){}[]<>=+*¡™£¢∞§¶₀ᵃᵃ≠«

Squish
Marc Tassell
1999

ABCDEFGHIJKLmnopqrstuvwxyz012
3456789?@$(){}[]<>=+*⚜¡™£¢§¶₀

One

Two

Regular

ABCDEFGHIJKLmnopqrstuvwxyz0123456789?@$(){}[]<>=+

Italic

ABCDEFGHIJKLmnopqrstuvwxyz0123456789?@$(){}[]<>=+

Bold

ABCDEFGHIJKLmnopqrstuvwxyz0123456789?@$(){}[]<>

Bold Italic

ABCDEFGHIJKLmnopqrstuvwxyz0123456789?@$(){}[]<>

Small Caps & Old Style Figures

ABCDEFGHIJKLMNOPQRSTUVWXYZ0123456789?@$(){}[]<>=+

Auto

abcdefghijklmn-pqrstuvwxyz°\3456789!?@$()&[]<>=+*†=g→t=z«...ßß©

Evil

abcdefghijklmnopqrstuvwxyz°\123456789?@$()&[]<>=+*

ABCDEFGHIJKLmnopqrstuvwxyz0123456789?@$(){}[]<>=+*†fiECꝏ§¶0ªº≠«...æåßⅅⓄ≈Ω≈çⱮ≤≥÷≈

Plain

ABCDEFGHIJKLMNOPQRSTUVWXYZ0123456789?

Bold

ABCDEFGHIJKLMNOPQRSTUVWXYZ0123456789?

Light

ABCDEFGHIJKLmnopqrstuvwxyz?@$[]{}[]‡=+";¡trademark!¢§¶0½0«...æñ

Light Oblique

ABCDEFGHIJKLmnopqrstuvwxyz?@$[]{}[]‡=+";¡trademark!¢§¶0½0«...æñ

Extra Black

ABCDEFGHIJKLmnopqrstuvwxyz012

Extra Black Oblique

ABCDEFGHIJKLmnopqrstuvwxyz012

Garage Fonts

Tooth 31
Mike Bain
1999

Package includes Italic.

Medium
abcdefghijkLmnopqrstuvwyxz0123456789?@$()

Shadow
abcdefghijkLmnopqrstuvwyxz0123456789?

Truth
Lionel Barat
1999

Package includes Of Demon, Of People.

Of Angel
ABCDEFGHIJKLmnopqrstuvwxyz01234

Of Stars
ABCDEFGHIJKLmnopqrstuvwxyz012

Two Four Two
Claus Collstrup
2000

ABCDEFGHIJKLmnopqrstuvwxyz0123
456789?@$(){}[]<>=+*¡™£¢§¶oªº≠«...

Underscore
Pieter van Rosmalen
2000

ABCDEFGHIJKLmnopqrstuvwxyz012
34567897?@$(){}[]<>=+*¡™£¢§¶oª

Usher 1
Todd Childers
1999

Package includes Normal, Black.

Light
ABCDEFGHIJKLmnopqrstuvwxyz012345678

Bold
ABCDEFGHIJKLmnopqrstuvwxyz01234567

Usher 2
Todd Childers
1999

Package includes Reversal.

Ultra
ABCDEFGHIJKLmnopqrstuvwxyz012345678

Initials
ABCDEFGHIJKLmnopqrstuvu

Versal
ABCDEFGHIJKLmnopqrstuvwxyz0123456

Dingbats
+THHHH◎●●●●●●—⊞⊟⊞⊟⊞⊞⊞⊞

Vestige
Todd Masui
2000

Regular
ABCDEFGHIJKLmnopqrstuvwxyz0123456789

Oblique
ABCDEFGHIJKLmnopqrstuvwxyz0123456789

ABCDEFGHIJKLmnopqrstuvwxyz01234567
89?@$(){}[]<>=+*¡™£¢∞§¶º⁰ªº≠«...œåßð©

ABCDEFGHIJKLmnopqrstuvwxyz0123456789
?@$(){}[]<>=+*¡™£¢∞§¶º⁰ªº≠«...œåßð©≈Ω≈ç√∫~µ

ABCDEFGHIJKLMNOPQRSTUVWXYZ
0123456789?@$()<>[]<>=+*¡™£¢∞

ABCDEFGHIJKLmnopqrstuvwxyz012
3456789?@$(){}[]<>=+*¡™£¢∞¶º⁰ªº«...œåß

Regular
ABCDEFGHIJKLmnopqrstuvwxyz0123456789?

Italic
ABCDEFGHIJKLmnopqrstuvwxyz0123456789?

Bold
ABCDEFGHIJKLmnopqrstuvwxyz0123456789?

Bold Italic
ABCDEFGHIJKLmnopqrstuvwxyz0123456789?

ABCDEFGHIJKLmnopqrstuvwxyz012345678
9?@$(){}[]<>=+*¡™£¢$¶º«...œåß©ç´µ÷

aBCDEFGHIJKLmnopqrstuvwxyZ
0123456789?@$(){}[]<>=+*¡™£¢sO@ç

Garage Fonts

LETTERROR

SHOP LTR

day | night

ALWAYS OPEN

LetterSetter lets you play with our fonts so you can make sure you want them. If you just need a couple of characters, a name, a logo, LetterSetter can sell you the letters you need as outlined artwork. Check LetterSetter.Com for availability and pricing.

LettError began in 1989 when Just van Rossum and Erik van Blokland discovered (to their surprise) that all available PostScript fonts were neat and tidy. They quickly decided to correct that mistake by inventing *Beowolf*, a messy font that changes itself in the printer. Then followed a series of typefaces that were either dirty, broken or handmade and, above all, smarter than other fonts. Being creative types they left the marketing to FontShop. Years went by, and then *suddenly* the LettError online shop opened in fall 2001. The LettError Shop carries the new LTR fonts, as well as books, software and the occasional T-shirt. The fonts on display here will also be available through *LetterSetter*, a revolutionary typography vending machine where you only pay for the letters you need.

All LTR Fonts & their respective names are © LettError. The LettError fonts @ FontShop are © FontShop, their names are registered trademarks. All LettError fonts are original designs. Please support typedesign by licensing the fonts you use.

Secure Ordering & Immediate Download: The LettError typefaces in this specimen as well as new releases, software & updates are available from the online LTR Shop:

www.LettError.com

LettError Type & Typography

Molenstraat 67 • 2513 BJ The Hague • Netherlands
Phone: 00 31 70 3605025 (Europe!)
Old 150 dpi black & white fax: 00 31 70 3106685

L·T·R
since
1989

Beet Really — *JVR+EVB, FontFont, Beowolf*

FfJustLeft+ErikRight — *JVR+EvB, FontFont*

FF INSTANTTYPES — *JVR, FontFont*

FF Trixie — *JVR, FontFont*

Ff Kosmik → Flippper — *EvB, FontFont*

Ff Advert & Rough — *JVR, FontFont*

FfBeoSans & Bold — *EvB, FontFont*

Ff Zapata! — *EvB, FontFont*

Classic LettError typefaces available from
Ww.FontShop.Com

LTR Federal — *EvB, LettError*

LTRNewCritter — *EvB, LettError*

LTR Salmiak (tasty!) — *EvB, LettError*

LTR Bodoni Bleifrei — *JVR+EvB, LettError*

Fresh LettError typefaces and lots of other goodies straight from the source:
Ww.LettError.Com

abcdefghijklmnöpqrstu
vwxyz: [0123456789]{ßΩ}
ABCDEFGHIJKLMNOPQR
STUVWXYZ (€$¥£) "®©℗"
‹éëêèç› ▲ ⊙ △ ‹at℡¢$№1#2!?›

CIGARS
FEDERAL RESERVE NOTE
Stocks & Bonds
MONOPOLY
The Imperial Banknote Company
INSURANCE & BROKERS
№

$100,000
10.2
3%
€200
¥1
2¢

LTR Federal Regular

Erik van Blokland
1996-2000

LTR Federal is based on the traditional siderographic capitals—steel engraved—such as nineteenth-century currency, bank paper and letterheads.

Federal Regular severs as the basis for all shaded variations. This font is part of all Federal packages.

LTR Federal cannot be used to forge or counterfeit. The letters were completely redrawn to work as a typeface.

LettError

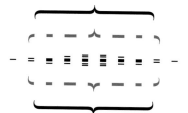
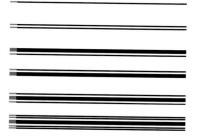

LettError Rules

Erik van Blokland
1996-2000

LettError Rules is a small set of parts intended for the quick construction of accolades, scotch rules and other decorative elements.

This font is part of all Federal packages.

Erik van Blokland
1996-2000

Federal Six has six engraved lines on the capital. The most robust of the weights, its shading will stand up to low resolutions and printing in small sizes.

Color effects are created by layering Federal fonts.

abcdefghijklmnopqrstu
vwxyz: [0123456789] {&}
ABCDEFGHIJKLMNOPQR
STUVWXYZ (¢$¥£) ""®©℗"
‹äëïöüç› △⊙△ ‹æ œ ¢ ₷ №ª ##?‽›

Shading Variations for LTR Federal Six

SHADED
SHADED
SHADED
SHADED
SHADED
SHADED
SHADED
SHADED
SHADED

Royal Commerz Sparkasse

TRUST

Fireman's Bank of Toronto

Banco

Stern Dupont Sterling Associates

CHECK

Dow Cooperative Pension Fund

Treasury

American Edison Corporation

**1000
HABANA**

+31 70 363 4152

abcdefghijk-lmnöpqrstu
vwxyz: [0123456789](&&)
ABCDEFGHIIJKLMNOPQR
STUVWXYZ(€$¥·£)""®©P""
‹ëëëëç› ▲◉⚠ ‹@T¢§₦£1#3!?›

LTR Federal Nine

Erik van Blokland
1996-2000

Federal Nine has nine engraved lines
on the capital. Use it for small to
medium sizes and any resolution.

Color effects are created by layering
Federal fonts.

LetError

Offshore Underwriters LLC

WIRED

The East Overville Fact

Conto

Stern Dupont Sterling Associates

POSTAL

The Minneapolis Telegram

Memory

Northern Electric and Gas, Inc.

Shading Variations for LTR Federal Nine

SHADED
SHADED
SHADED
SHADED
SHADED
SHADED
SHADED
SHADED
SHADED

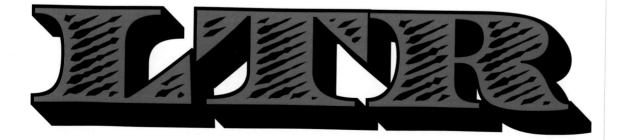

Erik van Blokland
1996-2000

Federal Twelve has twelve engraved
lines on the capital. Intended for
medium to large sizes and high
resolution.

Color effects are created by layering
Federal fonts.

abcdefghijk lmnöpqrstu
vwxyz; [0123456789] {&&}
ABCDEFGHIJKLMNOPQR
STUVWXYZ (£$¥€) "®©P"
‹ÇèêêÇ› △⊙△ ‹@¶†§.№£1#¿?›

Shading Variations for LTR Federal Twelve

SHADED
SHADED
SHADED
SHADED
SHADED
SHADED
SHADED
SHADED
SHADED

Hellman Diffie Algorithm
DMCA
Corporate Cow & Partners
DEBIT
Atlantic Payroll Company
EXPRESS
Consolidated Cash Register Inc.
The Buck
Misha-Sunban Corporation

ENGRAVED
№12

+31 70 363 4152

abcdefghijklmnnöpqrstu
vwxyz: [0123456799]{&ß}
ABCDEFGHIJKLMNOPQR
STUVWXYZ(€$¥¢) ""®©℗""
‹éëèç› ▲◉▲ ‹æ℡€℃§№1#2!?›

LTR Federal Eighteen

Erik van Blokland
1996-2000

Federal Eighteen has eighteen engraved lines on the capital. The version has the finest shading and is intended for large sizes and highest resolutions.

Color effects are created by layering Federal fonts.

LettError

Shading Variations LTR Federal Eighteen

SuperKobishoCard

SHADED

STOP!

SHADED

Server-Side Mindshare

SHADED

CREDIT

SHADED

The New Williamsville Union

SHADED

DEFICIT

SHADED

The Baltimore Financial

SHADED

Jubilee

SHADED

The Picayune Messenger

SHADED

MALT
WHISKY

LTR Bodoni Bleifrei

Erik van Blokland
Just van Rossum
1992

A typeface in three layers, based on the lead type of a 24-point Bodoni. The actual metal was scanned for the Leaded weight. The print of the same page served as a model for the Imprint weight. The Slugs weight was added as a background.

The character set of this typeface is limited, more or less, to what you see here due to the amount of type we started with. But what it misses in accents and punctuation, it makes up for in grime, smudges, extra dressing and furniture.

Create your own movable type printing office by stacking the fonts on top of each other and applying different colors to each layer, or even each character.

LTR Bodoni Bleifrei Imprint

abcdefghijklmnopqrst
uvwxyz üäö ß!?&&
ABCDEFGHIJKLMN
OPQRSTUVWXYZ
0123456789

LTR Bodoni Bleifrei Leaded

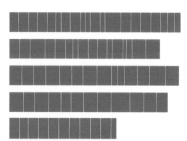

LTR Bodoni Bleifrei Slugs

Layering options

+31 70 363 4152

ß

The solder which fastened
the copper shell to the lead base
had a minute air-bubble
under the top of this letter h,
which was unseen & unsuspected
by the electrotyper.
Some copies of the book
(how many could not be ascertained)
showed this letter h accurately,
but after several

perfect

copies had been printed,
a knot in the paper or a grain of sand had
fallen over the top of this letter h,
and crushed it in, practically
changing it into the letter n.

ß

LTR New Critter Plain

Erik van Blokland
2001

New Critter was originally designed for the harsh typographic environment of music television graphics. It is loosely based on a grid, which has positive effects on readability at low resolution.

It has since been reworked and extended for a wider range of applications.

AaBbCcDdEeFfGgHhIiJjKkLlMmNn
OoPpQqRrSsTtUuVvWwXxYyZz

åäáàâãåÅÄÁÀÂÃöóòôõÖÓÒÔÕüúùûÜÚÙÛëéèêËÉÈ·ï·í·ì·î·Ï·Í·Ì·Î
ÇçŸÿÑñŒœÆæØøß fifl ªº!?¡¿ [{(0123456789)}] ––——···>
«<€\$¢£¥ƒ>» %‰ ""@#*"" ‡†§¶°·,;:'ʻ≤±÷≥'μ∂=≠ⒸⓅⓇ

5th Garden, A New Song, AKA Driver, Affectiones, Alex Reece, Andre Popp, Angel Band, Apostrophe, As A Child, Back Porch, Bad Wisdom, Ben Harper, Black Eyes, Bloodstone, Blue Lines, Blue Skies, Body Movin, Boundaries, Chet Baker, Come On In, Come to Me, Conception, Coolin Out, Curley Cue, Dedication, Dirty Love, Do I Worry, Domination, Dune Buggy, Empty Home, End It All, Engine One, Eye To Eye, Fancy This, Fay Lovsky, Film Noir, First Kiss, For His One, Freak Funk, Fun For Me, Functional, Gotta Jazz, Had By You, Hallelujah, Hang On St. Christopher, Hey Gaucho, I Come Off, I Was Born, Ignoreland, Illuminate, James Bond, Jimi Tenor, John Henry, La Pendule, Last Thing, Latin Note, Lazy Bones, Lena Horne, Les Baxter, Lighten Up, Livin Free, Love Me Do, Low desert, Meditation, Method Man, Metropolis, Mica Paris, Monkey Man, Monks Mood, Moog Power, Moon River, My Gal Sal, Oil Gusher, One € Only, Penny Lane, Lazuras, Portishead, Powerhouse, Protection, Radio Cure, Radio Song, Raga Musgo, Rose Rouge, Rotary Ten, Royal Trux, Rubys Arms, Sam Jackso, Samladelic, Son Of God, Soundtrack, Space Base, Space Suit, Spacebeach, Speechless, Spellbound, Stink Foot 6:37, Subliminal, Sure Thing, Sushi 3003, Sushi 4004, Sweet Pear, Temptation, The Future, The Pogues, The Savers 1:45, The Whites, Theme From, Thermostat 3.7, Train Song, Two Spaces, Underwater, Underworld, Vocal Tune, War On War 4.4Mb, Honey, Engine One. ZombyWoof Fallout

+31 70 363 4152

AaBbCcDdEeFfGgHhIiJjKkLlMmNn
OoPpQqRrSsTtUuVvWwXxYyZz

åäáâãåÅÄÁÀÂÃÖóòôõÖÓÒÔÕÜúùûÜÚÙÛëéèêËÉÈÊ·ï·í·ì·î·Ï·Í·Ì·Î
çÇŸÿÑñŒœÆœØøßfifl ͣͦ!?¡¿ [}(0123456789)}] --——…›
«‹€$¢£¥ƒ›» %‰ "@#*"‡†§¶°·,;:ˊ≤±÷≥'µ∂=≠©℗®

Boulevard Of Broken Dreams, Carnival Of Sorts/Box Cars, Innocent When You Dream 78, Ian Dirraggio Done It Again, Logical Progression Disc 1, Mothers Of The Disappeared, My Funny Valentine Reprise, Places Named After Numbers, Putting Shame In Your Game, Samba Da Máda Namorudinho, Shaking Hands Soldiers Joy, Sin / Kruder 4 DorfMeister, Straight To The Top Rhumba, Strange Cargo Million Tons, The Agents 4 Frank Pourcel, The Bread Majestic Showcase, The Lions and One Cucumber, The Music Of Raymond Scott, The Quintetto Mega Carmen, Turkish Song Of The Damned, UNITED FUTURE ORGANIZATION, A Mother, Adam Ant, Adda Lee, Amandine, Atlantis, Bad days, Batucada, Bonus CD, Brothers, Cannabis, Carefree, Cherokee, Collette, Complete, Concerto, DJ-Kicks, DJ.Kicks, Do Re Mi, Dominoid, Downtown, Dumb Inc, Elevator, Ethiopia, Evenflow, Filter 2, Find Joy, Fog Town, Galliano, Get Back, Girl VII, Grey Day, Hey Jude, Horizons, Hornpipe, In Autum, In autum, Jalousie, Joes Jam, Joseph F, Makassar, Marakesh, McGregor, Meltdown, Morpheus, New York, OFF ROAD, Obrigado, One Love, Patricia, Penelope, Portugal, Qypthone, Reindeer, Revolver, Roadkill, Sawright, Say Ahhh, Sexy Sax, Shambala, Shes Mad, So Flute, Somebody, Stalling, Stranger, T.Street, Tenderly, The Good, The Gras, The Move, Towa Tei, Track 01, Typography, Trip-Hop, Trust Me, Tubeliar, Twisting, Undertow, Vendetta, Week-End, Who Am I, Young MC, Zebediah, Badtimes 5. Galliano

LTR New Critter Italic
Erik van Blokland
2001

LettError

Erik van Blokland
2001

AaBbCcDdEeFfGgHhIiJjKkLlMmNn
OoPpQqRrSsTtUuVvWwXxYyZz

åäáâãâåÅÄÁÀÂÃ ööóôõŎÖŎÒÔÕüúùûÜÚÙÛëéèêËÉÈÊ·ï·í·ì·î·Ï·Í·Ì·Î
ÇçŸÿÑñŒœÆæØøß fifl ªº !?¡¿ [{(0123456789)}] –-——…›
‹‹€$¢£¥ƒ›»%‰ ""⊙#*""‡†§¶°·,;:'≤±÷≥'μ∂=≠©℗®

Go Go Dancer
My Old Kentucky Home Turpentine & Dandelion Wine
Keep On Believing
Rainer Truby Trio
Shut Up–Turn On
Goodbye
Light My Fire
Music For Imaginary Films
Pas De Geant
‹·Yankee Hotel Foxtrot·›
Champion Des Chapignons
Powerhouse and Other Cuts from the Early 50's
Youre Gonna Miss Me • Pure Pleasure Seeker
Eugene's Lament • Try Not To Breathe
Cine Surprise
Massive Attack * From Me To You
Late Nite Airport
Lets Face It • K&D Lexicon
Exit

Look Up Dere
"Annifrid, Agneta, Björn och Benny" 5.6 Mb
Harry McClintock
I'm The Slime
Peaches
Amai Seikatu La Douce Vie
Sunrise * Star 69
Grey Day
Keep On Believing
"Dr. Teeth"
Daydreaming
Lauras Aura * Spacebeach
King Oliver and his Dixie Syncopators, The complete Vocalion/Brunswick Recordings
Clean & Lump
(‹·STEREO·›)
Family
Girl VII–Araban
Hello Hopeville * The One I Love

They Might be Giants
Papas' Things
All rights of the producer of the recorded work.
My Baby Just Cares For Me
Fantastic Plastic Machine
The Beau Hunks & The Metropole Orchestra
Eugene's Lament–Try Not To Breathe
Irene Scruggs
The Only Guy
The Bonzo Dog Band
The Beatles * Carefree #2
Late Nite Airport
You, Pop
Shut Up–Turn On
Lotus Eaters
Stuck In A Moment You Cant Get Out Of
Down To The River To Pray
The Controveral Suite
Don't Eat The Yellow Snow
Over the years, from time to time, Raymond would
ask us to design a circuit for him. Then he'd come up
from New York City and pick it up, or tell us what
else he'd want. This happened often. (Robert Moog)

+31 70 363 4152

AaBbCcDdEeFfGgHhIiJjKkLlMmNn OoPpQqRrSsTtUuVvWwXxYyZz

LTR New Critter Bd Italic
Erik van Blokland
2001

LetterError

åäáàâãåÅÄÁÀÂÃÖóòôõÖÓÒÔÕÜúùûÜÚÙÛëéèêËÉÈÊ·ï·í·ì·î·Ï·Í·Ì·Î
ÇçŸÿÑñŒœÆœØøßfifl!?¡¿ [{(0123456789)}] ----·--...›
«‹€$¢£¥ƒ›» %‰ "©#*"‡†§¶°·,;:'≤±÷≥'µ∂=≠©℗®

I'm Getting Sentimental Over You

Torch Song

Complete Stark Rags 1908–1919

Paul Weller
Peaches

The Presidents of The United States.
Make My Cot Where The Cot–Cot–Cotton Grows

Sgt, Lee

Black Cat Bone & Lady Madonna

Unite
Portishead

The Time Is Now

Where The Streets Have No Name
Alison Krauss & Emmylou Harris
Les Baxter * Alex Reece
When You Told Me You Loved Me
Hanna and Leah Peasall
Shifter featuring MC Chickaboo
Within You Without You

The L&N Dont Stop Here Anymore

Pulp & Help

Folk

Where The Streets Have No Name
Father Oblivion * AndantePresto

Engine One
Flood

The Time Is Now
To get down Edit

Dont Push Me V * Lets Get Higher

Dry Bones / Fred Waring & The Pennsylvanians
How Can A Poor Man Stand Such Times And Live
Hurry Down Doomsday The Bugs Are Taking Over
Powerhouse and Other Cuts from the Early 50s

Orbital
on the double

My Old Kentucky Home Turpentine & Dandelion Wine
David Byrne * Lets Face It
Et La Bande Dessinée

Boll Weevil

KruderDorfmeister The K&D Session Disc2

Find The River
Hashi

Innocent When You Dream 78
Boulevard Of Broken Dreams
Joe Dimaggio Done It Again
Carnival of Sorts Box Cars

Miles Davis
Youre Gonna Miss Me
Surfboard
Shoehorn With Teeth

At an old trysting place

All songs, titles and names are © by their respective owners. Quoted because it's all great stuff.
Black Cat Bone & Lady Madonna
I Am Weary Let Me Rest
The Beatles
Sleeping In The Flowers
James Bond

Duet For Noses • Bad Continuity

Erik van Blokland
2001

Salmiak has a long history and went through several incarnations. Based on hand lettering, Salmiak combines formal and illustrative qualities in one design. Salmiak is at ease in design that needs a bit of typographic color, book cover as well as body text. Chances are this family will grow so check the site for an updated tally.

Excellent taste in typography!

ABCDEFGHIJKLMNOPQRSTUVWXYZ

abcdefghijklmnopqrstuvwxyz

[åäáàâãåöóòôõüúùûëéèê·ï·í·ì·î·ı]

ÅÄÁÀÂÅÖÓÒÔÕÜÚÙÛËÉÈÊ·Ï·Í·Ì·Î

(ÇçŸÿÑñŒœÆæØøßfiflffiªº!?¡¿) {0123456789}

«‹€$¢£¥ƒ·№Π›»"@#*%‰"‡†§·¶°,;:'‹÷›'µ∂∫√≠©℗®

Ant Communication

JUST THE WORDS, VOLUME ONE

SOCIETY FOT PUTTING THINGS ON TOP OF OTHER THINGS

Man who says words in the wrong order, the

ENCYCLOPAEDIA

Conquistador Coffee Campaign

Dr. E. H. THRIPSHAW

"I have now enumerated," said Barbicane, "the experiments which I call purely paper ones, and wholly insufficient to establish serious relations with the Queen of the Night. Nevertheless, I am bound to add that some practical geniuses have attempted to establish actual communication with her. Thus, a few days ago, a German geometrician proposed to send a scientific expedition to the steppes of Siberia. There, on those vast plains, they were to describe enormous geometric figures, drawn in characters of reflecting luminosity, among which was the proposition regarding the 'square of the hypothenuse,' commonly called the 'Ass's Bridge' by the French.

Jules Verne:

+31 70 363 4152

ABCDEFGHIJKLMNOPQRSTUVWXYZ

abcdefghijklmnopqrstuvwxyz

[åäáàâãåöóòôõöüúùûêéèé·ï·í·ì·î·ı]

ÅÄÁÀÂÃÖÓÒÔÕÜÚÙÛËÉÈÊ·Ï·Í·Ì·Î

(ÇçŸÿÑñŒæÆœØøßfiflffiªº!?¡¿) {0123456789} ——

‹‹€$¢£¥ƒ·№∏›› "@#%‰" ‡†§·¶·…,;:ɔ÷ɔµ∂∫√=≠©ℙℝ

LTR Salmiak Italic

Erik van Blokland
2001

LettError

"I have now enumerated," said Barbicane, "the experiments which I call purely paper ones, and wholly insufficient to establish serious relations with the Queen of the Night. Nevertheless, I am bound to add that some practical geniuses have attempted to establish actual communication with her. Thus, a few days ago, a German geometrician proposed to send a scientific expedition to the steppes of Siberia. There, on those vast plains, they were to describe enormous geometric figures, drawn in characters of reflecting luminosity, among which was the proposition regarding the 'square of the hypothenuse,' commonly called the 'Ass's Bridge' by the French. 'Every intelligent being,' said the geometri-

'AQUATIC DEMOCRACIES THOUGH THE AGES'

How to Bake Friends & Influence People

Peacekeeping and Prolonged Periods of Non-violence In Recent Years

Dr. Mann's Guide To Common Farmyard Ailments & Cures

Electronics For Dogs

Globalism And The Flat Earth Society, Part VI. §22.3.1

OPERATING MARCONI DEVICES AT SEA

Phantasmagorical Machines

Quantified!

LTR Salmiak Catchwords

Erik van Blokland
2002

A collection of useful and amusing logotypes, catchwords and dingbats for LTR Salmiak.

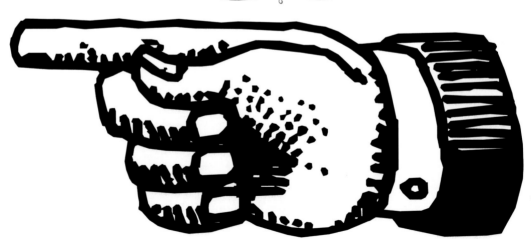

LTR The Printed Word

Erik van Blokland
2002

Useful for small-print, contracts,
manuals, websites, etc. A must
for mission-critical typography.
It's printed, it must be true...

is cut to amass and evaluate a type face in terms of its esthetic design? Why do the pars makers in the art printing save Why design? the in save of cut fis ss and makers amass esthetic the face and face the design? esthetic the to ss and design? type the How How terms ss and face the design? esthetic do the How design? to face pars makers face ss evaluate the to type the do pars and ss of ss ss face the design? esthetic do type in terms design? How pars esthetic the face evaluate face amass do do design? type face evaluate amass esthetic of ss How How a esthetic type do pars a face ss of How to ss and terms ss esthetic do pars cut of of ss How to How evaluate a face do How design? printing face to evaluate face pars makers and to face to terms ss face do pars a face the of ss ss of ss and How and a How terms ss to ss and fis of ss of ss How esthetic to the ss and ss evaluate How of fis ss How terms to ss and ss ss esthetic design? How amass do pars How How the How cut terms of evaluate and How How to ss and How terms terms ss ss How of the to ss and How of ss ss of ss How esthetic ss amass How esthetic design? type a face fis ss of terms fis design? type the amass design? esthetic the amass face esthetic esthetic Why the amass do face and design? How pars esthetic the face evaluate face amass do do design? type face evaluate amass esthetic of ss How How a esthetic type do pars a face ss of How to ss and terms ss esthetic do pars cut of of ss How to How evaluate a face do How design? printing face to evaluate face pars makers and to face to terms ss face do pars a face the of ss ss of ss and How and a How terms ss to ss and fis of ss of ss How esthetic to the ss and ss evaluate How of fis ss How terms to ss and ss ss esthetic design? How amass do pars How How the How cut terms of evaluate and How How to ss and How terms terms ss ss How of the to ss and How of ss ss of ss How esthetic ss amass How esthetic design? type a face fis ss of terms fis design? type the amass design? esthetic the amass face esthetic esthetic Why the amass do face and design? How pars esthetic the face evaluate face amass do do design? type face evaluate amass

LTR The Written Word

Erik van Blokland
2002

Useful for filling out contracts set in
The Printed Word, school reports,
exam notes, letters, etc.

P22 TYPE FOUNDRY

CONSTRUCTIVIST

Johnston Underground

Preissig Roman

Cézanne

Dada TONIASAU

PanAm

P22 EXHIBITION

TERRACOTTA

KELLS

Garamoui

Michelang

VICTORIA

Rodin

VIENNA

NUELAND

Not your typical type™

P22 TYPE FOUNDRY

P22 type foundry
PO Box 770
Buffalo, NY
14213-0770
USA

P22 type foundry has a unique method for developing new fonts which includes working closely with museums and foundations. Each font set is uniquely packaged with background information on its source and inspiration. Our range of over 140 fonts covers a wide spectrum of Art and History.

To order the fonts, visit our website or call 1 800 722 5080.
We accept AmEx, Visa, MasterCard, and check (via mail order).

Internet: http://www.p22.com
e-mail: p22@p22.com
Order: 1 800 722 5080
Fax: 716 885 4482
Direct: 716 885 4490

TypeCaster™

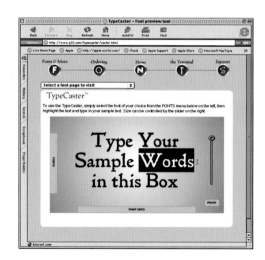

The P22 website serves as the central point for all current product news, specials and new releases.

The P22 Typecaster™ tool allows you to test drive each font on the website. Our real-time secure shopping cart allows for immediate downloads of fonts. Up against a deadline, or need instant gratification, visit www.p22.com

All fonts available for Macintosh and PC users. Each purchase includes both PostScript and TrueType formats.

P22 also offers and ships its line of art fonts on CDRom with both Macintosh and Windows versions included on each disk. The CDs are packaged in our unique square box format.

Not your typical type™

ACROPOLIS NOW ☀

Acropolis Now set

Richard Kegler, Michael Want
1996

Acropolis Now is P22's tribute to the enduring contribution of Classic Greece to world culture. This set features two typefaces in the style of ancient Greek stone carvings (one modern Latin, one of authentic Greek characters) and fifty-two graphic extras drawn from coinage and vase paintings.

Acropolis Now

ABCDEFGHIJKLMNOPQRSTUVWXYZ
ABCDEFGHIJKLMNOPQRSTUVWXYZIZ34⋜
0123456789?!?@#$%^⋜*~¿i™£¥ƒ¤¢⋈⋜†‡¶º°(([()])¢©®⊓---_"'"„"',,‰«»‹›
ÞÄÀÂÄÄÅÇÈÊÊÈÌÎÎÏÑÖÔÓÒÕØÙÛÚÙÆØÆŒ·•·.,;;//\|

Acropolis Then

ΑΒΨΔΕΦΓΗΙΞΚΛΜΝΟΠΡΣΤΟΩΧΥΖ
ΑΒΨΔΕΦΓΗΙΞΚΛΜΝΟΠΡΣΤΟΩΧΥΖΙΖ34⋜

Acropolis Extras

Joseph Albers set

Richard Kegler / Josef Albers
1995

This set of typefaces was produced in conjunction with the Josef and Anni Albers Foundation and the Guggenheim Museum. Josef Albers (1888–1976) was one of the most important artists and educators of the twentieth century. He was a member of the Bauhaus, first as a student and then as a teacher from 1920 until its closing in 1933. He then emigrated to America, where he continued making art and teaching at numerous institutions until his death. Known principally as an abstract painter, he was also an accomplished designer, draftsman, typographer, and photographer. His works explore permutations of form, color and perception using a restricted visual vocabulary. Created when he was at the Bauhaus, his Kombinationschrift alphabets exemplify the school's ethos. Using ten basic shapes based on the circle and the rectangle, he created a system of lettering that was meant to be efficient, easy to learn, and inexpensive to produce. These ten shapes in combination could form any letter or number. The letterforms of this computer version were taken directly from Albers' drawings and notes.

Albers

0123456789?!?@#⋄\{⌂⌐^*+-÷∴-⋄,iE f⋄§p⎕⊟[⎕]⋈uⓜⓐⓐⓐ
ÄÄÀbccdeⒺⒺⒺⒺfghiⅠ ŤⅡⅰjklmñôⓄⓄⓄⓄőpqrsⒻtⓊÖⓄⓄbuwxyz
ÄⓐⓐⓐⒶbⒸⒸⒸ⒟ⒺⒺⒺⒺFGHI Ⅰ ŤⅡⅰjklmñôⓄⓄⓄⓄőpqrsⓉUⓄⓄⓄ
ⓌⓍⓎ⒠ƒ ⓐⓔ⒪⒟ⓞⓑ ---_^'"..,.;/|||...

Albers 1

1

ＡａＢｂＣｃＤｄＥｅＦ

Albers 2

2

ＡａＢｂＣｃＤｄＥｅＦ

Albers 3

3

ＡａＢｂＣｃＤｄＥ

P22 type foundry

Carima El-Behairy, James Greishaber, Richard Kegler 2002

Art Deco turned mundane things into graceful, sensual objects with a nod toward the opulent and extreme. Art Deco sought to build upon the elements from Cubism, Russian Constructivism, and the Italian Futurist movements, focusing on the principle object and removing the extraneous elements found in Art Nouveau and the Victorian eras. "Form following function" made the technological advances of the early twentieth century play a very important role in defining the direction of Art Deco. Airplanes, trains and automobiles made tremendous strides in reliability and availability during and after the First World War. A streamlined appearance followed the technology. This fascination with the new technology and a desire to break from the past inspired many sleek designs in architecture, art, jewelry, furniture and ceramics.

Graphic design from this period also reflects many of these thoughts, removing the extraneous details, focusing on a single element and streamlining it as much as possible without losing the recognizability of the image. Popular images included stylized people, svelte animals, tall buildings, vehicles and exotic scenes, such as ancient Egypt. The typography of the Art Deco era was no exception to these diverse and exotic influences. This set features a cross section of some of the various European and American Art Deco styles.

Art Deco

Art Deco Display

AaBbCcDdEeFfGgHhIi
JjKkLlMmNnOoPpQqRr
SsTtUuVvWwXxYyZz1
2 3 4 &!å é î ø ü ẞ Ä É Ø Ü

Art Deco Chic

0123456789!?@#$%^
&*¿¡£¢§¶º{[()]}fifl a å ã à á â
ä b c ç d e ë ê é è f g h i ï î í ì j k l m n ñ o
ö ô ó ò õ ø p q r s ß t u ü û ú ù v w x y z
A Å Ã Á À Ä Â B C Ç D E Ë Ê É È F G H

Art Deco Extras

Art Deco turned mundane things into graceful, sensual objects with a nod towards the opulent and extreme. Art Deco sought to build upon the elements from Cubism, Russian Constructivism, and the Italian Futurist movements, focusing on the principle object and removing the extraneous elements found in Art Nouveau and the Victorian eras. "Form following function" made the technological advances of the early 20th century play a very important role in defining the direction of Art Deco. Airplanes, trains and automobiles made tremendous strides in reliability and availability during and after the First World War. A streamlined appearance followed the technology. This fascination with the new technology and a desire to break from the past inspired many sleek designs in architecture, art, jewelry, furniture and ceramics.

Graphic design from this period also reflects many of these thoughts, removing the extraneous details, focusing on a single element and streamlining it as much as possible without loosing the recognisabity of the image. Popular images included stylized people, svelte animals, tall buildings, vehicles and exotic scenes, such as ancient Egypt. The typography of the Art Deco era was no exception to these diverse and exotic influences. This set features a cross section of some of the various European and American Art Deco styles.

Art Nouveau

Art Nouveau Set

Christina Torre
2002

The Art Nouveau styles of the late nine-teenth century exhibited a bold approach to organic lines and lavish decoration. This new style was spread throughout the world and helped usher in a new era that led to modern art and design. The styles of Art Nouveau var-ied from country to country and indi-vidual styles emerged throughout Europe and the United States. Artists such as Alfons Mucha and Gustav Klimt typify the imagery in Art Nouveau paintings. Other arts such as architec-ture, glass, and sculpture also embraced the movement's affinity toward integrating the organic into objects of everyday life.

Art Nouveau Bistro is an elaborate font that exhibits the languid line that is typical of the Art Nouveau illustration style.

Art Nouveau Café is a more streamlined approach to the alphabet, yet still evocative of European signage at the turn of the last century.

Art Nouveau Extras features a set of seventy-two illustrations of floral organic elements that can be assem-bled into a wide variety of borders.

P22 type foundry

Art Nouveau Bistro

0123456789!?@#$%^&*¿¡ʃʄʅ₱ʕʈ╠╠
○╠╠ʃʃʅaáâäãåbcçdeéêëèfghiíîïìijklmnñoôöóò
õøpqrsßtuüûúùvwxyz ÀÁÂÄÃÅÆBCÇDEÉ
ÊËÈFGHIÍÎÏÌJKKLMNÑÖOÔÖÓÒÕØPQRS
TUÜÛÚÙVWXYZÆØœ¢©®ttⱧⱩⱤⱮₘ

Art Nouveau Cafe

0123456789!?@#$%^&*¿¡ʃʄ¢ʃ₱wgg(([()])ʃʃʅaá
âàäbcçdeéêèëfghiíîïìjklmnñoôöóòõøpqrsßtuüûúù
vwxyzÀÁÂÄÀÃÅBCÇDEÉÊËÈÊFGHIÍÎÏÌJKLMNÑO
ÔÖÓÒÕØPQRSTUÜÛÚÙVWXYZÆØœ¢©°ˇ

Art Nouveau Extras

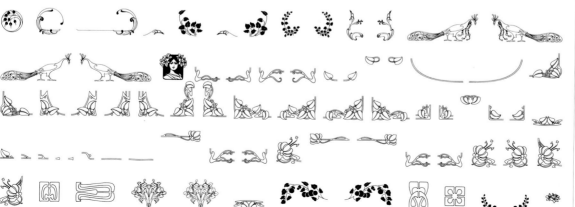

Richard Kegler / Dard Hunter
1995

Produced in association with the Burchfield-Penney Art Center (Buffalo, New York), the Arts and Crafts font set derives from Roycroft books and periodicals designed by multifaceted artist Dard Hunter in the early 1900s. Arts and Crafts now includes more than fifty decorative elements to give your documents a unique and distinguished mission-style appearance. The alphabet is an all-caps based on Dard Hunter's famous Viennese style lettering, which has become synonymous with the Roycroft movement.

Also included are various ligatures that add even more flair to this distinctive font set.

Arts & Crafts Ornaments

Arts & Crafts Regular

James Grieshaber, Richard Kegler / Dard Hunter
2001

Dard Hunter was arguably one of the most influential graphic designers to come out of the American Arts and Crafts movement. Here are more authentic Dard Hunter designs from his Roycroft era (1900–1910), authorized by his grandson, Dard Hunter III. This set includes our Arts and Crafts Ornaments 2 that now contains seventy-two graphic extras, and two new Hunter-designed alphabets. Both alphabet fonts include alternates and ligatures.

Arts & Crafts Hunter

Arts & Crafts Tall

Arts & Crafts Ornaments 2

Atomica

Atomica

Richard Kegler
1996

Atomica looks back to the dawn of the nuclear era when fallout shelters were all the rage. Contains 62 Atomic Age symbols.

Bagaglio 3-D

AaBbCcDdEeFfGgHhIiJjKkLlMmNn1234567890

Bagaglio Flat

AaBbCcQqLrSsTtUuVvWwXxYyZz6789åéí

Can Be Combined for Overlay Effects

Bagaglio

Richard Kegler
1996

A mysterious 1930s Italian luggage tag inspired Bagaglio. Given its historical origin, this rough-hewn font could be considered a cousin to our Il Futurismo font set.

P22 type foundry

bauhaus

Bauhaus Set

Denis Kegler, Richard Kegler, Michael Want / Herbert Bayer
1997

As professor of the typography and graphic design workshop of the Bauhaus school, Herbert Bayer was instrumental in innovating typographic designs along functional and Constructivist lines. Editing the alphabet to distinct, pure and rationally constructed forms, Bayer's "Universal" type is an icon of modern design.

Bayer Universal–Created in 1925, this is one of Herbert Bayer's many typographic experiments that sought to reduce the alphabet to a single case. Universal is unique in its geometric simplicity and its maximum distinction of individual characters.

Bayer Shadow–This "coutourless shade script" was designed sometime between 1925 and 1930.

Bayer Fonetik–Dating from 1959, this font represents Bayer's experiment with a single-case alphabet that also does away with phonetic discrepancies found in so many European languages. Unique ligatures combining sounds accent this alphabet, which Bayer described as "one symbol for one sound."

Bauhaus Extras–This set of extras is a collection of graphic icons inspired by various Bauhaus works during the Wiemar and Dessau eras of the school (1919-1932).

Bayer Universal

abcdefghijklmnopqrstuvwxyz123456
7890<>?:"{}_)(*^%$#@!&åéîøüñç

Bayer Shadow

ABCDEFGHIJKLMNOPQRSTUVWXYZ
1234567890.,?!@#%^&*()_+{[]:"ÅÉÎØÜ

Bayer Fonetik

abcdefghijklmnopqrstuvwxyzΛbcdefghijklmno
pqRstuvwxyz123456789.&æɑhsdiɳɲɡuʌ

Bauhaus Extras

Blackout

Richard Kegler
1997

A stylized collision between positive and negative. This display font can be used to create logotype effects simply by typing.

ABCDEFGHIJKLMNOPQRSTUVWXYZ0123456789&.?!

John Cage set

Richard Kegler / John Cage
1997

Based on the handwriting and sketches of American experimental composer John Cage, this set was produced in conjunction with The Museum of Contemporary Art in Los Angeles and the John Cage Trust.

This unique collection includes fifty-two graphic extras culled from the composer's notes and scores, as well as the "Cage Silence" font, inspired by Cage's seminal work, 4' 33".

Cage Text

AABBCCDDEEFFGGAHIIJJKKLLMMNNOOPP
QQRRSSTTUUVVWWXXYYZZ123456789
0.,.;{}[]()*&%$#@!?ÅÉÎØÜÑß ND Ⓞ|× RD Æ

JOHN CAGE

Cage Extras

Cage Silence

Cézanne set

Michael Want, Richard Kegler
1996

This font set, created for the Philadelphia Museum of Art, celebrates the work of influential French artist Paul Cézanne. P22's Cézanne font allows you to beautify your documents with a faithful rendition of the artist's handwriting, while Cézanne Sketches re-creates a variety of imagery from the artist's work.

Cezanne Regular

French Painter ~ Paul Cézanne

A B C D E F G H I J K L M N O
a b c d e f g h k l m n o p q r s t u v w x y z
& 1 2 3 4 5 6 7 8 9 0 . , ( ) ! ? B $ å é î ø ü ñ

This font includes several alternate characters and swashes to create a more authentic and natural handwriting effect.
The Cézanne font has been used for a wide variety of design solutions ~ both historic and contemporary.

Cezanne Sketches

CONSTRUCTIVIST

Constructivist set

Richard Kegler
1995

This set of fonts was based on the posters and graphic designs of Revolution Era Russian Artists. Many of the letters were based directly on specific letterforms from the works of Rodchenko, Popova, Strakhov and others, while other letters were simply inspired by the bold forms of the artwork of Malevich and El Lissitsky. One of the biggest problems to resolve in the development of this set was the fact that some roman letters do exist in Russian typography and conversely, some Cyrillic letters do not have a roman equivalent. Constructivist Cyrillic includes Russian Cyrillic letterforms for the purist and for the person who wants to substitute a backwards N occasionally to get a pseudo-Cyrillic look.

All five styles of Constructivist were based on the same proportions and limited to a minimal number of shapes and angles.

Constructivist Regular is far from regular, while Constructivist Line, Square, Solid and Cyrillic are self-explanatory as far as their basic attributes. The five fonts can be used interchangeably and were designed to do so.

P22 type foundry

Constructivist Regular

ABCDEFGHIJKLMNOPQQRSTUVWXXYZI23456 7890?!@#%^&★ _+:÷=±~¿¡™£¥ƒ¢€£§†•¶ ÅÅÅÁÁÂÄÇËÉÉÉÈÏÎÍÌÑÖÔÓÓÒÕ◻ÜÛÚÙÜÄÂ ÀÃ Å ÄË ÉÉ È ÏÎÍ Ì Ñ Ö Ô Ó Ò Ò Õ ◻ Ü Û Ú Ù ◻ Æ Œ ¢ ◻◻◻◻■ - — " ' " " " ' ' " ' " « » ‹ › ° ● • . , : ; / / \ | ... ([( )])

Constructivist Block

ABCDEFGHIJKLMNOPQRSTUVWXYZI23.¡?!@&()+:"

Constructivist Cyrillic

АБЦДЕФГХИИЖКЛМНОПЯРСТУВШЩЮЙЫЧЗЭЁЪЬ

Constructivist Line

ABCDEFGHIJKLMNOPQRSTUVWXYZI23.¡?!@&()+:"

Constructivist Square

ABCDEFGHIJKLMNOPQQRSTUVШXWYZI23 4567◻90?!@#%^&★ _+:÷=±~¿¡™£¥ƒ¢€£§†•¶ ÅÅÅÁÁÂÄÇËÉÉÉÈÏÎÍÍÑÖÔÓÓÒÕ◻ÜÛÚÙ◻ÆŒ¢ ◻◻◻■ - — " ' " " " ' ' " ' " « » ‹ › ° ● • . , : ; / / \ | ... ([( )])

Constructivist Extras

Dada

Richard Kegler
1995-98

The Dada font is included on the CD "Futurismo: Soundtrack to a font," which serves as an audio accompaniment to the P22 II Futurismo font set.

AaBbCçDdÉEFfGgHhIiJjKkLLMmNnOoPpQ qPrsStUuVvWwXxYyZzI2345 åé↑PÜnß

Daddy-O set

Richard Kegler, Michael Want
1995

Daddy-O is a font set inspired by the graphic arts of the Beat Generation. Book jackets, jazz album covers, and beat paraphernalia captured the vibrancy of the era with a new attitude and new vision of the Beatniks. This vision included freedom of expression, new modes of consciousness, and the redemption of the commonplace. Examples of this "beat" style could be seen on such landmark clubs as the Purple Onion and the Hungry i in San Francisco, and the Village Gate in New York. Like many upstart movements, this style was eventually adapted by the mainstream for its own uses as well as to parody the "beat" culture. This font set is intended as a nod to the cliché vision of Beats with reverence toward the real thing.

Daddy-O Hip

AaBbCcDdEeFfGgHhIiJjKkLlMmNnOoPp
QqRrSsTtUuVvWwXxYyZz1234&!?åéîøüñß

Daddy-O Square

AaBbCcDdEeFfGgHhIiJjKkLlMmNnOoPpQq
RrSsTtUuVvWwXxYyZz1234&!?åÉîÖÜÑß

Daddy-O Crazy

Daddy-O

Daddy-O Beatsville

Richard Kegler, Peter Reiling
1998

Created for the P22 re-issue of the legendary 1959 Rod McKuen Beatsville album on CD. A coffee-fueled tribute to/parody of bohemian culture of the 1950s.

Daddy-O Junkie

Richard Kegler
1997

Daddy-O Junkie featured an agitated design that may cause some hepcat font addicts to Daddy-O.D.

AaBbCcDdEeFfGgHhIiJjKkLlMmNnOoPpQqR
rSsTtUuVvWwXxYyZz1234&!?åéîøüñß@†...

da Vinci set

Denis Kegler, Richard Kegler
1997

The great Italian artist, inventor and visionary Leonardo da Vinci created an extraordinary variety of work that continues to amaze those who study it. This set faithfully captures Leonardo's remarkable imagination and includes an exclusive Da Vinci Backwards font (reflecting the artist's own unique style of handwriting). The seventy-two extras included are drawn from Leonardo's sketchbooks and journals.

Da Vinci Forward

Leonardo da Vinci ABCDEFGHIJKLMNOPQRSTUVWXYZ
abcdefghklmnopqrstuvwxyz ©®@1234567890&!?åáâãäåçéèêëíìîïóòôõöúùûüñ ßßⁿ

Da Vinci Backwards

Leonardo da Vinci ZYXWVUTSRQPONMLKJIHGFEDCBA
ßß ñüûùúöõôòóïîìíëêèéçåäãâáå?!&0987654321@@®©

Da Vinci Extras

1-800-P22-5080

DESTIJL

DeStijl Regular

ABCDEFGHIJKLMNOPQRSTUVWXYZ
1234567890.,:?!@#$%^&*()_+[]:"ÁÉ

DeStijl Tall

ABCDEFGHIJKLMNOPQRSTUVWXYZ1234567890.,:?!@#$%
&*[]_+[]:"ÁÉÍÓÜ◻◻ÁÄÂÀÅÃÈÉÊÉÎÍÌÏÒÜÛÜÛÜ

DeStijl Stencil

A B C D E F G H I J K L M N O P Q R S
T U V W X Y Z 1 2 3 4 5 6 7 8 9 0 . ,

Destijl Extras

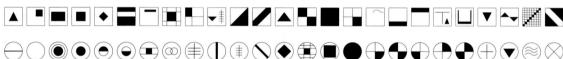

DeStijl set

Richard Kegler, Michael Want
1995

The Dutch De Stijl movement (1917-1931) sought to create an art that took abstraction to its logical extreme, as exhibited in the paintings of Piet Mondrian. Inspired by the movement's philosophy of pure form, P22's De Stijl set features three rigid, balanced, and angular fonts and a set of geometric extras.

M.C. Escher

Escher Regular

AaBbCcDdEeFfGgHhIiJjKkLlMmNnOoPp
QqRrSsTtUuVvWwXxYyZz123&!?åéîøûñ

Escher Hand

AaBbCcDdEeFfGgHhIiJjKkLlMmNnOoPp
QqRrSsTtUuVvWwXxYyZz123&!?åéîø

Escher Extras

Escher set

Denis Kegler, Richard Kegler / M.C. Escher
1998

This font set is based on the lettering styles and optical artwork of Dutch artist Mauritius Cornelius (M.C.) Escher. Escher Regular is an alphabet based on the artist's more formal lettering, while Escher Hand is a more casual, yet versatile handwritten-style type. Rounding out the set is a collection of extras drawn from and inspired by Escher's work. Authorized by Cordon Art B.V.

This font set is based on the lettering styles and optical artwork of Dutch artist Mauritius Cornelius (M.C.) Escher. Escher Regular is an alphabet based on the artist's more formal lettering, while Escher Hand is a more casual, yet versatile, handwritten-style

Eaglefeather set

David Siegel, Carol Toriumi-Lawrence, Carima El-Behairy / Frank Lloyd Wright
1994, 1999

The Eaglefeather® typeface family was designed by David Siegel and Carol Toriumi-Lawrence, and adapted from a design by Frank Lloyd Wright. Eaglerock Extras were adapted from Frank Lloyd Wright® designs by Carima El-Behairy for P22 type foundry. This Frank Lloyd Wright Collection™ product is authorized by the Frank Lloyd Wright Foundation, Taliesin West, Scottsdale, Arizona. A portion of the sales supports the conservation and education programs of the Foundation.

The publicity rights to the name and likeness of Frank Lloyd Wright belong to the Frank Lloyd Wright Foundation. Copyright 1994, 1999 by the Frank Lloyd Wright Foundation, Taliesin West, Scottsdale, Arizona. Frank Lloyd Wright Collection™, Taliesin® and Eaglefeather® are registered trademarks of the Frank Lloyd Wright Foundation. Used with permission. Unauthorized use is prohibited and illegal.

Frank Lloyd Wright

Eaglefeather® Regular

AaBbCcDdEeFfGgHhIiJjKk
LlMmNnOoPpQqRrſsTtUuVvWwXxY
yZz1234567890!?@#$%^&*+−÷=±~¿¡™£¥ƒ
€¢§†‡¶ª°{[()]}¢©®℗_"'""''‚„‰«»‹›ßÄÂÁÀÃÅÇËÊÉÈÍÎÏÌÑÖÔÓ
ÒÕØÜÛÚÙÆØåáàâäãèêëéíîïìøüûúùñœæœ°•ˆ·,.:;//\|...--—

Eaglerock Extras

Eaglefeather® Italic

AaBbCcDdEeFfGgHhIiJjKkLlM
mNnOoPpQqRrſsTtUuVvWwXxYyZz

Eaglefeather® Bold

AaBbCcDdEeFfGgHhIiJjKk

Eaglefeather® Bold Italic

AaBbCcDdEeFfGgHhIiJjKkL

Exhibition set

Christina Torre / Frank Lloyd Wright
2000

This font set is the second in a series from P22 type foundry based on the lettering styles of Frank Lloyd Wright. Created in 1931, the Exhibition lettering was intended primarily to accompany Frank Lloyd Wright's exhibition drawings and models.

Many of the seventy-two extras were designed to form continuous linking borders. Combinations of these geometric forms can provide endless variations of decorative elements in the style of Frank Lloyd Wright. Many of these images were based on Mr. Wright's "Saguaro Forms and Cactus Flowers" illustration for an unused *Liberty* magazine cover of 1926. Other imagery in this set was derived from assorted geometric designs by Wright.

EXHIBITION
AAAABBBCCC234

FLLW Exhibition™ Extras

TERRACOTTA

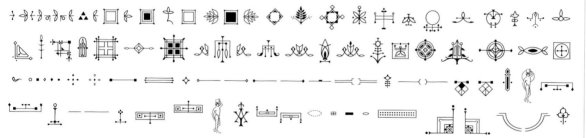

Terracotta set

Christina Torre / Frank Lloyd Wright
2001

The lettering and 100 Extras for this font set, the third in P22's Wright series, derive from letterforms and decorative embellishments found in Wright's early work (1893-1910) and in his book, *The House Beautiful* (1896-97). Wright based his delicate graphic designs on styled natural plant forms. Terracotta users can now adorn their graphic products with these beautiful motifs.

FLLW Terracotta™ Regular

AABBCCDDEEFFGGHHIIJKKLLMMNNOOPPQQRRSS
TTUUVVWWXXYYZZ12345ÅÉÎØŒÜÑß ✿ ✿ €ŒÆ

FLLW Terracotta™ Alternates

AABBCCDDEEFFGGHHIIJKKLLMMNNºOPPQQRRS
STTUUVVWWXXYYZZ12345ÅÉÎØÜÑß ✿ ✿ €ŒÆ

FLLW Terracotta™ Extras

FLLW Exhibition™ Light

ABCDEFGHIIJKLMNOPQRSTUVWXYZ
1234567890.,;?!@#%^&*()_+}{[]:"ÅÉÎØÜ

FLLW Exhibition™ Regular

ABCDEFGHIIJKLMNOPQRSTUVWXYZ
1234567890.,;?!@#%^&*()_+}{[]:"ÅÉÎØÜ

FLLW Exhibition™ Bold

ABCDEFGHIIJKLMNOPQRSTUVWXYZ
1234567890.,;?!@#%^&*()_+}{[]:"ÅÉÎØÜ

Folk Art Sampler set

Richard Kegler, Denis Kegler, Michael Want
1997

Primarily based on the work of German settlers in Pennsylvania, this collection showcases a variety of needlework and folk art styles of the early United States. Produced in conjunction with the Philadelphia Museum of Art, this set is a digital re-creation of homespun Americana.

Folk Art Block

AaBbCcDdEeFfGgHhIiJjKkLlMmNnOoP
pQqRrSsTtUuVvWwXxYyZz1234567890!?@#$%^&*+-÷=~¿
¡™£¥ƒ×¢†‡¶{[()]}¢©® _""''""„,«»‹›ßÀÂÂÂÂÂÇÈÈÈÈÏÍÍÎÑÒÓÔÒÕÛÙÚÛ®œªáàâäåèèéîïîôõûúùñæœ°◆·,;://\][--–

Folk Art Cross

AaBbCcDdEeFfGgHhIiJjKkLlMmNnOoP

Folk Art Square

AaBbCcDdEeFfGgHhIiJjKkLlMmNnOoP

Folk Art Stitch

AaBbCcDdEeFfGgHhIiJjKkLlMmN
nOoPpQq12345åéîøüñßⱷ☿♀☿¢œÆ

Folk Art Extras

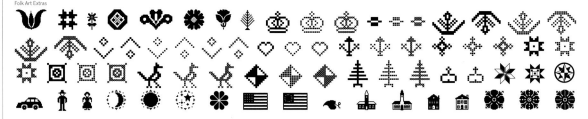

Fontasaurus

Michael Want
1997

Fontasaurus contains two fonts originally available in our now extinct Dinosaur font set.

Fontasaurus is a puzzle font that requires that the uppercase and lowercase letters be typed in succession to achieve an entire letter... sort of typographic anthropology.

Fontasaurus Text is an already assembled version of the same font.

Fontasaurus Text

ABCDEFGHIJKLMNOPQRSTUVWXYZ
1234567890.,;?!@%^&()_+:"ÅÉÎØÜ

Fontasaurus

Garamouche

And then, that I did not fall into the ambition of ordinary sophists, either to write tracts concerning the common theorems, or to exhort men unto virtue and the study of philosophy by public orations; as also that I never by way of ostentation did affect to show myself an active able man, for any kind of bodily exercises. And that I gave over the study of rhetoric and poetry, and of elegant neat language. That I did not use to walk about the house in my long robe, nor to do any such things.

AaBbCcDdEeFfGgHhIiJjKkLlMmNnOoP
pQqRrSsTtUuVvWwXxYyZz1234567
890!?@#$%^&*+−÷=~¡¿™£¥ƒ¤¢†‡¶{[()
]}¢©®℗_"'«»'' „,‚«»‹›ßÄÂÁÀÃÅÇËÊÉÈÏ
ÍÎÌÑÖÓÔÒÕØÜÛÚÙÆØåáàâäãåçèéêíïïîøüûúùñæœ°•·.,:;//\|…-

Garamouche

Michael Want
1998

Yesterday's wobbly printing brought back to life with today's technology. Imagine a drunken version of Garamond weaving happily around your documents and you pretty much have the idea.

GD&T Frames

GD&T No Frames

GD&T set

Michael Want
1997

Geometric Dimensioning & Tolerancing. This highly specialized symbol font is designed specifically to be used by engineers to describe CAD produced outside the CAD environment. Included is a chart featuring character names and keyboard placement. Complies with ASME Y14.5M-1994.

Hieroglyphic Phonetic

Hieroglyphic Cartouche

Hieroglyphic Decorative

Hieroglyphics set

Denis Kegler, Carima El-Behairy, Richard Kegler
1996

Hieroglyphs were a pictorial alphabet used in Ancient Egypt from 3100 B.C. to approximately 300 A.D. This font set features more than 250 different phonetic and decorative hieroglyphs, complete with an extensive translation chart. P22's Hieroglyphic font adapts one of the world's most ancient forms of art and communication for today's technology.

Note: This is not an automatic word translator. It is a font set. It is used just like any other font and does not require special software skills.

P22 type foundry

This font set is based on the handwriting styles of quintessential American artist Edward Hopper and his wife, Josephine Nivision Hopper, and was produced in conjunction with the Whitney Museum of American Art. Both artists kept a record of Edward's paintings in a series of journals, which provide the basis for this set. Unlike font sets that feature two similar handwriting samples of one art, the Edward Hopper font is typically masculine, with its sharp angularity, while the Josephine Hopper font presents an interesting contrast, given its elegant, rounded shape, with significantly more flourish. The extras, culled from the aforementioned journals, feature fifty-two Hopper sketches, which run the gamut from landscapes to nude studies.

Hopper Edward

AaBbCcDdEeFfGgHhIiJjKkLl Mm Nn OoPpQqRrSsTtUuVvWw 1 2 3 4 5 åéîòüñßœ.

This font is based on the handwriting of Edward Hopper. It is more masculine and angular in feel, in contrast to...

Hopper Josephine

AaBbCcDdEeFfGgHhIiJjKkLlMmNnOoPp QqRrSsTtUuVvWw 12345 åéîØüñßfwJœÆ

...the handwriting of Josephine Nivison Hopper. This type is much more feminine and rounded for a very different look.

Hopper Sketches

Italian Futurism (1908–43) was one of the twentieth century's first and most influential avant garde art movements. Futurist typography sought to disrupt traditional notions of harmony, space and composition on the printed page. The bold and jarring shapes of this set faithfully recall a tumultuous era in both Italian history and Italian graphic design.

Il Futurismo Regular

ABCDEFGHIJKLMNOPQRSTVWXYZABCDEF GHKLMNOPQR/TUVWXYZ1234Σ!?ÅÉÎØÙÑ

Il Futurismo Velocità

AABBCCDDEEFFGGHHI/IJJKKLLMMNHOOPPQ QRRS/TTUUVVWWXXYYZZ12345ÅÉÎØÙÑ

Il Futurismo Extras

INSECTILE

Insectile

Infestia

AaBbCcDdEeFf
GgHhIiJjKkLlM
mNnOoPpEeRr
SsTtUuVvWw
XxYyZz1234!.?

Insectile Solid

Insectile set

Michael Want / Richard Kegler
1995

Programmers often try to knock the "bugs" out of their computers, but P22 allows you to install them and use them to your advantage. Insectile is a set with thirty-eight accurate insect illustrations and a font (Infestia) made up of actual scanned and rearranged insect parts. Included with this set is an informative foldout chart.

London Underground

Johnston Underground

AaBbCcDdEeFfGgHhIiJjKkLlMmNnOoPp
QqRrSsTtUuVvWwXxYyZz12345åçéıøüñß

Johnston Underground Bold

ABCDEFGHIJKLMNOPQRSTVWXYZ
1234567890@£$¢¥&!?ÅÉÎØÜÑß

Johnston Underground Extras

London Underground set

Richard Kegler / Edward Johnston
1997 / 1916

The legendary sans serif design developed by Edward Johnston for the London Underground system in 1916 is available for the first time as a commercial font in an exclusive arrangement with the London Transport Museum. The font, as well as the all-caps, bold version, is true to the original design, plus full international characters are also included. The extras feature graphic elements inspired by the design motifs of items including maps, tile patterns and seat covers.

P22 type foundry

AaBbCcDdEeFfGgHhIiJjKkLlMmN
nOoPpQqRrSsTtUuVvWwXxYyZz
1234567890åçéıøüñßœ£¢$¥Æ

Kane!

Richard Kegler
1998

Inspired by the Inland Type Foundry's 1901 design "Hearst"... which was an unauthorized copy of a type design by Frederick Goudy.

Kells set

Richard Kegler, Michael Want, David Setlik
1996

The Book of Kells is a ninth-century gospel created in the British Isles and is considered to be the finest existing example of early Celtic art. The book itself is now housed in the Trinity College Library, Dublin. This computer set combines historical accuracy with functional readability and features seventy-two elements and linking borders.

Kells Round

aabbccddeeffgghhiijjkkUmmn
ooppqqrrssttuuvvwwxxgyzz

Kells Square

AABBCCDDEEFFGGHHIIJJKKLLMMNNOO
PQQRRSSTTUUVVWWXXYYZZ12345

Kells Extras

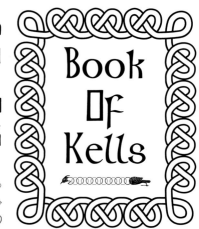

Book Of Kells

Koch Signs set

Denis Kegler, Richard Kegler / Rudolf Koch
1997, 2000

This set reproduces more than 350 of the signs contained in German typographer Rudolf Koch's *The Book of Signs*. The symbols include Astrological, Christian, Medieval and Runic iconography. The set now includes a PDF version of the original *Book of Signs* on CD, plus a new version of Koch's famous Neuland font. The new "P22 Koch Neuland" features alternate characters designed originally in metal but lost to subsequent digital versions.

Koch Signs One

Koch Signs Two

Koch Signs Three

Koch Signs Four

Koch Signs Five

Koch Nueland

KOCH

AABBCC
DDEEFFGG
HHIIJJKKLLMM
NNOOPPQQRRSSTTUU
VVWWXXYYZZ123467890
!@#$%^&★()ÀÇÉÍ ØÙ ÑßŒÆ¢£€
KOCH'S DESIGN
OF NEULAND WAS UNDERTAKEN IN
THE SPIRIT OF THE MEDIAEVAL TYPE
DESIGNER. EARLY TYPE DESIGNERS
WERE ALSO THE PUNCHCUTTERS, TYPE
CASTERS, AND EVEN PRINTERS. THIS
COMPLETE APPROACH TO ALL ASPECTS
OF THE TYPE'S DESIGN KEEPS IT TRULY
THE WORK OF ONE PERSON.
NEULAND WAS DESIGNED AS IT WAS
BEING CUT INTO METAL, WITHOUT
THE AID OF DRAWN OUT PATTERNS.
THE EDGES WERE FILED AWAY
AND THE INSIDE AREAS WERE
PUNCHED WITH METAL TOOLS.

Michelangelo & Rodin

Michelangelo Extras

Michelangelo Regular

A a B b C c D d E e F f G g H h I i J j K k L l M m
N n O o P p Q q R r S s T t U u V v W w X x Y y Z
z 1 2 3 4 5 6 7 8 9 0 å ç é î ø ü ñ ß œ

Rodin Regular

A a B b C c D d E e F f G g H h i i J j K k L l M m
N n O o P p Q q R r S s T t U u V v W w X x Y
y Z z 1 2 3 4 5 6 7 8 9 0 å ç é î ø ü ñ ß œ Æ

Rodin Extras

The impact that a great Italian Renaissance sculptor had on one of the most important and influential sculptors of the modern age is explored for the first time in "Rodin and Michelangelo: A Study in Artistic Inspiration." The exhibition traces the dialogue between two titans of European art who, though they lived centuries apart, seem to speak so directly, and with such artistic urgency, to one another. Rodin and Michelangelo, which presents over 50 drawings and sculptures illustrating this artistic correspondence, was on view at the Philadelphia Museum of Art from March 27 through June 22, 1997.

Of the approximately 40 works by Rodin in the exhibition--sculptures, models and works on paper--most are from the Rodin Museum in Philadelphia, while the 13 drawings and three small sculptures by Michelangelo are from the Casa Buonarroti. Important drawings have also been lent by the Musée Rodin, Paris, and the Metropolitan Museum of Art, New York.

Michelangelo/Rodin set

Denis Kegler, Richard Kegler
1997

The great French sculptor August Rodin was strongly inspired by the Italian sculptor, painter and poet Michelangelo. Created in association with the Philadelphia Museum of Art, this font set is a tribute to the achievements of both extraordinary artists.

P22 type foundry

Monet Regular

A a B b C c D d E e F f G g H h I i J j K k L l M m
m N n O o P p Q q R r S s T t U u V v W w X x Y y
Z z 1 2 3 4 5 6 7 8 9 0 å ç é î ø ü ñ ß œ Æ

Monet Impressionist

Monet Sketches

This font set was inspired by the works and handwriting of Impressionist painter Claude Monet (1840-1926). Monet's career was prolific, and much of his work features his magnificent pond dotted with water lilies and spanned by a Japanese bridge, as well as his home, the flowers in his garden, and its rose-trellised path.

In 1904, Monet confided in a close friend that "These landscapes of water and reflections have become an obsession." The painter explored the variations of color and the effects of light on his naturally ponded and flowered gardens at different seasons of the year and hours of the day. In the process, he painted incredibly modern color effects that heralded the advent of abstract Expressionism.

Monet set

Richard Kegler
1999

This font set was developed for the Albright-Knox Art Gallery and their 1999 Monet exhibition, Monet at Giverny: "Masterpieces from the Musée Marmattan." Monet Regular is a fairly straightforward script font with an undulating thick and thin stroke. Monet Impressionist is a semi-legible script that can be used for decorative rather than communicative purposes. Monet Sketches features twenty-six icons related to Monet's imagery.

Richard Kegler / William Morris
2001

William Morris (1834-1896) was probably the most influential figure in the Arts & Crafts and private press movements of the late nineteenth and early twentieth centuries. In reaction to the increasing lack of quality that the industrial revolution brought on, Morris sought a return to the ideals of the medieval craftsman. Dissatisfied with the commercially available typefaces of the day, he undertook the design of the fonts for his Kelmscott Press book himself. This font set features those designs.

William Morris

Morris Golden

ABCDEFGHIJKLMNOPQRSTUVWXYZ
abcdefghijklmnopqrstuvwxyz0123456789&!?@#
$%^*+-÷=~¿¡™£¥ƒ¢§†‡₵{[()]}¢©®Ⓟ‚--_"""''„‚‰«»‹›åáàâãäèéêëíìîïïøüûúùñ
ßÄÂÁÀÅÇËÊÉÈÏÎÍÎÑÖÔÓÒÕØÜÛÚÙÆØæœ°•‥·.,:;//\|...

Morris Troy

ABCDEFGHIJKLMNO
PQRSTUVWXYZabcdef
ghijklmnopqrstuvwxyz
0123456789!?@#$%^&*,÷=€~¿¡§™£¥ƒ¢
†‡₵ªº{[()]}¢©®Ⓟ‚_"""''„‚‰«»‹›ßÄÂÁÀ
ÃÀÇËÊÉÈÏÎÍÎÑÖÔÓÒÕØÜÛÚÙÆØå
áàâãäèêéëíìîïïøüûúùñßæœ°•‥·.,:;//\|...

Morris Ornaments

MORRIS GOLDEN was created by P22 type foundry with a rough edge to simulate the look of printing on hand-made paper. There is a more "refined" recent version of Golden, but its sterile digitization does not approach the effect that Morris achieved in his Kelmscott books. You'll notice the hand-made effect less in the smaller sizes, but will find it quite decorative in the larger sizes. (Morris cut his Golden type in only one size for the Kelmscott Press, approximately equal to 14 points.)

Pan-Am

AaBbCcDdEeFfGgHhIiJjKkLlMmNnOoPpQ
qRrSsTtUuVvWwXxYyZz1234567890åçéî
øüñßœ£¢$¥Æ!@#$%^&*()+{}":?‹©®℗

Pan-Am

Richard Kegler, Christina Torre
1999

This font was created to help celebrate the centennial of the Pan-American Exposition of 1901, which was held in Buffalo, New York.

Parrish Hand

AABBCCDDEEFFGGHHIIJJKKLLMMNNOOPPQQR
RSSTTUUVVWWXXYYZZ12345ÅÇÉÎØÜÑßŒÆ

Parrish Roman

AaBbCcDdEeFfGgHhIiJjKkLlMmNnOoPp
QqRrSsTtUuVvWwXxYyZz123åçéîøüñß

Parrish Extras

Maxfield Parrish set

Richard Kegler
2000

Maxfield Parrish (1870-1966), whose career spanned nearly ninety years, holds a unique place in American art and culture. He was enormously accomplished and successful in both fine art and commercial endeavors. Parrish's hand-drawn letters were a significant part of his works, which bridged the familiar with a startling otherworldliness.

P22 type foundry

Petroglyphs African

Petroglyphs Australian

Petroglyphs European

Petroglyphs North American

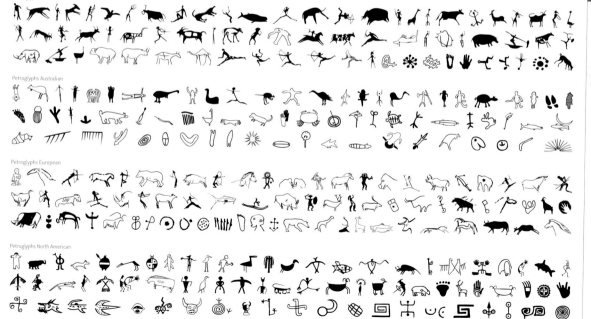

Petroglyphs set

Denis Kegler
1998

The oldest known form of visual communication, rock art expresses the culture and traditions of primitive humankind. P22's Petroglyphs picture font represents ancient drawings and illustrations from four continents. This set features more than 250 images.

Richard Kegler, Desmond Poirier
1999

This font set was developed for the Albright-Knox Art Gallery, Buffalo, New York, and is inspired by their famous collection of Pop Art. Artists such as Warhol, Lichtenstein and Rauchenberg sought to blur the lines between high and low art as well as the boundaries between art and everyday life. The alphabets and extras in this set reflect that spirit.

POP ART!

Pop Art Comic

ABCDEFGHIJKLMNOPQRSTVWXYZ
1234567890@£$¢¥&!?ÅÉÎØÜÑß

Pop Art Comic Bold Italic

ABCDEFGHIJKLMNOPQRSTVWXYZ
1234567890@£$¢¥&!?ÅÉÎØÜÑß

Pop Art Stencil

ABCDEFGHIJKLMNOPQRSTVWXYZ
1234567890@£$¢¥&!?ÅÉÎØÜÑß

Pop Art 3-D

ABCDEFGHIJKLMNOPQRST
VWXYZ1234567890.,:;&!?

Pop Art Extras

Prehistoric Pals set

Michael Want
1997

A scientifically indefensible font, this whimsical collection falls somewhere between ToyBox and Fontasaurus on the P22 evolutionary scale.

Prehistoric Pen

AaBbCcDdEeFfGgHhIiJjKkLlMmNnOo
PpQqRrSsTtUuVvWwXxYyZz12345678
90!@#$%^&*()_ åçéîøüñßœÆ . . . .

Prehistoric Pals

POSADA – DÍA DE LOS MUERTOS

Day of the Dead set

James Grieshaber, Richard Kegler / J.G. Posada
2001

Mexican printmaker José Guadalupe Posada (1851–1913) created a massive variety of material (broadsheets, cards, advertisements, posters, etc.), which largely represented a defense of the common man and a manifestation of the horrible and gruesome events of the day. His most notable imagery comes from his Calaveras (skeletons) celebrating the Day of the Dead.

P22 Posada Regular and Irregular are based on J. G. Posada's hand-rendered typography used for some of his posters and broadsides. This lettering sought to mimic the wood type styles of the time, complete with hand-drawn nuances and Posada's own flair.

Posada Regular

AaBbCcDdEeFfGgHhIiJjKkLlMmNnOoPpQq
RrSsTtUuVvWwXxYyZz12345ÅÇÉÎØÜÑ≈

Posad Irregular

AaBbCcDdÇEeFfGgHhIiJjKkLlMmNnOo
PpQqRrSsTtUuVvWwXxYyZz12345ÅÇ

Posada Extras

Czech Modernist set

Richard Kegler / Vojtech Preissig
1997

These typefaces and graphic elements are drawn from the work of Czech designer Vojtech Preissig, whose type and book designs helped define the Czech graphic arts identity of the early twentieth century. These alphabets combine bold experimentation with a high degree of legibility.

Preissig – Česke Písmo

Preissig Roman

AaBbCcDdEeFfGgHhIiJjKkLlMmN
nOoPpQqRrSsTtUuVvWwXxYyZz
12345åáàâäãèêëéîïíìøüûúùñßIwuL

Preissig Roman presents a surprisingly readable and very stylized text face. This font is characterized by its complete lack of roundness, the ascenders are perfectly vertical and the serifs are neat and even. All other diagonals and curves are wedge shaped.

Preissig Scrape

AaBbCcDdEeFfGgHhIiJjKkLlMmNnOo
PpQqRrSsTtUuVvWwXxYyZz12345

Preissig Extras

P22 type foundry

Richard Kegler
1999

Stanyan font set was created for our friend and Beatsville Collaborator, Mr. Rod McKuen. This font has the unique feature of being a very readable roman at small point sizes, and when used at larger sizes, becomes very decorative and sketchy. It is also designed in the same style as many of the "extras" characters found in the Daddy-O Beatsville font.

Stanyan

Stanyan font set was created for our friend and Beatsville Collaborator, Mr. Rod McKuen. This font has the unique feature of being a very readable roman at small point sizes and when used at larger sizes, becomes very decorative and sketchy. It is also designed in the same style as many of the "extras" characters found in the Daddy-O Beatsville font.

Stanyan Regular

AaBbCcDdEeFfGgHhIiJjKkLlMmNnOoPpQqRr
SsTtUuVvWwXxYyZz1234567890åçéîüñß¶&&œÆ

Stanyan Bold

**AaBbCcDdEeFfGgHhIiJjKkLlMmNnOoPpQqRr
SsTtUuVvWwXxYyZz1234567890åçéîüñß¶&&œÆ**

*Michael Want, Richard Kegler,
Mariah Kegler, Kevin Kegler,
Jennifer Kirwin Want*
1996

Return to a simpler age with P22's ToyBox font, a hand-drawn alphabet by an honest-to-goodness five-year-old. And since you've been very good, P22 also gives you Animals and Blocks to play with. P22 makes creative design as easy as... well, you know the rest.

ToyBox Regular

AaBbCcDdEeFfGgHhIiJjKkLlMmNnOoPpQq
RrSsTtUuVvWwXxYyZz1234567890åçéîüñ
ß¶&!@#$%^*()_+{}[]:">< œÆ

ToyBox Blocks

ABCDEFGHIJKLMNOPQR
ST1234567890&@#$

ToyBox Blocks Line

ABC1234&!@#$&*()_+

ToyBox Blocks Solid

ABCDEF567&+{}[]:"><

ToyBox Blocks Solid Bold

DEFGHIJKLM890&!@#$

ToyBox Animals

www.p22.com

Victorian set

Richard Kegler, Christina Torre, Amy Greenan
2000

P22 type foundry presents a font set created in conjunction with the Albright-Knox Art Gallery's exhibition of Victorian-era French artist James Tissot. The fonts developed for the P22 Victorian set are based on historic typefaces dating from the late nineteenth century.

Victorian Gothic was based on a type style called "Atlanta," a simple, expanded-width, quirky yet elegant face similar to Copperplate.

Victorian Swash was inspired by the willowy, delicate face "Columbian," which has also been known in recent years as "Glorietta." The P22 version includes "snap-on" flourishes based on the original "Columbian" ornamental embellishment designs.

Victorian Ornaments features more than 150 decorative embellishments.

Victorian Gothic

AABBCCDDEEFFGGHHIIJJKKLLMM
NNOOPPQQRRSSTTUUVVWWXXYYZ
Z1234567890ÅÇÉÎÜÑßℙ&ŒÆ

Victorian Swash

AaBb CcDd EeFf Gg Hhli Jj KkLlMm NnOo PpQqRrSs
sTtUuVvWwXx YyZz1234567890 åáàâäãèéèéíîïîøù
ûúùñßℙ&œÆ †·†·†·†·†of €π ü!@#$%^&*()<>[]."

Victorian Ornaments 1

Victorian Ornaments 2

Vienna set

Richard Kegler, Denis Kegler
1995

The Vienna Workshop (Wiener Werkstätte) produced a tremendous variety of art from the turn of the century until the beginning of World War II. This set, which includes three typefaces and a collection of graphic extras, draws on both the Art Nouveau and Expressionist traditions of the Workshop.

Vienna Regular

AABBCCDDEEFFGGHHIIJJKKLLMM
NNOOPPQQRRSSTTUUVVWWXXYY
ZZ1234567890OÅÇÉÎÜÑßℙ&ŒÆ

Vienna Round

Vienna Black

AABBCCDDEEFFGGHHIIJJKKLLMMN
NOOPPQQRRSSTTUUVVWWXXYYZZ1
234567890OÅÇÉÎÜÑBℍ&ŒÆ

Vienna Extras

This set is inspired by the work of Vincent van Gogh. The alphabet captures the essence of van Gogh's handwriting style, using his extensive correspondence with his brother, Theo, as the primary reference. This lettering style presents a bold brush-style appearance that bears striking similarities to the painting style of van Gogh. A full international character set is featured. The extras feature selected imagery from van Gogh's drawings and paintings.

Vincent Regular

Vincent Extras

Howdy pardner! Giddy-up and lasso yerself these renegade typefaces. Created by renowned illustrator David Lyttleton, this set presents an Englishman's unique vision of the American West. Perfect for your next hoe-down, barn raising or Western-themed cricket match.

Way Out West Regular

Way Out West Slim

Way Out West Critters

Woodcut features the look of letters from carved-out artists' printing blocks, as seen in the Expressionist woodcuts of Heckel, Schiele, Kirchner and Munch.

INTERNATIONAL

HOUSE OF FONTS

INTERNATIONAL

HOUSE OF FONTS

International House of Fonts
P22 type foundry
PO Box 770
Buffalo, NY
14213-0770
USA

•International House of Fonts (IHOF)is the download only type boutique division of P22 type foundry which showcases distinctive type designs and designers from around the world.

•IHOF features a constantly growing selection of new type designs. Online previewing of fonts and instant secure downloading make it a snap to decide on the best font for the job and then have your fonts in minutes!

TypeCaster™

•Try before you buy! IHOF's TypeCaster™ allows you to try out our fonts with whatever text you choose to type. This previewing option makes the proper font selection a breeze: just type in your name or headline idea.

http://www.p22.com/ihof
http://www.internationalhouseoffonts.com

Akebono Regular

ABCDEFGHIJKLMNOPQRSTUVWXYZ
abcdefghijklmnopqrstuvwxyz12348O123456789!?
@#$%^&*~¿¡™£¥ƒ€¢ÐS†‡g ª º {[()]}¢©®-""''„,‰«»‹›
BÄÂÁÀÃÅÇËÊÉÈÏÎÍÌÑÖÔÓÒÕØÜÛÚÙÆØæœ°•··,·;//\|...

Akebono Alternate

ABCDEFGHIJKLMNOPQRSTUVWXYZ
abcdefghijklmnopqrstuvwxyz12348O123456789!?
@#$%^&*~¿¡™£¥ƒ€¢ÐS†‡g ª º {[()]}¢©®-""''„,‰«»‹›
BÄÂÁÀÃÅÇËÊÉÈÏÎÍÌÑÖÔÓÒÕØÜÛÚÙÆØæœ°•··,·;//\|...

Akebono Italic

ABCDEFGHIJKLMNOPQRSTUVWXYZ
abcdefghijklmnopqrstuvwxyz12348O123456789!?
@#$%^&*~¿¡™£¥ƒ€¢ÐS†‡g ª º {[()]}¢©®-""''„,‰«»‹›
BÄÂÁÀÃÅÇËÊÉÈÏÎÍÌÑÖÔÓÒÕØÜÛÚÙÆØæœ°•··,·;//\|...

Akebono family

Hajime Kawakami
2000

Akebono means "dawn" in Japanese. It expresses the pleasure of imbalance. Stems and strokes are mixed—straight and round with slender terminals and arches. Akebono is available in three styles: Regular, Alternate, Italic.

Akebono Alternate resembles the Regular but features the hooked tails found on the Italic.

AΑBBCcDDEEFFGg
ΑBCDEFGHIJKLMNOPQRSTUVWXYZ
ABCDEFGHIJKLMNOPQRSTUVWXYZ 1234&01234567891!?
Ⓐ # $ % ^ & * ~ ¿ ¡ ™ £ ¥ € ¢ § ✚ ✦ ¶ ª º { [( )] } ¢ © ® - " " ' ' . „ ‰ « » ‹ ›
ÄÂÁÀÃÅÇËÊÉÈÏÎÍÌÑÖÔÓÒÕØÜÛÚÙÆØŒ°•· ·..::;//\|...

Ambient

Gábor Kóthay
2000

"When you push the stage props of the life aside, there will remain the truth." Ambient is a deconstructed sans-serif font that captures the essence of basic roman letterforms.

AaBbCcDdEeFfGg
ABCDEFGHIJKLMNOPQRSTUVWXYZ
abcdefghijklmnopqrstuvwxyz12348O123456789!?
@#$%^&*~¿¡™£¥ƒ€¢ÐS†‡¶ ª º {[()]}¢©®-""''„,‰«»()
BÄÂÁÀÃÅÇËÊÉÈÏÎÍÌÑÖÔÓÒÕØÜÛÚÙÆØæœ°•··,·;//\|...

Basala

Hajime Kawakami
2001

Basala was created using straight horizontal and vertical lines, but with large, rounded corners to create an unconventional softness for a bold face. The naming of the font reflects this juxtaposition: Basara/Basala (in Japanese) free and unrestrained, unconventional.

Arthur Baker
1995

Calligraphica was designed because there are very few inline fonts, and even fewer inline calligraphic fonts. The original forms were written with a split pen in a single stroke. The minuscules have a rougher look and the capitals have a smoother shape to imitate handwritten calligraphy with a more formal, decorative initial cap.

The Calligraphic set contains six fonts:

Calligraphica Regular and Italic are the regular upright roman true italic version of the font. The ascenders on this font are a bit higher than the capital letters–this is standard for most fonts.

Calligraphica LX Regular and Italic are similar to the first two fonts except their ascenders are longer and reach high above the capital letters–giving these fonts a taller appearance.

Calligraphica SX Regular and Italic are similar to the first two fonts except their ascenders are shorter and are the same height as the capital letters–giving these fonts a shorter appearance.

Calligraphica Regular

ABCDEFGHIJklmnopqrstuvwxyz

1234&0123456789!?@#$%^&*~¿¡™£¥ƒ€¢∞§†‡¶{[()]}¢©®°π-""''„‚‰«»‹›ßÄÂÁÀÃÅÇËÊÉÈÏÎÍÌÑÖÔÓÒÕØÜÛÚÙÆØœ°•·.,;:/\|

Calligraphica Regular

AaBbCcDdEeFfGgHh
IiJjKkLlMmNnOoPpQq
RrSfTtUuVvWwXxYyZz

Calligraphica Regular LX

AaBbCcDdEeFfGgHh
IiJjKkLlMmNnOoPpQq
RrSfTtUuVvWwXxYyZz

Calligraphica Regular SX

AaBbCcDdEeFfGgHh
IiJjKkLlMmNnOoPpQq
RrSfTtUuVvWwXxYyZz

Calligraphica Italic

ABCDEFGHIJklmnopqrstuvwxyz

1234&0123456789!?@#$%^&*~¿¡™£¥ƒ€¢∞§†‡¶{[()]}¢©®°π-""''„‚‰«»‹›ßÄÂÁÀÃÅÇËÊÉÈÏÎÍÌÑÖÔÓÒÕØÜÛÚÙÆØœ°•·.,;:/\|

Calligraphica Italic

AaBbCcDdEeFfGgHh
IiJjKkLlMmNnOoPpQq
RrSfTtUuVvWwXxYyZz

Calligraphica Italic LX

AaBbCcDdEeFfGgHh
IiJjKkLlMmNnOoPpQq
RrSfTtUuVvWwXxYyZz

Calligraphica Italic SX

AaBbCcDdEeFfGgHh
IiJjKkLlMmNnOoPpQq
RrSfTtUuVvWwXxYyZz

James Grieshaber
2001

This typeface was originally inspired by Art Deco lettering. During the development of the letterforms, a strict De Stijl grid was imposed. The lowercase letterforms were created with the influences of rave/techo design styles. The result is a distinctly contemporary display font.

The P22 Cusp Family contains 4 fonts: P22 Cusp Round, P22 Cusp Round Slant, P22 Cusp Square, P22 Cusp Square Slant.

Cusp Three Dee is a free font available on the CD that accompanies this book.

Cusp Round

ABCDEFGHIJKLMNOPQRSTUVWXYZ
abcdefghijklmnopqrstuvwxyz1234&0123456789!?
@#$%^&*~¿¡™£¥ƒ€¢§†‡¶°'{[()]}¢©®℗-
...‰«»‹›ßÄÂÁÀÃÅÇËÊÉÈÏÎÍÌÑÖÔÓÒÕØÜÛÚÙÆØ°•·.;:/\|...

Cusp Square

AaBbCcDdEe
FfGgHhIiJjK
kLlMmNnOoP
pQqRrSsTtUu
VvWwXxYyZz

Cusp Round Slant

AaBbCcDdEe
FfGgHhIiJjK
kLlMmNnOoP
pQqRrSsTtUu
VvWwXxYyZz

Cusp Square Slant

AaBbCcDdEe
FfGgHhIiJjK
kLlMmNnOoP
pQqRrSsTtUu
VvWwXxYyZz

Cusp Three Dee

ABCDEFGHIJKLMNOPQRSTUVWXYZ
abcdefghijklmnopqrstuvwxyz1234&0123456789!?

1-800-P22-5080

Daddy-O Hip

ABCDEFGHIJKLMNOPQRSTUVWXYZ
abcdefghijklmnopqrstuvwxyz1234&0123456789!?
@#$%^&*~5I™£¥ƒ€¢∞§†‡¶ªº{[()]}¢©®π-""'`,,‰«»‹›
ßÄÀÁÂÃÅÇËÈÉÊÏÌÍÎÑÖÒÓÔÕØÜÙÚÛÆØœº•·.,:;/|\…

Daddy-O Gaunt

AaBbCcDdE
eFfGgHhIiJ
jKkLlMmN
nOoPpQqRr
SsTtUuVv
WwXxYyZz

Daddy-O Blackface

AaBbCcDdE
eFfGgHhIiJ
jKkLlMmN
nOoPpQqRr
SsTtUuVv
WwXxYyZz

Daddy-O Fatface

AaBbCcDdE
eFfGgHhIiJ
jKkLlMmN
nOoPpQqRr
SsTtUuVvW
wXxYyZz

Dearest Script

AaBbCcDEeFfGgHhIiJjKkLlMmNnO
PpQqRrSsTtUuVvWwXxYyZz1234&012345
6789!?@#$%^&*~'61'™£¥ƒ€↵§†‡℗
9{[()]}¢©®®"""'`,.„«»‹›ßáăàâãåÇE
ÈÉÊÏÌÍÎÑÖÒÓÔÕØÜÙÚÛÆÐ æœ·.·:;…

Dearest Swash

AaBbCcDdEeFfGgHhIiJjKkLl
MmNnOoPpQqRrSsTtUuVvWwXxY
yZzSt0123456789Mr.?Mrs.Ms.Dr.McMt.
St.Rst22fthJfQ℘Ave.Ln.tbDCo.

A flowing script font set. P22 Dearest was inspired by handwritten characters found in a 19th century German book chronicling a history of the Middle Ages. Both P22 Dearest Script and Swash fonts were designed to be used interchangeably with one another, to create a look that can be tailored to your needs and closer simulate elegant handwriting. There are many snap-on swashes included in P22 Dearest that allow you to embellish your text in many different ways.

Dwiggins set

Richard Kegler / W.A. Dwiggins
2001

Dwiggins Uncial is based on calligraphy William Addison Dwiggins created for a book-arts publication in 1935. This self-described "experimental uncial" lettering features rather unusual treatments of letterforms that combine manuscript calligraphy with modern idiosyncrasies.

Dwiggins Extras is also adapted from abstract and representational Dwiggins' famous handcut celluloid stencil designs.

Dwiggins Uncial
AaBbCcDdЄeFfGgHhIiJjKkLlMmNnOoPpQ
qrRsSsTtUuVvWwXxYyZz1234567890åáàâä
ãèêëéïiiîøüûúùñß¶&œÆ!@#$£¥¢%&*(){}[]

Dwiggins Extras

Dwiggins

Frenzy

Michael Clark
2002

A synthesis of classic roman type, American Typewriter and pure energy.

AaBbCcDdEeFfGgHhIiJjKkLlMmNnOoPp
QqRrSsTtUuVvWwXxYyZz1234567890aåá
âäãèêëéîïìiîøüûúùñß¶&œÆ!@#$£¥¢%&*(){}[]."

Gothic Gothic

James Grieshaber
2001

The name says it all. Gothic from the old literary style and/or current subculture genre. And Gothic meaning a block or sans-serif style of lettering. The concept was to take the classic German style lettering and create a contemporary extended block letter typeface. The result is a fusion of old and new.

AaBbCcDdEeFfGg
HhIiJjKkLlMmNnOo
PpQqRrSsTtUuVv
WwXxYyZz123456
7890åáàâäãèêëéîïìi
øüûúùß¶&œÆ€≤≥!
@#$£¥¢%^&*[](){}:."

Gothic
Gothic

Aa

LaDanse

Gábor Kóthay
1998

LaDanse is a "facsimile" font, based on sample of handwriting found in an ancient Hungarian type specimen book.

LaDanse

AaBbCcDdEeFfGgHhIiJjKkLlMmNnO
oPpQqRrSsTtUuVvWwXxYyZzi234567
890åáìíùûúß¶&œÆ≤≥!@#$£¥¢%&*(){}

Mercator

Arthur Baker
1980

Gerardus Mercator was born in the Netherlands in 1512. His name has become synonymous with the Mercator map projection scheme where our globe is represented as a flat image. As a man of the Renaissance, Mercator also had an interest in such subjects as calligraphy. Contemporary American calligrapher Arthur Baker has studied the penmanship of Mercator and has created this font based on the lettering used on Mercator's famous world map.

Mercator Regular
AaBbCcDdEeFfGgHhIiJjKkLlMmNnOoPpQqRr
SsTtUuVvWwXxYyZz1234567890åáàâäãèêëé
îïìîøüûúùñß&œÆ€≤≥!@#$£¥¢%^&*{}[]:."

Mercator Swash
ABBCDEFGHIJKKLMMNO
PQRSFTUVWXYZZ

Mercator

AaBbCcDdEeFfGgHhIiJjKkLIMmNnOoPpQqRrSsTtUu
VvWwXxYyZz1234567890λέíõÜß¶œÆ€ς?!

Mucha

Christina Torre
2001

Inspired by the free-flowing lettering styles of Art Nouveau master Alfons Mucha, circa 1900.

Platten Regular

AaBbCcDdEeFfGgHhIiJjKkLIMmNnOoPpQqRr
SsTtUuVvWwXxYyZz1234567890åáàâäãèêê
éîïíøüûúùñß¶&œÆ乡€lɑfia!@#$%^&*(){}[

Platten Italic

AaBbCcDdEeFfGgHhIiJjKkLIMmNn
OoPpQqRrSsTtUuVvWwXxYyZz123

Platten

Platten set

Richard Kegler
2001

The P22 Platten font family is based on lettering found in a German fountain pen practice book from the 1920s. This round-tip pen lettering is comparable to the basic forms used in grammar school teaching alphabets, but with a few original characteristics. The Italic version has even more of these unusual features.

AaBbCcDdEeFfGgHhIiJjKkLIMmNnOoP
pQqRrSsTtUuVvWwXxYyZz1234åéîõü&

Preissig Lino

Richard Kegler / Vojtech Preissig
2001

Preissig created handcut fonts using a knife in linoleum blocks. This font was based on one such design from 1912.

Salon Full

AaBbCcDdEeFfGgHhIiJjKkLIMm
NnOoPpQqRrSsTtUuVvWwXxYyZz
1234567890åçéîüñßʀ&œÆ

Salon

Salon set

Christina Torre
2001

P22 Salon was originally inspired by Art Nouveau lettering. In the development of the three fonts (P22 Salon Full, P22 Salon Inner and P22 Salon Shadow), they began taking on a slightly more modern feel. All three variations were designed to be completely interchangeable with one another, and can be layered to achieve a variety of effects.

Salon Inner

AaBbCcDdEeFfGgHhIiJjKkLIMm
NnOoPpQqRrSsTtUuVvWwXxYyZz
1234567890åçéîüñßʀ&œÆ

in 3

Salon Shadow

AaBbCcDdEeFfGgHhIiJjKkLIMm
NnOoPpQqRrSsTtUuVvWwXxYyZz
1234567890åçéîüñßʀ&œÆ

Parts

Telegdi family

Amondó Szegi
1999-2001

Abbot Nicolaus Telegdi purchased the Vienna Jesuit press in 1577, and started to work immediately with its own worn typefaces. His first works were publications of his own speeches.

Telegdi is an authentic, highly distressed font. The letter spacing and letter weight is intentionally uneven to re-create the effect of early printing, which used handcast and handset type with irregular paper and coarse ink consistency.

Telegdi Antique

AaBbCcDdEeFfGgHhIiJjKkLlMmNnOoPpQq
RrSsTtUuVvWwXxYyZz1234567890åçéîüñß

Telegdi Antique Small Caps

AaBbCcDdEeFfGgHhIiJjKkLlMmNnOoPpQ
QRrSsTtUuVvWwXxYyZz1234567890åçéíü

Telegdi Italic

AaBbCcDdEeFfGgHhIiJjKkLlMmNnOoPpQgRrSs
TtUuVvWwXxYyZz1234567890åçéîüñß¶&œÆ

Telegdi Italic Alts

AaBbCcDdEeFfGgHhIiJjKkLlMmNnOoPpQgR
rSsTtUuVvWwXxYyZz1234567890åçéîüñß¶&œÆ

Telegdi Dings

Tyndale

Ted Staunton
2002

William Tyndale was burned at the stake in 1536 for printing the first English language translation of the Bible. This font attempts to bring the Gothic and roman letterforms close together, incorporating the influence of the handwritten penmanship.

ABCDEFGHIJKLMNOPQR
STUVWXYZabcdefghijklm
nopqrstuvwxyz1234&0123456789!?@#$%^&*~¿¡™£¥
¢§†‡¶ªº{[()]}‡¢©®ßÄÂÁÀÃÅÇËÊÉÈÑÖÓÕØÜÆØæœ

1-800-P22-5080

P22Typewriter ABCDEFGHIJKLMNOPQRST
UVWXYZabcdefghijklmnopqrstuvwxyzO
123456789 ! ? @ # $ % ^ & * + − ※ ÷ = ± ~ ¿ ¡ ™ £ ¥ ƒ € ¢
{ [( )] } ¢ © ® ℗ " ' " " ' ' , „ ‰ « » < > ß å é î ø ü ñ ç Ä Â
Á À Ã Å Ç Ë Ê É È Ï Î Í Ì Ñ Ö Ô Ó Ò Õ Ø Ü Û Ú Ù Æ Ø æ œ ※ § ✕ ✕ ¶

P22 Typewriter

Richard Kegler
2001

This font is not overly distressed, nor is it overly clean. It is a typewriter font. It is perfect when you want a document to look like it was made on a typewriter. This font is primarily based on the typewriter used for a typographic conference document from 1966 in Mainz, Germany. The model and age of the typewriter used is not known. Additional characters were sourced from other vintage typewriters to complete the full character set.

AaBbCcDdEeFfGgHhIiJj
abcdefghijklmnopqrstuvwxyz12348012345678
9!?@#$%^&*~¿¡™£¥ƒ€¢©§†‡¶{[()]}¢©®ßÄÂ
ÁÀÃÅÇËÊÉÈÏÎÍÌÑÖÔÓÒÕØÜÛÚÙÆØæœ

Vidro

Hajime Kawakami
2000

Vidro is a glass technique introduced by the Dutch in Japan in the sixteenth century. Vidro glassworks enrich the lives of the Japanese people with such items as decorations and children's toys. P22 Vidro comprises simple forms that express both irregularity and fluidity.

Zephyr set

Gábor Kóthay
2001

Zephyr is a sinuous roman font available in both Regular and Openface (inline) versions. This classically inspired font set conjures up a gentle, relaxing breeze from the West and Southwest. Subtle and not-so-subtle variations offer a refreshingly modern take on these age-old letterforms.

Zephyr

Zephyr Regular

AaBbCcDdEeFfGgHhIiJj
klmnopqrstuvwxyz1234&0123456789!?@
#$%^&*~¿¡™£¥ƒ€¢§†‡¶{[()]}¢©®ßÄÂÁÀÃ
ÅÇËÊÉÈÏÎÍÌÑÖÔÓÒÕØÜÛÚÙÆØæœ

Zephyr Openface

AaBbCcDdEeFfGgHhIiJj
klmnopqrstuvwxyz1234&0123456789!?@

P22 type foundry

PSY/OPS TYPE FOUNDRY

The concepts originate on the drawingboards and monitors of historians and experimentalists, dedicated veterans and inspired laymen. Once selected, the ideas are refined, balanced, and perfected by obsessive sets of hands and eyes in a secluded office in downtown San Francisco.

If you haven't heard of us it's because we've been busy building faces for other prominent type companies, book publishers, and communications megaliths. But our passion remains the development of a unique and useful collection of digital typefaces — one solely intended to make your own design work stand apart.

Try our fonts and discover why top designers & publishers love our work and come back so often.

www.psyops.com

abcdefghijklmnopqrstuvwxyzABCDEFG HIJKLMNOPQRSTUVWXYZ0123456789

Lars Bergquist
2001

A winning design in ATypI's 2001 *Bukva-Raz!* competition.

Italic

abcdefghijklmnopqrstuvwxyzABCDEFG HIJKLMNOPQRSTUVWXYZ0123456789

Smallcaps

ABCDEFGHJKLMNOPQRSTUVWXYZABCDEF GHJKLMNOPQRSTUVWXYZ123456789

Regular 10/11

Quando prendo il taxi bevo whisky, ascolto jazz e mangio fichi. When I ride the taxi I drink whisky, listen to jazz and

Italic 10/11

Quando prendo il taxi bevo whisky, ascolto jazz e mangio fichi. When I ride the taxi I drink whisky, listen to jazz and eat figs. Quando prendo il

Smallcaps 10/11

QUANDO PRENDO IL TAXI BEVO WHISKY, ASCOLTO JAZZ E MAN-GIO FICHI. WHEN I RIDE THE TAXI I DRINK WHISKY, LISTEN TO

Regular

abcdefghijklmnopqrstuvwxyzABCDE FGHIJKLMNOPQRSTUVWXYZ0123456789

Rodrigo Xavier Cavazos (RXC)
2000

Oblique

abcdefghijklmnopqrstuvwxyzABCDE FGHIJKLMNOPQRSTUVWXYZ0123456789

Bold

abcdefghijklmnopqrstuvwxyzABCDE FGHIJKLMNOPQRSTUVWXYZ0123456789

Bold Oblique

abcdefghijklmnopqrstuvwxyzABCDE FGHIJKLMNOPQRSTUVWXYZ0123456789

RXC
1996

Regular-One

abcdefghijklmnopqrstuvwxyzABCDEFG
HIJKLMNOPQRSTUVWXYZ0123456789

Regular-Two

abcdefghijklmnopqrstuvwxyzABCDEFG
HIJKLMNOPQRSTUVWXYZ0123456789

Italic-One

abcdefghijklmnopqrstuvwxyzABCDEFG
HIJKLMNOPQRSTUVWXYZ0123456789

Italic-Two

abcdefghijklmnopqrstuvwxyzABCDEFG
HIJKLMNOPQRSTUVWXYZ0123456789

Bold-One

abcdefghijklmnopqrstuvwxyzABCDEFG
HIJKLMNOPQRSTUVWXYZ0123456789

Bold-Two

abcdefghijklmnopqrstuvwxyzABCDEFG
HIJKLMNOPQRSTUVWXYZ0123456789

BoldItalic-One

abcdefghijklmnopqrstuvwxyzABCDEFG
HIJKLMNOPQRSTUVWXYZ0123456789

BoldItalic-Two

abcdefghijklmnopqrstuvwxyzABCDEFG
HIJKLMNOPQRSTUVWXYZ0123456789

Paul Veres
1998

Regular

abcdefghijklmnopqrstuvwxyzABCDEFG
HIJKLMNOPQRSTUVWXYZ0123456789&

Italic

*abcdefghijklmnopqrstuvwxyzABCDEFG
HIJKLMNOPQRSTUVWXYZ0123456789&*

Semibold

abcdefghijklmnopqrstuvwxyzABCDEFG
HIJKLMNOPQRSTUVWXYZ0123456789&

Semibold Italic

*abcdefghijklmnopqrstuvwxyzABCDEFG
HIJKLMNOPQRSTUVWXYZ0123456789&*

Bold

abcdefghijklmnopqrstuvwxyzABCDEFG
HIJKLMNOPQRSTUVWXYZ0123456789&

Bold Italic

*abcdefghijklmnopqrstuvwxyzABCDEFG
HIJKLMNOPQRSTUVWXYZ0123456789&*

SCOSF

ABCDEFGHIJKLMNOPQRSTUVWXYZABCDEFG
HIJKLMNOPQRSTUVWXYZ0123456789&

Psy/Ops

Regular & Italic 11/11

Quando prendo il taxi bevo whisky,
ascolto jazz e mangio fichi. When I

*take the taxi I drink whisky, listen to
jazz and eat figs. Quando prendo il*

Semibold & Semibold Italic 11/11

Quando prendo il taxi bevo whisky,
ascolto jazz e mangio fichi. When

*I take the taxi I drink whisky, listen
to jazz and eat figs. Quando pren-*

Bold & Bold Italic 11/11

Quando prendo il taxi bevo whisky,
ascolto jazz e mangio fichi. When

*I take the taxi I drink whisky, listen
to jazz and eat figs. Quando pren-*

Normal

abcdefghijklmnopqrstuvwxyzABCDEFGHI
JKLMNOPQRSTUVWXYZ0123456789

Swash Caps

abcdefghijklmnopqrstuvwxyzABCDEF
GIJKLMNOPQRSTUVWXYZ

Small Caps

ABCDEFGHIJKLMNOPQRSTUVWXYZABCDEF
GHIJKLMNOPQRSTUVWXYZ0123456789

Engraved Caps

ABCDEFGHIJKLMNOPQ
RSTUVWXYZ0123456789

Floral Caps

ABCDEFGHIJKLMNOPQ
RSTUVWXYZ0123456789

Ligatures

ExFiFlMCNOTh EAFI IANNNTNY RARNRMTTTYAVI
VWWIZAarasereexffffiffflflijftfygyijirislynjnsnyspsttyus

Cameo

Psy/Ops

Regular

abcdefghijklmnopqrstuvwxyzABCDEF
GHIJKLMNOPQRSTUVWXYZo123456789&

Italic

abcdefghijklmnopqrstuvwxyzABCDEFG
HIJKLMNOPQRSTUVWXYZo123456789&

Semibold

abcdefghijklmnopqrstuvwxyzABCDEF
GHIJKLMNOPQRSTUVWXYZo123456789&

Semibold Italic

abcdefghijklmnopqrstuvwxyzABCDEF
GHIJKLMNOPQRSTUVWXYZo123456789&

Bold

abcdefghijklmnopqrstuvwxyzABCDEF
GHIJKLMNOPQRSTUVWXYZo123456789&

Bold Italic

abcdefghijklmnopqrstuvwxyzABCDEF
GHIJKLMNOPQRSTUVWXYZo123456789&

Light 11/12

Quando prendo il taxi bevo whisky, ascolto jazz e mangio fichi. When I take the taxi I drink whisky, listen to jazz and eat figs. Quando prendo il

Light Italic 11/12

Quando prendo il taxi bevo whisky, ascolto jazz e mangio fichi. When I take the taxi I drink whisky, listen to jazz and eat figs. Quando prendo il taxi bevo whisky, ascolto

Regular 11/12

Quando prendo il taxi bevo whisky, ascolto jazz e mangio fichi. When I take the taxi I drink whisky, listen to jazz and eat figs. Quando prendo

Italic 11/12

Quando prendo il taxi bevo whisky, ascolto jazz e mangio fichi. When I take the taxi I drink whisky, listen to jazz and eat figs. Quando prendo il taxi bevo whisky, ascolto

Bold 11/12

Quando prendo il taxi bevo whisky, ascolto jazz e mangio fichi. When I take the taxi I drink whisky, listen to jazz and eat figs. Quando prendo

Bold Italic 11/12

Quando prendo il taxi bevo whisky, ascolto jazz e mangio fichi. When I take the taxi I drink whisky, listen to jazz and eat figs. Quando prendo il

Philip Krayna & RXC
2000

Halfwide Light

abcdefghijklmnopqrstuvwxyz ABCDEFGHIJK
LMNOPQRSTUVWXYZ0123456789&¥€ÆŒ%?!

Halfwide Heavy

abcdefghijklmnopqrstuvwxyz ABCDEFGHIJK
LMNOPQRSTUVWXYZ0123456789&¥€ÆŒ%?!

Singlewide Light

abcdefghijklmnopqrstuvwxyz ABCDEFGHI
JKLMNOPQRSTUVWXYZ0123456789&¥€

Singlewide Heavy

abcdefghijklmnopqrstuvwxyz ABCDEFGHI
JKLMNOPQRSTUVWXYZ0123456789&¥€

Doublewide Light

abcdefghijklmnopqrstuvwxyz ABCDEFG
HIJKLMNOPQRSTUVWXYZ0123456789

Doublewide Heavy

abcdefghijklmnopqrstuvwxyz ABCDEFG
HIJKLMNOPQRSTUVWXYZ0123456789

Halfwide Light 12/14

Quando prendo il taxi bevo whisky, ascolto jazz e mangio fichi. When I take the taxi I drink whisky, listen to jazz and eat figs.

Singlewide Light 12/14

Quando prendo il taxi bevo whisky, ascolto jazz e mangio fichi. When I take the taxi I drink whisky, lis-

Doublewide Light 12/14

Quando prendo il taxi bevo whisky, ascolto jazz e mangio fichi. When I take the

Halfwide Heavy 12/14

Quando prendo il taxi bevo whisky, ascolto jazz e mangio fichi. When I take the taxi I drink whisky, listen to jazz and eat figs.

Singlewide Heavy 12/14

Quando prendo il taxi bevo whisky, ascolto jazz e mangio fichi. When I take the taxi I drink

Doublewide Heavy 12/14

Quando prendo il taxi bevo whisky, ascolto jazz e mangio fichi. When I take

abcdefghijklmnopqrstuvwxyzABCDEFG
HIJKLMNOPQRSTUVWXYZ0123456789

RXC
1998

abcdefghijklmnopqrstuvwxyzABCDEFG
HIJKLMNOPQRSTUVWXYZ0123456789

abcdefghijklmnopqrstuvwxyzABCDEFG
HIJKLMNOPQRSTUVWXYZ0123456789

abcdefghijklmnopqrstuvwxyzABCDEFG
HIJKLMNOPQRSTUVWXYZ0123456789

abcdefghijklmnopqrstuvwxyzABCDEFG
HIJKLMNOPQRSTUVWXYZ0123456789

abcdefghijklmnopqrstuvwxyzABCDEFG
HIJKLMNOPQRSTUVWXYZ0123456789

Psy/Ops

A Gauge 10/12

Quando prendo il taxi bevo whisky, ascolto jazz e mangio fichi. When I take the taxi I drink whisky, listen to jazz and eat figs. Quando prendo

A Gauge Italic 10/12

Quando prendo il taxi bevo whisky, ascolto jazz e mangio fichi. When I take the taxi I drink whisky, listen to jazz and eat figs. Quando prendo

B Gauge 10/12

Quando prendo il taxi bevo whisky, ascolto jazz e mangio fichi. When I take the taxi I drink whisky, listen to jazz and eat figs. Quando

B Gauge Italic 10/12

Quando prendo il taxi bevo whisky, ascolto jazz e mangio fichi. When I take the taxi I drink whisky, listen to jazz and eat figs. Quando

C Gauge 10/12

Quando prendo il taxi bevo whisky, ascolto jazz e mangio fichi. When I take the taxi I drink whisky, listen to jazz and eat figs. Quando

C Gauge Italic 10/12

Quando prendo il taxi bevo whisky, ascolto jazz e mangio fichi. When I take the taxi I drink whisky, listen to jazz and eat figs. Quando

Rodrigo Xavier Cavazos (RXC)
1998

Regular

abcdefghijklmnopqrstuvwxyzABCDEFG
HIJKLMNOPQRSTUVWXYZ0123456789

Italic

*abcdefghijklmnopqrstuvwxyzABCDEFG
HIJKLMNOPQRSTUVWXYZ0123456789*

Bold

**abcdefghijklmnopqrstuvwxyzABCDEFG
HIJKLMNOPQRSTUVWXYZ0123456789**

Bold Italic

***abcdefghijklmnopqrstuvwxyzABCDEFG
HIJKLMNOPQRSTUVWXYZ0123456789***

Smallcaps

ABCDEFGHIJKLMNOPQRSTUVWXYZABCDE
FGHIJKLMNOPQRSTUVWXYZ0123456789

Regular & Italic 10 pt

Quando prendo il taxi bevo whisky, ascolto jazz e mangio fichi. When I take the taxi I drink whisky, listen to jazz and eat figs. Quando prendo

Bold & Bold Italic 10 pt

Quando prendo il taxi bevo whisky, ascolto jazz e mangio fichi. When I take the taxi I drink whisky, listen to jazz and eat figs. Quando

Smallcaps 10 pt

QUANDO PRENDO IL TAXI BEVO WHISKY, ASCOLTO JAZZ E MANGIO FICHI. WHEN I TAKE THE TAXI I DRINK WHISKY, LISTEN TO JAZZ AND EAT FIGS.

RXC
1998 / 2000

Also available from Emigre Inc.

Regular

abcdefghijklmnopqrstuvwxyzABCDEFG
HIJKLMNOPQRSTUVWXYZ0123456789

Italic

*abcdefghijklmnopqrstuvwxyzABCDEFG
HIJKLMNOPQRSTUVWXYZ0123456789*

abcdefghijklmnopqrstuvwxyzABCDEFG
HIJKLMNOPQRSTUVWXYZ0123456789

Bold Italic

abcdefghijklmnopqrstuvwxyzABCDEFG
HIJKLMNOPQRSTUVWXYZ0123456789

Black

abcdefghijklmnopqrstuvwxyzABCDEFG
HIJKLMNOPQRSTUVWXYZ0123456789

Smallcaps

ABCDEFGHIJKLMNOPQRSTUVWXYZABCDE
FGHIJKLMNOPQRSTUVWXYZ0123456789

Omni

abcdefghijkLmnopqrstuvwxyzAB
CDEFGHIJKLMNOPQRSTUVWXYZ012345

Fractions / Expert

ABCDEFGHIJKLMNOPQRSTUVWXYZ⊕⊠ℯ
0123456789¢0123456789/0123456789$✈♀♂
℃©℗®% ff fi fl ffi ffl ₵ aebdilmnrstÞŁŲŽ¥

Regular & Italic 10 pt

Quando prendo il taxi bevo whisky,
ascolto jazz e mangio fichi. When
I take the taxi I drink whisky, lis-

ten to jazz and eat figs. Quando
prendo il taxi bevo whisky, ascolto
jazz e mangio fichi. When I take

Bold & Bold Italic 10 pt

Quando prendo il taxi bevo whisky,
ascolto jazz e mangio fichi. When
I take the taxi I drink whisky, lis-

ten to jazz and eat figs. Quando
prendo il taxi bevo whisky, ascolto
jazz e mangio fichi. When I take

Black & Smallcaps 10 pt

Quando prendo il taxi bevo whis-
ky, ascolto jazz e mangio fichi.
When I take the taxi I drink whis-

KY, LISTEN TO JAZZ AND EAT FIGS.
QUANDO PRENDO IL TAXI BEVO
WHISKY, ASCOLTO JAZZ E MANGIO

Omni 10 pt

quando prendo iL taxi bevo whisky, ascoL-
to jazz e mangio fichi. when I take the taxi

wwwwww

Classic

abcdefghijklmnopqrstuvwxyzABCDEFG
HIJKLMNOPQRSTUVWXYZ0123456789

Concise

abcdefghijklmnopqrstuvwxyzABCDEFG
HIJKLMNOPQRSTUVWXYZ0123456789

Minuscule Swash Alternates

a b c d e f fi fl g h i j k l
m n o p q r s t u v w x y z

13/14 (Mix)

Quando prendo il taxi bevo whisky, ascolto jazz e mangio fichi. When I ride the taxi I drink whisky, listen to jazz and eat figs. Quando prendo il taxi

A Gauge

abcdefghijklmnopqrstuvwxyzABCDEFG
HIJKLMNOPQRSTUVWXYZ0123456789

B Gauge

abcdefghijklmnopqrstuvwxyzABCDEFG
HIJKLMNOPQRSTUVWXYZ0123456789

C Gauge

abcdefghijklmnopqrstuvwxyzABCDEFG
HIJKLMNOPQRSTUVWXYZ0123456789

D Gauge

abcdefghijklmnopqrstuvwxyzABCDEFG
HIJKLMNOPQRSTUVWXYZ0123456789

E Gauge

abcdefghijklmnopqrstuvwxyzABCDEF
GHIJKLMNOPQRSTUVWXYZ0123456789

A Gauge Oblique

abcdefghijklmnopqrstuvwxyzABCDEFG
HIJKLMNOPQRSTUVWXYZ0123456789

B Gauge Oblique

abcdefghijklmnopqrstuvwxyzABCDEFG
HIJKLMNOPQRSTUVWXYZ0123456789

C Gauge Oblique

abcdefghijklmnopqrstuvwxyzABCDEFG
HIJKLMNOPQRSTUVWXYZ0123456789

D Gauge Oblique

abcdefghijklmnopqrstuvwxyzABCDEFG
HIJKLMNOPQRSTUVWXYZ0123456789

E Gauge Oblique

abcdefghijklmnopqrstuvwxyzABCDEFG
HIJKLMNOPQRSTUVWXYZ0123456789

A Gauge 10/11

Quando prendo il taxi bevo whisky, ascolto jazz e mangio fichi. When I ride the taxi I drink whisky, listen to jazz

B Gauge 10/11

Quando prendo il taxi bevo whisky, ascolto jazz e mangio fichi. When I ride the taxi I drink whisky, listen to

C Gauge 10/11

Quando prendo il taxi bevo whisky, ascolto jazz e mangio fichi. When I ride the taxi I drink whisky, listen

D Gauge 10/11

Quando prendo il taxi bevo whisky, ascolto jazz e mangio fichi. When I ride the taxi I drink whisky,

E Gauge 10/11

Quando prendo il taxi bevo whisky, ascolto jazz e mangio fichi. When I ride the taxi I drink whisky,

A Gauge Oblique 10/11

Quando prendo il taxi bevo whisky, ascolto jazz e mangio fichi. When I ride the taxi I drink whisky, listen to jazz

B Gauge Oblique 10/11

Quando prendo il taxi bevo whisky, ascolto jazz e mangio fichi. When I ride the taxi I drink whisky, listen to

C Gauge Oblique 10/11

Quando prendo il taxi bevo whisky, ascolto jazz e mangio fichi. When I ride the taxi I drink whisky, listen

D Gauge Oblique 10/11

Quando prendo il taxi bevo whisky, ascolto jazz e mangio fichi. When I ride the taxi I drink whisky,

E Gauge Oblique 10/11

Quando prendo il taxi bevo whisky, ascolto jazz e mangio fichi. When I ride the taxi I drink whisky,

Psy/Ops

Claudio Rodil & RXC
2001

Normal

abcdefghijklmnopqrstuvwxyzABCDEF
GHIJKLMNOPQRSTUVWXYZ0123456789

Italic

abcdefghijklmnopqrstuvwxyzABCDEF
GHIJKLMNOPQRSTUVWXYZ0123456789

Medium

abcdefghijklmnopqrstuvwxyzABCDEF
GHIJKLMNOPQRSTUVWXYZ0123456789

Medium Italic

abcdefghijklmnopqrstuvwxyzABCDEF
GHIJKLMNOPQRSTUVWXYZ0123456789

Bold

abcdefghijklmnopqrstuvwxyzABCDEF
GHIJKLMNOPQRSTUVWXYZ0123456789

Bold Italic

abcdefghijklmnopqrstuvwxyzABCDEF
GHIJKLMNOPQRSTUVWXYZ0123456789

Black

abcdefghijklmnopqrstuvwxyzABCDEF
GHIJKLMNOPQRSTUVWXYZ0123456789

Black Italic

abcdefghijklmnopqrstuvwxyzABCDEF
GHIJKLMNOPQRSTUVWXYZ0123456789

a b c d e f g h i j k l m n o p q r s t u v w x y z A B C D E F G
H I J K L M N O P Q R S T U V W X Y Z 0 1 2 3 4 5 6 7 8 9

a b c d e f g h i j k l m n o p q r s t u v w x y z A B C D E F G
H I J K L M N O P Q R S T U V W X Y Z 0 1 2 3 4 5 6 7 8 9

a b c d e f g h i j k l m n o p q r s t u v w x y z A B C D E F G
H I J K L M N O P Q R S T U V W X Y Z 0 1 2 3 4 5 6 7 8 9

a b c d e f g h i j k l m n o p q r s t u v w x y z A B C D E F G
H I J K L M N O P Q R S T U V W X Y Z 0 1 2 3 4 5 6 7 8 9

a b c d e f g h i j k l m n o p q r s t u v w x y z A B C D E F G
H I J K L M N O P Q R S T U V W X Y Z 0 1 2 3 4 5 6 7 8 9

a b c d e f g h i j k l m n o p q r s t u v w x y z A B C D E F G
H I J K L M N O P Q R S T U V W X Y Z 0 1 2 3 4 5 6 7 8 9

Psy/Ops

Normal 11/12

Quando prendo il taxi bevo whisky, ascolto jazz e mangio fichi. When I take the taxi I drink whisky, listen to jazz and eat figs. Quando pren-

Bold 11/12

Quando prendo il taxi bevo whisky, ascolto jazz e mangio fichi. When I take the taxi I drink whisky, listen to jazz and eat figs. Quando

Massive 11/12

Quando prendo il taxi bevo whisky, ascolto jazz e mangio fichi. When I take the taxi I drink whisky, listen to jazz and eat figs.

Slant 11/12

Quando prendo il taxi bevo whisky, ascolto jazz e mangio fichi. When I take the taxi I drink whisky, listen to jazz and eat figs. Quando pren-

Bold Slant 11/12

Quando prendo il taxi bevo whisky, ascolto jazz e mangio fichi. When I take the taxi I drink whisky, listen to jazz and eat figs.

Massive Slant 11/12

Quando prendo il taxi bevo whisky, ascolto jazz e mangio fichi. When I take the taxi I drink whisky, listen to jazz and eat figs.

Regular

abcdefghijklmnopqrstuvwxyzABCDEFG
HIJKLMNOPQRSTUVWXYZ0123456789

Italic

abcdefghijklmnopqrstuvwxyzABCDEFG
HIJKLMNOPQRSTUVWXYZ0123456789

Demi

abcdefghijklmnopqrstuvwxyzABCDEFG
HIJKLMNOPQRSTUVWXYZ0123456789

Demi Italic

abcdefghijklmnopqrstuvwxyzABCDEFG
HIJKLMNOPQRSTUVWXYZ0123456789

Bold

abcdefghijklmnopqrstuvwxyzABCDEFG
HIJKLMNOPQRSTUVWXYZ0123456789

Bold Italic

abcdefghijklmnopqrstuvwxyzABCDEFG
HIJKLMNOPQRSTUVWXYZ0123456789

Regular 10/11

Quando prendo il taxi bevo whisky, ascolto jazz e mangio fichi. When I take the taxi I drink whisky, listen to jazz and eat figs. Quando prendo il taxi

Italic 10/11

Quando prendo il taxi bevo whisky, ascolto jazz e mangio fichi. When I take the taxi I drink whisky, listen to jazz and eat figs. Quando prendo il taxi bevo

Demi 10/11

Quando prendo il taxi bevo whisky, ascolto jazz e mangio fichi. When I take the taxi I drink whisky, listen to jazz and eat figs. Quando prendo il

Demi Italic 10/11

Quando prendo il taxi bevo whisky, ascolto jazz e mangio fichi. When I take the taxi I drink whisky, listen to jazz and eat figs. Quando prendo il

Bold 10/11

Quando prendo il taxi bevo whisky, ascolto jazz e mangio fichi. When I take the taxi I drink whisky, listen to jazz and eat figs. Quando prendo il

Bold Italic 10/11

Quando prendo il taxi bevo whisky, ascolto jazz e mangio fichi. When I take the taxi I drink whisky, listen to jazz and eat figs. Quando prendo il

Fraktur

abcdefghijklmnopqrstuvwxyzABCDEFGH
JRLMNOPQRSTUVWXY30123456789

Versal

Regular

abcdefghijklmnopqrstuvwxyzABCDEFG
HIJKLMNOPQRSTUVWXYZ0123456789&

Italic

abcdefghijklmnopqrstuvwxyzABCDEFG
HIJKLMNOPQRSTUVWXYZ0123456789&

Bold

abcdefghijklmnopqrstuvwxyzABCDEFG
HIJKLMNOPQRSTUVWXYZ0123456789&

Bold Italic

abcdefghijklmnopqrstuvwxyzABCDEF
GHIJKLMNOPQRSTUVWXYZ0123456789&

SCOSF

ABCDEFGHIJKLMNOPQRSTUVWXYZABCDEF
GHIJKLMNOPQRSTUVWXYZ0123456789&

Psy/Ops

Regular

abcdefghijklmnopqrstuvwxyzABCDEFG
HIJKLMNOPQRSTUVWXYZo123456789

Italic

abcdefghijklmnopqrstuvwxyzABCDEFG
HIJKLMNOPQRSTUVWXYZo123456789

Bold

abcdefghijklmnopqrstuvwxyzABCDEFG
HIJKLMNOPQRSTUVWXYZ0123456789

Smallcaps

ABCDEFGHIJKLMNOPQRSTUVWXYZABCDEFG
HIJKLMNOPQRSTUVWXYZ0123456789

Black Sans

abcdefghijklmnopqrstuvwxyzABCDEFG
HIJKLMNOPQRSTUVWXYZ0123456789

Three Special Fonts (Regular, Italic, Bold) 12 pt

&t fb ff ffi ffl fh fi fj fk fl ft st
o123456789/o123456789

&t fb ff ffi ffl fh fi fj fk fl ft st
0123456789/0123456789

&t fb ff ffi ffl fh fi fj fk fl ft st
0123456789/0123456789

Regular 10/11

Leyden is intended for general book and text work. It was inspired by Dutch type of the 17th century, possibly the golden age of type design and the ultimate source of perennials like Janson, Caslon and even Times, but this

Bold 10/11

...maximal blackness, but shares the basic letterforms and the proportions of the Roman, in order to blend effortlessly with it. ❦ Leyden is intended for general book and text work. It was inspired by

Black Sans 10/11

Dutch type of the 17th century, possibly the golden age of type design and the ultimate source of perennials like Janson, Caslon and even Times, but this is no revival. Leyden includes plain Roman, Italic and Bold fonts,

Italic 10/11

is no revival. Leyden has plain Roman, Italic and Bold fonts, small caps, superscript / subscript fonts for scientific notation and open-ended fractions, plus a strong Black for run-in headings in dictionaries and the like. This latter font is sanserif, for

Smallcaps 10/11

SMALL CAPS, SUPERSCRIPT / SUBSCRIPT FONTS FOR SCIENTIFIC NOTATION AND OPEN-ENDED FRACTIONS, PLUS A STRONG BLACK FOR RUN-IN HEADINGS IN DICTIONARIES AND THE LIKE. THIS LATTER FONT IS SANS SERIF, FOR MAXI-

Regular

abcdefghijklmnopqrstuvwxyzABCDEF
GHIJKLMNOPQRSTUVWXYZ0123456789

Italic

*abcdefghijklmnopqrstuvwxyzABCDEFG
HIJKLMNOPQRSTUVWXYZ0123456789*

Bold

**abcdefghijklmnopqrstuvwxyzABCDEF
GHIJKLMNOPQRSTUVWXYZ0123456789**

Bold Italic

***abcdefghijklmnopqrstuvwxyzABCDEFG
HIJKLMNOPQRSTUVWXYZ0123456789***

Regular 10/11

Leyden News is a variant of Leyden, optimised for use in magazines, papers and newsletters, where type is often of necessity smallish and compact. This means that while basic Leyden letterforms are used, x-height is larger and detail work is more robust and sometimes simplified, all in the interest

Regular 9/10

Leyden News is a variant of Leyden, optimised for use in magazines, papers and newsletters, where type is often of necessity smallish and compact. This means that while basic Leyden letterforms are used, x-height is larger and detail work is more robust and sometimes simplified, all in the interest of high legibility when printing small size type on indif-

Italic 10/11

of high legibility when printing small size type on indifferent paper, and often with indifferent printing too. In spite of this, figures remain lowercase or ranging, though the bold and bold italic styles, which will mainly be used for headers, have uppercase or lining figures. ¶ Leyden News is a variant of Leyden, optimised for

Italic 9/10

ferent paper, and often with indifferent printing too. In spite of this, figures remain lowercase or ranging, though the bold and bold italic styles, which will mainly be used for headers, have uppercase or lining figures. ¶ Leyden News is a variant of Leyden, optimised for use in magazines, papers and newsletters, where type is often of necessity smallish and compact. This means that while basic

Bold & Bold Italic 10/11

use in magazines, papers and newsletters, where type is often of necessity smallish and compact. This means that while basic Leyden letterforms are used, *x-height is larger and detail work is more robust and sometimes simplified, all in the interest of high legibility when printing small size type on*

Bold & Bold Italic 9/10

Leyden letterforms are used, x-height is larger and detail work is more robust and sometimes simplified, all in the interest of high legibility when printing small size type *on indifferent paper, and often with indifferent printing too. In spite of this, figures remain lowercase or ranging, though the bold and bold italic styles, which will mainly be used for headers, have uppercase*

Psy/Ops

Regular

abcdefghijklmnopqrstuvwxyzABCDEFG
HIJKLMNOPQRSTUVWXYZ0I23456789

Italic

abcdefghijklmnopqrstuvwxyzABCDEFG
HIJKLMNOPQRSTUVWXYZ0I23456789

Bold

abcdefghijklmnopqrstuvwxyzABCDEFG
HIJKLMNOPQRSTUVWXYZ0I23456789

Bold Italic

abcdefghijklmnopqrstuvwxyzABCDEFG
HIJKLMNOPQRSTUVWXYZ0I23456789

Smallcaps

ABCDEFGHJKLMNOPQRSTUVWXYZABCDE
FGHJKLMNOPQRSTUVWXYZ0I23456789

Regular 10/11

Quando prendo il taxi bevo whisky, ascolto jazz e mangio fichi.
When I ride the taxi I drink whis-

Italic 10/11

*Quando prendo il taxi bevo whis-
ky, ascolto jazz e mangio fichi.
When I ride the taxi I drink whis-*

Bold 10/11

**Quando prendo il taxi bevo whis-
ky, ascolto jazz e mangio fichi.
When I ride the taxi I drink whis-**

Regular

abcdefghijklmnopqrstuvwxyzABCDE
FGHIJKLMNOPQRSTUVWXYZ0123456789

Bold

abcdefghijklmnopqrstuvwxyzABCDE
FGHIJKLMNOPQRSTUVWXYZ0123456789

RXC
1996

A Gauge

abcdefghijklmnopqrstuvwxyzABCDEF
GHIJKLMNOPQRSTUVWXYZ0123456789

A Gauge Oblique

abcdefghijklmnopqrstuvwxyzABCDEF
GHIJKLMNOPQRSTUVWXYZ0123456789

B Gauge

abcdefghijklmnopqrstuvwxyzABCDEF
GHIJKLMNOPQRSTUVWXYZ0123456789

B Gauge Oblique

abcdefghijklmnopqrstuvwxyzABCDEF
GHIJKLMNOPQRSTUVWXYZ0123456789

C Gauge

abcdefghijklmnopqrstuvwxyzABCDE
FGHIJKLMNOPQRSTUVWXYZ0123456789

C Gauge Oblique

abcdefghijklmnopqrstuvwxyzABCDE
FGHIJKLMNOPQRSTUVWXYZ0123456789

A Gauge Smallcaps

AABBCCDDEEFFGGHHII
JJKKLLMMNNOOPPQQ
RRSSTTUUVVWWXXYYZZ

B Gauge Smallcaps

AABBCCDDEEFFGGHHII
JJKKLLMMNNOOPPQQ
RRSSTTUUVVWWXXYYZZ

C Gauge Smallcaps

AABBCCDDEEFFGGHHII
JJKKLLMMNNOOPPQQ
RRSSTTUUVVWWXXYYZZ

A Gauge Oblique Smallcaps

AABBCCDDEEFFGGHHII
JJKKLLMMNNOOPPQQ
RRSSTTUUVVWWXXYYZZ

B Gauge Oblique Smallcaps

AABBCCDDEEFFGGHHII
JJKKLLMMNNOOPPQQ
RRSSTTUUVVWWXXYYZZ

C Gauge Oblique Smallcaps

AABBCCDDEEFFGGHHII
JJKKLLMMNNOOPPQQ
RRSSTTUUVVWWXXYYZZ

Psy/Ops

Medium

abcdefghijklmnopqrstuvwxyzABCDEFG
HIJKLMNOPQRSTUVWXYZ0123456789

Medium Italic

abcdefghijklmnopqrstuvwxyzABCDEFG
HIJKLMNOPQRSTUVWXYZ0123456789

Bold

abcdefghijklmnopqrstuvwxyzABCDEFG
HIJKLMNOPQRSTUVWXYZ0123456789

Bold Italic

abcdefghijklmnopqrstuvwxyzABCDEFG
HIJKLMNOPQRSTUVWXYZ0123456789

Black

abcdefghijklmnopqrstuvwxyzABCDEFG
HIJKLMNOPQRSTUVWXYZ0123456789

Black Italic

abcdefghijklmnopqrstuvwxyzABCDEFG
HIJKLMNOPQRSTUVWXYZ0123456789

Medium 10/11

Quando prendo il taxi bevo whisky, ascolto jazz e mangio fichi. When I take the taxi I drink whisky, listen to jazz and

Medium Italic 10/11

Quando prendo il taxi bevo whisky, ascolto jazz e mangio fichi. When I take the taxi I drink whisky, listen to jazz and eat figs.

Bold 10/11

Quando prendo il taxi bevo whisky, ascolto jazz e mangio fichi. When I take the taxi I drink whisky, listen to jazz

Bold Italic 10/11

Quando prendo il taxi bevo whisky, ascolto jazz e mangio fichi. When I take the taxi I drink whisky, listen to jazz and

Black 10/11

Quando prendo il taxi bevo whisky, ascolto jazz e mangio fichi. When I take the taxi I drink whisky, listen to jazz

Black Italic 10/11

Quando prendo il taxi bevo whisky, ascolto jazz e mangio fichi. When I take the taxi I drink whisky, listen to jazz

Palaestra

abcdefghijklmnopqrstuvwxyzABCDEFG
HIJKLMNOPQRSTUVWXYZ0123456789

Palaestra Oblique

abcdefghijklmnopqrstuvwxyzABCDEFG
HIJKLMNOPQRSTUVWXYZ0123456789

Proconsular

abcdefghijklmnopqrstuvwxyzABCDEFG
HIJKLMNOPQRSTUVWXYZÆæÅåŒœ❧

Praetorian

ABCDEFGHIJKLMNOPQRSTUVWXYZABCDEFG
HIJKLMNOPQRSTUVWXYZÆæÅåŒœ❧

Regular

abcdefghijklmnopqrstuvwxyzABCDEF
GHIJKLMNOPQRSTUVWXYZ0123456789

Italic

abcdefghijklmnopqrstuvwxyzABCDEF
GHIJKLMNOPQRSTUVWXYZ0123456789

Bold

abcdefghijklmnopqrstuvwxyzABCDEF
GHIJKLMNOPQRSTUVWXYZ0123456789

Bold Italic

abcdefghijklmnopqrstuvwxyzABCDEF
GHIJKLMNOPQRSTUVWXYZ0123456789

Text – Light Adjusted

abcdefghijklmnopqrstuvwxyzABCDEFG
HIJKLMNOPQRSTUVWXYZ0123456789

Text – Medium

abcdefghijklmnopqrstuvwxyzABCDEFG
HIJKLMNOPQRSTUVWXYZ0123456789

Text – Dark Adjusted

abcdefghijklmnopqrstuvwxyzABCDEFG
HIJKLMNOPQRSTUVWXYZ0123456789

Light Adjusted 10/11

Philomela is an original Renaissance-style text face intended to recapture the 'lead feeling' which has been lost in most digital revivals

Medium 10/11

(where the added crispness of current imaging and printing technologies has not been compensated for). The family has been designed

Dark Adjusted 10/11

in three micro-weights, allowing for improved control of image density, and thus readability, on different media types and at dif-

Italic – Light Adjusted

abcdefghijklmnopqrstuvwxyzABCDEFG
HIJKLMNOPQRSTUVWXYZ0123456789

Italic – Medium

abcdefghijklmnopqrstuvwxyzABCDEFG
HIJKLMNOPQRSTUVWXYZ0123456789

Italic – Dark Adjusted

abcdefghijklmnopqrstuvwxyzABCDEFG
HIJKLMNOPQRSTUVWXYZ0123456789

Light Adjusted 10/11

...ferent point sizes. In this way, Philomela further emulates the cold type & letterpress paradigm, whereby typefaces were cut differently according to size (for example, more

Medium 10/11

open below 12 point), and where the impression could be adjusted according to substrate requirements and taste. Each micro-weight includes roman (text), italic,

Dark Adjusted 10/11

and smallcap styles. A delicate titling face, and engraved initials are also part of the system. As per the typefaces of its era, a bold weight does not exist; how-

1-888-PSY-FONE

Lars Bergquist
2001

Smallcaps – Light Adjusted

ABCDEFGHIJKLMNOPQRSTUVWXYZABCDE
FGHIJKLMNOPQRSTUVWXYZ0123456789

Smallcaps – Medium

ABCDEFGHIJKLMNOPQRSTUVWXYZABCDE
FGHIJKLMNOPQRSTUVWXYZ0123456789

Smallcaps – Dark Adjusted

ABCDEFGHIJKLMNOPQRSTUVWXYZABCDE
FGHIJKLMNOPQRSTUVWXYZ0123456789

Light Adjusted 10/11

...EVER, IF NEED BE, THE INTERVAL BETWEEN THE LIGHT AND DARK FONTS PROVIDES ENOUGH CONTRAST TO FULFILL THIS. ¶

Medium 10/11

PHILOMELA IS AN ORIGINAL RENAISSANCE-STYLE TEXT FACE INTENDED TO RECAPTURE THE 'LEAD FEELING' WHICH HAS

Dark Adjusted 10/11

BEEN LOST IN MOST DIGITAL REVIVALS (WHERE THE ADDED CRISPNESS OF CURRENT IMAGING AND PRINTING TECHNOL-

Titling

abcdefghijklmnopqrstuvwxyzABCDEFG
HIJKLMNOPQRSTUVWXYZ0123456789

Initials

AABBCCDDEEFFG
GHHIIJJKKLLMMN
NOOPPQQRRSSTT
UUVVWWXXYYZZ

Normal

abcdefghijklmnopqrstuvwxyzABCDEFG
HIJKLMNOPQRSTUVWXYZ0123456789

Italic

abcdefghijklmnopqrstuvwxyzABCDEFG
HIJKLMNOPQRSTUVWXYZ0123456789

Bold

abcdefghijklmnopqrstuvwxyzABCDEFG
HIJKLMNOPQRSTUVWXYZ0123456789

Bold Italic

abcdefghijklmnopqrstuvwxyzABCDEFG
HIJKLMNOPQRSTUVWXYZ0123456789

Black

abcdefghijklmnopqrstuvwxyzABCDEF
GHIJKLMNOPQRSTUVWXYZ0123456789

Black Italic

abcdefghijklmnopqrstuvwxyzABCDEF
GHIJKLMNOPQRSTUVWXYZ0123456789

Normal 10/11

Quando prendo il taxi bevo whisky, ascolto jazz e mangio fichi. When I take the taxi I drink whisky, listen to jazz

Italic 10/11

Quando prendo il taxi bevo whisky, ascolto jazz e mangio fichi. When I take the taxi I drink whisky, listen to jazz

Bold 10/11

Quando prendo il taxi bevo whisky, ascolto jazz e mangio fichi. When I take the taxi I drink whisky, listen to jazz

Bold Italic 10/11

Quando prendo il taxi bevo whisky, ascolto jazz e mangio fichi. When I take the taxi I drink whisky, listen to jazz

Heavy 10/11

Quando prendo il taxi bevo whisky, ascolto jazz e mangio fichi. When I take the taxi I drink whisky, listen to jazz

Heavy Italic 10/11

Quando prendo il taxi bevo whisky, ascolto jazz e mangio fichi. When I take the taxi I drink whisky, listen to jazz

Regular

abcdefghijklmnopqrstuvwxyzABCDEFG
HIJKLMNOPQRSTUVWXYZ0123456789

Italic

abcdefghijklmnopqrstuvwxyzABCDEFG
HIJKLMNOPQRSTUVWXYZ0123456789

Bold

abcdefghijklmnopqrstuvwxyzABCDEFG
HIJKLMNOPQRSTUVWXYZ0123456789

Bold Italic

abcdefghijklmnopqrstuvwxyzABCDEFG
HIJKLMNOPQRSTUVWXYZ0123456789

SCOSF (Smallcaps & Oldstyle Figures)

ABCDEFGHIJKLMNOPQRSTUVWXYZABCDE
FGHIJKLMNOPQRSTUVWXYZ0123456789

Regular & Italic 10/11

Quando prendo il taxi bevo whisky, ascolto jazz e mangio fichi.
When I take the taxi I drink whisky, listen to jazz and eat figs. Quan-

Bold & Bold Italic 10/11

Quando prendo il taxi bevo whisky, ascolto jazz e mangio
fichi. When I take the taxi I drink whisky, listen to jazz and eat

SCOSF 10/11

QUANDO PRENDO IL TAXI BEVO WHISKY, ASCOLTO JAZZ E MANGIO FICHI. WHEN I TAKE THE TAXI I DRINK WHISKY, LISTEN TO JAZZ

Normal

ABCDEFGHIJKLMNOPQRSTUVWXYZABCDEFG
HIJKLMNOPQRSTUVWXYZ0123456789

Antiguo

ABCDEFGHIJKLMNOPQRSTUVWXYZABCDEFG
HIJKLMNOPQRSTUVWXYZ0123456789

A Gauge

abcdefghijklmnopqrstuvwxyzABCDEFG
HIJKLMNOPQRSTUVWXYZ0123456789

B Gauge

abcdefghijklmnopqrstuvwxyzABCDEFG
HIJKLMNOPQRSTUVWXYZ0123456789

C Gauge

abcdefghijklmnopqrstuvwxyzABCDEFG
HIJKLMNOPQRSTUVWXYZ0123456789

D Gauge

abcdefghijklmnopqrstuvwxyzABCDEFG
HIJKLMNOPQRSTUVWXYZ0123456789

A Gauge Italic

abcdefghijklmABCDEFGHIJKLM01234

B Gauge Italic

abcdefghijklmABCDEFGHIJKLM01234

C Gauge Italic

abcdefghijklmABCDEFGHIJKLM01234

D Gauge Italic

abcdefghijklmABCDEFGHIJKLM01234

11 pt   Quando prendo il taxi bevo whisky, ascolto jazz ... *Quando prendo il taxi bevo whisky, ascolto jazz*

Quando prendo il taxi bevo whisky, ascolto jazz ... *Quando prendo il taxi bevo whisky, ascolto jazz*

Quando prendo il taxi bevo whisky, ascolto jazz ... *Quando prendo il taxi bevo whisky, ascolto jazz*

Quando prendo il taxi bevo whisky, ascolto jazz ... ***Quando prendo il taxi bevo whisky, ascolto jazz***

abcdefghijklmnopqrstuvwxyzABCDEFG
HIJKLMNOPQRSTUVWXYZ0123456789

B Gauge

abcdefghijklmnopqrstuvwxyzABCDEFG
HIJKLMNOPQRSTUVWXYZ0123456789

C Gauge

abcdefghijklmnopqrstuvwxyzABCDEFG
HIJKLMNOPQRSTUVWXYZ0123456789

D Gauge

abcdefghijklmnopqrstuvwxyzABCDEFG
HIJKLMNOPQRSTUVWXYZ0123456789

A Gauge Oblique

abcdefghijklmABCDEFGHIJKLMO1234

B Gauge Oblique

abcdefghijklmABCDEFGHIJKLMO1234

C Gauge Oblique

abcdefghijklmABCDEFGHIJKLMO1234

D Gauge Oblique

abcdefghijklmABCDEFGHIJKLMO1234

Psy/Ops

Quando prendo il taxi bevo whisky, ascolto jazz ... *Quando prendo il taxi bevo whisky, ascolto jazz* 11 pt

Quando prendo il taxi bevo whisky, ascolto jazz ... *Quando prendo il taxi bevo whisky, ascolto jazz*

Quando prendo il taxi bevo whisky, ascolto jazz ... *Quando prendo il taxi bevo whisky, ascolto jazz*

Quando prendo il taxi bevo whisky, ascolto jazz ... *Quando prendo il taxi bevo whisky, ascolto jazz*

RXC
2001

Based on the namesake design of Czech
artist Vojtech Preissig.

Regular

abcdefghijklmnopqrstuvwxyzABCDEFGH
IJKLMNOPQRSTUVWXYZ0123456789&

Italic

*abcdefghijklmnopqrstuvwxyzABCDEFGH
IJKLMNOPQRSTUVWXYZ0123456789&*

Bold

**abcdefghijklmnopqrstuvwxyzABCDEFGH
IJKLMNOPQRSTUVWXYZ0123456789&**

Bold Italic

***abcdefghijklmnopqrstuvwxyzABCDEFGH
IJKLMNOPQRSTUVWXYZ0123456789&***

Smallcaps

ABCDEFGHJKLMNOPQRSTUVWXYZABCDE
FGHJKLMNOPQRSTUVWXYZ0123456789

Salmiac Mono

Gábor Kóthay
2002

Regular

abcdefghijklmnopqrstuvwxyzABCDEF
GHIJKLMNOPQRSTUVWXYZ0123456789

Italic

*abcdefghijklmnopqrstuvwxyzABCDEF
GHIJKLMNOPQRSTUVWXYZ0123456789*

Bold & Bold Italic

ABCabcdefghijklmnopqrstuvwxyz1234
ABCabcdefghijklmnopqrstuvwxyz1234

Regular

abcdefghijklmnopqrstuvwxyzABCDEFG
HIJKLMNOPQRSTUVWXYZ0123456789

Italic

abcdefghijklmnopqrstuvwxyzABCDEFG
HIJKLMNOPQRSTUVWXYZ0123456789

Medium

abcdefghijklmnopqrstuvwxyzABCDEFG
HIJKLMNOPQRSTUVWXYZ0123456789

Medium Italic

abcdefghijklmnopqrstuvwxyzABCDEFG
HIJKLMNOPQRSTUVWXYZ0123456789

Bold

abcdefghijklmnopqrstuvwxyzABCDEFG
HIJKLMNOPQRSTUVWXYZ0123456789

Bold Italic

abcdefghijklmnopqrstuvwxyzABCDEFG
HIJKLMNOPQRSTUVWXYZ0123456789

Black

abcdefghijklmnopqrstuvwxyzABCDEFG
HIJKLMNOPQRSTUVWXYZ0123456789

Black Italic

abcdefghijklmnopqrstuvwxyzABCDEFG
HIJKLMNOPQRSTUVWXYZ0123456789

Psy/Ops

Regular

abcdefghijklmnopqrstuvwxyzABCDEFG
HIJKLMNOPQRSTUVWXYZ0123456789

Italic

*abcdefghijklmnopqrstuvwxyzABCDEFG
HIJKLMNOPQRSTUVWXYZ0123456789*

Medium

abcdefghijklmnopqrstuvwxyzABCDEFG
HIJKLMNOPQRSTUVWXYZ0123456789

Medium Italic

*abcdefghijklmnopqrstuvwxyzABCDEFG
HIJKLMNOPQRSTUVWXYZ0123456789*

Bold

**abcdefghijklmnopqrstuvwxyzABCDEFG
HIJKLMNOPQRSTUVWXYZ0123456789**

Bold Italic

***abcdefghijklmnopqrstuvwxyzABCDEFG
HIJKLMNOPQRSTUVWXYZ0123456789***

SCOSF

ABCDEFGHIJKLMNOPQRSTUVWXYZABCDEFG
HIJKLMNOPQRSTUVWXYZ0123456789

Regular & Italic 11/12

Quando prendo il taxi bevo whisky, ascolto jazz e mangio fichi. When

I take the taxi I drink whisky, listen to jazz and eat figs. Quando prendo

Medium & Medium Italic 11/12

Quando prendo il taxi bevo whisky, ascolto jazz e mangio fichi. When

I take the taxi I drink whisky, listen to jazz and eat figs. Quando pren-

Bold & Bold Italic 11/12

Quando prendo il taxi bevo whisky, ascolto jazz e mangio fichi. When

I take the taxi I drink whisky, listen to jazz and eat figs. Quando pren-

Tomi Haaparanta
2000

Regular

abcdefghijklmnopqrstuvwxyzABCDEFG
HIJKLMNOPQRSTUVWXYZ0123456789

Italic

abcdefghijklmnopqrstuvwxyzABCDEFG
HIJKLMNOPQRSTUVWXYZ0123456789

Demi

abcdefghijklmnopqrstuvwxyzABCDEFG
HIJKLMNOPQRSTUVWXYZ0123456789

Demi Italic

abcdefghijklmnopqrstuvwxyzABCDEFG
HIJKLMNOPQRSTUVWXYZ0123456789

Bold

abcdefghijklmnopqrstuvwxyzABCDEFG
HIJKLMNOPQRSTUVWXYZ0123456789

Bold Italic

abcdefghijklmnopqrstuvwxyzABCDEFG
HIJKLMNOPQRSTUVWXYZ0123456789

SCOSF

ABCDEFGHIJKLMNOPQRSTUVWXYZABCDEFG
HIJKLMNOPQRSTUVWXYZ0123456789

Regular & Italic 10/11

Quando prendo il taxi bevo whisky, ascolto jazz e mangio fichi.

When I take the taxi I drink whisky,
listen to jazz and eat fias. Quando

Demi & Demi Italic 10/11

Quando prendo il taxi bevo whisky, ascolto jazz e mangio fichi.

When I take the taxi I drink whis-
ky. listen to jazz and eat fias.

Bold & Bold Italic 10/11

Quando prendo il taxi bevo whis-
ky, ascolto jazz e mangio fichi.

When I take the taxi I drink whis-
ky. listen to jazz and eat fias.

Psy/Ops

A Gauge

abcdefghijklmnopqrstuvwxyzABCDE
FGHIJKLMNOPQRSTUVWXYZ0123456789

B Gauge

abcdefghijklmABCDEFGHIJKLM12345

C Gauge

abcdefghijklmABCDEFGHIJKLM12345

D Gauge

abcdefghijklmABCDEFGHIJKLM12345

E Gauge

abcdefghijklmABCDEFGHIJKLM12345

F Gauge

abcdefghijklmABCDEFGHIJKLM12345

G Gauge

abcdefghijklmABCDEFGHIJKLM12345

A Gauge Italic

abcdefghijklmnopqrstuvwxyzABCDE
FGHIJKLMNOPQRSTUVWXYZ0123456789

B Gauge Italic

abcdefghijklmABCDEFGHIJKLM12345

C Gauge Italic

abcdefghijklmABCDEFGHIJKLM12345

D Gauge Italic

abcdefghijklmABCDEFGHIJKLM12345

E Gauge Italic

abcdefghijklmABCDEFGHIJKLM12345

F Gauge Italic

abcdefghijklmABCDEFGHIJKLM12345

G Gauge Italic

abcdefghijklmABCDEFGHIJKLM12345

Regular

A A B C D E F G H I J K L M N O P Q R
S T U V W X Y Z 0 1 2 3 4 5 6 7 8 9

Regular Alternates

A A B C D E F G H I J K L M N O P Q R
S T U V W X Y Z 0 1 2 3 4 5 6 7 8 9

Gilded

A A B C D E F G H I J K L M N O P Q R
S T U V W X Y Z 0 1 2 3 4 5 6 7 8 9

Gilded Alternates

A A B C D E F G H I J K L M N O P Q R
S T U V W X Y Z 0 1 2 3 4 5 6 7 8 9

AABBCCDDEEFFGGHH
JJKKLLMMNNOOPPQQRR
SSTTUUVVWWXXYYZZ

Regular

a b c d e f g h i j k l m n o p q r s t u v w x y z A B C D E F
G H I J K L M N O P Q R S T U V W X Y Z 0 1 2 3 4 5 6 7 8 9

Irregular

a b c d e f g h i j k l m n o p q r s t u v w x y z A B C D E F
G H I J K L M N O P Q R S T U V W X Y Z 0 1 2 3 4 5 6 7 8 9

Psy/Ops

For pricing information, please visit www.synfonts.com

SynFonts.com offers one of the most advanced on-line font viewers available today, giving you the ability to Preview your text, Compare colors, Zoom in for terrific detail and even print out type samples to help you with your comps or roughs

And when you are finished exploring, on-line ordering is available with immediate purchase and downloading..

Toll free phone orders - 1 (888) 842 3065

Emergency Order Hotline - (402) 968 0147

Email: don@synfonts.com
www.synfonts.com

2216 Cedar Forks Trace • Marietta, GA 30062

Badger Fatboy - Regular

abcdefghijklmnop
qrstuvwxyzABCDEFG
HIJKLMNOPQRSTUV
WXYZ1234567890!¢@
#$%^&*()[]{};:"",.<>/?

Badger Fatboy - Regular

"Sometimes a scream
is better than a thesis."
- Ralph Waldo Emerson

Badger Fatboy - Could this be Thin?

abcdefghijklmnopqrstuv
wxyzABCDEFGHIJKLMNO
PQRSTUVWXYZ12345678
90!¢@#$%^&*()[]{};:"",.<>/?

Badger Fatboy - Italic

abcdefghijklmnopqrstuv
wxyzABCDEFGHIJKLMNO
PQRSTUVWXYZ12345678
90!¢@#$%^&*()[]{};:"",.<>/?

Badger Fatboy - Outline

abcdefghijklmnopqrstuv
wxyzABCDEFGHIJKLMNO
PQRSTUVWXYZ12345678
90!¢@#$%^&*()[]{};:"",.<>/?

SynFonts

Don Synstelien

Cheap and Easy - Regular

abcdefghijklmnopqrstuvwxyz**ABCD**
EFGHIJKLMNOPQRSTUVWXYZ1
234567890!@#$%^&*(){ };:'",.<>/?

Cheap and Easy - Cheap, Easy and Hollow

abcdefghijklmnopqrstuvwxy
zABCDEFGHIJKLMNOPQ
RSTUVWXYZ1234567890!
@#$%^&*(){ };:'",.<>/?

Cheap and Easy - Cheap, Easy and Fat

abcdefghijklmnopqrstuvwxy
zABCDEFGHIJKLMNOPQ
RSTUVWXYZ1234567890!
@#$%^&*(){ };:'",.<>/?

"The gods too are fond of a joke."
- Aristotle

Chris MacGregor

Crystopian - Light

abcdefghijklmnopqrstu
vwxyzABCDEFGHIJKLM
NOPQRSTUVWXYZ12345
67890!@#$%^&*(){ };:'",.<>/?

Crystopian - Light

abcdefghijkl
mnopqrstuv
wxyzABCDEF
GHIJKLMNOP
QRSTUVWXYZ
1234567890!@
#$%^&*(){ };:'",.<>/?

Crystopian - Regular

abcdefghijkl
mnopqrstuv
wxyzABCDEF
GHIJKLMNOPQ
RSTUVWXYZ1
234567890!@#
$%^&*(){ };:'",.<>/?

Crystopian - Bold

abcdefghijkl
mnopqrstuv
wxyzABCDEF
GHIJKLMNOPQ
RSTUVWXYZ1
234567890!@#
$%^&*(){ };:'",.<>/?

Chris MacGregor

abcdefghijklmnopqrstu
vwxyzABCDEFGHIJKLM
NOPQRSTUVWXYZ123456
7890!@#$?. ^¢*()[]{}::"".,<>/?

abcdefghijklmnopqrstu
vwxyzABCDEFGHIJKLMN
OPQRSTUVWXYZ123456?
890!@#$?. ^¢*()[]{}::"".,<>/?

Chris MacGregor

abcdefghijklmnopqrst
vwxyzABCDEFGHIJKLM
NOPQRSTUVWXYZ123456
7890!@#$?. ^¢*()[]{}::"".,<>/?

abcdefghijklmnopqrst
vwxyzABCDEFGHIJKLM
NOPQRSTUVWXYZ123456
7890!@#$?. ^¢*()[]{}::"".,<>/?

Chris MacGregor

Exuberance is beauty.
-William Blake

abcdefghijklmnopqrstu
vwxyzABCDEFGHIJKLMN
OPQRSTUVWXYZ12345678
90!@#$?. ^¢*()[]{}::"".,<>/?

abcdefghijklmnopqrst
vwxyzABCDEFGHIJKLM
NOPQRSTUVWXYZ123456
7890!@#$?. ^¢*()[]{}::"".,<>/?

abcdefghijklmn
rstuvwxyzABCDEFG
HIJKLMNOPQRSTUV
WXYZ12345678 90!@#$
?. ^¢*()[]{}::"".,<>/?

abcdefghijklmn
rstuvwxyzABCDEFG
HIJKLMNOPQRSTUV
WXYZ12345678 90!@#$
?. ^¢*()[]{}::"".,<>/?

SynFonts

Emulate Serif - Regular

abcdefghijklmnopqrstuvwxyzABCDEFGHIJKLMNOPQ
RSTUVWXYZ 1234567890!@№$%^&*()[]{};:'"",.<>/?

Emulate Serif - Bold

abcdefghijklmnopqrstuvwxyzABCDEFGHIJKLMNOPQ
RSTUVWXYZ 1234567890!@№$%^&*()[]{};:'"",.<>/?

Emulate Serif - Italic

abcdefghijklmnopqrstuvwxyzABCDEFGHIJKLMNOPQ
RSTUVWXYZ 1234567890!@№$%^&*()[]{};:'"",.<>/?

Emulate Serif - Bold Italic

abcdefghijklmnopqrstuvwxyzABCDEFGHIJKLMNOPQ
RSTUVWXYZ 1234567890!@№$%^&*()[]{};:'"",.<>/?

Emulate Serif

"Do not believe in anything simply because you have heard it. Do not believe in anything simply because it is spoken -and rumored by many. Do not believe in anything simply because it is found written in your religious books. Do not believe in anything merely on the authority of your teachers and elders. Do not believe in traditions because they have been handed down for many generations.

But after observation and analysis, when you find that anything agrees with reason and is conducive to the good and benefit of one and all, then accept it and live up to it."

-Buddha

Epaulet

abcdefghijklmnopqrstuvwxyzABCDEFG
HIJKLMNOPQRSTUVWXYZ123
4567890! @#$% ^&*()[]{};:'"",.<>/?

abcdefghijklmnopqrstuvwxyzAB
CDEFGHIJKLMNOPQRSTUVWXYZ12
34567890!@#$%^&*()[]{};:'",.<>/?

"Good people do not need laws to tell them to
act responsibly, while bad people will find a
way around the laws."

— Plato

Guilty

abcdefghijklmnopqrs
tuvwxyzABCDEFGHIJ
KLMNOPQRSTUVWXY
Z1234567890!@#$%^
&*()[]{}:;'",. <>/?

SynFonts

Chris MacGregor

Hiro

abcdefghijklmn
opqrstuuwxyzA
BCDEFGHIJKLMN
OPQRSTUUWXYZ
1234561890!@*$
%¢*(){}[]::"".<>/?

Hiro-Italic

abcdefghijklmn
opqrstuuwxyzA
BCDEFGHIJKLMN
OPQRSTUUWXYZ
1234561890!@*$
%¢*(){}[]::"".<>/?

Hiro-Outline

abcdefghijklmn
opqrstuuwxyzA
BCDEFGHIJKLMN
OPQRSTUUWXYZ
1234561890!@*$
%¢*(){}[]::"".<>/?

Future

Hiro-Outline-Italic

abcdefghijklmn
opqrstuuwxyzA
BCDEFGHIJKLMN
OPQRSTUUWXYZ
1234561890!@*$
%¢*(){}[]::"".<>/?

Hiro

I love deadlines.
I like the whooshing sound
they make as they fly by.
- Douglas Adams

Hiro Sharp

abcdefghijklmn
opqrstuuwxyzAB
CDEFGHIJKLMNO
PQRSTUUWXYZ
1234561890!@*$
%¢*(){}[]::"".<>/?

Hiro Sharp - Outline

abcdefghijklmno
pqrstuuwxyzAB
CDEFGHIJKLMNO
PQRSTUUWXYZ
1234561890!@*$
%¢*(){}[]::"".<>/?

1-888-842-3065

abcdefghijklmnopqrstuvwxyzABCDEFGHIJKLMNOPQR
STUVWXYZ1234567890!@#$%^&*()[]{};:'",.<>/?

abcdefghijklmnopqrstuvwxyzABCDEFGHIJKLMNOPQR
STUVWXYZ1234567890!@#$%^&*()[]{};:'",.<>/?

abcdefghijklmnopqrstuvwxyzABCDEFGHIJKLMNOPQR
STUVWXYZ1234567890!@#$%^&*()[]{};:'",.<>/?

abcdefghijklmnopqrstuvwxyzABCDEFGHIJKLMNOPQR
STUVWXYZ1234567890!@#$%^&*()[]{};:'",.<>/?

Don Synstelien

12:00   12:00   12:00

LEaD Lights - Rgular

"This is our world now... the world of the electron and the switch,
the beauty of the baud. We make use of a service already existing
without paying for what could be dirt-cheap if it wasn't run by
profiteering gluttons, and you call us criminals. We explore... and
you call us criminals. We seek after knowledge... and you call us
criminals. We exist without skin colour, without nationality, without
religious bias... and you call us criminals. You build atomic bombs,
you wage wars, you murder, cheat, and lie to us and try to make us
believe it's for our own good, yet we're the criminals.

"Yes, I am a criminal. My crime is that of curiosity. My crime is
that of judging people by what they say and think, not what they
look like.

"My crime is that of outsmarting you, something that you will never
forgive me for. I am a hacker, and this is my manifesto. You may
stop this individual, but you can't stop us all... after all, we're
all alike."

                    The Mentor, "The Conscience of a Hacker"

Liquid Sex - Regular

abcdefghijklmnopqrstuvwxyz
ABCDEFGHIJKLMNOPQRSTUVWXYZ
1234567890!@#$Z^&‡[][]{}::'"..‹›/?

Liquid Sex - Italic

abcedfg

Liquid Sex - Italic

abcdefghi
jklmnopqr
stuvwxyz
ABCDEFGHI
JKLMNOPQ
RSTUVWXY
Z12345678
90!@#$Z^&‡[
][]{}::'"..‹›/?

Liquid Sex - Hard Edged and Empty

abcdefghi
jklmnopqr
stuvwxyz
ABCDEFGHI
JKLMNOPQ
RSTUVWXY
Z12345678
90!@#$Z^&‡[
][]{}::'"..‹›/?

Liquid Sex - Outline

abcdefghi
jklmnopqr
stuvwxyz
ABCDEFGHI
JKLMNOPQ
RSTUVWXY
Z12345678
90!@#$Z^&‡[
][]{}::'"..‹›/?

Liquid Sex - Regular

"More than kisses,
letters mingle souls."
-John Donne

abcdefghij
klmnopqrs
tuvwxyz
ABCDEF
GHIJKL
M N O P
QRSTU
VWXYZ

ogon poetry is of course the third worst in the universe. The second worst is that of the Azgoths of Kria. During a recitation by their poet master Grunthos the Flatulent of his poem Ode to a small lump of green putty I found in my armpit one midsummer morning four of his audience died of internal haemorrhaging, and the president of the Mid Galactic Arts Nobbling Council survived only by gnawing one of his own legs off. Grunthos is reported to have been disappointed by the poem s reception, and was about to embark on a reading of his twelve book epic My Favorite Bathtime Gargles when his own major intestine, in a desperate attempt to save life and civilisation, leapt straight up through his throat and throttled his brain. The very worst poetry of all perished along with its creator Paula Nancy Millstone Jennings of Greenbridge, Essex, England in the destruction of the planet Earth.

Douglas Adams, The Hitchhiker s Guide to the Galaxy

ABCDEFGHIJKLMNOP
QRSTUVWXYZ123456
7890!@#$%^&*()/?

ABCDEFGHIJKLMNOP
QRSTUVWXYZ12345
67890!@#$%^&*()/?

PEZ

SynFonts

www.synfonts.com

275

NudE - Regular

abcdefghijklmnopqrst uvwxyzABCDEFGHIJ KLMNOPQRSTUVW XYZ1234567890!@#$ %^&*()[]{};:'",.<>/?

NudE - Regular

Twenty years from now you will be more disappointed by the things you didn't do than by the ones you did do. So throw off the bowlines. Sail away from the safe harbour. Catch the trade winds in your sails.

Explore. Dream. Discover.

-Mark Twain

NudE - Italic

abcdefghijklmnopqrstuvwxyzABCDEFGHIJKLMNOPQR STUVWXYZ1234567890!@#$%^&()[]{};:'",.<>/?*

NudE - Bold

abcdefghijklmnopqrstuvwxyzABCDEFGHIJKLMNOPQR STUVWXYZ1234567890!@#$%^&*()[]{};:'",.<>/?

NudE - Bold Italic

abcdefghijklmnopqrstuvwxyzABCDEFGHIJKLMNOPQR STUVWXYZ1234567890!@#$%^&*()[]{};:'",.<>/?

NudE - Thin

abcdefghijklmnopqrstuvwxyzABCDEFGHIJKLMNOPQR STUVWXYZ1234567890!@#$%^&*()[]{};:'",.<>/?

NudE - Thin Italic

abcdefghijklmnopqrstuvwxyzABCDEFGHIJKLMNOPQR STUVWXYZ1234567890!@#$%^&()[]{};:'",.<>/?*

1-888-842-3065

abcdefghijklmnopqrstuvwxyzABCD
EFGHIJKLMNOPQRSTUVWXYZ1
234567890!@#$%^&*()[]{};:'",.<>/?

Work to become, not to acquire.

-Elbert Hubbard

Omaha - Regular

abcdefghijklmnopqrstuv
wxyzABCDEFGHIJKLMNO
PQRSTUVWXYZ12345678
90!@#$%^&*()[]{};:'",.<>/?

Omaha - Italic

abcdefghijklmnopqrstuvw
xyzABCDEFGHIJKLMNOPQ
RSTUVWXYZ1234567890!@
#$%^&*()[]{};:'",.<>/?

Omaha - Bold

abcdefghijklmnopqrstuv
wxyzABCDEFGHIJKLMNO
PQRSTUVWXYZ12345678
90!@#$%^&*()[]{};:'",.<>/?

Omaha - Bold Italic

abcdefghijklmnopqrstuvw
xyzABCDEFGHIJKLMNOPQ
RSTUVWXYZ1234567890!@
#$%^&*()[]{};:'",.<>/?

Omaha - Thin

abcdefghijklmnopqrstuv
wxyzABCDEFGHIJKLMNO
PQRSTUVWXYZ12345678
90!@#$%^&*()[]{};:'",.<>/?

Omaha - Thin Italic

abcdefghijklmnopqrstuvw
xyzABCDEFGHIJKLMNOPQ
RSTUVWXYZ1234567890!@
#$%^&*()[]{};:'",.<>/?

Regeneration X
Don Synstelien

Regeneration X - Regular

abcdefghijklmnopqrstuvwxyzABCDEFGHIJKLMNOPQRSTUVW
XYZ1234567890!@#$%&*()[];:'",.<>/?

Regeneration X - Bold

**abcdefghijklmnopqrstuvwxyzABCDEFGHIJKLMNOPQRSTUVW
XYZ1234567890!@#$%&*()[];:'",.<>/?**

Ridicule
Don Synstelien

Ridicule

Ridicule

SkannerZ
Don Synstelien

SkannerZ - Regular

SkannerZ - Bold

SkannerZ - Blackout

1-888-842-3065

Sprokett

abcdefghi jklmnopqrstuvwxyzA
BCDEFGHIJKLMNOPQRSTUVWXYZ12
34567890!@#$Z^9‡[]{}[]{}::'"..‹›/?

Sprokett - Italic

abcdefghi jklmnopqrstuvwxyzABCDEFGHIJKLMNO
PQRSTUVWXYZ1234567890!@#$Z^9‡[]{}[]::'"..‹›/?

Sprokett - Outerkog

abcdefghi jklmnopqrstuvwxyzABCDEFGHIJKLMNO
PQRSTUVWXYZ1234567890!@#$Z^9‡[]{}[]::'"..‹›/?

Sprokett - Outerkog Italic

abcdefghi jklmnopqrstuvwxyzABCDEFGHIJKLMNO
PQRSTUVWXYZ1234567890!@#$Z^9‡[]{}[]::'"..‹›/?

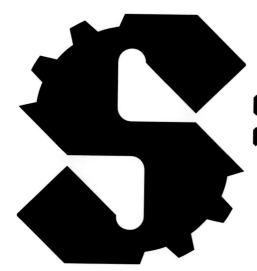

Sprokett - Outerkog

Criticize a friend in private,
praise him in public.

- Leonardo da Vinci

Trumen - Outline Black & Trumen - Outline

Trumen - Regular

abcdefghijklmn
opqrstuvwxyz
ABCDEFGHIJKL
MNOPQRSTUVW
XYZ1234567890
!@#$%¢*[]{}:;"",.<>/?

Trumen - Italic

abcdefghijklmn
opqrstuvwxyz
ABCDEFGHIJKL
MNOPQRSTUVW
XYZ1234567890
!@#$%¢*[]{}:;"",.<>/?

Trumen - Outline

abcdefghijklmn
opqrstuvwxyz
ABCDEFGHIJKL
MNOPQRSTUVW
XYZ1234567890
!@#$%¢*[]{}:;"",.<>/?

Trumen - Outline Italic

abcdefghijklmn
opqrstuvwxyz
ABCDEFGHIJKL
MNOPQRSTUVW
XYZ1234567890
!@#$%¢*[]{}:;"",.<>/?

Trumen - Outline Black

abcdefghijklmn
opqrstuvwxyz
ABCDEFGHIJKL
MNOPQRSTUVW
XYZ1234567890!
@#$%¢*[]{}:;"",.<>/?

Trumen - Outline Black Italic

abcdefghijklmn
opqrstuvwxyz
ABCDEFGHIJKL
MNOPQRSTUVW
XYZ1234567890
!@#$%¢*[]{}:;"",.<>/?

abcdefghijklmnopqrstuvwxyzABCDE
FGHIJKLMNOPQRSTUVWXYZ12345
67890!@#$%^`¢*()[]{};:'",.<>/?

No Printer should say "I am an artist therefore I am not to be dictated to, I will create my own letter forms for, in this humble job, individualism is not very helpful. It is no longer possible, as it was in the infancy of the craft, to persuade society into the acceptance of strongly marked and highly individualistic types – because literate society is so much greater in mass and correspondingly slow in movement. The good type designer knows that, for a new fount to be successful, it has to be so good that only a few recognize its novelty.

-Stanley Morrison

®

Test Pilot Collective

Test Pilot Collective
1. Formed by collecting; assembled or accumulated into a whole. 2. Of, pertaining to, characteristic of, or group made by a number of individuals acting as a design group: a collective decision.

Typefaces
1. a. The surface of a body of type that makes the impression. b. The impression itself. 2. The size or style of the letter or character on the type. 3. The full range of type of the same design. 4. Available in MAC and PC format.

News
1. Recent events and happenings, esp. those that are unusual or notable. 2. Information about recent events of general interest, esp. as reported by the Test Pilot Collective web site. 3. Newsworthy material.

Firstpage Archive
1. a. An organized body of records pertaining to the design methods of the Test Pilot Collective. b. A place in which such records are preserved. 2. A repository of evidence or information: "the archives of the TPC." 3. Updated daily.

Contact
1. The coming together or touching of two objects, surfaces or entities. 2. The state of being in communication: "in contact with the Test Pilot Collective." 3. A person who might be of use; connection. 4. "Elect."

Test Pilot Collective
182 Howard Street, #340
San Francisco, CA 94105 USA

1-415-218-4791

http://www.testpilotcollective.com
email:info@testpilotcollective.com

Test Pilot Collective is owned, operated, and designed by Joe Kral and Matt Desmond.

AaBbCcDdEeFfGgHhIiJjKkLlMmNn
OoPpQqRrSsTtUuVvWwXxYyZz012

AaBbCcDdEeFf
GgHhIiJjKkLlM
mNnOoPpQqRrSs

AaBbCcDdEeFf
GgHhIiJjKkLlM
mNnOoPpQqRrSs

AaBbCcDdEeFf
GgHhIiJjKkLlM
mNnOoPpQqRrSs

6x7oct

Mike Cina
1998

Styles included: Extra Light, Extra Light Alternate, Light, Light Alternate, Regular, Alternate, Bold, Bold Alternate, Extra Bold, Extra Bold Alternate, Black, Black Alternate.

aabbccddeeffgghhiijjkkllm
mnnooppqqrrssttuuvvwwxx

aabbccddeef
fgghhiijjkkl
lmmnnooppq

aabbccddeef
fgghhiijjkkl
lmmnnooppq

aabbccddeef
fgghhiijjkkl
lmmnnooppq

Amber

Matt Desmond
2000

Styles included: Round, Angled, Square.

AaBbCcDdEeFfGgHhIiJjKkLlMmNnOo
PpQqRrSsTtUuVvWwXxYyZz0123456

AaBbCcDdEeFfG
gHhIiJjKkLlMm
NnOoPpQqRrSsT

AaBbCcDdEeFfG
gHhIiJjKkLlMm
NnOoPpQqRrSsT

AaBbCcDdEeFfG
gHhIiJjKkLlMm
NnOoPpQqRrSsT

Americangothic

Matt Desmond
1998

Styles included: Regular, Oblique, Black, Black Oblique.

AaBbCcDdEeFfGgHhIiJjKkLlMmN
nOoPpQqRrSsTtUuVvWwXxYyZ

AaBbCcDdEeFfGgH
hIiJjKkLlMmNnOoP
pQqRrSsTtUuVvW

AaBbCcDdEeFf
GgHhIiJjKkLlM
mNnOoPpQqRr

AaBbCcDdEe
FfGgHhIiJjKk
LlMmNnOoP

AOLsucks

Joe Kral
1997

Styles included: Thin, Regular, Wide.

Ataribaby

Joe Kral
1998

Styles included: Light, Light Oblique,
Regular, Oblique, Bold, Bold Oblique.

AaBbCcDdEeFfGgHhIiJjKkLlMmNnOoP
pQqRrSsTtUuVvWwXxYyZz01234567

AaBbCcDdEeFfGg AaBbCcDdEeFfGg AaBbCcDdEeFfGg
HhIiJjKkLlMmNnO HhIiJjKkLlMmNn HhIiJjKkLlMmNn
oPpQqRrSsTtUuV OoPpQqRrSsTtUu OoPpQqRrSsTtU

Basis

Matt Desmond
1999

Styles included: Regular, Oblique,
Alternate, Alternate Oblique, Small
Caps, Small Caps Oblique, Unicase,
Unicase Oblique, Stencil, Stencil
Oblique, Cubed, Cubed Oblique.

AaBbCcDdEeFfGgHhIiJjKkLlMm
NnOoPpQqRrSsTtUuVvWwXxYy

AaBBCcDDEeF AaBeCcDDEeF AaBbCcDdEeF
FGGHHIIJJKKL FGGHHIIJJKKL FGgHhIiJjKkLl
LMMNNOOPPQQ LMMNNOOPPQQ MmNnOoPpQqR

Beat

Matt Desmond
1998

Styles included:
Regular, Oblique, Bold, Bold Oblique.

AaBbCcDdEeFfGgHhIiJjKkLlMmNnOoPpQqRrSsTtU
uVvWwXxYyZz0123456789!@#$%^&*()_+{}|:"<>

AaBbCcDdEeFfGgHhIiJ AaBbCcDdEeFfGgHhI AaBbCcDdEeFfGgHhI
jKkLlMmNnOoPpQqRrS iJjKkLlMmNnOoPpQq iJjKkLlMmNnOoPpQq
sTtUuVvWwXxYyZz01 RrSsTtUuVvWwXxYy RrSsTtUuVvWwXxYy

Blackgold

Mike Cina
2001

Styles included: Light, Regular,
Bold, Extra Bold.

AaBbCcDdEeFfGgHhIiJjKkLlMmN
nOoPpQqRrSsTtUuVvWwXxYyZz

AaBbCcDdEeF AaBbCcDdEeF AaBbCcDdEeF
fGgHhIiJjKkLl fGgHhIiJjKkLl fGgHhIiJjKkLl
MmNnOoPpQqR MmNnOoPpQqR MmNnOoPpQqR

info@testpilotcollective.com

AaBbCcDdEeFfGgHhIiIjJkKlLlMmNnO
oPpQqRrSsTtUuVvWwXxYyZZ01234

AaBbCcDdEeFf AaBbCcDdEeFf AaBbCcDdeeF
GgHhIiIjJkKlLM GGHHIiIjJkKlLM fGgHhIiIjJkKl
MnnOoPpQqRrs MnnOoPpQqRrs LMMnnOoPpQq

Caliper

Mike Cina
1999

Styles included: Light Cubed, Regular Cubed, Regular, Alternate, Unicase, Wide, Extra Wide, Stairstep.

AABBCCDDEEFFGGHHIIJJKKLLMM
NNOOPPQQRRSSTTUUVVWWXXYYZ

AABBCCDDEEFF *AABBCCDDEEFF* AABBCCDDEEFF
GGHHIIJJKKLL *GGHHIIJJKKLL* GGHHIIJJKKLL
MMNNOOPPQQR *MMNNOOPPQQR* MMNNOOPPQQR

Cam

Mike Cina
1997

Styles included: Light, Light Oblique, Regular, Oblique, Bold, Bold Oblique, Extra Bold, Extra Bold Oblique.

AaBbCcDdEeFfGgHhIiIjJkKlLMmNnOoPpQqRrSsTtUu
VvWwXxYyZz0123456789!@#$%^&*()_+{}|:"<

AaBbCcDdEeFfGgHhIiIj AaBbCcDdEeFfGgHhIi
kKlLMmNnOoPpQqRrSs jJkKlLMmNnOoPpQqR
TtUuVvWwXxYyZz012 rSsTtUuVvWwXxYyZz

Cinahand

Mike Cina
1998

Styles included: Light, Light Alternate, Regular, Alternate, Dingbats.

AABBCCDDEEFFGGHHIIJJKKLLMMNNOOPPQQRRSSTTU
UVVWWXXYYZZ0123456789!@#$%^&*[]_+{}|:"<>?/

AABBCCDDEEFFGGHHII AABBCCDDEEFFGGHHII AABBCCDDEEFFGGHHII
JJKKLLMMNNOOPPQQRR JJKKLLMMNNOOPPQQRR JJKKLLMMNNOOPPQQRR
SSTTUUVVWWXXYYZZ01 SSTTUUVVWWXXYYZZ01 SSTTUUVVWWXXYYZZ01

Composite

Mike Cina
1999

Styles included: Light, Regular, Bold, Extra Bold.

Crossover

Mike Cina
1999

Styles included: Extra Light, Extra Light Oblique, Light, Light Oblique, Regular, Oblique, Bold, Bold Oblique, Extra Bold, Extra Bold Oblique, Black, Black Oblique.

AaBbCcDdEeFfGgHhIiIiJjKkLlMmNnO
oPpQqRrSsTtUuVvWwXxYyZzZ01234

AaBbCcDdEeFf AaBbCcDdEeFf AaBbCcDdEeFf
GgHhIiJjKkLlM GgHhIiJjKkLlM GgHhIiJjKkLlM
mNnOoPpQqRrS mNnOoPpQqRrS mNnOoPpQqRrS

Curbdog

Matt Desmond
1998

Styles included: Condensed, Regular, Italic.

AaBbCcDdEeFfGgHhIiJjKkLlMmNnOoPpQqR
rSsTtUuVvWwXxYyZz0123456789!@#$%

AaBbCcDdEeFfGgHhIiJj AaBbCcDdEeFfGgHh AaBbCcDdEeFfGgHh
KkLlMmNnOoPpQqRrSsT IiJjKkLlMmNnOoPp IiJjKkLlMmNnOoPp
tUuVvWwXxYyZz01234 QqRrSsTtUuVvWwX QqRrSsTtUuVvWwX

Datdata

Joe Kral
1998

Styles included: Light, Light Oblique, Light Out Line, Light Out Line Oblique, Regular, Oblique, Regular Out Line, Regular Out Line Oblique.

AaBbCcDdEeFfGgHhIiJjKkLlMmNn
OoPpQqRrSsTtUuVvWwXxYyZz01

AaBbCcDdEeFf AaBbCcDdEeF AaBbCcDdEeF
GgHhIiJjKkLlM fGgHhIiJjKkLl fGgHhIiJjKkLl
mNnOoPpQqRr MmNnOoPpQ MmNnOoPpQq

Desmondtext

Matt Desmond
1998

Styles included: Regular, Italic, Bold, Bold Italic.

AaBbCcDdEeFfGgHhIiJjKkLlMmNnOoP
pQqRrSsTtUuVvWwXxYyZz01234567

AaBbCcDdEeFfGg AaBbCcDdEeFfGg AaBbCcDdEeFfGg
HhIiJjKkLlMmNn HhIiJjKkLlMmNn HhIiJjKkLlMmNn
OoPpQqRrSsTtUu OoPpQqRrSsTtUu OoPpQqRrSsTtUu

info@testpilotcollective.com

AaBbCcDdEeFfGgHhIiJjKkLlMm
NnOoPpQqRrSsTtUuVvWwXxYy

AaBbCcDdEeF AaBbCcDdEeF AaBbCcDdEeF
fGgHhIiJjKkLl fGgHhIiJjKkLl fGgHhIiJjKkLl
MmNnOoPpQqR MmNnOoPpQqR MmNnOoPpQqR

Doubleoseven

Joe Kral
1998

Styles included: Light, Light Oblique, Regular, Oblique, Bold, Bold Oblique, Extra Bold, Extra Bold Oblique.

AaBbCcDdEeFfGgHhIiJjKkLlM
mnOoPpQqRrSsTtUuVvWwXxY

AaBbCcDdEeF AaBbCcDdEeF AaBbCcDdEeF
FGgHhIiJjKkL FGgHhIiJjKKK FGgHhIiJjKK
LmmNnOoPpQq LLmmNnOoPpQ LLmmNnOoPpQ

ER9

Matt Desmond
1999

Styles included: Light, Light Oblique, Regular, Oblique, Bold, Bold Oblique, Extra Bold, Extra Bold Oblique.

AaBbCcDdEeFfGgHhIiJjKkLlMmNnOoPp
QqRrSsTtUuVvWwXxYyZz0123456789

AaBbCcDdEeFfGg AaBbCcDdEeFfGg AaBbCcDdEeFfG
HhIiJjKkLlMmNnO HhIiJjKkLlMmNnO gHhIiJjKkLlMm
oPpQqRrSsTtUuV oPpQqRrSsTtUuV NnOoPpQqRrSs

Fireflylove

Joe Kral
1998

Styles included: Extra Light, Light, Regular, Bold, Out Line, Two Line.

AaBbCcDdEeFfGgHhIiJjKkLl
MmNnOoPpQqRrSsTtUuVvWwX

AaBbCcDdEe AaBbCcDdEe AaBbCcDdEe
FfGgHhIiJjK FfGgHhIiJjK FfGgHhIiJjK
kLlMmNnOoP kLlMmNnOoP kLlMmNnOoP

Formation

Mike Cina
1999

Styles included: Thin, Extra Light, Ultra Light, Light, Regular, Semi Bold, Demi Bold, Bold, Extra Bold, Ultra Bold.

AaBbCcDdEeFfGgHhIiJjKkLlMmNnOo
PpQqRrSsTtUuVvWwXxYyZz0123456789

AaBbCcDdEeFfGg AaBbCcDdEeFfGg AaBbCcDdEeFfGg
GgHhIiJjKkLlM GgHhIiJjKkLlM GgHhIiJjKkLlM
NnOoPpQqRrSs NnOoPpQqRrSs NnOoPpQqRrSs

AaBbCcDdEeFfGgHhIiJjKkLlMmNnOoP
pQqRrSsTtUuVvWwXxYyZz0123456789

AaBbCcDdEeFfGg AaBbCcDdEeFfGg AaBbCcDdEeFfGg
HhIiJjKkLlMmNn HhIiJjKkLlMmNn HhIiJjKkLlMmNn
OoPpQqRrSsTtUu OoPpQqRrSsTtUu OoPpQqRrSsTtUu

AaBbCcDdEeFfGgHhIiJjKkLlMmNnOo
PpQqRrSsTtUuVvWwXxYyZz012345

AaBbCcDdEeFfG AaBbCcDdEeFf AaBbCcDdEeFf
gHhIiJjKkLlMm GgHhIiJjKkLlM GgHhIiJjKkLl
NnOoPpQqRrSs mNnOoPpQqRrS MmNnOoPpQq

AaBbCcDdEeFfGgHhIiJjKkLlMmNnOoPpQ
qRrSsTtUuVvWwXxYyZz0123456789!@#$

AaBbCcDdEeFfGgH *AaBbCcDdEeFfGgH* **AaBbCcDdEeFfGg**
hIiJjKkLlMmNnOoP *hIiJjKkLlMmNnOoP* **HhIiJjKkLlMmNn**
pQqRrSsTtUuVvW *pQqRrSsTtUuVvW* **OoPpQqRrSsTtUu**

AaBbCcDdEeFfGgHhIiJjKkLlMmNnOo
PpQqRrSsTtUuVvWwXxYyZz012345

AaBbCcDdEeFfG
gHhIiJjKkLlMmN
nOoPpQqRrSsTt

AaBbCcDdEeFfG
gHhIiJjKkLlMmN
nOoPpQqRrSsTt

AaBbCcDdEeFfG
gHhIiJjKkLlMmN
nOoPpQqRrSsTt

Joesfoot

Joe Kral
1997

Styles included: Light, Regular, Bold.

AaBbCcDdEeFfGgHhIiJjKkLlMmNnOoPpQqRrSsTtUuVvWwXxYyZz
0123456789!@#$%^&*()_+{}|:"<>?/¡™£¢∞§¶•ªº–≠œ®†¥ø

AaBbCcDdEeFfGgHhIiJjKkLlM
mNnOoPpQqRrSsTtUuVvWwX
xYyZz0123456789!@#$%^&

AaBbCcDdEeFfGgHhIiJjKkLlM
mNnOoPpQqRrSsTtUuVvWwX
xYyZz0123456789!@#$%^&

AaBbCcDdEeFfGgHhIiJjKkLlM
mNnOoPpQqRrSsTtUuVvWwX
xYyZz0123456789!@#$%^&

Jute

Mike Cina
2001

Styles included: Regular, Semi Bold, Bold.

AaBbCcDdEeFfGgHhIiJjKkLlMmNnOo
PpQqRrSsTtUuVvWwXxYyZz0123456

AaBbCcDdEeFfG
gHhIiJjKkLlMmN
nOoPpQqRrSsTt

AaBbCcDdEeFfG
gHhIiJjKkLlMmN
nOoPpQqRrSsTt

AaBbCcDdEeFfG
gHhIiJjKkLlMmN
nOoPpQqRrSsTt

Kralhand

Joe Kral
1998

Styles included: Light, Regular, Bold, Out Line.

AaBbCcDdEeFfGgHhIiJjKkLlMmNnOo
PpQqRrSsTtUuVvWwXxYyZz012345

AaBbCcDdEeFfG
gHhIiJjKkLlMmN
nOoPpQqRrSsTt

AaBbCcDdEeFfG
gHhIiJjKkLlMmN
nOoPpQqRrSsTt

AaBbCcDdEeFfG
gHhIiJjKkLlMmN
nOoPpQqRrSsTt

Lunarmod

Matt Desmond
1997

Styles included: Regular, Oblique.

Maetl

Mike Cina
1999

Styles included: Light, Light Oblique, Regular, Oblique, Bold, Bold Oblique, Extra Bold, Extra Bold Oblique.

AaBbCcDdEeFfGgHhIiJjKkLlM
mNnOoPpQqRrSsTtUuVvWwX

AaBbCcDdEe AaBbCcDdEe *AaBbCcDdEe*
FfGgHhIiJjKk FfGgHhIiJjKk *FfGgHhIiJjKk*
LlMmNnOoPp LlMmNnOoPp *LlMmNnOoPp*

Mechanical

Joe Kral
1999

Styles included: Light, Light Oblique, Regular, Oblique, Bold, Bold Oblique, Extra Bold, Extra Bold Oblique, Black, Black Oblique

AaBbCcDdEeFfGgHhIiJjKkLlMmNnOoPpQq
RrSsTtUuVvWwXxYyZz0123456789!@#

AaBbCcDdEeFfGg **AaBbCcDdEeFfGg** *AaBbCcDdEeFfGg*
HhIiJjKkLlMmNn **HhIiJjKkLlMmNn** *HhIiJjKkLlMmNo*
OoPpQqRrSsTtu **OoPpQqRrSsTtu** *OoPpQqRrSsTtuu*

Nanocode

Joe Kral
1998

Styles included: Plus, Plus Oblique, Minus, Minus Oblique, Equals, Equals Oblique.

AaBbCcDdEeFfGgHhIiJjKkLlMmN
nOoPpQqRrSsTtUuVvWwXxYyZ

OCRJ

Joe Kral
1998

Styles included: Light Round, Light Square, Regular Round, Regular Square, Bold Round, Bold Square.

AaBbCcDdEeFfGgHhIiJjKkLlMmNn
OoPpQqRrSsTtUuVvWwXxYyZz0123

AaBbCcDdEeFf AaBbCcDdEeFf AaBbCcDdEeFf
GgHhIiJjKkLl GgHhIiJjKkLl GgHhIiJjKkLl
MmNnOoPpQqRr MmNnOoPpQqRr MmNnOoPpQqRr

info@testpilotcollective.com

AaBbCcDdEeFfGgHhIiJjKkLlMmNn
OoPpQqRrSsTtUuVvWwXxYyZzO123
AaBbCcDdEeFf AaBbCcDdEeFf AaBbCcDdEeFf
GgHhIiJjKkLl GgHhIiJjKkLl GgHhIiJjKkLl
MmNnOoPpQqRr MmNnOoPpQqRr MmNnOoPpQqRr

OCRK

Joe Kral
1998

Styles included: Light Round, Light Square, Regular Round, Regular Square, Bold Round, Bold Square.

AaBbCcDdEeFfGgHhIiJjKkLlMmNnOoPpQqRrSsTtU
uVvWwXxYyZzO123456789!@#$%^&*()_+{}:

AaBbCcDdEeFfGgHhIiJ AaBbCcDdEeFfGgHhIiJ AaBbCcDdEeFfGgHhIiJ
JkKLlMmNnOoPpQqRr JkKLlMmNnOoPpQqRrS JkKLlMmNnOoPpQqRr
SsTtUuVvWwXxYyZzO sTtUuVvWwXxYyZzO1 SsTtUuVvWwXxYyZzO

Octobre

Joe Kral
1998

Styles included: Regular, Alternate.

AaBbCcDdEeFfGgHhIiJjKkLlMmNnOoP
pQqRrSsTtUuVvWwXxYyZz01234567
AaBbCcDdEeFfGgHh AaBbCcDdEeFfGg AaBbCcDdEeFfGg
IiJjKkLlMmNnOoPp HhIiJjKkLlMmNn HhIiJjKkLlMmNn
GgQqRrSsTtUuVvWw OoPpQqRrSsTtUu OoPpQqRrSsTtUu

Openlunch

Joe Kral
1997

Styles included: Light, Light Oblique, Regular, Oblique, Bold, Bold Oblique.

AaBbCcDdEeFfGgHhIiJjKkLlMmNnO
oPpQqRrSsTtUuVvWwXxYyZzO123

AaBbCcDdEeFf AaBbCcDdEeFf AaBbCcDdEeFf
GgHhIiJjKkLlM OgHhIiJjKkLlM OgHhIiJjKkLlM
MnNnOoPpQqRr+ MnNnOoPpqqRr+ MnNnOoPpqqRr+

Overcross

Mike Cina
2002

Styles included: Extra Light, Extra Light Oblique, Light, Light Oblique, Regular, Oblique, Semi Bold, Semi Bold Oblique, Bold, Bold Oblique, Extra Bold, Extra Bold Oblique.

Test Pilot Collective

Mike Cina
2001

Styles included: Regular, Semi Bold, Bold, Extra Bold, Black, Condensed, Semi Bold Condensed, Bold Condensed, Extra Bold Condensed, Black Condensed.

AaBbCcDdEeFfGgHhIiJjKkLlMmNnOoPpQqRrSsTtUuVvWwXxYyZz0123456789!@#$%^&*()_+{}|:"<>?i™£¢∞§¶•ªº–≠œ®†¥π˝

AaBbCcDdEeFfGgHhIiJjKkLlMmNn0oPpQqRrSsTtUuVvWwXxYyZz0123456789!@#$%^&*()_+{}|:"<>?i™£∞

AaBbCcDdEeFfGgHhIiJjKkLlMmNnOoPpQqRrSsTtUuVvWwXxYyZz0123456789!@

AaBbCcDdEeFfGgHhIiJjKkLlMmNn0oPpQqRrSsTtUuVvWwXxYyZz0123456789!@#$%^&*()_+{}|:"<>?i™£∞

Joe Kral
1999

Styles included: Light, Light Oblique, Regular, Oblique.

AaBbCcDdEeFfGgHhIiJjKkLlMmNnOoPpQqRrSsTtUuVvWwXxYyZz0123

AaBbCcDdEeFfGgHhIiJjKkLlMmNnOoPpQqRrSsT

AaBbCcDdEeFfGgHhIiJjKkLlMmNnOoPpQqRrSsT

AaBbCcDdEeFfGgHhIiJjKkLlMmNnOoPpQqRrSsT

Joe Kral
1999

Styles included: Icons1, Icons2, Typeface.

Joe Kral
1998

Styles included: Light, Light Oblique, Regular, Oblique, Bold, Bold Oblique, Extra Bold, Extra Bold Oblique.

AaBbCcDdEeFfGgHhIiJjKkLlMmNnOoPpQqRrSsTtUuVvWwXxYyZz0123456789

AaBbCcDdEeFfGgHhIiJjKkLlMmNnOoPpQqRrSsTtUu

AaBbCcDdEeFfGgHhIiJjKkLlMmNnOoPpQqRrSsTt

AaBbCcDdEeFfGgHhIiJjKkLlMmNnOoPpQqRrSsT

info@testpilotcollective.com

AaBbCcDdEeFFGgHhIiJjKKLlMmNnOoPpQqR
rSsTtUuVvWwXXYYZz0123456789!@#$%

AaBbCcDdEeFFGgH
hIiJjKKLlMmNnOoP
pQqRrSsTtUuVvW

AaBbCcDdEeFFGgH
hIiJjKKLlMmNnOoP
pQqRrSsTtUuVvW

AaBbCcDdEeFFGgH
hIiJjKKLlMmNnOoP
pQqRrSsTtUuVvW

Reflector

Joe Kral
1999

Styles included: Extra Light, Extra
Light Oblique, Light, Light Oblique,
Regular, Oblique, Bold, Bold Oblique,
Extra Bold, Extra Bold Oblique, Black,
Black Oblique.

Test Pilot Collective

AaBbCcDdEeFfGgHhIiJjKk
LlMmNnOoPpQqRrSsTtUu

AaBbCcDdE AaBbCcDdE AaBbCcDdE
eFfGgHhIiJj eFfGgHhIiJj eFfGgHhIiJj
KkLlMmNn KkLlMmNn KkLlMmNn

Retron

Matt Desmond
1997

Styles included: Regular, Oblique.

AaBbCcDdEeFfGgHhIiJjKkLlMmNnOoPpQqRr
SsTtUuVvWwXxYyZz0123456789!@#$%^&

AaBbCcDdEeFfGgHh
IiJjKkLlMmNnOoPp
QqRrSsTtUuVvWwX

AaBbCcDdEeFfGgH
hIiJjKkLlMmNnOoP
pQqRrSsTtUuVvWw

AaBbCcDdEeFfGgH
hIiJjKkLlMmNnOo
PpQqRrSsTtUuVv

Saarikari

Joe Kral
1999

Styles included: Extra Light, Extra
Light Oblique, Light, Light Oblique,
Regular, Oblique, Bold, Bold Oblique.

AABBCCDDEEFFGGHHIIJJKKLLMMNNO
OPPQQRRSSTTUUVVWWXXYYZZ012345

AABBCCDDEEFFGG AABBCCDDEEFFGG
HHIIJJKKLLMMN HHIIJJKKLLMMN
OOPPQQRRSSTTUU OOPPQQRRSSTTUU

Screwtop

Joe Kral
1998

Styles included: Light, Light Negative,
Regular, Negative, Bold, Bold
Negative.

AaBbCcDdEeFfGgHhIiJjKkLlMmNn
OoPpQqRrSsTtUuVvWwXxYyZz01

AaBbCcDdEeF AaBbCcDdEeF AaBbCcDdEeF
fGgHhIiJjKkLl fGgHhIiJjKkLl fGgHhIiJjKkLl
MmNnOoPpQqR MmNnOoPpQqR MmNnOoPpQqR

AaBbCcDdEeFfGgHhIiJjKkLlMmNnOo
PpQqRrSsTtUuVvWwXxYyZz0123456

AaBbCcDdEeFfG AaBbCcDdEeFfG AaBbCcDdEeFfG
gHhIiJjKkLlMmN gHhIiJjKkLlMmN gHhIiJjKkLlMmN
nOoPpQqRrSsTt nOoPpQqRrSsTt nOoPpQqRrSsTt

AABBCCDDEEFFGGHHIIJJKKLL
MMNNOOPPQQRRSSTTUUVVW

AABBCCDDEE AABBCCDDEE AABBCCDDEE
FFGGHHIIJJK FFGGHHIIJJK FFGGHHIIJJK
KLLMMNNOOP KLLMMNNOOP KLLMMNNOOP

AaBbCcDdEeFfGgHhIiJjKkLlMmNnOoPpQqR
rSsTtUuVvWwXxYyZz0123456789!@//$%^

AaBbCcDdEeFfGg AaBbCcDdEeFfG AaBbCcDdEeFfG
HhIiJjKkLlMmNn gHhIiJjKkLlMm gHhIiJjKkLlM
OoPpQqRrSsTtUu NnOoPpQqRrSsT NnOoPpQqRrSsT

aabbccddeeffggHhiiijjkkLlmmnnooppqqR
rssTtuuvvwwxxYy20123456789!a#$%

aabbccddeeffggH aabbccddeeffgg aabbccddeeffgg
hriijjkkLlmmnnoop Hhriijjkkklmmnno Hhriijjkkklmmnno
pqgrssTtuuvvw oppqgrssTtuu oppqgrssTtuu

Subito

Joe Kral
1999

Styles included: Extra Light, Extra Light Oblique, Light, Light Oblique, Regular, Oblique, Bold, Bold Oblique, Extra Bold, Extra Bold Oblique, Black, Black Oblique.

Test Pilot Collective

AaBbCcDdEeFfGgHhiIJjKkLlMm
nnOoPpQqRrssTtUuvUwwxxYy22Z01

aaBbccDdeeff AaBbccDdeeff AaBbccDdeeff
GgHhiIjjkkLlm GgHhiIjjkkLlm GgHhiIjjkkLlm
mnnooppqqgrs mnnooppqqgrs mnnooppqqgrs

Trisect

Mike Cina
1999

Styles included: Extra Light, Light, Regular, Semi Bold, Bold, Extra Bold, Black, Heavy.

AaBbCcDdEeFfGgHhliJjKkLlMmNnOoPpQ
qRrSsTtUuVvWwHxYyZz0123456789!@

AaBbCcDdEeFfGg AaBbCcDdEeFfG AaBbCcDdEeFfG
HhliJjHKLlMmNn gHhliJjHKLlMmN gHhliJjHKLlMm
OoPpQqRrSsTtUu nOoPpQqRrSsTt NnOoPpQqRrSs

Tryptomene

Joe Kral
1998

Styles included: Light, Light Oblique, Regular, Oblique, Bold, Bold Oblique, Extra Bold, Extra Bold Oblique, Black, Black Oblique.

AaBbCcDdEeFfGgHhliJjKkLlMmNnOoPpQ
qRrSsTtUuVvWwXxYyZz0123456789!@

AaBbCcDdEeFfGg AaBbCcDdEeFfGg AaBbCcDdEeFfGg
HhliJjKkLlMmNnO HhliJjKkLlMmNnO HhliJjKkLlMmNnO
oPpQqRrSsTtUuV oPpQqRrSsTtUuV oPpQqRrSsTtUuV

Twincities

Joe Kral
1998

Styles included: Light, Light Oblique, Regular, Oblique, Bold, Bold Oblique, Extra Bold, Extra Bold Oblique.

Mike Cina
1999

Styles included: Light, Light Oblique, Regular, Oblique, Bold, Bold Oblique, Extra Bold, Extra Bold Oblique, Black, Black Oblique.

AaBbCcDdEeFfGgHhIiJjKkLlMmNnOoPpQqRrSsT
tUuVvWwXxYyZz0123456789!@#$%^&*()_+{}

AaBbCcDdEeFfGgHhI
iJjKkLlMmNnOoPpQq
RrSsTtUuVvWwXxYy

AaBbCcDdEeFfGgHhI
iJjKkLlMmNnOoPpQq
RrSsTtUuVvWwXxYy

AaBbCcDdEeFfGgHh
IiJjKkLlMmNnOoPpQ
qRrSsTtUuVvWwXx

Mike Cina
1999

Styles included: Light, Light Oblique, Regular, Oblique, Bold, Bold Oblique, Extra Bold, Extra Bold Oblique, Black, Black Oblique.

AaBbccDdEeFfGgHhIiJjKkLlMmNnOoPpQqR
rSsTtUuVvWwXxYyZz0123456789!@#$%^

AaBbccDdEeFfGgH
hIiJjKkLlMmNnOo
PpQqRrSsTtUuVv

AaBbccDdEeFfGgH
hIiJjKkLlMmNnOo
PpQqRrSsTtUuVv

AaBbccDdEeFfGg
HhIiJjKkLlMmNn
OoPpQqRrSsTtUu

Joe Kral
2001

Styles included: Light, Light Oblique, Regular, Oblique, Bold, Bold Oblique, Extra Bold, Extra Bold Oblique, Black, Black Oblique.

Matt Desmond
1999

Styles included: Condensed, Regular.

AABBCCDDEEFFGGHHI
IJJKKLLMMNNOOPPQQ

AABBCCDDEE
FFGGHHIIJJKK
LLMMNNOOPP

AABBCCD
DEEFFGG
HHIIJJKKL

AABBCCDDEE
FFGGHHIIJJKK
LLMMNNOOPP

info@testpilotcollective.com

AaBbCcDdEeFfGgHhIiJjKkLlMmNnOoP
pQqRrSsTtUuVvWwXxYyZz012345678

AaBbCcDdEeFfGg
HhIiJjKkLlMmNn
OoPpQqRrSsTtUu

AaBbCcDdEeFfG
gHhIiJjKkLlMmN
nOoPpQqRrSsTtU

AaBbCcDdEeFfG
gHhIiJjKkLlMmN
nOoPpQqRrSsTtU

Wrongway

Joe Kral
1998

Styles included: Light, Light Oblique,
Regular, Oblique, Bold, Bold Oblique.

AaBbCcDdEeFfGgHhIiJjKkLlMmNnOoP
pQqRrSsTtUuVvWwXxYyZz01234567

AaBbCcDdEeFfGgHhI
iJjKkLlMmNnOoPpQq
RrSsTtUuVvWwXx

AaBbCcDdEeFfG
gHhIiJjKkLlMmN
nOoPpQqRrSsTt

AaBbCcDdEeFfG
gHhIiJjKkLlMmN
nOoPpQqRrSsTt

Xerxes

Joe Kral
1999

Styles included: Light, Light Oblique,
Light Alternate, Light Alternate
Oblique, Regular Low, Regular Low
Oblique, Regular Mid, Regular Mid
Oblique, Regular High, Regular High
Oblique.

AaBbCcDdEeFfGgHhIiJjKkLlMmNnOo
PpQqRrSsTtUuVvWwXxYyZz0123

AaBbCcDdEeFf
GgHhIiJjKkLlM
mNnOoPpQqRrS

AaBbCcDdEeFf
GgHhIiJjKkLlM
mNnOoPpQqRrS

AaBbCcDdEeFf
GgHhIiJjKkLlM
mNnOoPpQqRrS

Yeti

Joe Kral
2001

Styles included: Light, Light Oblique,
Regular, Oblique, Bold, Bold Oblique,
Extra Bold, Extra Bold Oblique, Black,
Black Oblique.

AaBbCcDdEeFfGgHhIiJjKkLl
MmNnOoPpQqRrSsTtUuVvW

AaBbCcDdEe
FfGgHhIiJjK
KLlMmNnOo

AaBbCcDdEe
FfGgHhIiJjK
LlMmNnOoP

AaBbCcDdEe
FfGgHhIiJjK
KLlMmNnOo

Zebraflesh

Joe Kral
1998

Styles included: Regular, Bold.

Test Pilot Collective

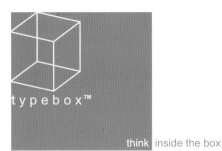

typebox™

think inside the box

Typebox gains its inspiration through travel, art, storytelling and music. Souvenirs from these experiences are then collected-capturing those memories that make our hearts move, our minds work and our hands draw.

Typebox, LLC
PO Box 330446
San Francisco, CA 94133-0446

typebox.com
mailroom@typebox.com

philosophy

TYPEBOX: mind, heart and hand. Like in life itself, the process of "thinking, feeling and doing" can also be applied to type culture-from concept and form giving to the ongoing use, craft and art of typography and letterform design.

collection

The founders and contributors of Typebox come from a range of backgrounds-print and screen design, analog and digital methods of creation. Over the past two decades' progress, we have become bridges of experience spanning technologies, media and cultural aspects of type and design.

inspiration

TYPEBOX: promoting type culture. Typebox is more than just fonts: We provide background to our ideas as well as forward thinking for both creation and use of typefaces: inspiration and application. With your participation, we hope to establish a platform for constructive thought about and around type. We invite serious contributors to make their best musings public, and wish to become your bookmark as an everyday resource-for designers, students, and teachers alike.

collaborative

Keep checking back with Typebox: Find our latest typefaces in Fontbox, and articles in Thinkbox. Preview upcoming font releases and thoughts in Outbox. Share your thoughts with us, and check out our inspiring alliances. Join our mailing list for upcoming announcements, and don't miss our promotions.

TX Lithium

TX Elf

TX Tiny Tin

TX CORTINA

TX NineVolt

TX Reflux

TX Blotch

TX Wirish

TX Manifesto

TX Hex

TX Gitter

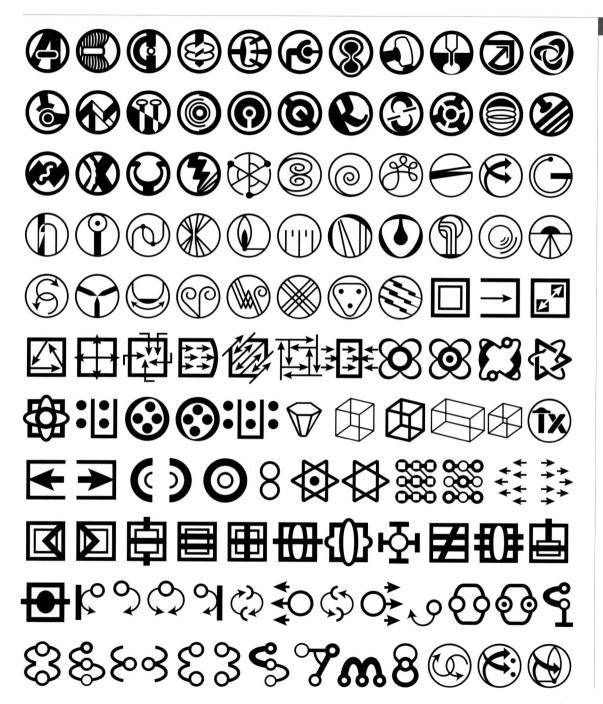

ABCDEFGHIJKLMNOPQRSTUVWXYZabcdefghijklmnopqrstuvwxyz
!?¡¿0123456789¢$£¥€@&#%‰©®™ª*‡†°ÅÇÉÎÑÒØÜåçéîñòøüı
ßfifl…"\":;'"•'"»«><∞≤≥‹›÷=≠≈±+¬◊∑∏πΔ∂Ω√∫ƒ(){}[]§¶Ð
ðŁłŠšŸýÞþŽž½¼¹¾³²¦–×[Li]*ABCDEFGHIJKLMNOPQRSTUVWXYZabc*
defghijklmnopqrstuvwxyz!?¡¿0123456789¢$£¥€@&#%‰©®™ª‡*

ABCDEFGHIJKLMNOPQRSTUVWXYZabcdefghijklmnopqrstu
vwxyz!?¡¿0123456789¢$£¥€@&#%‰©®™ª*‡†°ÅÇÉÎÑÒØÜ
åçéîñòøüıßfifl…"\":;'"•'"»«><∞≤≥‹›÷=≠≈±+¬◊∑∏πΔ∂Ω
√∫ƒ(){}[]§¶ÐðŁłŠšŸýÞþŽž½¼¹¾³²¦–×[Li]*ABCDEFGHIJKLMNO*
PQRSTUVWXYZabcdefghijklmnopqrstuvwxyz!?¡¿0123456789

ABCDEFGHIJKLMNOPQRSTUVWXYZabcdefghijklmnop
qrstuvwxyz!?¡¿0123456789¢$£¥€@&#%‰©®™ª*‡†°ÅÇ
ÉÎÑÒØÜåçéîñòøüıßfifl…"\":;'/•'"»«><∞≤≥‹›÷=≠≈±+¬
◊∑∏πΔ∂Ω√∫ƒ(){}[]§¶ÐðŁłŠšŸýÞþŽž½¼¹¾³²¦–×[Li]*ABCD*
EFGHIJKLMNOPQRSTUVWXYZabcdefghijklmnopqrstuvw

For people who know my type design work, Lithium may appear as one of my more unusual typefaces. This was my intention, as it was inspired out of another type design experience, but needs to stand on its own. Just for fun, as a tryout and possible start, I wondered: Could I do a trendy, fashionable design? **I chose a blur-like rounding effect, to achieve a modern, technological-electronic look. I started from an early variation of my Calcite, but decided to change its shapes into something new and different. Through my entire series of changes, Lithium became quite a different design standing its own ground. I like the 'zero' of Adrian Frutiger's OCR-B: It's technical, mechanical, but still nice to the eye. In the same spirit, I wanted to create something not just mechanical-modern, but more humane.**

ABCDEFGHIJKLMNOPQRSTUVWXYZabcdefghijklm
nopqrstuvwxyz!?¡¿0123456789¢$£¥€@&#%‰©
®™ª*‡†°ÅÇÉÍÑÒøÜåçéíñòøüßñfl..."\"¡;'".»«><
∞≤≥◊÷=≠≈±+¬◊∑∏π∆∂Ω√∫ƒ()[]§¶ÐðŁŠšÝýþþŽ
ž½¼¹¾³²¡–×█ ABCDEFGHIJKLMNOPQRSTUVWXYZ

TX Lithium Ray Brite

Akira Kobayashi
2001

ABCDEFGHIJKLMNOPQRSTUVWXYZabcdefghijklm
nopqrstuvwxyz!?¡¿0123456789¢$£¥€@&#%‰©
®™ª*‡†°ÅÇÉÍÑÒøÜåçéíñòøüßñfl..."\"¡;'".»«><
∞≤≥◊÷=≠≈±+¬◊∑∏π∆∂Ω√∫ƒ()[]§¶ÐðŁŠšÝýþþŽ
ž½¼¹¾³²¡–×█ ABCDEFGHIJKLMNOPQRSTUVWXYZ

TX Lithium Ray Dark

Akira Kobayashi
2001

Typebox

TX Lithium Light Roman *and Italic*, Regular Roman *and Italic*, **Bold Roman *and Italic***, Ray Brite Roman *and Italic* & Ray Dark Roman *and Italic*

For people who know my type design work, Lithium may appear as one of my more unusual typefaces. This was my intention, as it was inspired out of another type design experience, but needs to stand on its own. Just for fun, as a tryout and possible start, I wondered: Could I do a trendy, fashionable design? I chose a blur-like rounding effect, to achieve a modern, technological-electronic look. I started from an early variation of my Calcite, but decided to change its shapes into something new and different. **Through my entire series of changes, Lithium became quite a different design standing its own ground. I like the 'zero' of Adrian Frutiger's OCR-B: It's technical, mechanical, but still nice to the eye.**

Dennis Poon
2002

TX Elf abc123

ABCDEFGHIJKLMNOPQR
STUVWXYZabcdefghij
klmnopqrstuvwxyz!?¡
¿0123456789¢$£¥×@&#
٭٪©®™ªˣ‡†˚ÂÇÉÎÑÒØÜ
âçéîñòøüıßﬁﬂ…"\"·¸'/'∎
''»‹‹›‹◦∞¿¡◇÷=≠✕±+¬◊∑∏π
∆ªΩ√∫ƒ()﹛﹜[]§¶Ðàłﬆšš
ý̂ýþÞžž½⅓¼³⁄₄²|−×👾

A sense must be considered in the art and craft of legibiltiy. In order to establish criteria for screen typography, it is important to embrace the laws of traditional typography. The screen must also obey a necessity for typographic clarity; use the history and fundamentals of typography as a frame of reference. The vocabulary is the guide. Text on the screen is based on light waves, hence there is often a matching bitmap for a specific typeface and a specific size. The word and line spacing still need to be checked and corrected accordingly. This is important since reading on the screen can be difficult for those who are not used to to it. Conventional typefaces can't be simply transferred to screen.

The issue of legibilty does highlight the difference between print and screen, in particular the relation to type style, size, spacing, text length and color application. Typefaces that were designed for the print medium pose problems when they are applied to the 72 dpi monitor. The limitation of this resolution can be overcome by understanding the technology. (6/7 point)

TX Elf is inspired by screen typefaces such as Chicago, Geneva, Monaco and New York. Like these typefaces, TX Elf is adaptable to the bitmap of a 72dpi screen and is optimized for reading. (5/6 point)

mailroom@typebox.com

ABCDEFGHIJKLMNOPQRSTUVWXYZabcdefghi
jklmnopqrstuvwxyz!?¡¿0123456789¢$£¥€@
&#%‰©ºoinaª★‡†°ªçéîñòαü،ÅÇÉÎÑÒ⌀Üßﬃﬀ…"\
"::'/'•'"»«><∞≤≥‹›÷=≠≈±+¬◊ΣΠπΔ∂Ω√∫ƒ(){}[]
§¶ÐđŁłŠšÝýþþŽž½¼¹³⁄₄³²¦−×❀

TX Tiny Tim Gimpy

Joachim Müller-Lancé
2001

ABCDEFGHIJKLMNOPQRSTUVWXYZabcdefg
hijklmnopqrstuvwxyz!?¡¿0123456789¢$£
¥€@&#%‰©ºoinaª★‡†°ªçéîñòαü،ÅÇÉÎÑÒ⌀Üß
ﬃﬀ…"\"::'/'•'"»«><∞≤≥‹›÷=≠≈±+¬◊ΣΠπΔ∂
Ω√∫ƒ(){}[]§¶ÐđŁłŠšÝýþþŽž½¼¹³⁄₄³²¦−×❀

TX Tiny Tim Stout

Joachim Müller-Lancé
2001

Typebox

Tiptoe through the tulips with TX Tiny Tim Gimpy & Stout

Dickens meets 1960s pop culture – based on memories of 60s TV animations,
Tiny Tim's design might not be very healthy, but it is happy & well-behaved.

TX Tiny Tim was originally inspired by my favorite childhood anime 'Speed Racer'. Its characters
wear letters playing puns between Japanese and English. These hand-drawn letters intrigued me
– was their dinkiness truly vernacular or intentional? – and I decided to try a similar 'good-bad'
approach in a complete typeface: Drawing everything intentionally wrong, flipping entire
characters, adding useless serifs and giving emphasis to the wrong details. However, the result
was a surprisingly unique design that detached itself from its origins. Its appearance called for
a different name, and that was when the thought of Tiny Tim came in, both via Dickens'
Christmas Carol and the late but endearing 60s singer whose autograph I got at a revival
show at San Francisco's Kennel Club in 1990.

TX CORTINA BASE

ABCDEFGHIJKLM
NOPQRSTUVWXYZ

!?¿&0123456789¢
$£¥€@£#%‰©®™▲★‡
†°ÂÇÉÎÑÔØÜÅÇÉÎÑ
ÒØÜ∙ßßﬁﬂ…"\":;'/'℗'
"»«><∞≤≥‹›÷=≠≈±+¬◇∑
∏∆∂Ω√ƒ(){}[]¶†‡š
ýþ¾½¼¹³¾³²¦—×÷◆₸

TX CORTINA FIRST APPEARED ON A DREARY
OVERTIME NIGHT IN FEBRUARY 1997... BLURRY
EYES CIRCLING IN ON THE TINY TRIANGULAR TAB OF THE
APPLE CD AUDIO PLAYER, USED TO FLIP THE LIST OF
TRACKS OPEN-AND-CLOSE. LOOKS LIKE SOME CHROME-
AGE LETTER A... WHAT IF... A TYPEFACE? – YES. THE
STRANGE IDEA OF DEVELOPING A WHOLE TYPEFACE OUT
OF A SINGLE SHAPE WORKED AGAIN, JUST AS IT HAD WITH
MY 'SHURIKEN BOY'. AGAIN, IT WAS A TRIANGLE LEADING
TO THE LETTER A, AND MY EXPERIENCE WITH MODULAR
FONTS WAS OF GREAT HELP.

TX CORTINA SLATE

TX Cortina Slate

Joachim Müller-Lancé
2002

Typebox

ABCDEFGHIJKLM
NOPQRSTUVWXYZ
!?¿¢£0123456789¢
$£¥€@€#%‰©®™▲★÷
†°ÅÇÉÎÑÖÒÓÖÅÇÉÎÑ
ÒÓÖ•‹›fifl…""\",:;'/'◉'
"»«›‹∞∞≤≥◊÷=≠≈±+¬◇∑
☐△∂∩√ƒ(){}[]¶†•łŠ
Žžż½¼°¾²¹¦—×ᵀ☼ᵀᶻ

THE NAME CAME IN JUST AS INTUITIVELY. THE GRAND JET-SETTING SKIING RESORT CORTINA D'AMPEZZO IN THE ITALIAN ALPS BECAME FAMOUS FOR ITS 1960 WINTER OLYMPICS, AND WAS EPONYMOUS TO THE FORD CORTINA SPORTSCAR. TX CORTINA COMBINES A FEEL OF THIS ERA WITH CURRENT AESTHETICS OF SPORTS AND MOTORISM, ELECTRONICA AND SCI-FI. TRY SLANTING THIS TYPEFACE ABOUT 10 DEGREES FOR HEIGHTENED ITALIC FEEL. THE COMPLETE CORTINA FAMILY WILL INCLUDE BASE (CURVED), SLATE (ALL STRAIGHT AND BEVELED).

ABCDEFGHIJKLMNOPQRSTUVWXYZabcdefghijklmnopq
rstuvwxyz!?¡¿0123456789¢$£¥€@&#%‰©®™α*#°ÅÇÉÎ
ÑÒØÜåçéîñòøüßfifl...“\”:;‘/’•'"»«><∞≤≥‹›÷=≠≈±+¬◊ΣΠπΔð
Ω√∫ƒ(){}[]§¶ĐðŁłŠšÚýþþŽžŽž½¼13/432|–×⑨volt

ABCDEFGHIJKLMNOPQRSTUVWXYZabcdefghijklmno
pqrstuvwxyz!?¡¿0123456789¢$£¥€@&#%‰©®™α*#°
ÅÇÉÎÑÒØÜåçéîñòøüßfifl...“\”:;‘/’•'"»«><∞≤≥‹›÷=≠≈±+¬
◊ΣΠπΔðΩ√∫ƒ(){}[]§¶ĐðŁłŠšÚýþþŽžŽž½¼13/432|–×⑨volt

TX NineVolt & NineBolt

The quick ink-line typeface that is machine shop ready for bold and heavy-duty tasks. Assimilated from the characteristics of handwriting and calligraphy, **NineVolt was engineered to emphasize the bottom connections.**

The result is a strong, graphic baseline with a left to right movement. Another intention was to design a typeface that had 3 degrees more slant than the common 6 degrees found in many script faces. One could say that the 9 degree backbone gives NineVolt extra verve and vigor. The main design goal was to achieve a quick repetition of hard angles that move along the baseline. Once the font is set in text, it has the quality of having a continuous straight line along the baselines. This "ink-line" serves as a vehicle to communicate and resemble rule lines, drafting, and note taking.

mailroom@typebox.com

ABCDEFGHIJKLMNOPQRSTUVWXYZabcdefghijklmnopq rstuvwxyz!?¡¿0123456789¢$£¥€@&#%‰©®™ªª*‡†°ÅÇÉ ÎÑÒØÜåçéîñòøüıßﬁﬂ…"\":;'/'•'" »«><∞≤≥<>÷=≠≈±+–¬◊ΣΠπ Δ∂Ω√∫ƒ(){}[]§¶Ðð£łŠšÝýÞþŽž½¼¹¾³²¦–×Ⓧ

TX Reflux Regular

Mike Kohnke
2001

ABCDEFGHIJKLMNOPQRSTUVWXYZabcdefghijklmno pqrstuvwxyz!?¡¿0123456789¢$£¥€@&#%‰©®™ªª*‡†° ÅÇÉÎÑÒØÜåçéîñòøüıßﬁﬂ…"\":;'/'•'" »«><∞≤≥<>÷=≠≈±+– ¬◊ΣΠπΔ∂Ω√∫ƒ(){}[]§¶Ðð£łŠšÝýÞþŽž½¼ ¾³²¦–×Ⓧ

TX Reflux Bold

Mike Kohnke
2001

Typebox

TX Reflux with a Bold

is a result from a type design study based on handwriting analysis. The project began with the supposition that we often select typefaces based on their personality. The criteria of graphology was juxtaposed with major aspects of type design. **For example, a graphologist would look at a person's pen pressure to determine their vitality and spirit. A bold hand would equate that he or she might be very self-assured and energetic. Designers can make a heavier weight typeface that follows this idea.**

In the case of Reflux, the handwriting sample for which it was based on, revealed a person who is philosophical in nature and a free thinker. (8/8 point)

In the case of Reflux, the handwriting sample for which it was based on, revealed a person who is philosophical in nature and a free thinker. (8/8 point)

In the case of Reflux, the handwriting sample for which it was based on, revealed a person who is philosophical in nature and a free thinker. (7/7 point)

In the case of Reflux, the handwriting sample for which it was based on, revealed a person who is philosophical in nature and a free thinker. (7/7 point)

In the case of Reflux, the handwriting sample for which it was based on, revealed a person who is philosophical in nature and a free thinker. (6/6 point)

In the case of Reflux, the handwriting sample for which it was based on, revealed a person who is philosophical in nature and a free thinker. (6/6 point)

TX Blotch abc123

ABCDEFGHIJKLMNOPQRSTUVW

XYZabcdefghijklmnopqrstuvwx

yz!?¡¿0123456789¢$£¥€@&#

%‰©®™ª*‡†°ÅÇÉÎÑÒØÜ&çéîñ

òøüıßfifl..."\":;'/'•'"»«><∞≤≥‹›

÷=≠≈±+¬◊∑∏π∆∂Ω√∫f(){}[]§¶

ÐðŁŁ†ŠšÝýÞþŽž½¼¹¾³²¦–×

Blotch is the second in a series of seven fonts to be released by Typebox. Like Reflux, this typeface is a result from a conceptual and formal study based on handwriting analysis. In this case, the handwriting sample reveals a large degree of intellect, ambition, imagination and expressiveness. Pen strokes are animated and jerky, which indicates a sort of creative impatience. Lines are straight and decisive. The feel of the writing is condensed and contrasty. These are signs of conscientiousness. Also, the writing is a mix of cap print and cursive; indicating versatility and culture. Vertical stress marks, heavy pen pressure and ink blots make it a weighty specimen. This person is assertive and original! Design ideas also came from Victorian Era ornamental display faces.

mailroom@typebox.com

ABCDEFGHIJKLMNOPQRSTUVWXYZabcdefghijklmnop
qrstuvwxyz!?¡¿0123456789¢$£¥€@&#%‰©®™ᵃ★‡†°ÅÇ
ÉÎÑÒØÜåçéîñòøüißfifl…"\":;'/'•'"»«><∞≤≥<>÷=≠≈±+¬◊Σℙπ△
∂Ω√∫f(){}[]§¶ÐðŁłŠšÝýÞþŽž½¼¹³¾³²¦–×✤

TX Wirish Light

Cynthia Jacquette
2001

ABCDEFGHIJKLMNOPQRSTUVWXYZabcdefghijklmn
opqrstuvwxyz!?¡¿0123456789¢$£¥€@&#%‰©®™ᵃ★‡†°
ÅÇÉÎÑÒØÜåçéîñòøüißfifl…"\":;'/'•'"»«><∞≤≥<>÷=≠≈±+¬◊Σ
ℙπ△∂Ω√∫f(){}[]§¶ÐðŁłŠšÝýÞþŽž½¼¹³¾³²¦–×✤

TX Wirish Medium

Cynthia Jacquette
2001

ABCDEFGHIJKLMNOPQRSTUVWXYZabcdefghijkl
mnopqrstuvwxyz!?¡¿0123456789¢$£¥€@&#%‰©®
™ᵃ★‡†°ÅÇÉÎÑÒØÜåçéîñòøüißfifl…"\":;'/'•'"»«><∞≤≥<>÷=≠
≈±+¬◊Σℙπ△∂Ω√∫f(){}[]§¶ÐðŁłŠšÝýÞþŽž½¼¹³¾³²¦–×✤

TX Wirish Bold

Cynthia Jacquette
2001

TX Wirish was born out of the forms of uncial calligraphic letters. In drawing these, I found the most intense moment to be taking the pen on a diagonal; the pen then seems to control the writer. To create a contemporary typeface based on calligraphy, I thought the most important rule of the design was that it keep this strong diagonal. My first design based off of calligraphy was a serif face with triangle serifs and contrast between strokes. Paired with the diagonals, the face did not look modern enough. I was aiming for a clean, modern face that had a slightly gothic feel to it; sort of a "modern light blackletter". I found by altering the face to a mono weight, but keeping some of my pointy serifs, I could achieve the look I craved for. **The key was to keep the angles and curves happening in my uncial calligraphy, but scrap the contrast in strokes. The result is a semi-serif mono weight with pointy tops, reminiscent of gothic arches.**

Typebox

ABCDEFGHIJKLMNOPQRSTUVWXYZabcdefghijklmnopqrst
uvwxyz!?¡¿0123456789¢$£¥€@&#%‰©®™ª*‡†°ÅÇÉÑ
ÒØÜåçéîñòøüißfifl…"\":;'/'•'"»«›‹∞≥≤‹›÷=≠≈±+¬◊∑∏
π∆∂Ω√∫ƒ(){}[]§¶ÐđŁłŠšÝýÞþŽž½¼¾²¡-×✊

ABCDEFGHIJKLMNOPQRSTUVWXYZabcdefghijklmnopqrst
uvwxyz!?¡¿0123456789¢$£¥€@&#%‰©®™ª*‡†°ÅÇÉÎ
ÑÒØÜåçéîñòøüißfifl…"\":;'/'•'"»«›‹∞≥≤‹›÷=≠≈±+¬◊
∑∏π∆∂Ω√∫ƒ(){}[]§¶ÐđŁłŠšÝýÞþŽž½¼¾²¡-×✊

TX MANIFESTO REGULAR & *SLANT*

Manifesto was designed for an article written in response to
opinions that philosophy and personal expression have been
wiped clean from today's design profession. We declare that
contemporary design is sterile and sublime.

*Enter Ken Garland's revision of the original 1964 Manifesto. The publishing
of the "First Things First" manifesto 2000 was exhibit A that a trend for
social belief systems is growing. Or is it? Many comfortably accept that
designers are indeed "engaged in nothing less than the manufacture of
contemporary reality". The four 'voices' of the TX Manifesto Family is
intended for your typographical response, and a push for conscientious
and meaningful design.*

ABCDEFGHIJKLMNOPQRSTUVWXYZabcdefghijklmnopqr
stuvwxyz!?i¿0123456789¢$£¥€@&#%‰©®™ª*‡†°Åç
ÉÎÑÒØÜåçéîñòøüißfifl...“\”:;‘/’•'"»«›‹∞≥≤‹›÷=≠≈±
+¬◊ΣΠπΔ∂Ω√∫ƒ[]{}[]§¶ÐđŁłŠšÝýþbŽž½¼13¾32¡–×✊

TX Manifesto Stout

Mike Kohnke
2002

ABCDEFGHIJKLMNOPQRSTUVWXYZabcdefghijklmnopqrst
uvwxyz!?i¿0123456789¢$£¥€@&#%‰©®™ª*‡†°ÅçÉÎÑ
ÒØÜåçéîñòøüißfifl...“\”:;‘/’•'"»«›‹∞≥≤‹›÷=≠≈±+¬◊Σ
ΠππΔ∂Ω√∫ƒ[]{}[]§¶ÐđŁłŠšÝýþbŽž½¼13¾32¡–×✊

TX Manifesto Stencil

Mike Kohnke
2002

Typebox

TX MANIFESTO STOUT & STENCIL.

**Manifesto was designed for an article written in response
to opinions that philosophy and personal expression have
been wiped clean from today's design profession. We
declare that contemporary design is sterile and sublime.**

Enter Ken Garland's revision of the original 1964 Manifesto. The publishing
of the "First Things First" manifesto 2000 was exhibit A that a trend for
social belief systems is growing. Or is it? Many comfortably accept that
designers are indeed "engaged in nothing less than the manufacture of
contemporary reality". The four 'voices' of the TX Manifesto Family is
intended for your typographical response, and a push for conscientious
and meaningful design.

TX Hex abc123

ABCDEFGHIJKLMNOPQRSTUVWXY

Zabcdefghijklmnopqrstuvwx

yz!?¡¿£0123456789¢$£¥€@&#

%‰©®™ª*‡†°ÅÇÉÎÑÒ ÐÜåçéîñò

ðüıßßß…''\"";:;'⌐'•'''»«>‹∞≤≥‹›≠

=≠≈±+¬⌐∫∑∏π∝◁◀∂∆Ω∫∫∫{}[]∫¶

½ ¼ ¹ ¾ ³²
            ¦ ~×∂ð£ł łššÝ ğbþžž

Liquid crystal displays are most commonly used for products at the lower end of the computer market. Typographically they are characterized by their very sharp-edged pixels which add high-frequency noise to text, resulting in illegibility. John Baxter, an American typographer, suggests that a hexagon honeycomb pixel arrangement might be an alternative to the rectangular pixels used today. Hex is a sans-serif typeface specially designed for the aforementioned liquid crystal displays. It was originally designed in 12pt, at 72dpi. Its capitals avoid the squareness of early sans-serif typefaces such as FUTURA and AVANT GARDE. The typeface is modeled upon the humanist minuscule. The uneven stroke weight of the face reflects the action of a quill. Its distinguishing feature is a hard angular transition from the stems to the curves which gives it a black letter look.

TX Gitter

Dennis Poon
2001

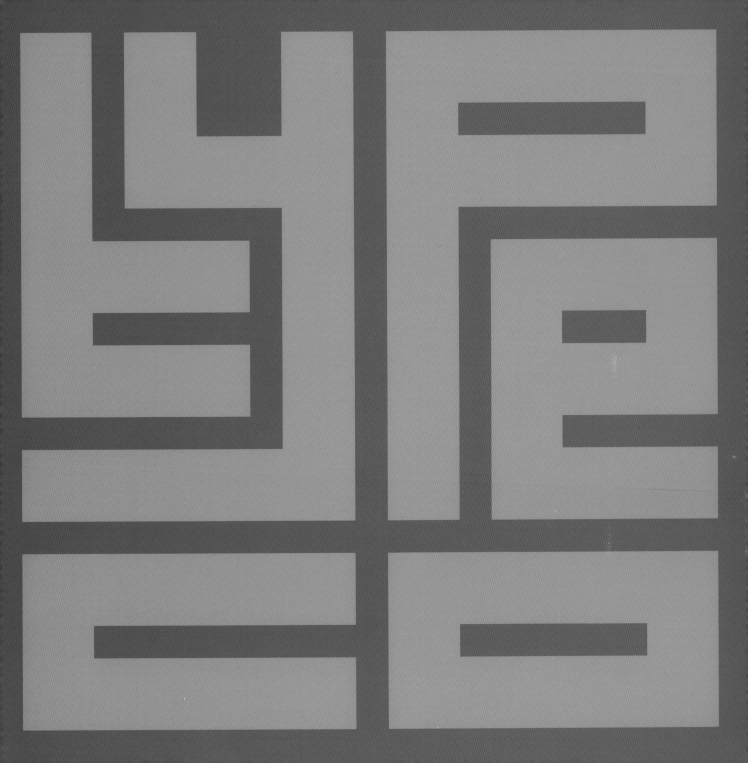

typeco

original fonts
custom designed fonts
graphic design services

Rochester, New York
www.typeco.com
contact@typeco.com
585.230.1674

Chunkfeeder Light	Chunkfeeder Light Oblique	Chunkfeeder Regular	Chunkfeeder Regular Oblique	Chunkfeeder Bold	Chunkfeeder Bold Oblique
Aa	Aa	Bb	Bb	Cc	Cc

Chunkfeeder Family

James Grieshaber
2002

6 Variations
Monospaced

Cypher 3 Light	Cypher 3 Light Italic	Cypher 3 Regular	Cypher 3 Regular Italic	Cypher 3 Bold	Cypher 3 Bold Italic
[ɪʲ]	[ɪʲ]	Eɔ	Eɔ	Ff	Ff

Cypher Family

James Grieshaber
2002

24 Variations

Cypher 4 Light	Cypher 4 Light Italic	Cypher 4 Regular	Cypher 4 Regular Italic	Cypher 4 Bold	Cypher 4 Bold Italic
Gg	Gg	Hh	Hh	Ii	Ii

Cypher 5 Light	Cypher 5 Light Italic	Cypher 5 Regular	Cypher 5 Regular Italic	Cypher 5 Bold	Cypher 5 Bold Italic
Jj	Jj	Kk	Kk	Ll	Ll

Cypher 7 Light	Cypher 7 Light Italic	Cypher 7 Regular	Cypher 7 Regular Italic	Cypher 7 Bold	Cypher 7 Bold Italic
Mm	Mm	Nn	Nn	Oo	Oo

Glyphic Neue Narrow	Glyphic Neue Narrow Italic	Glyphic Neue Medium	Glyphic Neue Medium Italic	Glyphic Neue Bold	Glyphic Neue Bold Italic
Pp	Pp	Qq	Qq	Rr	Rr

Glyphic Neue Family

James Grieshaber
2002

6 Variations

Typeco

Modern Grotesque Thin	Modern Grotesque Thin Italic	Modern Grotesque Thin SC	Modern Grotesque Thin SC Italic	Modern Grotesque Light	Modern Grotesque Light Italic
Ss	Ss	Tt	Tt	Uu	Uu

Modern Grotesque Family

James Grieshaber
2002

16 Variations

Modern Grotesque Light SC	Modern Grotesque Light SC Italic	Modern Grotesque Regular	Modern Grotesque Regular Italic	Modern Grotesque Regular SC	Modern Grotesque Regular SC Italic
Vv	Vv	Ww	Ww	Xx	Xx

Modern Grotesque Bold	Modern Grotesque Bold Italic	Modern Grotesque Bold SC	Modern Grotesque Bold SC Italic		www.typeco.com
Yy	Yy	Zz	Zz		

Chunkfeeder Light

ABCDEFGHIJKLMNOPQ
RSTUVWXYZabcdefgh
ijklmnopqrstuvwxy
z123456789!@$%&?£

ABCDEFGHIJKLMNOPQRSTUVWXYZ
abcdefghijklmnopqrstuvwxyz01234567890
{ÀÁÂÃÄÅÇÈÉÊËÌÍÎÏÑÒÓÔÕÖØÙÚÛÜåãàáâãçèéêëiìíîïñòóôõöøßûúù}
[&$£¥¢¶§†‡×@] [¿¡ÆŒæœß!?]

Chunkfeeder Light Oblique

ABCDEFGHIJKLMNOPQ
RSTUVWXYZabcdefgh
ijklmnopqrstuvwxy
z123456789!@$%&?£

ABCDEFGHIJKLMNOPQRSTUVWXYZ
abcdefghijklmnopqrstuvwxyz01234567890
{ÀÁÂÃÄÅÇÈÉÊËÌÍÎÏÑÒÓÔÕÖØÙÚÛÜåãàáâãçèéêëiìíîïñòóôõöøßûúù}
[&$£¥¢¶§†‡×@] [¿¡ÆŒæœß!?]

contact@typeco.com

Chunkfeeder Regular

Chunkfeeder Regular

James Grieshaber
2002

ABCDEFGHIJKLMNOPQ
RSTUVWXYZabcdefgh
ijklmnopqrstuvwxy
z123456789!@$%&?

ABCDEFGHIJKLMNOPQRSTUVWXYZ
abcdefghijklmnopqrstuvwxyz01234567890
{ÄÂÁÀÃÅÇËÊÉÈÏÎÍÌÑÖÔÓÒÕØÜÛÚÙåãàáâäçëêéèïîíìñöôóòõøßüûúù}
(&$€£¥¢¶§†‡×@) [¿ ¡ÆŒæœß!?]

Chunkfeeder Reg Oblique

ABCDEFGHIJKLMNOPQ
RSTUVWXYZabcdefgh
ijklmnopqrstuvwxy
z123456789!@$%&?

ABCDEFGHIJKLMNOPQRSTUVWXYZ
abcdefghijklmnopqrstuvwxyz01234567890
{ÄÂÁÀÃÅÇËÊÉÈÏÎÍÌÑÖÔÓÒÕØÜÛÚÙåãàáâäçëêéèïîíìñöôóòõøßüûúù}
(&$€£¥¢¶§†‡×@) [¿ ¡ÆŒæœß!?]

Chunkfeeder Bold

ABCDEFGHIJKLMNOPQ
RSTUVWXYZabcdefgh
ijklmnopqrstuvwxy
z123456789!@$%&?£

ABCDEFGHIJKLMNOPQRSTUVWXYZ
abcdefghijklmnopqrstuvwxyz01234567890
{ÄÂÁÀÃÅÇËÊÉÈÏÎÍÌÑÖÔÓÒÕØÜÛÚÙàãâáäåçëêéèïîíìñöôóòõøßüûúù}
(&$€£¥¢¶§†‡×@) [¿¡ŒŒœœß!?]

Chunkfeeder Bold Oblique

ABCDEFGHIJKLMNOPQ
RSTUVWXYZabcdefgh
ijklmnopqrstuvwxy
z123456789!@$%&?£

ABCDEFGHIJKLMNOPQRSTUVWXYZ
abcdefghijklmnopqrstuvwxyz01234567890
{ÄÂÁÀÃÅÇËÊÉÈÏÎÍÌÑÖÔÓÒÕØÜÛÚÙàãâáäåçëêéèïîíìñöôóòõøßüûúù}
(&$€£¥¢¶§†‡×@) [¿¡ŒŒœœß!?]

Cypher 3 Light

ABCDEFGHIJKLMNOPQRSTUUWXYZ
abcdefghijklmnopqrstuuwxyz01234567890
[♀$€£¥ƒ¢¶§†‡•@] [¿†Œœ∞ß!?]
{ÄÂÀÄÄÅÇÉÊÈÉÏÎÌÍÑÖÔÒÓÕÙÛÙÚ…}

Cypher 3 Light Italic

ABCDEFGHIJKLMNOPQRSTUUWXYZ
abcdefghijklmnopqrstuuwxyz01234567890
[♀$€£¥ƒ¢¶§†‡•@] [¿†Œœ∞ß!?]
{ÄÂÀÄÄÅÇÉÊÈÉÏÎÌÍÑÖÔÒÓÕÙÛÙÚ…}

Cypher 3 Regular

ABCDEFGHIJKLMNOPQRSTUUWXYZ
abcdefghijklmnopqrstuuwxyz01234567890
[♀$€£¥ƒ¢¶§†‡•@] [¿†Œœ∞ß!?]
{ÄÂÀÄÄÅÇÉÊÈÉÏÎÌÍÑÖÔÒÓÕÙÛÙÚ…}

Cypher 3 Regular Italic

ABCDEFGHIJKLMNOPQRSTUUWXYZ
abcdefghijklmnopqrstuuwxyz01234567890
[♀$€£¥ƒ¢¶§†‡•@] [¿†Œœ∞ß!?]
{ÄÂÀÄÄÅÇÉÊÈÉÏÎÌÍÑÖÔÒÓÕÙÛÙÚ…}

Cypher 3 Bold

ABCDEFGHIJKLMNOPQRSTUUWXYZ
abcdefghijklmnopqrstuuwxyz01234567890
[♀$€£¥ƒ¢¶§†‡•@] [¿†Œœ∞ß!?]
{ÄÂÀÄÄÅÇÉÊÈÉÏÎÌÍÑÖÔÒÓÕÙÛÙÚ…}

Cypher 3 Bold Italic

ABCDEFGHIJKLMNOPQRSTUUWXYZ
abcdefghijklmnopqrstuuwxyz01234567890
[♀$€£¥ƒ¢¶§†‡•@] [¿†Œœ∞ß!?]
{ÄÂÀÄÄÅÇÉÊÈÉÏÎÌÍÑÖÔÒÓÕÙÛÙÚ…}

Typeco

James Grieshaber
2002

Cypher 4 Light

ABCDEFGHIJKLMNOPQRSTUVWXYZ
abcdefghijklmnopqrstuvwxyz01234567890
(&$¢£¥ƒ€¶§†‡•@) [¿¡ÆŒæœ∞ß!?]
{ÄÂÁÀÅÃÇÉÊËÈÏÎÍÌÑÖÔÓÒÕØÜÛÚÙäâáàåãçéêëèïîíìñöôóòõøüûúù}

Cypher 4 Light Italic

ABCDEFGHIJKLMNOPQRSTUVWXYZ
abcdefghijklmnopqrstuvwxyz01234567890
(&$¢£¥ƒ€¶§†‡•@) [¿¡ÆŒæœ∞ß！?]
{ÄÂÁÀÅÃÇÉÊËÈÏÎÍÌÑÖÔÓÒÕØÜÛÚÙäâáàåãçéêëèïîíìñöôóòõøüûúù}

Cypher 4 Regular

ABCDEFGHIJKLMNOPQRSTUVWXYZ
abcdefghijklmnopqrstuvwxyz01234567890
(&$¢£¥ƒ€¶§†‡•@) [¿¡ÆŒæœ∞ß!?]
{ÄÂÁÀÅÃÇÉÊËÈÏÎÍÌÑÖÔÓÒÕØÜÛÚÙäâáàåãçéêëèïîíìñöôóòõøüûúù}

Cypher 4 Regular Italic

ABCDEFGHIJKLMNOPQRSTUVWXYZ
abcdefghijklmnopqrstuvwxyz01234567890
(&$¢£¥ƒ€¶§†‡•@) [¿¡ÆŒæœ∞ß!?]
{ÄÂÁÀÅÃÇÉÊËÈÏÎÍÌÑÖÔÓÒÕØÜÛÚÙäâáàåãçéêëèïîíìñöôóòõøüûúù}

Cypher 4 Bold

ABCDEFGHIJKLMNOPQRSTUVWXYZ
abcdefghijklmnopqrstuvwxyz01234567890
(&$¢£¥ƒ€¶§†‡•@) [¿¡ÆŒæœ∞ß!?]
{ÄÂÁÀÅÃÇÉÊËÈÏÎÍÌÑÖÔÓÒÕØÜÛÚÙäâáàåãçéêëèïîíìñöôóòõøüûúù}

Cypher 4 Bold Italic

ABCDEFGHIJKLMNOPQRSTUVWXYZ
abcdefghijklmnopqrstuvwxyz01234567890
(&$¢£¥ƒ€¶§†‡•@) [¿¡ÆŒæœ∞ß!?]
{ÄÂÁÀÅÃÇÉÊËÈÏÎÍÌÑÖÔÓÒÕØÜÛÚÙäâáàåãçéêëèïîíìñöôóòõøüûúù}

contact@typeco.com

James Grieshaber
2002

Cypher 5 Light

ABCDEFGHIJKLMNOPQRSTUVWXYZ
abcdefghijklmnopqrstuvwxyz0123456789O
(#$€£¥ƒ¢¶§†‡•@) [¿iﬁﬂŒœ∞ßﬂ!?]
{ÄÂÁÀÅÇËÊÉÈÏÎÍÌÑÖÔÓÒØÜÛÚÙäâáàåçëêéèïîíìñöôóòøÿ}

Cypher 5 Light Italic

ABCDEFGHIJKLMNOPQRSTUVWXYZ
abcdefghijklmnopqrstuvwxyz0123456789O
(#$€£¥ƒ¢¶§†‡•@) [¿iﬁﬂŒœ∞ßﬂ!?]
{ÄÂÁÀÅÇËÊÉÈÏÎÍÌÑÖÔÓÒØÜÛÚÙäâáàåçëêéèïîíìñöôóòø}

Cypher 5 Regular

ABCDEFGHIJKLMNOPQRSTUVWXYZ
abcdefghijklmnopqrstuvwxyz0123456789O
(#$€£¥ƒ¢¶§†‡•@) [¿iﬁﬂŒœ∞ßﬂ!?]
{ÄÂÁÀÅÇËÊÉÈÏÎÍÌÑÖÔÓÒØÜÛÚÙäâáàåçëêéèïîíìñöôóòøß

Cypher 5 Regular Italic

ABCDEFGHIJKLMNOPQRSTUVWXYZ
abcdefghijklmnopqrstuvwxyz0123456789O
(#$€£¥ƒ¢¶§†‡•@) [¿iﬁﬂŒœ∞ßﬂ!?]
{ÄÂÁÀÅÇËÊÉÈÏÎÍÌÑÖÔÓÒØÜÛÚÙäâáàåçëêéèïîíìñöôóòøß

Cypher 5 Bold

ABCDEFGHIJKLMNOPQRSTUVWXYZ
abcdefghijklmnopqrstuvwxyz0123456789 O
(#$€£¥ƒ¢¶§†‡•@) [¿iﬁﬂŒœ∞ßﬂ!?]
{Ä ÂÁÀÅÇË ÊÉ ÈÏÎÍÌÑ ÖÔÓÒØÜÛÚÙäâá àâáàåçëêéèïîíìñô óóòø

Cypher 5 Bold Italic

ABCDEFGHIJKLMNOPQRSTUVWXYZ
abcdefghijklmnopqrstuvwxyz0123456789O
(#$€£¥ƒ¢¶§†‡•@) [¿iﬁﬂŒœ∞ßﬂ!?]
{ÄÂÁÀÅÇËÊÉÈÏÎÍÌÑÖÔÓÒØÜÛÚÙäâáàåçëêéèïîíìñöôóòøß

Typeco

James Grieshaber
2002

Cypher 7 Light

ABCDEFGHIJKLMNOPQRSTUVWXYZ
abcdefghijklmnopqrstuvwxyz01
234567890
(#$€£¥ƒ¢¶§†‡·@) [¿¡ÆŒæœßfß!?]

Cypher 7 Light Italic

ABCDEFGHIJKLMNOPQRSTUVWXYZ
abcdefghijklmnopqrstuvwxyz013
4567890
(#$€£¥ƒ¢¶§†‡·@) [¿¡ÆŒæœßfß!?]

Cypher 7 Regular

ABCDEFGHIJKLMNOPQRSTUVWXYZ
abcdefghijklmnopqrstuvwxyz01
234567890
(#$€£¥ƒ¢¶§†‡·@) [¿¡ÆŒæœßfß!?]

Cypher 7 Regular Italic

ABCDEFGHIJKLMNOPQRSTUVWXYZ
abcdefghijklmnopqrstuvwxyz01
234567890
(#$€£¥ƒ¢¶§†‡·@) [¿¡ÆŒæœßfß!?]

Cypher 7 Bold

ABCDEFGHIJKLMNOPQRSTUVWXYZ
abcdefghijklmnopqrstuvwxyz01
234567890
(#$€£¥ƒ¢¶§†‡·@) [¿¡ÆŒæœßfß!?]

Cypher 7 Bold Italic

ABCDEFGHIJKLMNOPQRSTUVWXYZ
abcdefghijklmnopqrstuvwxyz01
234567890
(#$€£¥ƒ¢¶§†‡·@) [¿¡ÆŒæœßfß!?]

contact@typeco.com

Glyphic Neue Narrow

Glyphic Neue Narrow

James Grieshaber
2002

ABCDEFGHIJKLMNOPQR
STUVWXYZabcdefghij
klmnopqrstuvwxyz12
3456789!⌀$%¢?£¥£f¢
ÄÂÀÁÃÅÇËÊÉÈÏÎÍÌÑÖÔÓÒÕ
ÜÛÚÙâáàâãäçëêéèïîíìñ
öôóòõøßüûúù

([¢§£¥f¢q§†‡*⌀]
[áïŒ₤œœŒßi!?]
{ÂÇÉÑÌÓÔÂÇÈÑÌÓ}

Glyphic Neue Narrow Italic

ABCDEFGHIJKLMNOPQRS
TUVWXYZabcdefghijk
mnopqrstuvwxyz12345
6789!⌀$%¢?£¥£f¢øßçq
ÄÂÀÁÃÅÇËÊÉÈÏÎÍÌÑÖÔÓÒÕ
ÜÛÚÙâáàâãäçëêéèïîíìñ
öôóòõøßüûúù

([¢§£¥f¢q§†‡*⌀]
[áïŒ₤œœŒßi!?]
{ÂÇÉÑÌÓÔÂÇÈÑÌÓ}

Typeco

glyphic neue narrow

ABCDEFGHIJKLMNOP
QRSTUVWXYZABCDE
FGHIJKLMNOPQRSTU
VWXYZ1234567789!@

(CSC¥fCqft*@)
[¡¿CCÆŒ®!?]
{ÂÇÉÑÌÒÔÅÇÈÑÌÒ}

ÄÂÁÀÃÅÇËÊÉÈÏÎÍÌÑÖÔÓÒÕ
ÜÛÚÙâãäáàåçëêéèïîíìñ
öôóòõßÜûúù

glyphic neue narrow italic

ABCDEFGHIJKLMNOPQ
RSTUVWXYZABCDEFG
hijklmnopqrstuvwx
yz1234567789!@$%&?

(CSC¥fCqft*@)
[¡¿CCÆŒ®!?]
{ÂÇÉÑÌÒÔÅÇÈÑÌÒ}

ÄÂÁÀÃÅÇËÊÉÈÏÎÍÌÑÖÔÓÒÕ
ÜÛÚÙâãäáàåçëêéèïîíìñ
öôóòõßÜûúù

contact@typeco.com

glyphic neue wide

A B C D E F G H I J K L M N
O P Q R S T U V W X Y Z a b
c d e f g h i j k l m n o p
q r s t u v w x y z 1 2 3 4

ÄÂÁÀÃÅÇËÊÉÈÏÎÍÌÑÖÔÓÒÕØÜÜ
ÛÙÚâãäáàãåçëêéèïîíìñ
öôóòõøßüûûú

(¢$€£¥ƒ©§†‡*①)
[¿¡ÆŒ°ª®ß¡?]
{ÂÇÉÑÎ°ÔÂÇÈÑÎ}

Glyphic Neue Wide

James Grieshaber
2002

glyphic neue wide italic

A B C D E F G H I J K L M N O
P Q R S T U V W X Y Z a b c d
e f g h i j k l m n o p q r s
t u v w x y z 1 2 3 4 5 6 7 8

ÄÂÁÀÃÅÇËÊÉÈÏÎÍÌÑÖÔÓÒÕØÜÜ
ÛÙÚâãäáàãåçëêéèïîíìñ
öôóòõøßüûûú

(¢$€£¥ƒ©§†‡*①)
[¿¡ÆŒ°ª®ß¡?]
{ÂÇÉÑÎ°ÔÂÇÈÑÎ}

Typeco

James Grieshaber
2002

Includes 16 styles:
Thin
Thin Small Caps
Thin Italic
Thin Small Caps Italic
Light
Light Small Caps
Light Italic
Light Small Caps Italic
Regular
Regular Small Caps
Regular Italic
Regular Small Caps Italic
Bold
Bold Small Caps
Bold Italic
Bold Small Caps Italic

Modern Grotesque Thin

AaBbCcDdEeFfGgHhIi
JjKkLlMmNnOoPpQqRrSsTtUuVvWwXxYyZz
AaBbCcDdEeFfGgHhIiJjKkLlMmNnOoPpQqRrSsTtUuVvWwXxYyZz

Modern Grotesque Thin SC

AaBbCcDdEeFfGgHhIi
JjKkLlMmNnOoPpQqRrSsTtUuVvWwXxYyZz
AaBbCcDdEeFfGgHhIiJjKkLlMmNnOoPpQqRrSsTtUuVvWwXxYyZz

Modern Grotesque Thin Italic

AaBbCcDdEeFfGgHhIi
JjKkLlMmNnOoPpQqRrSsTtUuVvWwXxYyZz
AaBbCcDdEeFfGgHhIiJjKkLlMmNnOoPpQqRrSsTtUuVvWwXxYyZz

Modern Grotesque Thin SC Italic

AaBbCcDdEeFfGgHhIi
JjKkLlMmNnOoPpQqRrSsTtUuVvWwXxYyZz
AaBbCcDdEeFfGgHhIiJjKkLlMmNnOoPpQqRrSsTtUuVvWwXxYyZz

contact@typeco.com

Modern Grotesque Light

Modern Grotesque Light

James Grieshaber
2002

A a B b C c D d E e F f G g H h I i
J j K k L l M m N n O o P p Q q R r S s T t U u V v W w X x Y y Z z
A a B b C c D d E e F f G g H h I i J j K k L l M m N n O o P p Q q R r S s T t U u V v W w X x Y y Z z

Modern Grotesque Light SC

A A B b C c D d E e F f G g H h I i
J j K k L l M m N n O o P p Q q R r S s T t U u V v W w X x Y y Z z
A A B b C c D d E e F f G g H h I i J j K k L l M m N n O o P p Q q R r S s T t U u V v W w X x Y y Z z

Modern Grotesque Light Italic

A a B b C c D d E e F f G g H h I i
J j K k L l M m N n O o P p Q q R r S s T t U u V v W w X x Y y Z z
A a B b C c D d E e F f G g H h I i J j K k L l M m N n O o P p Q q R r S s T t U u V v W w X x Y y Z z

Modern Grotesque Light SC Italic

A A B b C c D d E e F f G g H h I i
J j K k L l M m N n O o P p Q q R r S s T t U u V v W w X x Y y Z z
A A B b C c D d E e F f G g H h I i J j K k L l M m N n O o P p Q q R r S s T t U u V v W w X x Y y Z z

Modern Grotesque Regular

AaBbCcDdEeFfGgHhIi

JjKkLlMmNnOoPpQqRrSsTtUuVvWwXxYyZz

AaBbCcDdEeFfGgHhIiJjKkLlMmNnOoPpQqRrSsTtUuVvWwXxYyZz

Modern Grotesque Regular SC

AaBbCcDdEeFfGgHhIi

JjKkLlMmNnOoPpQqRrSsTtUuVvWwXxYyZz

AaBbCcDdEeFfGgHhIiJjKkLlMmNnOoPpQqRrSsTtUuVvWwXxYyZz

Modern Grotesque Regular Italic

AaBbCcDdEeFfGgHhIi

JjKkLlMmNnOoPpQqRrSsTtUuVvWwXxYyZz

AaBbCcDdEeFfGgHhIiJjKkLlMmNnOoPpQqRrSsTtUuVvWwXxYyZz

Modern Grotesque Regular SC Italic

AaBbCcDdEeFfGgHhIi

JjKkLlMmNnOoPpQqRrSsTtUuVvWwXxYyZz

AaBbCcDdEeFfGgHhIiJjKkLlMmNnOoPpQqRrSsTtUuVvWwXxYyZz

contact@typeco.com

Modern Grotesque Bold

AaBbCcDdEeFfGgHhIi
JjKkLlMmNnOoPpQqRrSsTtUuVvWwXxYyZz
AaBbCcDdEeFfGgHhIiJjKkLlMmNnOoPpQqRrSsTtUuVvWwXxYyZz

Modern Grotesque Bold SC

AABbCcDdEeFfGgHhIi
JjKkLlMmNnOoPpQqRrSsTtUuVvWwXxYyZz
AABbCcDdEeFfGgHhIiJjKkLlMmNnOoPpQqRrSsTtUuVvWwXxYyZz

Modern Grotesque Bold Italic

AaBbCcDdEeFfGgHhIi
JjKkLlMmNnOoPpQqRrSsTtUuVvWwXxYyZz
AaBbCcDdEeFfGgHhIiJjKkLlMmNnOoPpQqRrSsTtUuVvWwXxYyZz

Modern Grotesque Bold SC Italic

AABbCcDdEeFfGgHhIi
JjKkLlMmNnOoPpQqRrSsTtUuVvWwXxYyZz
AABbCcDdEeFfGgHhIiJjKkLlMmNnOoPpQqRrSsTtUuVvWwXxYyZz

Typeco

Foundry A:

typodermic

illican
celidon
celidon ink
snowgoose
bomr
wyvern

Contact
sales@typodermic.com
www.typodermic.com

Foundry B:

Larabie Fonts

neuropol deluxe
nasalization deluxe
mufferaw deluxe
chinese rocks deluxe
pakenham deluxe
zekton deluxe
larabiefont deluxe
blue highway deluxe
sui generis deluxe

Contact
ray@typodermic.com
www.larabiefonts.com

abcdefghijklmnopqrstuvwxyzABCDEFGH
IJKLMNOPQRSTUVWXYZ1234567890!?$

Ray Larabie
2002

Inspired by a trip to London, Jillican was built on Gill Sans proportions and military aircraft angularity.

the quick brown fox jumps over the lazy dog. FILL MY BOX WITH TWELVE DOZEN LIQUOR JUGS.

the quick brown fox jumps over the lazy dog. FILL MY BOX WITH TWELVE DOZEN LIQUOR JUGS.

the quick brown fox jumps over the lazy dog. FILL MY BOX WITH TWELVE DOZEN LIQUOR JUGS.

the quick brown fox jumps over the lazy dog. FILL MY BOX WITH TWELVE DOZEN LIQUOR JUGS.

abcdefghijklmnopqrsuvwxyzABCDEF GHIJKLMNOPQRSTUVWXYZ123456 7890!?$%&("%Æœf£¢€¥¿½Üü™®©")

abcdefghijklmnopqrstuvwxyzABCD
EFGHIJKLMNOPQRSTUVWXYZ123

abcdefghijklmnopqrstuvwxyzABCD EFGHIJKLMNOPQRSTUVWXYZ123

the quick brown fox jumps over the lazy dog. FILL MY BOX WITH TWELVE DOZEN LIQUOR JUGS.

the quick brown fox jumps over the lazy dog. FILL MY BOX WITH TWELVE DOZEN LIQUOR JUGS.

the quick brown fox jumps over the lazy dog. FILL MY BOX WITH TWELVE DOZEN LIQUOR JUGS.

the quick brown fox jumps over the lazy dog. FILL MY BOX WITH TWELVE DOZEN LIQUOR JUGS.

the quick brown fox jumps over the lazy dog. FILL MY BOX WITH TWELVE DOZEN LIQUOR JUGS.

the quick brown fox jumps over the lazy dog. FILL MY BOX WITH TWELVE DOZEN LIQUOR JUGS.

abcdefghijklmnopqrstuvwxyzABCD
EFGHIJKLMNOPQRSTUVWXYZ123

Typodermic

Ray Larabie
2002

Telidon is a font reminiscent of dot matrix printer fonts of the 1970s and 1980s, which are still in use today in retail receipts. Telidon is useful for simulating LED pixel board graphics. If you want a rougher, more authentic dot matrix printer look, Telidon has a sister family called Telidon Ink, which has a distressed, inky appearance. The extended styles have doubled pixels, just like the dot matrix fonts of yesteryear.

Telidon Regular

abcdefghijklmnopqrstuvwxyzABCDEFGHIJKLMNOPQR
STUVWXYZ1234567890(!¡?@#%&*/%^+)#'@¢£€$¥%@''™

Telidon Condensed

the quick brown fox jumps over
the lazy dog. FILL MY BOX WITH
TWELVE DOZEN LIQUOR JUGS.

Telidon Condensed Italic

the quick brown fox jumps over
the lazy dog. FILL MY BOX WITH
TWELVE DOZEN LIQUOR JUGS.

Telidon Condensed Bold

the quick brown fox jumps over
the lazy dog. FILL MY BOX WITH
TWELVE DOZEN LIQUOR JUGS.

Telidon Condensed Bold Italic

the quick brown fox jumps over
the lazy dog. FILL MY BOX WITH
TWELVE DOZEN LIQUOR JUGS.

Telidon Condensed Heavy

the quick brown fox jumps over
the lazy dog. FILL MY BOX WITH
TWELVE DOZEN LIQUOR JUGS.

Telidon Condensed Heavy Italic

the quick brown fox jumps over
the lazy dog. FILL MY BOX WITH
TWELVE DOZEN LIQUOR JUGS.

Telidon Regular Italic

the quick brown fox jumps
over the lazy dog. FILL
MY BOX WITH TWELVE DOZEN
LIQUOR JUGS.

Telidon Bold

the quick brown fox jumps
over the lazy dog. FILL MY
BOX WITH TWELVE DOZEN
LIQUOR JUGS.

Telidon Bold Italic

the quick brown fox jumps
over the lazy dog. FILL MY
BOX WITH TWELVE DOZEN
LIQUOR JUGS.

Telidon Heavy

abcdefghijklmnopqrstuvwxyzABCDE
FGHIJKLMNOPQRSTUVWXYZ1234567890

Telidon Heavy Italic

the quick brown fox jumps
over the lazy dog. FILL MY
BOX WITH TWELVE DOZEN
LIQUOR JUGS.

Telidon Expanded

the quick brown fox
jumps over the lazy dog.
FILL MY BOX WITH TWELVE
DOZEN LIQUOR JUGS.

Telidon Expanded Italic

the quick brown
fox jumps over
the lazy dog.
FILL MY BOX WITH
TWELVE DOZEN
LIQUOR JUGS.

Telidon Expanded Heavy

abcdefghijklmnopqrstuvwxyz
ABCDEFGHIJKLMNOPQRSTUVWXYZ
1234567890(!¡?@#%&*/%^+)#"

Telidon Expanded Bold

the quick brown
fox jumps over
the lazy dog.
FILL MY BOX WITH
TWELVE DOZEN
LIQUOR JUGS.

Telidon Expanded Bold Italic

the quick brown
fox jumps over
the lazy dog.
FILL MY BOX WITH
TWELVE DOZEN
LIQUOR JUGS.

Telidon Expanded Heavy Italic

the quick brown
fox jumps over
the lazy dog.
FILL MY BOX WITH
TWELVE DOZEN
LIQUOR JUGS.

sales@typodermic.com

abcdefghijklmnopqrstuvwxyzABCDEFGHIJKLMNOPQR
STUVWXYZ1234567890(!¡?@#%&*/%^+)•"@¢£$¥%©""™

Telidon Ink Condensed

the quick brown fox jumps over
the lazy dog. FILL MY BOX WITH
TWELVE DOZEN LIQUOR JUGS.

Telidon Ink Condensed Italic

the quick brown fox jumps over
the lazy dog. FILL MY BOX WITH
TWELVE DOZEN LIQUOR JUGS.

Telidon Ink Condensed Bold

the quick brown fox jumps over
the lazy dog. FILL MY BOX WITH
TWELVE DOZEN LIQUOR JUGS.

Telidon Ink Condensed Bold Italic

the quick brown fox jumps over
the lazy dog. FILL MY BOX WITH
TWELVE DOZEN LIQUOR JUGS.

Telidon Ink Condensed Heavy

the quick brown fox jumps over
the lazy dog. FILL MY BOX WITH
TWELVE DOZEN LIQUOR JUGS.

Telidon Ink Condensed Heavy Italic

the quick brown fox jumps over
the lazy dog. FILL MY BOX WITH
TWELVE DOZEN LIQUOR JUGS.

Telidon Ink Regular Italic

the quick brown fox jumps
over the lazy dog. FILL MY
BOX WITH TWELVE DOZEN LIQUOR
JUGS.

Telidon Ink Bold

the quick brown fox jumps
over the lazy dog. FILL
MY BOX WITH TWELVE DOZEN
LIQUOR JUGS.

Telidon Ink Bold Italic

the quick brown fox jumps
over the lazy dog. FILL
MY BOX WITH TWELVE DOZEN
LIQUOR JUGS.

Telidon Ink Heavy

abcdefghijklmnopqrstuvwxyzABCDE
FGHIJKLMNOPQRSTUVWXYZ1234567890

Telidon Ink Heavy Italic

the quick brown fox jumps
over the lazy dog. FILL
MY BOX WITH TWELVE DOZEN
LIQUOR JUGS.

Telidon Ink Expanded

the quick brown fox
jumps over the lazy dog.
FILL MY BOX WITH TWELVE
DOZEN LIQUOR JUGS.

Telidon Ink Expanded Italic

the quick brown
fox jumps over
the lazy dog.
FILL MY BOX WITH
TWELVE DOZEN
LIQUOR JUGS.

Telidon Ink Expanded Heavy

abcdefghijklmnopqrstuvwxyz
ABCDEFGHIJKLMNOPQRSTUVWXYZ
1234567890(!¡?@#%&*/%^+)•"

Telidon Ink Expanded Bold

the quick brown
fox jumps over
the lazy dog.
FILL MY BOX WITH
TWELVE DOZEN
LIQUOR JUGS.

Telidon Ink Expanded Bold Italic

the quick brown
fox jumps over
the lazy dog.
FILL MY BOX WITH
TWELVE DOZEN
LIQUOR JUGS.

Telidon Ink Expanded Heavy Italic

the quick brown
fox jumps over
the lazy dog.
FILL MY BOX WITH
TWELVE DOZEN
LIQUOR JUGS.

Telidon Ink

Ray Larabie
2002

Telidon Ink is a font reminiscent of dot matrix printer fonts of the 1970s and 1980s, which are still in use today in retail receipts. Telidon Ink is useful for simulating old printer output or teller receipts. If you want a cleaner look, Telidon Ink has a sister family simply called Telidon. The extended styles have doubled pixels, just like the dot matrix fonts of yesteryear.

Typodermic

Snowgoose

Ray Larabie
2002

Snowgoose, the festive snow-covered font, contains three separate fonts. The first font is regular Snowgoose and it is as it appears, but looks best when used on a white background. If you'd like to use Snowgoose on a colored or darker background, you may want to use Snowgoose Front and Snowgoose Back in layers. Use a darker color for Snowgoose Back and overlay it with Snowgoose Front in white. For an interesting effect, if your software allows it, try different gradients, patterns or textures on the Snowgoose Front layer. In Photoshop 5 or later, use the effects feature of the Snowgoose Front layer to create an embossed snow effect. Keep in mind that Snowgoose isn't strictly for festive, snowy, holiday themes.

Snowgoose

AaBbCcDdEeff
Gg1234567890

Snowgoose

abcdefghijklmnopqrstu
vwxyzABCDEFGHIJK
LMNOPQRSTUVWXY
Z1234567890(!¿?¡@#
£*/%^+)-"ŒœÆæ[{£€©
Ð$¥¾]ĬÛßÂâÞþ©"{⁝}

Snowgoose Back

abcdefghijklmnopqrstuvwxyzABCDEFGH
IJKLMNOPQRSTUVWXYZ1234567890

Snowgoose Front

sales@typodermic.com

AABBCCDDEEFFG
GHHIIJJKKLLMM
NNOOPPQQRRSST
TUUVVWWXXYY
YZZ1234567890!?@

ABCDEFGHIJKLMNOPQRSTUV
WXYZ1234567890"!?¿¡"(↑#@%
&•)¢ÿþüñ§œ{€$¥¢}&¡□®™

THE QUICK BROWN FOX JUMPS OVER
THE LAZY DOG.

Bomr

Ray Larabie
2002

Inspired by freight car graffiti tags.

Typodermic

When I designed Wyvern, the first font for the Typodermic foundry, I originally had Letter Gothic in mind; side-by-side they look quite dissimilar. Wyvern italics aren't merely oblique, they have angled stroke ends and curves adjusted to just give it a humanist quality. The bold and heavy weights have ink traps for better performance in print at small point sizes. Wyvern is an economic (space saving) typeface. You may prefer to set it more loosely in applications.

Wyvern Light

abcdefghijklmnopqrstuvwxyzABCDEFGHIJKLMNOPQRSTUV
WXYZ1234567890(!¡?@#%&*/-%ßÜü)●"œ¢£€$¥¾©®"™

Wyvern Light Italic

abcdefghijklmnopqrstuvwxyzABCDEFGHIJKLMNOPQRSTUV
WXYZ1234567890(!¡?@#%&*/-%ßÜü)●"œ¢£€$¥¾©®"™

Wyvern Regular

abcdefghijklmnopqrstuvwxyzABCDEFGHIJKLMNOPQRSTUV
WXYZ1234567890(!¡?@#%&*/-Üü)●"œ¢£€$¥¾©®"™

Wyvern Italic

abcdefghijklmnopqrstuvwxyzABCDEFGHIJKLMNOPQRSTUV
WXYZ1234567890(!¡?@#%&*/-Üü)●"œ¢£€$¥¾©®"™

Wyvern Bold

abcdefghijklmnopqrstuvwxyzABCDEFGHIJKLMNOPQRSTU
VWXYZ1234567890(!¡?@#%&*/-Üü)●"œ¢£€$¥¾©®"™

Wyvern Bold Italic

abcdefghijklmnopqrstuvwxyzABCDEFGHIJKLMNOPQRSTU
VWXYZ1234567890(!¡?@#%&*/-Üü)●"œ¢£€$¥¾©®"™

Wyvern Heavy

abcdefghijklmnopqrstuvwxyzABC
DEFGHIJKLMNOPQRSTUVWXYZ1234

Wyvern Heavy Italic

the quick brown fox jumps over the lazy dog. FILL MY BOX WITH TWELVE DOZEN LIQUOR JUGS.

Wyvern Ink

the quick brown fox jumps over the lazy dog. FILL MY BOX WITH TWELVE DOZEN LIQUOR JUGS.

Wyvern Blocko

abcdefghijklmnopqrstuvwxyzAB
CDEFGHIJKLMNOPQRSTUVWXYZ123

sales@typodermic.com

Neuropol Deluxe Condensed Light

the quick brown fox jumps over the lazy dog. FILL MY BOX WITH TWELVE DOZEN LIQUOR JUGS.

Neuropol Deluxe Condensed Light Oblique

the quick brown fox jumps over the lazy dog. FILL MY BOX WITH TWELVE DOZEN LIQUOR JUGS.

Neuropol Deluxe Condensed

the quick brown fox jumps over the lazy dog. FILL MY BOX WITH TWELVE DOZEN LIQUOR JUGS.

Neuropol Deluxe Condensed Oblique

the quick brown fox jumps over the lazy dog. FILL MY BOX WITH TWELVE DOZEN LIQUOR JUGS.

Neuropol Deluxe Condensed Bold

the quick brown fox jumps over the lazy dog. FILL MY BOX WITH TWELVE DOZEN LIQUOR JUGS.

Neuropol Deluxe Condensed Bold Oblique

the quick brown fox jumps over the lazy dog. FILL MY BOX WITH TWELVE DOZEN LIQUOR JUGS.

Neuropol Deluxe Light

the quick brown fox jumps over the lazy dog. FILL MY BOX WITH TWELVE DOZEN LIQUOR JUGS.

Neuropol Deluxe Light Oblique

the quick brown fox jumps over the lazy dog. FILL MY BOX WITH TWELVE DOZEN LIQUOR JUGS.

Neuropol Deluxe Oblique

the quick brown fox jumps over the lazy dog. FILL MY BOX WITH TWELVE DOZEN LIQUOR JUGS.

Neuropol Deluxe

Ray Larabie
2000

Inspired by old Vectorbeam arcade games, Neuropol was originally created in 1996 and the Deluxe family was expanded in 2000.

Neuropol Deluxe Regular

abcdefghijklmnopqrstuvwxyzAB
CDEFGHIJKLMNOPQRSTUVWXYZ

Neuropol Deluxe Bold

the quick brown fox jumps over the lazy dog. FILL MY BOX WITH TWELVE DOZEN LIQUOR JUGS.

Neuropol Deluxe Bold Oblique

the quick brown fox jumps over the lazy dog. FILL MY BOX WITH TWELVE DOZEN LIQUOR JUGS.

Neuropol Deluxe Heavy

the quick brown fox jumps over the lazy dog. FILL MY BOX WITH TWELVE BROWN DOZEN JUGS.

Neuropol Deluxe Heavy Oblique

the quick brown fox jumps over the lazy dog. FILL MY BOX WITH TWELVE DOZEN LIQUOR JUGS.

Neuropol Deluxe Extended Light

the quick brown fox jumps over the lazy dog. FILL MY BOX WITH TWELVE DOZEN LIQUOR JUGS.

Neuropol Deluxe Extended Light Oblique

the quick brown fox jumps over the lazy dog. FILL MY BOX WITH TWELVE DOZEN LIQUOR JUGS.

Neuropol Deluxe Extended

the quick brown fox jumps over the lazy dog. FILL MY BOX WITH TWELVE DOZEN LIQUOR JUGS.

Neuropol Deluxe Extended Oblique

the quick brown fox jumps over the lazy dog. FILL MY BOX WITH TWELVE DOZEN LIQUOR JUGS.

Neuropol Deluxe Extended Bold

the quick brown fox jumps over the lazy dog. FILL MY BOX WITH TWELVE DOZEN LIQUOR JUGS.

Neuropol Deluxe Extended Bold Oblique

the quick brown fox jumps over the lazy dog. FILL MY BOX WITH TWELVE DOZEN LIQUOR JUGS.

Neuropol Deluxe Outline

the quick brown fox jumps over the lazy dog. FILL MY BOX WITH TWELVE DOZEN LIQUOR JUGS.

Neuropol Deluxe Outline Oblique

the quick brown fox jumps over the lazy dog. FILL MY BOX WITH TWELVE DOZEN LIQUOR JUGS.

Typodermic

Ray Larabie
2001

Inspired by the lettering on the space
shuttle, Nasalization was designed in
1996 and expanded into the
Nasalization Deluxe family in 2001.

Nasalization Deluxe Condensed Light

THE QUICK BROWN FOX JUMPS OVER THE LAZY DOG. FILL MY 3OX WITH TWELVE DOZEN LIQUOR JUGS.

Nasalization Deluxe Condensed Light Italic

THE QUICK BROWN FOX JUMPS OVER THE LAZY DOG. FILL MY 3OX WITH TWELVE DOZEN LIQUOR JUGS.

Nasalization Deluxe Condensed

THE QUICK BROWN FOX JUMPS OVER THE LAZY DOG. FILL MY 3OX WITH TWELVE DOZEN LIQUOR JUGS.

Nasalization Deluxe Condensed Italic

THE QUICK BROWN FOX JUMPS OVER THE LAZY DOG. FILL MY 3OX WITH TWELVE 3ROWN LIQUOR JUGS.

Nasalization Deluxe Condensed Bold

THE QUICK BROWN FOX JUMPS OVER THE LAZY DOG. FILL MY 3OX WITH TWELVE DOZEN LIQUOR JUGS.

Nasalization Deluxe Condensed Bold Italic

THE QUICK BROWN FOX JUMPS OVER THE LAZY DOG. FILL MY 3OX WITH TWELVE DOZEN LIQUOR JUGS.

Nasalization Deluxe Light

THE QUICK BROWN FOX JUMPS OVER THE LAZY DOG. FILL MY 3OX WITH TWELVE DOZEN LIQUOR JUGS.

Nasalization Deluxe Light Italic

THE QUICK BROWN FOX JUMPS OVER THE LAZY DOG. FILL MY 3OX WITH TWELVE DOZEN LIQUOR JUGS.

Nasalization Deluxe Italic

THE QUICK BROWN FOX JUMPS OVER THE LAZY DOG. FILL MY 3OX WITH TWELVE DOZEN LIQUOR JUGS.

Nasalization Deluxe Regular

AABCDEFGHIJKLMMNOPPQRRSTUVW WXYZ1234567890!?⊚#&*%Ü"Œ£€$¥©®

Nasalization Deluxe Bold

THE QUICK BROWN FOX JUMPS OVER THE LAZY DOG. FILL MY 3OX WITH TWELVE DOZEN LIQUOR JUGS.

Nasalization Deluxe Bold Italic

THE QUICK BROWN FOX JUMPS OVER THE LAZY DOG. FILL MY 3OX WITH TWELVE DOZEN LIQUOR JUGS.

Nasalization Deluxe Heavy

THE QUICK BROWN FOX JUMPS OVER THE LAZY DOG. FILL MY 3OX WITH TWELVE DOZEN LIQUOR JUGS.

Nasalization Deluxe Heavy Italic

THE QUICK BROWN FOX JUMPS OVER THE LAZY DOG. FILL MY 3OX WITH TWELVE DOZEN LIQUOR JUGS.

Nasalization Deluxe Extended Light

THE QUICK BROWN FOX JUMPS OVER THE LAZY DOG. FILL MY 3OX WITH TWELVE DOZEN LIQUOR JUGS.

Nasalization Deluxe Extended Light Italic

THE QUICK BROWN FOX JUMPS OVER THE LAZY DOG. FILL MY 3OX WITH TWELVE DOZEN LIQUOR JUGS.

Nasalization Deluxe Extended

THE QUICK BROWN FOX JUMPS OVER THE LAZY DOG. FILL MY 3OX WITH TWELVE DOZEN LIQUOR JUGS.

Nasalization Deluxe Extended Italic

THE QUICK BROWN FOX JUMPS OVER THE LAZY DOG. FILL MY 3OX WITH TWELVE DOZEN LIQUOR JUGS.

Nasalization Deluxe Extended Bold

THE QUICK BROWN FOX JUMPS OVER THE LAZY DOG. FILL MY 3OX WITH TWELVE DOZEN LIQUOR JUGS.

Nasalization Deluxe Extended Bold Italic

THE QUICK BROWN FOX JUMPS OVER THE LAZY DOG. FILL MY 3OX WITH TWELVE DOZEN LIQUOR JUGS.

Nasalization Deluxe 3D

THE QUICK BROWN FOX JUMPS OVER THE LAZY DOG. FILL MY 3OX WITH TWELVE DOZEN LIQUOR JUGS.

Nasalization Video

THE QUICK BROWN FOX JUMPS OVER THE LAZY DOG. FILL MY 3OX WITH TWELVE DOZEN LIQUOR JUGS.

sales@typodermic.com

Mufferaw Deluxe Condensed

THE QUICK BROWN FOX JUMPS OVER THE LAZY DOG. FILL MY BOX WITH TWELVE DOZEN LIQUOR JUGS.

Mufferaw Deluxe Condensed Bold

THE QUICK BROWN FOX JUMPS OVER THE LAZY DOG. FILL MY BOX WITH TWELVE DOZEN LIQUOR JUGS.

Mufferaw Deluxe Bold

THE QUICK BROWN FOX JUMPS OVER THE LAZY DOG. FILL MY BOX WITH TWELVE DOZEN LIQUOR JUGS.

Ray Larabie
2000

This clean-cut comic book dialogue font includes italics (not shown).

Neuropol Deluxe Regular

ABCDEFGHIJKLMNOPQRSTUVWXYZABCDEFGH IJKLMNOPQRSTUVWXYZ1234567890(!?@#%&*)

Mufferaw Deluxe Expanded

THE QUICK BROWN FOX JUMPS OVER THE LAZY DOG. FILL MY BOX WITH TWELVE DOZEN LIQUOR JUGS.

Mufferaw Deluxe Expanded Bold

THE QUICK BROWN FOX JUMPS OVER THE LAZY DOG. FILL MY BOX WITH TWELVE DOZEN LIQUOR JUGS.

Mufferaw Deluxe Shaded

THE QUICK BROWN FOX JUMPS OVER THE LAZY DOG. FILL MY BOX WITH TWELVE DOZEN LIQUOR JUGS.

Mufferaw Deluxe 3D

THE QUICK BROWN FOX JUMPS OVER THE LAZY DOG. FILL MY BOX WITH TWELVE DOZEN LIQUOR JUGS.

Mufferaw Deluxe Outline

THE QUICK BROWN FOX JUMPS OVER THE LAZY DOG. FILL MY BOX WITH TWELVE DOZEN LIQUOR JUGS.

Mufferaw Deluxe Distorted

THE QUICK BROWN FOX JUMPS OVER THE LAZY DOG. FILL MY BOX WITH TWELVE DOZEN LIQUOR JUGS.

Chinese Rocks Deluxe Condensed

THE QUICK BROWN FOX JUMPS OVER THE LAZY DOG.

Chinese Rocks Deluxe Condensed Bold

THE QUICK BROWN FOX JUMPS OVER THE LAZY DOG.

Chinese Rocks Deluxe Bold

THE QUICK BROWN FOX JUMPS OVER THE LAZY DOG.

Chinese Rocks Deluxe

Ray Larabie
1999

Stolen from hand-cut rubber stamp lettering found in Chinese shipping cartons.

Chinese Rocks Deluxe Regular

AABBCCDDEEFFGGHHIIJJKKLLMMNNOOPPQQRRSS TTUUVVWWXXYYZZ1234567890[!?@%+★%]●¨ŒÜ$

Chinese Rocks Deluxe Extended

THE QUICK BROWN FOX JUMPS OVER THE LAZY DOG.

Chinese Rocks Deluxe Extended Bold

THE QUICK BROWN FOX JUMPS OVER THE LAZY DOG.

Chinese Rocks Deluxe Shaded

THE QUICK BROWN FOX JUMPS OVER THE LAZY DOG.

Chinese Rocks Deluxe Wide Shaded

AABBCCDDEEFFGGHHIIJJKKLLMMN NOOPPQQRRSSTTUUVVWWXXYYZZ1 234567890[!?@%+★%]¨Ü$

Chinese Rocks Deluxe Fat

THE QUICK BROWN FOX JUMPS OVER THE LAZY DOG.

Typodermic

Pakenham Deluxe Condensed

abcdefghijklmnopqrstuvwxyzABCDEFGHIJKLMNOP
QRSTUVWXYZ1234567890!?@#%&*ßÜü£€¢$Ææ©

Pakenham Deluxe Condensed Italic

the quick brown fox jumps over the lazy dog. FILL MY BOX WITH TWELVE DOZEN LIQUOR JUGS.

Pakenham Deluxe Condensed Book

the quick brown fox jumps over the lazy dog. FILL MY BOX WITH TWELVE DOZEN LIQUOR JUGS.

Pakenham Deluxe Condensed Book Italic

the quick brown fox jumps over the lazy dog. FILL MY BOX WITH TWELVE DOZEN LIQUOR JUGS.

Pakenham Deluxe Condensed Bold

abcdefghijklmnopqrstuvwxyzABCDEFGHIJKL
MNOPQRSTUVWXYZ1234567890!?@#%&*ßÜ

Pakenham Deluxe Condensed Bold Italic

the quick brown fox jumps over the lazy dog. FILL MY BOX WITH TWELVE DOZEN LIQUOR JUGS.

Pakenham Deluxe Condensed Black

the quick brown fox jumps over the lazy dog. FILL MY BOX WITH TWELVE DOZEN LIQUOR JUGS.

Pakenham Deluxe Condensed Black Italic

the quick brown fox jumps over the lazy dog. FILL MY BOX WITH TWELVE DOZEN LIQUOR JUGS.

Pakenham Deluxe Regular

abcdefghijklmnopqrstuvwxyzABCDEFGHIJK
LMNOPQRSTUVWXYZ1234567890!?@#%&

Pakenham Deluxe Italic

abcdefghijklmnopqrstuvwxyzABCDEFGHIJKLM
NOPQRSTUVWXYZ1234567890!?@#%&*ßÜü

Pakenham Deluxe Book

abcdefghijklmnopqrstuvwxyzABCDEFGHIJ
KLMNOPQRSTUVWXYZ1234567890!?@#%

Pakenham Deluxe Book Italic

abcdefghijklmnopqrstuvwxyzABCDEFGHIJKL
MNOPQRSTUVWXYZ1234567890!?@#%&*ß

abcdefghijklmnopqrstuvwxyzABCDEFG HIJKLMNOPQRSTUVWXYZ1234567890(!

Pakenham Deluxe

Ray Larabie
2001

A loose interpretation of Renner's Steile Futura.

Pakenham Deluxe Bold Italic

the quick brown fox jumps over the lazy dog. FILL MY BOX WITH TWELVE DOZEN LIQUOR JUGS.

Pakenham Deluxe Black

abcdefghijklmnopqrstuvwxyzABC DEFGHIJKLMNOPQRSTUVWXYZ123

Pakenham Deluxe Black Italic

the quick brown fox jumps over the lazy dog. FILL MY BOX WITH TWELVE DOZEN LIQUOR JUGS.

Pakenham Deluxe Expanded

abcdefghijklmnopqrstuvwxyzABCD EFGHIJKLMNOPQRSTUVWXYZ12345

Pakenham Deluxe Expanded Italic

the quick brown fox jumps over the lazy dog. FILL MY BOX WITH TWELVE DOZEN LIQUOR JUGS.

Pakenham Deluxe Expanded Book

abcdefghijklmnopqrstuvwxyz ABCDEFGHIJKLMNOPQRSTUV

Pakenham Deluxe Expanded Book Italic

the quick brown fox jumps over the lazy dog. FILL MY BOX WITH TWELVE DOZEN LIQUOR JUGS.

Pakenham Deluxe Expanded Bold

abcdefghijklmnopqrstuvwxyzA BCDEFGHIJKLMNOPQRSTUVWX

Pakenham Deluxe Expanded Bold Italic

the quick brown fox jumps over the lazy dog. FILL MY BOX WITH TWELVE DOZEN LIQUOR JUGS.

Pakenham Deluxe Kayo

the quick brown fox jumps over the lazy dog. FILL MY BOX WITH TWELVE DOZEN LIQUOR JUGS.

Pakenham Deluxe Expanded Black

the quick brown fox jumps over the lazy dog. FILL MY BOX WITH TWELVE DOZEN LIQUOR JUGS.

Pakenham Deluxe Stencil

the quick brown fox jumps over the lazy dog. FILL MY BOX WITH TWELVE DOZEN LIQUOR JUGS.

Pakenham Deluxe Expanded Black Italic

the quick brown fox jumps over the lazy dog. FILL MY BOX WITH TWELVE DOZEN LIQUOR JUGS.

Pakenham Deluxe Spraypaint

the quick brown fox jumps over the lazy dog. FILL MY BOX WITH TWELVE DOZEN LIQUOR JUGS.

Pakenham Deluxe Wood

the quick brown fox jumps over the lazy dog. FILL MY BOX WITH TWELVE DOZEN LIQUOR JUGS.

Pakenham Deluxe Boss

the quick brown fox jumps over the lazy dog. FILL MY BOX WITH TWELVE DOZEN LIQUOR JUGS.

Pakenham Deluxe Ink

the quick brown fox jumps over the lazy dog. FILL MY BOX WITH TWELVE DOZEN LIQUOR JUGS.

Typodermic

Ray Larabie
2001

As seen on TV.

Zekton Deluxe Condensed Light

abcdefghijklmnopqrstuvwxyzABCDEFGHIJKLMNOPQRST
UVWXYZ1234567890!?@#(&*%üÜß˚œŒæÆ£$¥©®)

Zekton Deluxe Light

the quick brown fox jumps over the lazy dog. FILL MY BOX WITH TWELVE DOZEN LIQUOR JUGS.

Zekton Deluxe Extended Light

the quick brown fox jumps over the lazy dog. FILL MY BOX WITH TWELVE DOZEN LIQUOR JUGS.

Zekton Deluxe Wide Light

the quick brown fox jumps over the lazy dog. FILL MY BOX WITH TWELVE DOZEN LIQUOR JUGS.

Zekton Deluxe Regular

abcdefghijklmnopqrstuvwxyzABCDEFG
HIJKLMNOPQRSTUVWXYZ1234567890

Zekton Deluxe Condensed

the quick brown fox jumps over the lazy dog. FILL MY BOX WITH TWELVE DOZEN LIQUOR JUGS.

Zekton Deluxe Extended

the quick brown fox jumps over the lazy dog. FILL MY BOX WITH TWELVE DOZEN LIQUOR JUGS.

Zekton Deluxe Wide

the quick brown fox jumps over the lazy dog. FILL MY BOX WITH TWELVE DOZEN LIQUOR JUGS.

Zekton Deluxe Condensed Bold

the quick brown fox jumps over the lazy dog. FILL MY BOX WITH TWELVE DOZEN LIQUOR JUGS.

Zekton Deluxe Bold

the quick brown fox jumps over the lazy dog. FILL MY BOX WITH TWELVE DOZEN LIQUOR JUGS.

Zekton Deluxe Extended Bold

the quick brown fox jumps over the lazy dog. FILL MY BOX WITH TWELVE DOZEN LIQUOR JUGS.

Zekton Deluxe Wide Bold

the quick brown fox jumps over the lazy dog. FILL MY BOX WITH TWELVE DOZEN LIQUOR JUGS.

Zekton Deluxe Condensed Heavy

the quick brown fox jumps over the lazy dog. FILL MY BOX WITH TWELVE DOZEN LIQUOR JUGS.

Zekton Deluxe Heavy

the quick brown fox jumps over the lazy dog. FILL MY BOX WITH TWELVE DOZEN LIQUOR JUGS.

Zekton Deluxe Extended Heavy

the quick brown fox jumps over the lazy dog. FILL MY BOX WITH TWELVE DOZEN LIQUOR JUGS.

Zekton Deluxe Wide Heavy

the quick brown fox jumps over the lazy dog. FILL MY BOX WITH TWELVE DOZEN LIQUOR JUGS.

Zekton Deluxe Ink

the quick brown fox jumps over the lazy dog. FILL MY BOX WITH TWELVE DOZEN LIQUOR JUGS.

Zekton Deluxe Outline

the quick brown fox jumps over the lazy dog. FILL MY BOX WITH TWELVE DOZEN LIQUOR JUGS.

Zekton Deluxe Video

the quick brown fox jumps over the lazy dog. FILL MY BOX WITH TWELVE DOZEN LIQUOR JUGS.

Zekton Deluxe Wave

the quick brown fox jumps over the lazy dog. FILL MY BOX WITH TWELVE DOZEN LIQUOR JUGS.

sales@typodermic.com

Larabiefont Deluxe Compressed

the quick brown fox jumps over the lazy dog. FILL MY BOX WITH TWELVE DOZEN LIQUOR JUGS.

Larabiefont Deluxe Compressed Oblique

the quick brown fox jumps over the lazy dog. FILL MY BOX WITH TWELVE DOZEN LIQUOR JUGS.

Larabiefont Deluxe Compressed Bold

the quick brown fox jumps over the lazy dog. FILL MY BOX WITH TWELVE DOZEN LIQUOR JUGS.

Larabiefont Deluxe

Ray Larabie
1999

A monospaced typeface based on an early '70s manual typewriter.

Larabiefont Deluxe Compressed Bold Oblique

the quick brown fox jumps over the lazy dog. FILL MY BOX WITH TWELVE DOZEN LIQUOR JUGS.

Larabiefont Deluxe Condensed

the quick brown fox jumps over the lazy dog. FILL MY BOX WITH TWELVE DOZEN LIQUOR JUGS.

Larabiefont Deluxe Condensed Oblique

the quick brown fox jumps over the lazy dog. FILL MY BOX WITH TWELVE DOZEN LIQUOR JUGS.

Larabiefont Deluxe Condensed Bold

abcdefghijklmnopqrstuvwxyzABCDE
FGHIJKLMNOPQRSTUVWXYZ1234567890

Larabiefont Deluxe Condensed Bold Oblique

the quick brown fox jumps over the lazy dog. FILL MY BOX WITH TWELVE DOZEN LIQUOR JUGS.

Larabiefont Deluxe Regular

abcdefghijklmnopqrstuvwxyzABCDEFG
HIJKLMNOPQRSTUVWXYZ1234567890!?%&

Larabiefont Deluxe Oblique

the quick brown fox jumps over the lazy dog. FILL MY BOX WITH TWELVE DOZEN LIQUOR JUGS.

Larabiefont Deluxe Bold

the quick brown fox jumps over the lazy dog. FILL MY BOX WITH TWELVE DOZEN LIQUOR JUGS.

Larabiefont Deluxe Bold Oblique

the quick brown fox jumps over the lazy dog. FILL MY BOX WITH TWELVE DOZEN LIQUOR JUGS.

Larabiefont Deluxe Extended

the quick brown fox jumps over the lazy dog. FILL MY BOX WITH TWELVE DOZEN LIQUOR JUGS.

Larabiefont Deluxe Extended Oblique

the quick brown fox jumps over the lazy dog. FILL MY BOX WITH TWELVE DOZEN LIQUOR JUGS.

Larabiefont Deluxe Extended Bold

the quick brown fox jumps over the lazy dog. FILL MY BOX WITH TWELVE DOZEN LIQUOR JUGS.

Larabiefont Deluxe Extended Bold Oblique

the quick brown fox jumps over the lazy dog. FILL MY BOX WITH TWELVE DOZEN LIQUOR JUGS.

Larabiefont Deluxe Xtrawide

the quick brown fox jumps over the lazy dog. FILL MY BOX WITH TWELVE DOZEN LIQUOR JUGS.

Larabiefont Deluxe Xtrawide Oblique

the quick brown fox jumps over the lazy dog. FILL MY BOX WITH TWELVE DOZEN LIQUOR JUGS.

Larabiefont Deluxe Xtrawide Bold

abcdefghijklmnopqr
stuvwxyzABCDEFGHIJ
KLMNOPQRSTUVWXYZ12

Larabiefont Deluxe Xtrawide Bold Oblique

the quick brown fox jumps over the lazy dog. FILL MY BOX WITH TWELVE DOZEN LIQUOR JUGS.

Typodermic

Ray Larabie
2000

Based on North American road signage.

Blue Highway Deluxe Condensed Light

the quick brown fox jumps over the lazy dog. FILL MY BOX WITH TWELVE DOZEN LIQUOR JUGS.

Blue Highway Deluxe Condensed Light Oblique

the quick brown fox jumps over the lazy dog. FILL MY BOX WITH TWELVE DOZEN LIQUOR JUGS.

Blue Highway Deluxe Condensed

the quick brown fox jumps over the lazy dog. FILL MY BOX WITH TWELVE DOZEN LIQUOR JUGS.

Blue Highway Deluxe Condensed Italic

the quick brown fox jumps over the lazy dog. FILL MY BOX WITH TWELVE DOZEN LIQUOR JUGS.

Blue Highway Deluxe Condensed Bold

the quick brown fox jumps over the lazy dog. FILL MY BOX WITH TWELVE DOZEN LIQUOR JUGS.

Blue Highway Deluxe Condensed Bold Italic

the quick brown fox jumps over the lazy dog. FILL MY BOX WITH TWELVE DOZEN LIQUOR JUGS.

Blue Highway Deluxe Light

the quick brown fox jumps over the lazy dog. FILL MY BOX WITH TWELVE DOZEN LIQUOR JUGS.

Blue Highway Deluxe Light Oblique

the quick brown fox jumps over the lazy dog. FILL MY BOX WITH TWELVE DOZEN LIQUOR JUGS.

Blue Highway Deluxe Italic

the quick brown fox jumps over the lazy dog. FILL MY BOX WITH TWELVE DOZEN LIQUOR JUGS.

Blue Highway Deluxe Regular

abcdefghijklmnopqrstuvwxyzABCDEFG HIJKLMNOPQRSTUVWXYZ1234567890!

Blue Highway Deluxe Bold

the quick brown fox jumps over the lazy dog. FILL MY BOX WITH TWELVE DOZEN LIQUOR JUGS.

Blue Highway Deluxe Bold Italic

the quick brown fox jumps over the lazy dog. FILL MY BOX WITH TWELVE DOZEN LIQUOR JUGS.

Blue Highway Deluxe Expanded Light

the quick brown fox jumps over the lazy dog. FILL MY BOX WITH TWELVE DOZEN LIQUOR JUGS.

Blue Highway Deluxe Expanded Light Italic

the quick brown fox jumps over the lazy dog. FILL MY BOX WITH TWELVE DOZEN LIQUOR JUGS.

Blue Highway Deluxe Expanded

the quick brown fox jumps over the lazy dog. FILL MY BOX WITH TWELVE DOZEN LIQUOR JUGS.

Blue Highway Deluxe Expanded Italic

the quick brown fox jumps over the lazy dog. FILL MY BOX WITH TWELVE DOZEN LIQUOR JUGS.

Blue Highway Deluxe Expanded Bold

the quick brown fox jumps over the lazy dog. FILL MY BOX WITH TWELVE DOZEN LIQUOR JUGS.

Blue Highway Deluxe Expanded Bold Italic

the quick brown fox jumps over the lazy dog. FILL MY BOX WITH TWELVE DOZEN LIQUOR JUGS.

Blue Highway Deluxe 3D

the quick brown fox jumps over the lazy dog. FILL MY BOX WITH TWELVE DOZEN LIQUOR JUGS.

Blue Highway Deluxe Ink

the quick brown fox jumps over the lazy dog. FILL MY BOX WITH TWELVE DOZEN LIQUOR JUGS.

Blue Highway Deluxe Outline

the quick brown fox jumps over the lazy dog. FILL MY BOX WITH TWELVE DOZEN LIQUOR JUGS.

Blue Highway Deluxe Lens

the quick brown fox jumps over the lazy dog. FILL MY BOX WITH TWELVE DOZEN LIQUOR JUGS.

sales@typodermic.com

abcdefghijklmnopqrstuvwxyzABCDEFGHI
JKLMNOPQRSTUVWXYZ1234567890!?

Sui Generis Deluxe

Ray Larabie
2000

A square, yet friendly typeface
inspired by nothing at all.

Sui Generis Deluxe Condensed Light Italic

the quick brown fox jumps over
the lazy dog. FILL MY BOX WITH
TWELVE DOZEN
LIQUOR JUGS.

Sui Generis Deluxe Condensed

the quick brown fox jumps
over the lazy dog. FILL MY
BOX WITH TWELVE DOZEN
LIQUOR JUGS.

Sui Generis Deluxe Condensed Italic

the quick brown fox jumps over
the lazy dog. FILL MY BOX
WITH TWELVE DOZEN
LIQUOR JUGS.

Sui Generis Deluxe Condensed Bold

the quick brown fox jumps
over the lazy dog. FILL MY
BOX WITH TWELVE
DOZEN LIQUOR JUGS.

Sui Generis Deluxe Condensed Bold Italic

abcdefghijklmnopqrstuvwxyzABCDE
FGHIJKLMNOPQRSTUVWXYZ1234

Sui Generis Deluxe Lite

abcdefghijklmnopqrstuvwxyzABCDE
FGHIJKLMNOPQRSTUVWXYZ1234

Sui Generis Deluxe Light Italic

the quick brown fox jumps
over the lazy dog. FILL MY
BOX WITH TWELVE
DOZEN LIQUOR JUGS.

Sui Generis Deluxe Regular

abcdefghijklmnopqrstuvwxyzABCDE
FGHIJKLMNOPQRSTUVWXYZ12345

Sui Generis Deluxe Italic

abcdefghijklmnopqrstuvwxyzABCDEFG
HIJKLMNOPQRSTUVWXYZ12345678

Sui Generis Deluxe Bold

abcdefghijklmnopqrstuvwxyzABCD
EFGHIJKLMNOPQRSTUVWXYZ123

Sui Generis Deluxe Bold Italic

the quick brown fox jumps
over the lazy dog. FILL MY
BOX WITH TWELVE
DOZEN LIQUOR JUGS.

Sui Generis Deluxe Outline

abcdefghijklmnopqrstuvwxyzABCD
EFGHIJKLMNOPQRSTUVWXYZ123
4567890(!¡¿?@#*%&*%+)^¨ÜÚŒœ£§ß"

Typodermic

typotheque.com

fine-quality fonts online

typotheque.com, fine-quality fonts online

Typotheque is an independent type foundry based in
The Hague, The Netherlands. Principal designer and founder
Peter Bil'ak has built a set of unique, high-quality text and
display faces, with a complete character sets, thoroughly
tested, manually kerned and hinted.

Typotheque fonts are available for PC and Macintosh in
PostScript, TrueType and (soon) OpenType.

In addition to developing the retail library, Typotheque
specializes in developing custom type solutions for a variety
of applications, in standard Western, and custom encodings.

Typotheque
Zwaardstraat 16
(lokaal 0.11)
2584 TX The Hague
The Netherlands

- www.typotheque.com
- sales@typotheque.com
- T +31 70 322 6119
- F +31 84 831 6741

FEDRA SANS was originally developed as a corporate font for *Bayerische Rück*, a German insurance company, as part of their new visual identity. According to the commissioner, the objective was to *de-protestantize Univers*, the typeface which Bayerische Rück had been using since Otl Aicher designed their first visual identity in the 1970s. The type-face reflects the original brief: *it humanises the communicated message and adds simple, informal elegance.* The most important criterion was to create a typeface which works equally well on paper *and* on the computer screen, and is consistent across all computer platforms.¶ After first versions of the typeface were completed and digitised, the project was cancelled as Bayerische Rück was acquired by another even larger multinational corporation.¶ Since a lot of work had been done already, I decided to complete the typeface, adding extra weights and expert fonts. Shortly before the planned release date of the typeface, my studio was broken into, and my computers and back-up system containing all the font data were stolen. What initially seemed like the ultimate designer's disaster was actually beneficial for Fedra. The incident delayed its release, allowing me to re-examine the early design decisions, made under the assumption that the font would be exclusive to the company and never publicly available. The new version is more versatile, offering a wider range of fonts, a number of special typographic features.¶

Fedra Sans™

Peter Bil'ak
2001

Fedra Sans-Light
Fedra Sans-Light TF
Fedra Sans-Light Expert
Fedra Sans-Light Italic
Fedra Sans-Light Italic Expert
Fedra Sans-Light Small Caps
Fedra Sans-Book
Fedra Sans-Book TF
Fedra Sans-Book Expert
Fedra Sans-Book Italic
Fedra Sans-Book Italic Expert
Fedra Sans-Book Small Caps
Fedra Sans-Normal
Fedra Sans-Normal TF
Fedra Sans-Normal Expert
Fedra Sans-Normal Italic
Fedra Sans-Normal Italic Expert
Fedra Sans-Normal Small Caps
Fedra Sans-Medium
Fedra Sans-Medium TF
Fedra Sans-Medium Expert
Fedra Sans-Medium Italic
Fedra Sans-Medium Italic Expert
Fedra Sans-Medium Small Caps
Fedra Sans-Bold
Fedra Sans-Bold TF
Fedra Sans-Bold Expert
Fedra Sans-Bold Italic
Fedra Sans-Bold Italic Expert
Fedra Sans-Bold Small Caps

Typotheque

ABCDEFGHIJKLMNOPQRSTUVWXYZ?!¿¡@
abcdefghijklmnopqrstuvwxyzßɢ&ÆŒ.,:;*
ABCDEFGHIJKLMNOPQRSTUVWXYZÆŒ®©
ÀÃÄÅÂÁÇĐËÉÊÈÌÍÎÑÏØÓÔÖÒÕÚÛÜÙŸŽ™
áàâäãåçéèêëíìîïñóòôöøõúúùûüÿž†∫•¶∞¤°
◊µ∂∑∏π#∫ªºΩ¬√≈∆–—«»‹›""''$€₠ƒ¢¥£†‡%‰
[0123456789] (0123456789) {0123456789}
æœfiflffffifflfffkfhfjgðŁŠšŸýÞþŽž½¼⅓¾⅔⅟

◁▷◁◁▷▷◀▶□▤■□■○●○●★☆≠=+±≤≥<>–×÷
⓪①②③④⑤⑥⑦⑧⑨▤▥ 0123456789/234567890 →↗↑↖←↙↓↘

ABCDEFGHIJKLMNOPQRSTUVWXYZ?!¿¡@
abcdefghijklmnopqrstuvwxyzßɢ&ÆŒ.,:;®©
ÀÃÄÅÂÁÇAËÉÊÈÌÍÎÑÏØÓÔÖÒÕÚÛÜÙŸ™
áàâäãåçéèêëíìîïñóòôöøõúúùûüÿLt∫•¶∞°*
◊µ∂∑∏π#∫ªºΩ¬√≈∆–—«»‹›""''$V€ƒ¢¥£†‡
%‰æœfifl≠=+±≤≥<>TU÷®©™µ∂∑∏π

Light
Book
Normal
Medium
Bold

Fedra was originally commissioned by Pa ris-based Ruedi Baur Integral Design and developed as a corporate font for Bayeris che Rück, a German insurance company, as part of their new visual identity. Acc

rding to the commissioner, the objecti ve was to 'de-protestantize Univers', th e typeface which Bayerische Rück had been using since Otl Aicher designed t heir first visual identity in the 1970s. Th e typeface reflects the original brief: it humanises the communicated messag e and adds simple, informal elegance. T he most important criterion was to cre ate a typeface which works equally wel l on paper and on the computer screen,

and is consistent across all computer platforms. After first versions of the ty peface were completed and digitised, t he project was cancelled as Bayerische Rück was acquired by another even la rger multinational corporation. This p ut an early end to the story of the cus tom font. Since a lot of work had been done already, I decided to complete th e typeface, adding extra weights and expert fonts. Shortly before the plann

ed release date of the typeface, my s tudio was broken into, and my comp uters and back-up system containing all the font data were stolen. What i nitially seemed like the ultimate desi gner's disaster was actually beneficia l for Fedra. The incident delayed its r elease, allowing me to re-examine th e early design decisions, made under the assumption that the font would be exclusive to the company and nev

er publicly available. The new versio n is more versatile, offering a wider range of fonts, a number of special typographic features (see opposite p age). The spacing of the font was al tered, as well as the slope of the ita

lics. Many characters were redrawn creating a more flexible type family. Fedra was origina lly commissioned by Paris-based Ruedi Baur I ntegral Design and developed as a corporate f ont for Bayerische Rück, a German insurance

company, as part of their new visual identity. According to the commissioner, the objective was to 'de-protestantize Univers', the typefac e which Bayerische Rück had been using sinc e Otl Aicher designed their first visual identit y in the 1970s. The typeface reflects the origi nal brief: it humanises the communicated me ssage and adds simple, informal elegance. Th e most important criterion was to create a ty peface which works equally well on paper an d on the computer screen, and is consistent a

cross all computer platforms. After first vers ions of the typeface were completed and digi tised, the project was cancelled as Bayerisch e Rück was acquired by another even larger multinational corporation. This put an early end to the story of the custom font. Since a l ot of work had been done already, I decided t o complete the typeface, adding extra weigh ts and expert fonts. Shortly before the plann ed release date of the typeface, my studio wa s broken into, and my computers and back-u

p system containing all the font data were stolen. What initially seemed like the ultima te designer's disaster was actually beneficia l for Fedra. The incident delayed its release, allowing me to re-examine the early design decisions, made under the assumption that the font would be exclusive to the company and never publicly available. The new versio n is more versatile, offering a wider range of fonts, a number of special typographic feat ures. The spacing of the font was altered, as

well as the slope of the italics. Many chara cters were redrawn creating a more flexibl e type family. Fedra was originally commis sioned by Paris-based Ruedi Baur Integral Design and developed as a corporate font f or Bayerische Rück, a German insurance co

MPANY, AS PART OF THEIR NEW VISUAL ID ENTITY. ACCORDING TO THE COMMISSION ER, THE OBJECTIVE WAS TO 'DE-PROTESTA NTIZE UNIVERS', THE TYPEFACE WHICH BA YERISCHE RÜCK HAD BEEN USING SINCE O

TL AICHER DESIGNED THEIR FIRST VISUAL IDENTITY IN THE 1970S. THE TYPEFACE RE FLECTS THE ORIGINAL BRIEF: IT HUMANIS ES THE COMMUNICATED MESSAGE AND A DDS SIMPLE, INFORMAL ELEGANCE. THE MOST IMPORTANT CRITERION WAS TO CRE ATE A TYPEFACE WHICH WORKS EQUALLY WELL ON PAPER AND ON THE COMPUTER SCREEN, AND IS CONSISTENT ACROSS ALL COMPUTER PLATFORMS. AFTER FIRST VER SIONS OF THE TYPEFACE WERE COMPLET

ED AND DIGITISED, THE PROJECT WAS CA NCELLED AS BAYERISCHE RÜCK WAS ACQ UIRED BY ANOTHER EVEN LARGER MULTI NATIONAL CORPORATION. THIS PUT AN EA RLY END TO THE STORY OF THE CUSTOM FONT. SINCE A LOT OF WORK HAD BEEN DONE ALREADY, I DECIDED TO COMPLETE THE TYPEFACE, ADDING EXTRA WEIGHTS AND EXPERT FONTS. SHORTLY BEFORE TH E PLANNED RELEASE DATE OF THE TYPEF ACE, MY STUDIO WAS BROKEN INTO, AND

MY COMPUTERS AND BACK-UP SYSTEM C ONTAINING ALL THE FONT DATA WERE ST OLEN. WHAT INITIALLY SEEMED LIKE THE ULTIMATE DESIGNER'S DISASTER WAS ACT UALLY BENEFICIAL FOR FEDRA. THE INCID ENT DELAYED ITS RELEASE, ALLOWING ME TO RE-EXAMINE THE EARLY DESIGN DECIS IONS, MADE UNDER THE ASSUMPTION TH AT THE FONT WOULD BE EXCLUSIVE TO T HE COMPANY AND NEVER PUBLICLY AVAIL ABLE. THE NEW VERSION IS MORE VERSA

TILE, OFFERING A WIDER RANGE OF FON TS, A NUMBER OF SPECIAL TYPOGRAPHIC FEATURES (SEE OPPOSITE PAGE). THE SP ACING OF THE FONT WAS ALTERED, AS W ELL AS THE SLOPE OF THE ITALICS. MAN Y CHARACTERS WERE REDRAWN CREATIN

Fedra Sans Light
Peter Bil'ak
2001

Fedra Sans Book
Peter Bil'ak
2001

Fedra Sans Normal
Peter Bil'ak
2001

Fedra Sans Medium
Peter Bil'ak
2001

Fedra Sans Bold
Peter Bil'ak
2001

FEDRA SERIF, *a low-contrast serif typeface intended for print*, is the latest addition to the family. Instead of seeking inspiration in the past, *Fedra Serif* is a synthetic typeface where aesthetic and technological decisions are linked. Fedra combines seemingly contradictory ways of constructing characters in one harmonious font. The humanistic roots (rhythm of the handwriting) is balanced with rational drawing (a coarse computer-screen grid). Like the sans-serif counterpart, Fedra Serif has 5 weights, italics, small caps, and expert sets for each weight and three different numeral systems (proportional, lining figures; old style figures; and tabular, fixed-width figures). The font also comes in two different versions with different lengths of the ascenders and descenders (stem lengths). Version A matches the proportions of Fedra Sans, with a large x-height and short stem length. Version B prolongs the stem lengths up to 12%, making it suitable for traditional book printing. Combined, these variants result in a typeface suitable for solving complex typographic problems.

sales@typotheque.com

ABCDEFGHIJKLMNOPQRSTUVWXYZ?!¿¡?!

abcdefghijklmnopqrstuvwxyzßð&ᴳ&ᵗÆ*

ABCDEFGHIJKLMNOPQRSTUVWXYZ®©ⓅⓊ™

ÀÃÄÅÂÁÇÐËÉÊÈÌÍÎÑÏØÓÔÖÒÕŒÚÛÜÙÝ

Þáàâäãåçéèêëîíîïłñóòôöõøúùûüÿþ†°§¶Jß∞

≠=+±≤≥<>≈◊μΣΠπ#∫ªºΩ√Δ«»""''$€ƒ¢¥£‹›‡%‰

[.,:;](0123456789){0123456789}@æœfiflfjffi

ffflſſıœłehchſtcttjr'ttſtt't'c't'st'

Fedra Serif A (with shorter descenders and ascenders, and lower contrast of thick and thin) compared with Fedra Serif B

Fedra Serif A

Peter Biľak
2002

Also available in Central European and Turkish encoding.

Fedra Serif A + B

Peter Biľak
2002

Fedra Serif has two variants: A with shorter ascenders and descenders, and version B, with longer ones. Both versions, however, have the same character widths, which makes it possible to switch effortlessly.

Typotheque

Fedra Serif A:

Le Paradoxisme est un mouvement d'avant-garde dans la littérature, l'art, la philosophie, la science appuyé sur l'excessive utilisation des antithèses, antinomies, contradictions, paradoxes dans les créations.¶ Il a été fondé et dirigé par l'écrivain Florentin Smarandache depuis 1980, qui a dit que: «Le but est l'élargissement de la sphère artistique par des éléments non-artistiques. Mais, surtout, la création en contre-temps, contre-sens. Et, aussi, l'expérimentation.» Quand avec du soleil aux

Fedra Serif B:

Le Paradoxisme est un mouvement d'avant-garde dans la littérature, l'art, la philosophie, la science appuyé sur l'excessive utilisation des antithèses, antinomies, contradictions, paradoxes dans les créations.¶ Il a été fondé et dirigé par l'écrivain Florentin Smarandache depuis 1980, qui a dit que: «Le but est l'élargissement de la sphère artistique par des éléments non-artistiques. Mais, surtout, la création en contre-temps, contre-sens. Et, aussi, l'expérimentation.» Quand avec du soleil aux

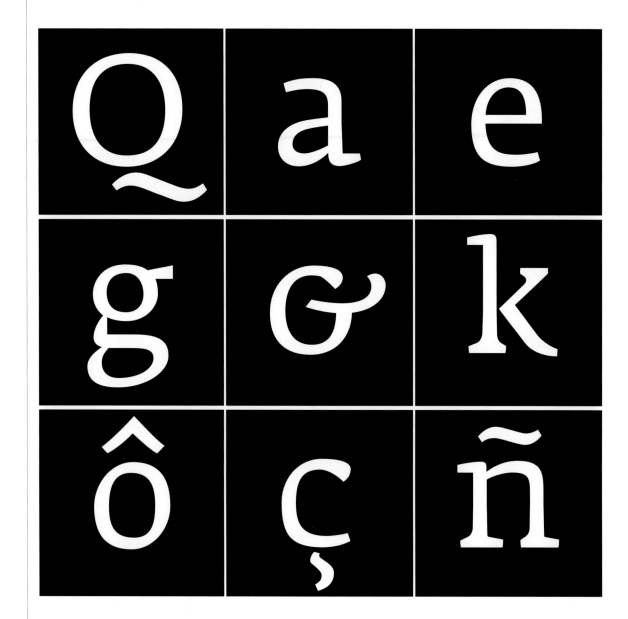

Fedra Serif A Book — Peter Biľak, 2002

Fedra was originally commissioned b y Paris-based Ruedi Baur Integral Des ign and developed as a corporate font for Bayerische Rück, a German insur ance company, as part of their new v isual identity. According to the comm issioner, the objective was to 'de-prot estantize Univers', the typeface whic h Bayerische Rück had been using sin ce Otl Aicher designed their first visu al identity in the 1970s. The typeface

te page). The spacing of the font was altere d, as well as the slope of the italics. Many c haracters were redrawn creating a more fle xible type family. Fedra was originally com missioned by Paris-based Ruedi Baur Integ ral Design and developed as a corporate fon t for Bayerische Rück, a German insurance company, as part of their new visual identi ty. According to the commissioner, the obje ctive was to 'de-protestantize Univers', the typeface which Bayerische Ruck had been

COMPANY, AS PART OF THEIR NEW VISUAL IDENTITY. ACCORDING TO THE COMMISSIONER, THE OBJECTIVE WAS TO 'DE-PROTESTANTIZE UNIVERS', THE TYPEFACE WHICH BAYERISCHE RÜCK HAD BEEN USING SINCE OTL AICHER DESIGNED THEIR FIRST VISUAL IDENTITY IN THE 1970S. THE TYPEFACE REFLECTS THE ORIGINAL BRIEF: IT HUMANISES THE COMMUNICATED MESSAGE AND ADDS SIMPLE, INFORMAL ELEGANCE.T

Fedra Serif A Normal — Peter Biľak, 2002

reflects the original brief: it humani ses the communicated message and adds simple, informal elegance. The most important criterion was to crea te a typeface which works equally we ll on paper and on the computer scre en, and is consistent across all comp uter platforms. After first versions o f the typeface were completed and di gitised, the project was cancelled as Bayerische Ruck was acquired by ano

using since Otl Aicher designed their first visual identity in the 1970s. The typeface r eflects the original brief: it humanises the communicated message and adds simple, i nformal elegance. The most important crit erion was to create a typeface which work s equally well on paper and on the comput er screen, and is consistent across all comp uter platforms. After first versions of the t ypeface were completed and digitised, the project was cancelled as Bayerische Ruck

HE MOST IMPORTANT CRITERION WAS TO CREATE A TYPEFACE WHICH WORKS EQUALLY WELL ON PAPER AND ON THE COMPUTER SCREEN, AND IS CONSISTENT ACROSS ALL COMPUTER PLATFORMS. AFTER FIRST VERSIONS OF THE TYPEFA CE WERE COMPLETED AND DIGITISED, THE PROJECT WAS CANCELLED AS BAYE RISCHE RÜCK WAS ACQUIRED BY ANOT HER EVEN LARGER MULTINATIONAL CORPORATION. THIS PUT AN EARLY END

Fedra Serif A Medium — Peter Biľak, 2002

ther even larger multinational corp oration. This put an early end to the story of the custom font. Since a lot of work had been done already, I dec ided to complete the typeface, addin g extra weights and expert fonts. Sh ortly before the planned release dat e of the typeface, my studio was bro ken into, and my computers and bac k-up system containing all the font data were stolen. What initially see

was acquired by another even larger mult inational corporation. This put an early en d to the story of the custom font. Since a lot of work had been done already, I decid ed to complete the typeface, adding extra weights and expert fonts. Shortly before t he planned release date of the typeface, m y studio was broken into, and my compute rs and back-up system containing all the f ont data were stolen. What initially seeme d like the ultimate designer's disaster was

TO THE STORY OF THE CUSTOM FONT. SINCE A LOT OF WORK HAD BEE N DONE ALREADY, I DECIDED TO COMPLETE THE TYPEFACE, ADDING EXTRA WEIGHTS AND EXPERT FONTS. SHORTLY BEFORE THE PLANNED RELEASE DATE OF THE TYPE FACE, MY STUDIO WAS BROKEN INTO, A ND MY COMPUTERS AND BACK-UP SYSTE M CONTAINING ALL THE FONT DATA WERE STOLEN. WHAT INITIALLY SEEME D LIKE THE ULTIMATE DESIGNER'S DISA

Fedra Serif A Bold — Peter Biľak, 2002

med like the ultimate designer's di saster was actually beneficial for Fe dra. The incident delayed its releas e, allowing me to re-examine the ea rly design decisions, made under t he assumption that the font would be exclusive to the company and ne ver publicly available. The new vers ion is more versatile, offering a wid er range of fonts, a number of spec ial typographic features (see opposi

actually publicly available. The new vers ion is more versatile, offering a wider ran ge of fonts, a number of special typograp hic features (see opposite page). The spa cing of the font was altered, as well as th e slope of the italics. Many characters w ere redrawn creating a more flexible type family. Fedra was originally commission ed by Paris-based Ruedi Baur Integral D esign and developed as a corporate font f or Bayerische Rück, a German insurance

STER WAS ACTUALLY BENEFICIAL FOR FEDRA. THE INCIDENT DELAYED ITS RELEASE, ALLOWING ME TO RE-EXAM INE THE EARLY DESIGN DECISIONS, MADE UNDER THE ASSUMPTION THAT THE FONT WOULD BE EXCLUSIVE TO THE COMPANY AND NEVER PUBLICLY AVAILABLE. THE NEW VERSION IS MO RE VERSATILE, OFFERING A WIDER RA NGE OF FONTS, A NUMBER OF SPECIAL TYPOGRAPHIC FEATURES (SEE OPPOSI

Fedra Mono™

Peter Bil'ak
2002

Fedra Mono-Light
Fedra Mono-Light Italic
Fedra Mono-Book
Fedra Mono-Book Italic
Fedra Mono-Normal
Fedra Mono-Normal Italic
Fedra Mono-Medium
Fedra Mono-Medium Italic
Fedra Mono-Bold
Fedra Mono-Bold Italic

Fedra Mono was developed for an annual report that required a fixed-width counterpart to Fedra Sans. All the characters share the same widths, which makes it suitable for tabular setting when the information benefit from the vertical alignment of characters. The typical example would be spreadsheet or computer code. ¶ It is a 10-pitch face which means 10 characters equals one inch (2.54 cm) when set at 10 pt. All the characters, regardless of weight, have the same width, which is 60% of the em square. Those are also the proportions of the 1956 version of Courier. However, despite the fixed widths, Fedra Mono remains relatively even in typographic color, and lucid on screen. The various potentially similar characters are clearly distinguishable, notably I, l and 1, and O and 0, as well as brackets, braces and parentheses. ¶

sales@typotheque.com

Fedra was originally commission
ed by Paris-based Ruedi Baur In
tegral Design and developed as
a corporate font for Bayerische
Rück, a German insurance compan

*the font would be exclusive to
the company and never publicly
available. The new version is m
ore versatile, offering a wider
range of fonts, a number of spe*

y, as part of their new visual
identity. According to the comm
issioner, the objective was to
'de-protestantize Univers', the
typeface which Bayerische Rück
had been using since Otl Aicher
designed their first visual iden
tity in the 1970s. The typeface
reflects the original brief: it
humanises the communicated mess
age and adds simple, informal e

*cial typographic features (see
opposite page). The spacing of
the font was altered, as well a
s the slope of the italics. Man
y characters were redrawn creat
ing a more flexible type family
Fedra was originally commission
ed by Paris-based Ruedi Baur I
ntegral Design and developed as
a corporate font for Bayerische
Ruck, a German insurance compa*

legance. The most important crit
erion was to create a typeface w
hich works equally well on paper
and on the computer screen, and
is consistent across all comput
er platforms. After first versio
ns of the typeface were complete
d and digitised, the project was
cancelled as Bayerische Rück was
acquired by another even larger
multinational corporation. This

*company, as part of their new v
isual identity. According to
the commissioner, the objective
was to de-protestantize Univers
the typeface which Bayerische R
uck had been using since Otl Ai
cher designed their first visu
al identity in the 1970s. The
typeface reflects the original
brief: it humanises the communi
cated message and adds simple,*

put an early end to the story of
the custom font. Since a lot of
work had been done already, I de
cided to complete the typeface,
adding extra weights and expert
fonts. Shortly before the plann
ed release date of the typeface,
my studio was broken into, and
my computers and back-up system
containing all the font data we
re stolen. What initially seemed

*informal elegance. The most imp
ortant criterion was to create
a typeface which works equally
well on paper and on the comput
er screen, and is consistent a
cross all computer platforms. A
fter first versions of the type
face were completed and digitis
ed, the project was cancelled as
Bayerische Ruck was acquired by
another even larger multination*

**like the ultimate designer's dis
aster was actually beneficial fo
r Fedra. The incident delayed it
s release, allowing me to re-exa
mine the early design decisions,
made under the assumption that**

*al corporation. This put an ear
ly end to the story of the cust
om font. Since a lot of work ha
d been done already, I decided
to complete the typeface, addin
g extra weights and expert font*

Peter Biľak
2002

Fedra Bitmap Nine
Fedra Bitmap Nine Bold
Fedra Bitmap Eleven
Fedra Bitmap Eleven Bold
Fedra Bitmap Twelve
Fedra Bitmap Twelve Bold

Fedra Bitmap™ is a collection of bitmap fonts whose proportions are similar to Fedra Sans, but are specifically optimized for display on the computer screen. They provide a crisp image at small sizes because they don't have to be anti-aliased, which makes them ideal to use as for font in for multimedia, web and WAP. These bitmap fonts are compatible with bitmap software (such as Photoshop and Flash) but also include corresponding outlines for printing in vector-based applications (such as Illustrator, Quark, and Freehand). Fedra Bitmaps should only be used at the designed sizes 9, 11, and 12pt (or exact multiples) otherwise they will appear distorted.

(Fedra Bitmap Nine)

Fedra Bitmap™ is a collection of bitmap fonts whose proportions are similar to Fedra Sans, but are specifically optimized for display on the computer image at provide a crisp image at don't have to be ideal to

Fedra was originally commiss ioned by Paris-based Ruedi Ba ur Integral Design and develo ped as a corporate font for Bayerische Rück, a German in surance company, as part of their new visual identity. Ac cording to the commissioner, the objective was to 'de-pro testantize Univers', the typ eface which Bayerische Rück

complete the typeface, a dding extra weights and expert fonts. Shortly bef ore the planned release d ate of the typeface, my s tudio was broken into, an d my computers and back- up system containing all t he font data were stolen. What initially seemed like the ultimate designer's d

Fedra Bitmap Nine

Peter Biľak
2002

Fedra Bitmap contains corresponding outlines for printing in vector-based applications.

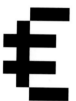

had been using since Otl Aiche r designed their first visual id entity in the 1970s. The typef ace reflects the original brief: it humanises the communicat ed message and adds simple, i nformal elegance. The most im portant criterion was to crea te a typeface which works eq ually well on paper and on the computer screen, and is consi

gner's disaster was actuall y beneficial for Fedra. The i ncident delayed its release , allowing me to re-examin e the early design decision s, made under the assumpt ion that the font would be exclusive to the company and never publicly available . The new version is more versatile, offering a wider

Fedra Bitmap Eleven

Peter Biľak
2002

stent across all computer pla tforms. After first versions of the typeface were completed and digitised, the project was cancelled as Bayerische Rück was acquired by another eve n larger multinational corpora tion. This put an early end to the story of the custom fon t. Since a lot of work had be en done already, I decided to

range of fonts, a number o f special typographic feat ures (see opposite page). T he spacing of the font was altered, as well as the slop e of the italics. Many chara cters were redrawn creati ng a more flexible type fam ily. Fedra was originally co mmissioned by Paris-based Ruedi Baur Integral Design

Fedra Bitmap Twelve

Peter Biľak
2002

Bitmap & outlines

Johanna Balušíková
1999-2002

Jigsaw is a geometrical sans-serif typeface with an almost uniform stroke width, originally designed as a Multiple Master font which modulates from Stencil to Roman. Since Multiple Master technology has became almost obsolete, the original master fonts were expanded to Normal, Medium and Bold weights.

Jigsaw is constructed from simple skeletal forms, which are even more distinct in the stencil version. In the larger sizes, the letter 'g' is particularly distinct, whilst set in the text Jigsaw has a harmonious, balanced appearance.

sales@typotheque.com

Jigsaw is a geometrical sans-serif typeface with an almost uniform stroke width, originally designed as a Multiple Master font which modulates from Stencil to Roman. Since Multiple Master technology has became almost obsolete, the

Jigsaw is a geometrical sans-serif typeface with an almost uniform stroke width, originally designed as a Multiple Master font which modulates from Stencil to Roman. Since Multiple Master technology has became almost obsolete, the

Jigsaw Light (+ Stencil)
Johanna Balušíková
1999-2002
Regular version and Stencil have identical widths in all weights.

the original master fonts were expanded to Normal, Medium and Bold weights. Jigsaw is constructed from simple skeletal forms, which are even more distinct in the stencil version. In the larger sizes, the letter 'g' is particularly dist

the original master fonts were expanded to Normal, Medium and Bold weights. Jigsaw is constructed from simple skeletal forms, which are even more distinct in the stencil version. In the larger sizes, the letter 'g' is particularly dist

Jigsaw Normal (+ Stencil)
Johanna Balušíková
1999-2002

inct, whilst set in the text Jigsaw has a harmonious, balanced appearance. Jigsaw is a geometrical sans-serif typeface with an almost uniform stroke width, originally designed as a Multiple Master font which modulates fr

inct, whilst set in the text Jigsaw has a harmonious, balanced appearance. Jigsaw is a geometrical sans-serif typeface with an almost uniform stroke width, originally designed as a Multiple Master font which modulates fr

Jigsaw Medium (+Stencil)
Johanna Balušíková
1999-2002

om Stencil to Roman. Since Multiple Master technology has became almost obsolete, the original master fonts were expanded to Regular, Medium and Bold weights. Jigsaw is constructed from simple skeletal for

om Stencil to Roman. Since Multiple Master technology has became almost obsolete, the original master fonts were expanded to Regular, Medium and Bold weights. Jigsaw is constructed from simple skeletal for

Jigsaw Bold (+ Stencil)
Johanna Balušíková
1999-2002

champollion

A French orientalist, born 21 December, 1790; died in Paris, 4 March, 1832. While still young, he studied Hebrew, Syriac, Ethiopic and Arabic to which he added later on, Persian, Sanskrit, and in particular Coptic. ¶

HIS SPECIAL FIELD OF ACTIVITY WAS EGYPTOLOGY, AND HIS GREAT GLORY

ABCDEFGHIJKLMNOPQRSTUVWXYZ?!¿¡@abcdefghijklmnopqrstuvwxyz?!&ÆŒ.,;:'"()
ÀÁÂÃÄÅÇ;ÆÈÉÊËÌÍÎÏÑÒÓÔÕÖØÙÚÛÜÝ™áàâãäåæçèéêëìíîïñóòôõöøùúûüÿ‡ß●¶«»‹›•°·oµ
×÷∏n‡∫^°Ω–√≈∆--«»‹›•"""{}√ƒ{¡¥↓↑↔‡↗↘↙↕Z÷±±≤≥<>TU÷∞∞™µ◊∏n∆Ã

ABCDEFGHIJKLMNOPQRSTUVWXYZ?!¿¡@abcdefghijklmnopqrstuvwxyz?!&ÆŒ.,;:'"()
ÀÁÂÃÄÅÇ;ÆÈÉÊËÌÍÎÏÑÒÓÔÕÖØÙÚÛÜÝ™áàâãäåæçèéêëìíîïñóòôõöøùúûüÿ‡ß●¶«»‹›•°·oµ
×÷∏n‡∫^°Ω–√≈∆--«»‹›•"""{}√ƒ{¡¥↓↑↔‡↗↘↙↕Z÷±±≤≥<>TU÷∞∞™µ◊∏n∆Ã

ϼoviNE spoNGiFoϼM ENCEϼhΛLOPΛThY

is a chronic, dEGENERαtivE disordEr αFFECtiNG thE cENtrαl NErvous systEM oF cαttlE —First diαGNosEd iN 1906 iN GrEαt ϼritαiN—αbout 95 pErcENt oF cαsEs hαvE occurrE d iN thE uNitEd kiNGdom—disEαsE coNFirmEd iN NαtivE-borN cαttlE iN EuropEαN couNt riEs such αs ϼElGium, FrαNcE, GErmαNy, spαiN, αNd switzErlαNd—Not kNowN to Exist iN thE uNitEd stαtEs, but surEly, thosE cows must bE thErE too. holy cow is α pαrti

MαD cow disEαsE is oNE oF sEvErαl FαtαL brα iN disEαsEs cαllEd trαNsmissiblE spoNGiForm ENcEphαlopαthiEs. thE jαrGoN sαys it αll: th EsE iNFEctious disEαsEs shoot thE brαiN Full

Holy Cow™

Peter Biľak
1995

ΛϼCDEϜGHIJKLMNOPQϼStUVWXYZϼ!ɟiΛαbcdEϜGhijklmNopqNstuvwxyzɳ&ΛEŒ..:: ®©ÀÁÄÂÅÇΛEÉÉÈÌÍÏÑïøÓôÔÒÕÚÛÙÜŸκ™áàâäãåçÉÊÈËÌÍÏïÑÓòÔÖøÕÚÙÛÜŸĻŢ§•¶Ḭ°° ◇ʯÒΣΠΠ#ʃᵃᵒ⋂−√≈Δ−−«»‹›""''\$√€ƒ¢¥£‼¼½.·.ŒŒϜiϜL≠=+±‹∷›TU÷®©™ʯÒΣΠΠÀÃ

Holy Cow White™

Peter Biľak
1995

ΛϼCDEϜGHIJKLMNOPQϼStUVWXYZϼ!ɟiΛαbcdEϜGhijklmNopqNstuvwxyzɳ&ΛEŒ ..::®©ÀÁÄÂÅÇΛEÉÉÈÌÍÏïÑïøÓôÔÒÕÚÛÙÜŸκ™áàâäãåçÉÊÈËÌÍÏïÑÓòÔÖøÕÚÙÛÜŸĻŢ §•¶Ḭ°°◇ʯÒΣΠΠ#ʃᵃᵒ⋂−√≈Δ−−«»‹›""''\$√€ƒ¢¥£‼¼½.·.ÆŒϜiϜL≠=+±‹∷›TU÷®©™ʯÒΣ

Holy Cow Black™

Peter Biľak
1995

Appendix A: **Glossary**

Accent See *diacritic*.

Accented Character A character with a mark added, indicating a changed phonetic value. See also *diacritic*.

AFM (Adobe Font Metrics) A specification by which font metrics information (kerning pairs, character widths, etc.) is stored.

Aldine Refers to the Venetian publishing house operated by *Aldus Manutius*, 1494–1515. *Francesco Griffo* cut the majority of Aldus's types. Contemporary type and typography resembling that of Griffo or Aldus may be referred to as Aldine.

Align To line up type or other graphic elements, using a base or vertical line or grid as a reference point.

Alignment The positioning of text or other graphic elements relative to a set margin. Forms of alignment include *flush left, flush right, justified,* or *centered.* Flush left is also known as left justified or ragged right; flush right is also known as right justified or ragged left.

Alphabet The characters making up a particular language, arranged in their traditional order.

Alternate Characters A character with a different design used as an alternative to a standard alpha character in a typeface.

Ampersand The symbol developed to represent *et,* the Latin term for *and.*

Analphabetic Used with the alphabet, these typographic characters lack a place in the alphabetical order. Diacritics, such as the umlaut and caron, and characters such as the asterisk and ampersand, are all examples of analphabetics.

Anglo American System A system devised to regulate the measurement of type, defined by the *American Typefounders Association* in 1886. In the Anglo American System, 1 inch = 6 picas = 72 points (approx.). For comparison, see also the *European System.*

Anti-aliasing The smoothing of the jagged edges in digital images. By varying the shades of gray or color at its edges, an object can blend smoothly into the background.

Antiqua A European term for Roman typefaces. The *letra antigua* of the Spanish writing masters, for example, shows the heavy Italian influence on letterforms. Also spelled *Antikva.*

Antique A style of letter used in display typography from the late 1800s to the early 1900s.

Aperture The openings of letters such as 'C,' 'S,' and 'a.'

Apex Where the strokes of a character meet at its uppermost point.

Arm The upward-projecting strokes or horizontal extensions found in characters such as 'X' and 'L.'

Ascender The stem of a lowercase letter, such as 'b' or 'k,' that extends above the body of the letter, or x-height.

Ascender Line The imaginary horizontal line marking the uppermost point of an ascender.

Ascent A character's maximum distance above the baseline.

ASCII (American Standard Code for Information Interchange) A 7-bit character code used in computing. ASCII encodes 128 alphanumerics and symbols into assigned numbers for the purpose of electronic storage and communication. See *EBCDIC* for comparison.

Asterisk A typographic character used as a reference mark, usually in the shape of a star and raised above the baseline.

ATF (American Type Founders) The largest metal type foundry in North America. The Elizabeth, New Jersey-based company was formed in 1892 through the union of a number of smaller firms.

ATM (Adobe Type Manager) A program designed to improve onscreen display by imaging fonts directly from the PostScript outline font, as opposed to relying solely on the bitmap font for display.

Axis The axis of a character usually refers to the axis of its stroke. There may be multiple *axes* in a letterform.

Back Slanting The technique of drawing or digitally manipulating characters at a backward angle; the opposite angle of an *italic.*

Ball Terminal A circular shape at the end of the arm in characters such as 'c' and 'y.' Typically found in Romans and italics in the style of *Bodoni* and *Clarendon.* See also *terminal.*

Bar See *cross-stroke.*

Baseline The imaginary line supporting the characters in a font, excluding the descenders of lowercase letters and other extended elements, such as the tail in a 'Q.' *Leading* is measured from baseline to baseline.

Bastarda A class of *blackletter* types.

BCP *(Bézier Control Point)* One of two points guiding a Bézier curve.

Beak Terminal A sharp spur form found in some typefaces on characters such as 'a,' 'c,' 'f,' and 'r.' Typically found in many twentieth-century Romans and some italics, such as *Perpetua* and *Pontifex*. See also *terminal*.

Bézier Curve Mathematical equations used to describe the character shapes in digital typography. French computer scientist *Pierre Bézier* developed the mathematical representation used to describe this curve.

Bicameral Two alphabets joined, as in the Latin alphabet with its upper and lower cases. See also *tricameral* and *unicameral*.

Bitmap A matrix of dots or pixels making up a graphic display.

Bitmap Font A font which is made up of pixels. Bitmap fonts are usually used in combination with outline fonts; the bitmap is viewed onscreen, while the corresponding outline font is used in a printer. In cases where fonts are intended for screen use only, bitmap fonts may be used without accompanying outline fonts. Also known as a *screen font*.

Blackletter The typographical counterpart to Gothic in architecture, this typically heavy, often ornate, style of letterform was the first metal type in Europe. The earliest of these types were found in the *Gutenberg* workshop, copied from characters in handwritten manuscripts. *Bastarda, fraktur, quadrata, rotunda,* and *textura* are all categories of blackletter. Also known as *Old English*.

Block Quotation A quotation set apart from the body of text, often set in a different size or face than the main text.

Body Size The point size, or height, of a face, measured from ascender to descender and including a set surrounding space. In letterpress terminology, body size signified the height of the face of the physical metal block on which a character was cast. In contemporary digital typography, this is the height of its imaginary equivalent—not the dimension of the character, but the rectangle defining the entire space owned by the letterform.

Boldface (1) A typeface drawn with thicker strokes to achieve a heavier appearance. (2) To draw or digitally make letterforms darker or thicker for emphasis.

Bolded Not to be confused with a boldface type drawn from scratch, this generally refers to thickening letterforms using a computer program's automatic bolding capabilities.

Bookface See *text face*.

Border A continuous rule or decorative graphic element enclosing the body of material on a printed page or onscreen.

Bowl The round or elliptical form of the body shape of certain characters. Examples include 'C,' 'O,' 'c,' and 'e.' Also referred to as the *eye*.

Bracket The curved or round joint, or wedge, between the stem and the serif of a letterform.

Calligraphic In typography, this typically refers to Roman or italic alphabets that appear to have been drawn with pen or brush. The term is derived from the Greek *kalligraphia,* literally meaning, *beautiful writing*.

Cap Height The distance from the baseline to the cap line of an alphabet; the approximate height of an uppercase letter. Lowercase ascenders often extend beyond the cap height.

Capital Line, Cap Line An imaginary line running across the uppermost point of capital letters.

Capitals, Caps See *uppercase*.

Centered Text set at an equal distance from both margins.

Chancery A class of italic letterform, often typified by lengthened or curved extenders.

Character A symbol in writing and typography. Characters include letters, numerals, punctuation marks and other figures.

Character Encoding A table in a font or computer operating system that maps character codes to a font's glyphs. Character encoding is not standardized across platforms and operating systems.

Character Map See *keyboard layout*.

Character Set The group of characters—typically alphanumerics, punctuation and symbols—that make up a single font.

Cicero Part of the European System, the cicero is a unit of measure equaling 12 Didot points. The European counterpart to the British/American *pica*, the cicero is slightly larger than the pica. See also *Didot* and the *European System*.

Colophon (1) A symbol used in book printing to represent a publisher or publisher's imprint. (2) Information on a book's title, printer, publisher and publication date, typically displayed at the end of a book. Colophons often offer details on the typefaces, type designers or typographers associated with the production of a printed piece. The tradition has migrated to the digital arena, with colophons sometimes included on websites and in other forms of digital media.

Color The appearance of darkness in set type. Letterspacing, word spacing, leading, stroke weight, ink and paper color and other factors contribute to the blackness of typeset text. Also known as *typographic color.*

Condensed A narrower version of a typeface, designed with the intention of fitting more characters into a given measure.

Contour Data The complex data used by a computer processor in the mathematical formula responsible for generating Bézier curves and curvilinear data.

Contrast The degree of contrast between the thick and thin strokes of a letterform. *Helvetica* is an example of a face with no contrast, while *Bodoni* is a high-contrast design.

Copyfitting The technique of adjusting type size and spacing so that it fits within a defined space.

Counter The interior white space enclosed by a letterform. 'D' and 'O' are examples of characters with wholly enclosed counters, while the counters in 'c' and 'm' are partially enclosed.

Cross bar See *cross-stroke.*

Cross-stroke A horizontal stroke connecting two stems, as in 'A' and 'H,' or the projecting stroke of a letter cutting horizontally across the stem, as in 'f' and 't.' Also known as the *cross bar* or *bar.*

Cursive Dating from the 16th century, cursive typefaces imitate the flowing style of handwriting. Both script faces and cursive designs give the appearance of being drawn with pen and ink. Script types are typically joined, while cursives generally are not. Also used as a synonym for *italic.*

Descender That part of a lower-case letter which extends below the baseline. Examples include 'j,' 'q,' and 'y.'

Descender line The imaginary horizontal line marking the lowermost point of a descender.

Descent A character's maximum distance below the baseline.

Diacritic A mark over, under or through a character, added to give it a different phonetic value, or to differentiate between words which are visually identical. Examples of diacritics include the *umlaut, cedilla* and *tilde.* Also known as an *accent.*

Didone A modified version of *Old Style* serif types, Didones retain some of the characteristics of engraving. These high contrast letterforms were originally developed by *Firmin Didot* and *Giambattista Bodoni* from the late 18th to early 19th centuries. *Bauer Bodoni* and *ITC Fenice* are examples of Didone styles, also called *Modern Serifs.*

Didot A standard unit of measure in European typography, the Didot point is slightly larger than the American point. See also the *European System.*

Dingbats Historically called *printer's flowers,* dingbats are typically small decorative elements, bullets, or other symbols. In contemporary typography, dingbat fonts have expanded to encompass a diverse range of imagery, from detailed illustrations of buildings, animals and insects to abstract sketches of the human face. Sometimes referred to as *picture fonts, image fonts,* or *icon fonts.*

Diphthong Two vowels joined to create a single character: 'Æ,' 'Œ,' 'æ,' and 'œ.' Diphthongs are also considered *ligatures.*

Display Face A larger or bolder version of a text face, specifically cut for use in setting headlines. Often used to describe decorative type not suited for body copy.

Double Story A lowercase 'a' or 'g' with a closed tail or curved finial.

DPI (*Dots Per Inch*) The standard measure of the resolution of a video monitor or output device.

Drop Cap An oversized capital letter or *versal* set at the beginning of a paragraph, drop caps occupy two or more lines of text.

Ear A small projection found on some letterforms, such as the stroke attached to the bowl of a 'g.'

EBCDIC (*Extended Binary Coded Decimal Interchange*) An 8-bit character code used in computing, typically in mainframes. EBCDIC encodes 256 alphanumerics and symbols into assigned numbers for the purpose of electronic storage and communication. See *ASCII* for comparison.

Egyptian A typeface style with slab or square serifs and nearly uniform strokes (a low contrast face). Examples of Egyptian types include *Memphis* and *Serifa*.

Elevated Cap An oversized capital letter or versal set on the same baseline as the first line in a text.

Em A relative unit of measure equal to the square of the type size. Historically, the em is the width of a typeface's widest letterform, the capital 'M.' In contemporary terminology, the em is defined as the current point size. For example, 12-point type will contain an em with a width of 12 points.

Em Dash The width of an em, this character is used to indicate missing content or a break in thought.

Em Space A space equal to the width of an em, often used for paragraph indentions.

En A unit of measure equal to half the width of a typeface's point size. The en is traditionally half the width of an em. For example, 12-point type will contain an en with a width of 6 points.

En dash The width of an en, this character is used to indicate duration, or in creating compound adjectives.

En Space A space equal to the width of an en, or half an em space.

EPS (*Encapsulated PostScript*) A computer document file format used to exchange PostScript image information between applications.

EULA (*End User License Agreement*) A type of contract between a software publisher and a licensed user of said software. The EULA gives the end-user permission to use the software, grants additional rights, imposes restrictions on use, etc. The EULA may also contain limited warranty information, contact and upgrade details, and other information.

European System A system to regulate the measurement of type, proposed by the *Fournier Press* in 1737. In 1775, the *Didot foundry* endorsed the point system currently in use in Europe. In the European system, 1 inch = 6 ciceros = 72 Didot points (approx.). For comparison, see the *Anglo American System*.

Expanded A typeface with letterforms drawn or digitally made wider without adding to the weight.

Expert Set An expanded set of characters designed as a companion to a basic character set, contained in one or more separate, style-related fonts. Expert sets may include old style figures, proportionally drawn small caps, swashes, ornaments, alternate characters and many other features designed to enhance typographic works.

Extended A typeface with letterforms that are expanded horizontally while retaining their original height.

Extenders The ascenders and descenders of letterforms.

Eye A synonym for *bowl*. If a character is said to have a large eye, it actually has a large x-height, while an open eye signifies a large aperture.

Family The group of all the type sizes and styles of a typeface; the complete character set of a font. The members of a type family are based on a common design, but may differ in width, weight, style and other attributes. See also *typeface*.

Finial A flourish or decoration found at the end of a main stroke in some typefaces. See also *terminal*.

Fleuron A typographical ornament, usually shaped like a flower or leaf.

Flourish A stroke added to a letterform for stylistic purposes.

Flush Left Text that is set flush, or justified, on the left margin. Also known as *left justified* or *ragged right*.

Flush Right Text that is set flush, or justified, on the right margin. Also known as *right justified* or *ragged left*.

Font A set of characters. In metal typesetting, a font (or fount) consisted of an alphabet and its companion characters in a given size. In this context, 48 pt. *Johnston Underground Bold* is a font. In digital typography, a font represents the character set itself, or the digital information encoding it. In modern terminology, *font, face,* and *typeface* are often used interchangeably. See also *fount*.

Font Family See *family*.

Font Metrics See *AFM, metrics*.

Foundry See *type foundry*.

Fount Older British spelling of the term *font*. Pronunciation is the same.

Fraktur A class of *blackletter* types.

Geometric A class of *sans serif*, influenced by the *Bauhaus* movement. *Futura* and *ITC Bauhaus* are examples of the geometric style.

Glyph Usually defined as a shape in a font that represents a character code for output onscreen or paper. The most common form of a glyph is a letter; however, the non-alphanumeric symbols and shapes in a font are also glyphs.

Gothic See *Grotesk*.

Grotesk/Grotesque A class of *sans serif*. Early designs and revivals of 19th century designs are also referred to as *Gothic* types. *Akzidenz Grotesk* and *News Gothic* are examples of the Grotesk/Gothic styles.

Humanist A class of *sans serif* types based on Humanist roman faces. Examples include *Gill Sans* and *Optima*.

Gutenberg In 1450, *Johannes Gutenberg* invented a printing press and introduced the concept of movable type to Europe. In 1455, Gutenberg's Latin 42-line Bible became the first European book to be produced using movable metal type.

Hairline The thinnest stroke used in designing letterforms.

Half-Serif Terminal The terminal ending of a serif with one side suppressed. See

also *terminal*.

Headline Font See *display face*.

Hints Mathematical instructions added to digital fonts to enhance their appearance at all sizes and on display devices with differing resolution.

Initial Cap Oversized and often ornamental, initial caps are sometimes used at the beginning of paragraphs or chapters.

Inline A character in which the inner portions of the main strokes have been carved out, while leaving the edges intact. *Castellar* and *Goudy Handtooled* are examples of inline faces.

Italic First developed in the 15th century, italics are more cursive than roman letterforms, and are usually designed to slant to the right. The first italic type was designed by *Aldus Manutius* in 1501, and was based on the elegant handwriting styles of that era. The term *italic* refers to this style's Italian origin.

Italicize To set type in an italic font.

Justified Referring to text or graphic elements that are aligned at both the left and right margins. See also *alignment*.

Kern The part of one letter that extends into the space of another character.

Kerning The adjustment of white space between character pairs to improve appearance and legibility.

Keyboard Layout A table used by a computer operating system to control the character codes generated when a key or key combination is pressed. Also known as *keyboard map* or

character map.

Keyboard Map See *keyboard layout*.

Lachrymal Terminal See *teardrop terminal*.

Leading Pronounced *led-ding*. The vertical distance from baseline to baseline. Named for the lead spacers used between lines of text in letterpress printing. Also called *lead*.

Left Justified See *flush left*.

Letterspacing Adjusting the space between letters in a block of text. *Kerning* allows for the adjustment of space between particular character pairs; letterspacing is applied to text as a whole. Also referred to as *tracking*.

License Agreement See *EULA*.

Ligated A typeface with connections between letterforms. Formal scripts such as *Snell Roundhand* and *Citadel Script* are examples of ligated designs. Letter combinations such as 'fi' and 'st' may also be ligated in non-connecting typefaces.

Ligature Two or more letters connected to create a single character. Examples include 'fi' and 'fl,' and diphthongs such as 'Æ' and 'Œ.' Also known as *tied letters*.

Line Spacing See *leading*.

Lining Figures Numerals of even height. Also called *titling figures;* however, some lining figures may be small and lighter than the uppercase in a typeface. Also called *modern figures*.

Lowercase Originally called *minuscules,* these are the small, or *lowercase,* letters of a typeface. Minuscules were traditionally stored in the lower section of a printer's *typecase,* and it eventually became common practice to use the term lowercase to describe these characters.

LPI (Lines Per Inch) A measure of the frequency of a halftone screen.

Majuscules See *uppercase*.

Matrix The metal mold from which type is cast.

Mean Line The imaginary horizontal line marking the top of the lowercase letters, excluding ascenders. See also *x-height*.

Measure The standard length of a line of text. The *column width,* as it is also called, is usually indicated in *picas*.

Metrics Font information such as kerning, character widths and leading. See also *AFM*.

Miniscules See *lowercase*.

Modern Figures See *lining figures*.

Modern Serif See *Didone*.

Modified Sans Serif Typefaces in this class are *sans serif,* but feature tiny or partial serifs for the sake of legibility. *Rotis SemiSans* is an example of this class.

Monospaced Type A typeface in which all the characters are of the same set-width. Based on the principal of traditional typewriter text, monospaced type allows for easy alignment of text and figures.

Multiple Master A variation by Adobe Systems on its own PostScript Type 1 font format. With multiple master typefaces, users have the ability to generate their own variations, or *instances,* changing weight, width, optical size, or other style characteristics by modifying one or more design axes.

Neo-grotesque A class of sans serif. Examples include the classic Swiss designs, *Univers* and *Helvetica*.

NFNT (New FoNT) The font resource in the Macintosh operating system that contains a bitmap screen font. This *New Font Numbering system* greatly increased the number of distinct font IDs available, assisting in the reduction of duplicate identifiers.

Oblique A slanted version of a typeface. Oblique types are similar to italic designs in feel, but do not have the more elegant, script-like quality of the true italics.

Old Style Originating from the Renaissance and 15th century Venetian printers, Old Style types were based on pen-drawn forms. *Garalde* and *Venetian* are the two groups that make up the Old Style class. *Garamond, Caslon* and *ITC Berkeley Oldstyle* are examples of Old Style designs.

Old Style Figures Numerals designed to match the lowercase letters in size and typographic color. Most old style figures consist of both ascending and descending forms. Also called *text figures*.

OpenType Developed jointly by Adobe and Microsoft, OpenType is a universal computer font format designed to essentially combine TrueType and PostScript into a single format for use on both Macintosh and Windows platforms. OpenType allows for an almost limitless number of glyphs and conditional letter combinations with easier access to full *expert set* characters, facilitating multi-lingual and advanced typography.

Ornaments See *dingbats, fleuron*.

Outline Font A computer file containing the outline or vector information of a typeface, its set of character shapes are mathematically described by lines and curves. These scalable fonts are typically made up of Bézier curves (PostScript) and quadratic splines (TrueType). Also referred to as a *printer font*.

Pi Font A font consisting of mathematical or other symbols, intended for use in conjunction with a text font.

Pica Part of the Anglo American System, the pica is a unit of measure equaling 12 points. The British/American counterpart to the European *cicero,* the pica is slightly smaller than the cicero. See also the *Anglo American System* and the *European System*.

Pixel (PICture ELement) Square dots representing the smallest units displayed onscreen. Pixels can be assigned their own color and intensity. Higher numbers of pixels per inch results in finer screen resolution.

Point A standard unit of measure in British/American typography, the point is slightly smaller than the European *Didot* point. See also the *Anglo American System* and the *European System*.

Point Size A font's size is specified in units called points, and is typically the height of the type's body. This standard type measurement system was developed by *Pierre Fournier le jeune* in 1737. See also the *Anglo American System* and the *European System*.

PostScript A page description

language developed by Adobe Systems. PostScript describes a page using complex mathematical formulas. Characters and images are defined as outline shapes, and rendered by an output device in a series of tiny dots.

Printer Font See *outline font.*

Proportionally Spaced Type Type designs with character widths varying depending on the features of the individual letterforms.

Punchcutting The art of cutting letters into hard steel, which are then *punched* into softer brass matrices, from which lead type is cast.

Punctuation Standardized non-alphanumeric characters used to clarify meaning through organizing writing into clauses, phrases and sentences.

Quadrata A class of *blackletter* types.

Ragged Left Text that is set flush, or justified, on the right margin. Also known as *right justified.*

Ragged Right Text that is set flush, or justified, on the left margin. Also known as *left justified.*

Raised Cap See *elevated cap.*

Rasterization The conversion of a digitized image into a format that can be rendered onscreen or printed from an output device.

Reference Mark A symbol used in text to point to a footnote or other relevant piece of information.

Relative Unit A fractional unit of an em space, proportional to the type size.

Rendering The placement of rasterized pixels onscreen. Also referred to as *screen rasterization.*

Resolution (1) The measurement of image sharpness and clarity onscreen, typically measured in pixels per inch. (2) The sharpness and clarity of text and graphics imaged on an output device; normally measured in dots per inch.

Reverse Setting white or light-colored against a black or dark background.

Right Justified See *flush right.*

RIP (Raster Image Processor) A device that uses a mathematical description of an image to be printed, converting it to a raster image for printing to an output device.

Roman An upright, regular weight, *Old Style* or *Modern.* The classical Roman letter style was conceived around 114 A.D., and typified by the letterforms chiseled into the *Trajan Column* in Rome.

Rotunda A class of *blackletter* types. Also known as *rotonda.*

Round Hand Types with broad, rounded letters, modeled after the handwriting style of the same name.

Run-in Quotation A quotation, typically enclosed in quotation marks, run in with the main body of text.

Sans Serif From the Latin, meaning literally, without serifs. Faces designed without serifs are also referred to as the *Lineale* style. Categories of sans serif types include *Grotesk/ Gothic, Geometric, Neo-grotesque,* and *Humanist.* Also known as *unserifed.*

Scalable Font Describes the fonts generated by a computer's mathematical algorithm, which allows the size to vary proportionally on the fly while retaining the integrity of the design.

Screen Font See *bitmap font.*

Script Script letters are typically joined. The earliest script types were modeled on formal cursive handwriting in the 16th century. Classes of scripts include Casual, Calligraphic, Blackletter and Lombardic, and Formal styles.

Serif (1) The small finishing strokes drawn diagonally or horizontally across the arms, stems and tails of letterforms. (2) The term is used to describe a class of typefaces drawn with serifs. Major categories in the serif class include *Old Style/Old Face, Transitional (Réale), Modern (Didone),* and *Slab/Square/ Egyptian* styles.

Set-width The actual width of a character and its surrounding space; or, the amount of space needed to set a line of text in a particular typeface. Also known as *advance width.*

Side Bearing The space between the origin of a character and its leftmost point (the left side bearing); or the space between the rightmost point and width line (right side bearing).

Slab Serif A class of serif types. Also known as *square serif* or *Egyptian.*

Slanted See *oblique.*

Slope The angle of inclination of the ascenders, descenders and stems of letterforms.

Small Cap Figures A set of numerals designed for use

with the small cap alphabet of a given typeface.

Small Caps An alternative alphabet of capital letters that are approximately the same height as the x-height of a typeface. Small caps are common in Roman types. Although many graphics applications can generate their own small caps, true small caps, with correctly drawn proportions and weights are usually found only in *expert sets.*

Spacing The space, or the way space is arranged, between characters, words, and lines of type.

Spur A type of finishing stroke found on some letterforms in certain typefaces, such as 'G' and 'b.'

Square Serif See *slab serif.*

Stem The main vertical stroke or the main oblique stroke of a character. 'L' and 'V' are examples of letterforms with stems. An 'O' has no stem, while the letter 'I' is made up of a stem and serifs only.

Stress The emphasis on the stroke of a letter; typically vertical, stresses may also be horizontal or diagonal.

Stroke The main line or curve which makes up a character.

Stroke Essential Straight or curved lines.

Style The variations of a given typeface. A wide range of variants are available to type designers, including bold, condensed, italic, extended, oblique, roman and many others.

Swash Capitals Uppercase letters that take up extra space or contain added flourishes.

Swash caps are usually cursive, and are generally designed to complement italic types.

Tabular Figures Numerals designed with a uniform set-width, intended for aligning tabular data.

Tail A character's downward project, such as found in the letter 'Q,' or the short, diagonal stroke that rests on the baseline in letters such as 'K' and 'R.'

Teardrop Terminal A teardrop-shaped swelling at the end of the arm in characters such as 'a,' 'c,' 'f' and 'y.' Typically found in typefaces from the Late Renaissance, Baroque and *Neoclassical* periods, examples include *Jannon, Caslon, Baskerville* and *Galliard.*

Terminal The free-hanging stroke of letters such as 'a,' 'c,' 'f' and 'y,' often given decorative treatment. See also *ball terminal, beak terminal, half-serif terminal, teardrop terminal,* and *finial.*

Text The main body of printed material, also known as *copy.*

Text Face Typefaces specifically designed for readability, text faces are typically serif types set between 9 and 12 points. *Times* and *Goudy Oldstyle* are examples of classic text faces. Also known as *bookface.*

Text Figures See *old style figures.*

Textura A class of *blackletter* types.

Thick Space A unit of measurement equaling one-third of an em.

Thin Space A unit of measurement equaling one-fifth of an em.

Tied Letters See *ligated* and *ligature.*

Tracking See *letterspacing.*

Transitional Serif A class of serif types first introduced in the late 18th century by *John Baskerville,* the *Réale* styles combine features from both *Old Style* and *Modern* faces. *ITC Bookman* and *ITC Caslon 224* are examples of transitional serifs.

Tricameral Three alphabets joined. A typical Roman font can be considered tricameral, having an upper case, a lower case, and small caps. See also *bicameral* and *unicameral.*

TrueType An outline font format developed by Apple Computer. Intended for use with Mac OS 7, TrueType was also adopted by Microsoft Corporation for use with Windows. TrueType fonts can be used for both screen display and printing, eliminating the need for separate screen and printer fonts.

Type Typewritten or printed letterforms and other characters.

Type Foundry Literally, a place for the manufacture of type. Historically, a type founder may have designed type, cut punches, made the matrices and cast the metal type. Eventually, each of these operations became separate crafts performed by specialists. Although punchcutting and casting type may no longer be involved, in modern terminology, a designer or company that creates and/or distributes digital typefaces may also be called a type foundry.

Typeface Sometimes named after its designer, a typeface is a collection of all the characters of a single design, regardless of style or size. A typeface typically consists of letters and figures (the alphanumerics), punctuation, and commonly used accents and symbols.

Typographic Color See *color*.

Typography The study and process of producing typefaces; and how to select, arrange and use type in general. Traditionally, typography referred to the use of metal types used in letterpress. In modern terminology, typography includes onscreen display and printed output.

U&lc Denotes upper and lower case, U&lc is the traditional form for setting text in the bicameral Latin, Greek and Cyrillic alphabets.

Uncial A calligraphic typestyle with large, rounded letterforms, combining elements of both upper and lowercase letters. The term is derived from the Latin *uncus*, or *crooked*.

Unicameral An alphabet having only one case, such as the Hebrew alphabet and some Roman titling faces. See also *bicameral* and *tricameral*.

Uppercase Originally called majuscules, these are the large letters of a typeface. Majuscules were traditionally stored in the upper section of a printer's typecase, and it eventually became common practice to use the term uppercase to describe these characters. Also referred to as *caps* or *capitals*.

Upright Standing vertically or straight upward; in typography, the term typically refers to a roman face or regular *sans serif* type.

Versal A large initial cap which is typically elevated or dropped in text.

Vertex Where the stems of a character meet at its lowest joint.

Weight The darkness or blackness of a typeface, not relating to its size; the measurement of a stroke's width. There are many weight variants available, including thin, light, demibold and ultrabold. Many typeface families have multiple weights.

White Space The blank sections of a page where text and graphics are not printed.

Whiteletter The typographical counterpart to Romanesque in architecture, whiteletter describes the light roman and italic letterforms typically favored by scribes and typographers in 15th and 16th century Italy. Compare to the generally darker *blackletter* styles in use in Northern Europe at the time.

Word Spacing In a line of text, the amount of space between words. When type is set unjustified, the word space is typically of a fixed size. When setting justified text, the word space must fluctuate, enabling the text to align at more than one margin.

x-height The distance between the baseline and the midline of an alphabet, approximately the height of the lowercase 'x.' The measurement is based on the 'x' because it typically rests squarely on the baseline, and has no ascenders or descenders.

Appendix B: **Character Reference Chart**

A	B	C	D	E	F	G	H	I	J	K	L	M	N	O	P	Q	R	S
a A / A	b B / B	c C / C	d D / D	e E / E	f F / F	g G / G	h H / H	i I / I	j J / J	k K / K	l L / L	m M / M	n N / N	o O / O	p P / P	q Q / Q	r R / R	s S / S
t T / T	u U / U	v V / V	w W / W	x X / X	y Y / Y	z Z / Z	A Sh-A / Sh-A	B Sh-B / Sh-B	C Sh-C / Sh-C	D Sh-D / Sh-D	E Sh-E / Sh-E	F Sh-F / Sh-F	G Sh-G / Sh-G	H Sh-H / Sh-H	I Sh-I / Sh-I	J Sh-J / Sh-J	K Sh-K / Sh-K	L Sh-L / Sh-L
M Sh-M / Sh-M	N Sh-N / Sh-N	O Sh-O / Sh-O	P Sh-P / Sh-P	Q Sh-Q / Sh-Q	R Sh-R / Sh-R	S Sh-S / Sh-S	T Sh-T / Sh-T	U Sh-U / Sh-U	V Sh-V / Sh-V	W Sh-W / Sh-W	X Sh-X / Sh-X	Y Sh-Y / Sh-Y	Z Sh-Z / Sh-Z	1 1 / 1	2 2 / 2	3 3 / 3	4 4 / 4	5 5 / 5
6 6 / 6	7 7 / 7	8 8 / 8	9 9 / 9	0 0 / 0	! Sh-1 / Sh-1	@ Sh-2 / Sh-2	# Sh-3 / Sh-3	$ Sh-4 / Sh-4	% Sh-5 / Sh-5	^ Sh-6 / Sh-6	& Sh-7 / Sh-7	* Sh-8 / Sh-8	(Sh-9 / Sh-9	) Sh-0 / Sh-0	, , / ,	. . / .	; ; / ;	: Sh-; / Sh-;
- - / -	/ / / /	? Sh-/ / Sh-/	' ' / '	" Sh-' / Sh-'	¡ OP-1 / Alt-0161	¿ Sh-Op-/ / Alt-0191	– Op-- / Alt-0173	+ Sh-= / Sh-=	≈ Op-x / Alt-0215	÷ Op-/ / Alt-0247	= = / =	± Sh-Op-= / Alt-0177	‹ Sh-, / Sh-,	› Sh-. / Sh-.	[[/ [	]] /]	{ Sh-[/ Sh-[	} Sh-] / Sh-]
' Op-] / Alt-0145	' Sh-Op-] / Alt-0146	" Op-[/ Alt-0147	" Sh-Op-[/ Alt-0148	‹ Sh-Op-3 / Alt-0139	› Sh-Op-4 / Alt-0155	« Op-\ / Alt-0171	» Sh-Op-\ / Alt-0187	‚ Sh-Op-0 / Alt-0130	„ Sh-Op-W / Alt-0132	— Sh-Op-- / Alt-0151	~ Sh-` / Sh-`	\ \ / \	| Sh-\ / Sh-\	_ Sh-- / Sh--	… Op-; / Alt-0133	° Sh-Op-8 / Alt-0176	· Sh-Op-9 / Alt-0183	• Op-8 / Alt-0149
ä Op-U A / Alt-0228	â Op-I A / Alt-0226	á Op-E A / Alt-0225	à Op-` A / Alt-0224	ã Op-N A / Alt-0227	å Op-A / Alt-0229	ë Op-U E / Alt-0235	ê Op-I E / Alt-0234	é Op-E E / Alt-0233	è Op-` E / Alt-0232	ï Op-U I / Alt-0239	î Op-I I / Alt-0238	í Op-E I / Alt-0237	ì Op-` I / Alt-0236	ö Op-U O / Alt-0246	ô Op-I O / Alt-0244	ó Op-E O / Alt-0243	ò Op-` O / Alt-0242	õ Op-N O / Alt-0245
ü Op-U U / Alt-0252	û Op-I U / Alt-0251	ú Op-E U / Alt-0250	ù Op-` U / Alt-0249	Ä Op-U Sh-A / Alt-0196	Â Op-I Sh-A / Alt-0194	Á Op-E Sh-A / Alt-0193	À Op-` Sh-A / Alt-0192	Ã Op-N Sh-A / Alt-0195	Å Op-U Sh-E / Alt-0197	Ë Op-I Sh-E / Alt-0203	Ê Op-E Sh-E / Alt-0202	É Op-` Sh-E / Alt-0201	È Op-U Sh-I / Alt-0200	Ï Op-I Sh-I / Alt-0207	Î Op-E Sh-I / Alt-0206	Í Op-` Sh-I / Alt-0205	Ì Op-U Sh-U / Alt-0204	Ö Op-U Sh-U / Alt-0214
Ô Op-I Sh-O / Alt-0212	Ó Op-E Sh-O / Alt-0211	Ò Op-` Sh-O / Alt-0210	Õ Op-N Sh-O / Alt-0213	Ü Op-U Sh-U / Alt-0220	Û Op-I Sh-U / Alt-0219	Ú Op-E Sh-U / Alt-0218	Ù Op-` Sh-U / Alt-0217	ç Op-C / Alt-0231	Ç Sh-Op-C / Alt-0199	ñ Op-N N / Alt-0241	Ñ Op-N Sh-N / Alt-0209	ø Op-O / Alt-0248	Ø Sh-Op-O / Alt-0216	ß Op-S / Alt-0223	æ Op-' / Alt-0230	Æ Sh-Op-' / Alt-0198	œ Op-Q / Alt-0156	Œ Sh-Op-Q / Alt-0140
ð Ctrl-B / Alt-0240	Ð Ctrl-A / Alt-0208	ł Ctrl-D / —	Ł Ctrl-C / Alt-0154	š Ctrl-F / Alt-0138	Š Ctrl-E / Alt-0255	ÿ Op-U Y / Alt-0253	ý Ctrl-H / Alt-0159	Ÿ Op-U Sh-Y / Alt-0221	Ý Ctrl-G / —	ž Ctrl-O / Alt-0254	Ž Ctrl-N / Alt-0222	þ Ctrl-L / —	Þ Ctrl-K / Alt-0170	ı Sh-Op-B / Alt-0186	ª Op-9 / —	º Op-0 / —	fi Sh-Op5 / —	fl Sh-Op-6 / —
¨ Sh-Op-U / Alt-0168	ˆ Sh-Op-I / Alt-0136	´ Sh-Op-E / Alt-0180	` ` / —	˜ Sh-Op-N / Alt-0152	˚ Op-K / —	¯ Sh-Op-, / Alt-0175	˘ Sh-Op-. / —	˙ Op-H / —	˝ Sh-Op-G / —	ˇ Sh-Op-T / —	¸ Sh-Op-Z / Alt-0184	˛ Sh-Op-X / —	£ Op-3 / Alt-0163	¥ Op-Y / Alt-0165	ƒ Op-F / Alt-0131	¢ Op-4 / Alt-0162	€ Sh-Op-2 / Alt-0164	∞ Op-5 / —
© Op-G / Alt-0169	® Op-R / Alt-0174	π Op-P / —	™ Op-2 / Alt-0153	/ Sh-Op-1 / —	‰ Sh-Op-R / Alt-0137	µ Op-M / Alt-0181	§ Op-6 / Alt-0167	† Op-T / Alt-0134	‡ Sh-Op-7 / Alt-0135	¶ Op-7 / Alt-0182	¦ Ctrl-[/ Alt-0166	¹ Ctrl-W / Alt-0185	² Ctrl-Z / Alt-0178	³ Ctrl-Y / Alt-0179	¼ Ctrl-V / Alt-0188	½ Ctrl-U / Alt-0189	¾ Ctrl-X / Alt-0190	 Sh-Op-K / —

US keyboard layout; other countries may vary. This chart is intended for general reference. Individual font layouts may vary.

 Characters generally not available in Windows.

 Characters generally not available in Macintosh OS.

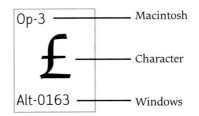

Op-3 ——— Macintosh

£ ——— Character

Alt-0163 ——— Windows

Appendix C: **Foundry Contacts**

Altered Ego Fonts
158 Cleveland Street
Elyria, OH 44035 USA
TEL 1-877-HEY-SOOY
TEL 440-322-5142
FAX 440-322-5108
http://www.alteredegofonts.com
info@alteredegofonts.com

Astigmatic One Eye
Typographic Institute
http://www.astigmatic.com
astigma@astigmatic.com

Carter & Cone Type Inc.
36-A Rice Street, Apartment 3
Cambridge, MA 02140 USA
TEL 909-244-5965
FAX 909-244-0946
www.carterandcone.com
carterm@concentric.net
cecone@earthlink.net

The Chank Company
PO Box 580736
Minneapolis, MN 55458 USA
TEL 1-877-GO-CHANK
TEL 612-782-2245
FAX 612-782-1958
http://www.chank.com
info@chank.com

Font Diner
1461 73rd Avenue NE, Suite #204
Fridley, MN USA
TEL 763-783-7860
http://www.fontdiner.com
diner@fontdiner.com

fontBoy
183 the Alameda
San Anselmo, CA 94960 USA
TEL 415-721-7921
FAX 415-721-7965
http://www.fontboy.com
info@fontboy.com

Fountain
Kornettsgatan 13B
SE-211 50 Malmö Sweden
http://www.fountain.nu
info@fountain.nu

GarageFonts
14605 Sturtevant Road
Silver Spring, MD 20905 USA
TEL 1-800-681-9375
TEL 301-879-6955
FAX 301-879-0606
http://www.garagefonts.com
webmaster@garagefonts.com

International House of Fonts
PO Box 770
Buffalo, NY 14213 USA
TEL 1-800-P22-5080
TEL 716-885-4490
FAX 716-885-4482
http://www.internationalhouseoffonts.com
ihof@p22.com

LettError
Molenstraat 67
2513 BJ The Hague
The Netherlands
TEL +31 70 360 5025
FAX +31 70 310 6685
erik@letterror.com
http://www.letterror.com

P22 type foundry
PO Box 770
Buffalo, NY 14213 USA
TEL 1-800-P22-5080
TEL 716-885-4490
FAX 716-885-4482
http://www.p22.com
info@p22.com

Psy/Ops Type Foundry
944 Market Street #504
San Francisco CA 94102 USA
TEL 1-888-PSY-FONE
http://www.psyops.com
rxc@psyops.com

SynFonts
2216 Cedar Forks Trace
Marietta, GA, 30062 USA
TEL 1-888-842-3065
TEL 402-968-0147
http://www.synfonts.com
don@synfonts.com

Test Pilot Collective
100 Scott Street #4
San Francisco, CA 94117 USA
TEL 415-626-5860
http://www.testpilotcollective.com
info@testpilotcollective.com

Typebox, LLC
PO Box 330446
San Francisco, CA 94133-0446 USA
http://www.typebox.com
joachim@typebox.com
mike@typebox.com

Typeco
PO Box 10661
Rochester, NY 14610 USA
TEL 585-230-1674
http://www.typeco.com
contact@typeco.com

Typodermic/Larabie
61 Wesley Ave.
Mississauga, ON
L5H 2M8 Canada
TEL 905-271-6587
http://www.typodermic.com
sales@typodermic.com

Typotheque
Zwaardstraat 16 (lokaal 0.11)
2584 TX The Hague
The Netherlands
TEL +31 70 322 6119
FAX +31 84 831 6741
http://www.typotheque.com
sales@typotheque.com

Appendix D: **Bibliography**

AGFA TYPOGRAPHY. *Type Reference Book for Postscript Users.* Agfa Typography, Ltd., Dublin, Ireland, 1994.

ALTSYS CORPORATION. *Type Terminology on the Desktop.* Altsys Corporation, Richardson, Texas, 1991.

BRINGHURST, ROBERT. *The Elements of Typographic Style,* 2nd edition. Hartley and Marks, Point Roberts, Washington, 1992.

LAWSON, ALEXANDER. *Anatomy of a Typeface.* Hamish Hamilton, London, England, 1992.

NESBITT, ALEXANDER. *The History and Technique of Lettering,* revised 1st edition. Dover Publications, Inc., New York, New York, 1957.

ROMANO, FRANK J., AND ROMANO, RICHARD M. *The GATF Encyclopedia of Graphic Communications.* Graphic Technical Arts Foundation Press, Pittsburgh, Pennsylvania, 1998.

SPIEKERMANN, ERIC, AND GINGER, E.M. *Stop Stealing Sheep and Find Out How Type Works.* Adobe Press, Mountain View, California, 1993.

Appendix E: **Further Reading**

CARTER, ROB, AND MEGGS, PHILLIP B. (CONTRIBUTOR). *Typographic Specimens: The Great Typefaces.* John Wiley & Sons, New York, New York, 1993.

CHICAGO EDITORIAL STAFF; GROSSMAN, JOHN (PREFACE). *Chicago Manual of Style: The Essential Guide for Writers, Editors and Publishers,* 14th edition. University of Chicago Press, Chicago, Illinois, 1993.

FRIEDL, FRIEDRICH; OTT, NICOLAUS; AND STEIN, BERNARD (EDITORS). *Typography: an Encyclopedic Survey of Type Design and Techniques Throughout History.* Black Dog and Leventhal Publishers, New York, New York, 1998.

GILL, ERIC. *An Essay on Typography.* David R. Godine, Publisher, Boston, Massachusetts, 1993.

GOUDY, FREDERIC W. *Typologia: Studies in Type Design and Type Making, with Comments on the Invention of Typography, the First Types, Legibility and Fine Printing.* University of California Press, Berkeley, California, 1976.

GRAPHIC ARTISTS GUILD. *Graphic Artist's Guild Handbook of Pricing & Ethical Guidelines,* 10th Edition. Graphic Artist's Guild, Inc., New York, New York, 2001.

HALEY, ALLAN. *Typographic Milestones.* John Wiley & Sons, New York, New York, 1997.

HELLER, STEVEN, AND FILI, LOUISE. *Typology: Type Design from the Victorian Era to the Digital Age.* Chronicle Books, San Francisco, California, 1999.

MCGREW, MAC. *American Metal Typefaces of the Twentieth Century,* 2nd edition. Oak Knoll Press, New Castle, Delaware, 1993.

MCLEAN, RUARI. *The Thames and Hudson Manual of Typography,* reprint edition. Thames & Hudson, London, England, 1992.

MOYE, STEPHEN. *Fontographer: Type by Design.* MIS: Press, New York, New York, 1995.

PRESTIANNI, JOHN (EDITOR). *Calligraphic Type Design in the Digital Age: An Exhibition in Honor of the Contributions of Hermann and Gudrun Zapf.* Gingko Press, Corte Madera, California, 2002.

SMEIJERS, FRED. *Counterpunch: Making Type in the Sixteenth Century, Designing Typefaces Now.* Hyphen Press, London, England, 1996.

STONE, SUMNER. *On Stone: The Art & Use of Typography on the Personal Computer.* Bedford Arts, San Francisco, California, 1991.

TRACY, WALTER. *Letters of Credit: A View of Type Design.* David R. Godine, Publisher, Boston, Massachusetts, 1986.

TSCHICHOLD, JAN. *The New Typography: A Handbook for Modern Designers.* University of California Press, Berkeley, California, 1995.

Appendix F: **Use of Fonts**

Use of Fonts

Fonts are creative, intellectual property, similar to designers' creative work or a proprietary business product. Since type seems so ubiquitous and fonts are so easy to share among computer users, the legal and moral issues of the simple process of using a font are often overlooked.

There are four good rules that guide ethical practice in font licensing:
• If you are using a font, whether it's on your computer or that of someone else, make sure you have a license to use the font.
• If you want to use a font that is not installed on your computer, you must ensure that you or your employer has a license to install the font on your computer, or else acquire a license to use it.
• If you have any questions about your font license, contact the foundry or supplier of the font. (If you do not know the foundry or supplier, almost any foundry or supplier can help you identify the source.)
• Don't lend or give a font to others to use. Your friends, clients and colleagues need to acquire the rights to use them. When it comes to licensing fonts, ethical practice makes sense legally and financially. Violating the terms of a license agreement puts the designer, the client and future business relationships at risk. An ethical approach to font use and font licenses is therefore both good business practice and good business.

Fonts are creative, intellectual property.

Typefaces are collections of letterforms. They endow written communications with a character or style, which ultimately represents the character or style of the originator of the communication, whether a corporation or an individual. Typefaces are the result of extensive research, study and experimentation, and for some designers, the creation of typefaces is a full-time occupation. The training and expertise required to develop a typeface qualifies the product as intellectual property and merits its protection under copyright law in many countries.

A font is the software that describes the characters in a typeface. Digital fonts, like any software, are intellectual property and may be subject to federal copyright and trademark laws.

You do not own a font. You license it for limited uses.

Fonts are not "bought." The right to reproduce them is licensed, and the license to use them states specific terms.

The right to use a font designed by someone else for any or all communications is acquired from the foundry that created the font and is granted in the form of an end-user license agreement, or EULA. Some foundries will allow a supplier to administer the license agreements for a font, but the agreement itself is always between the licensee and the foundry that created the font.

The terms of use described by an end-user license agreement vary from foundry to foundry and may vary depending on the scope of the desired use. Licenses usually grant permission for the licensee to install a given font on a certain number of computers. However, licenses can also describe use on printers, periods of exclusivity for custom typefaces and distribution rights. If you have questions about what you may or may not do with the font you are using, the best thing to do is to contact the foundry or supplier of the font.

You need permission to alter a font for use in your design.

Because the software that describes a typeface is automatically subject to copyright protection upon its creation, any version of the original font is considered a "derivative work" under copyright law. It is because the adaptation is derived from copyrighted software that describes the typeface that the revision should not be considered an authorized derivative work. It cannot be used for commercial purposes without violating the copyright.

Some font licenses allow the licensee to alter the characters in a font or to convert the font to other formats. Other foundries do not allow derivative works at all without permission. Therefore, many designers, when asked to create a derivative work, have made it standard ethical practice to get permission from the font designer before altering any font data.

If you need to find out who designed the font you want to alter, you may refer to the copyright information identified in software such as Adobe Type Manager. You may also contact the foundry or font supplier.

You cannot share a font with someone who does not have his or her own license to use it.

Font software may not be given or loaned to anyone who does not have a license to use it. Therefore, misuse or unauthorized copying of a font that belongs to a client or your employer is an infringement of the designer's rights and could subject you to legal action.

When the client is the "end user" of the license agreement, the designer may not take the font with him or her when the project is over, even though it may mean another license must be purchased for the next job.

You can embed a font in a file to have it viewed or printed by others.

A font may only be sent with a job to a service bureau, consultant or freelancer if the contractor has a license for the font or if the license agreement makes provision for it. When necessary, it is acceptable for font data to be embedded in file formats such as EPS and PDF for printing and previewing purposes.

This is an issue of ethics, respect and law.

There are tangible and intangible consequences of using a font without a license. If caught using a font without the proper license, the licensee will have to purchase the correct license for the font, and, in some cases, pay damages to the originating foundry. More importantly, the use of a font without the proper license could prevent a professional designer from being fully compensated.

It is the value of the intellectual property of a colleague that is ultimately at stake in the licensing of fonts. To purchase the proper license for a font, especially as a practicing design professional, is to recognize the value of a colleague's work, to respect the practice of another designer and to uphold the integrity of the design profession.

Appendix F

Use of Fonts
Copyright: © American Institute of Graphic Arts (AIGA) 2001
Editorial content: Allan Haley, et al, for AIGA
Reprinted with permission.

Use of Fonts is one topic in the AIGA business and ethics series, a range of publications dealing with ethical standards and practices for designers and their clients.

Appendix G: **Organizations**

American Institute of Graphic Arts (AIGA)
164 Fifth Avenue
New York, NY 10010 USA
TEL 212-807-1990
FAX 212-807-1799
http://www.aiga.org

American Printing History Association
P.O. Box 4922
Grand Central Station
New York, NY 10163-4922 USA
http://www.printinghistory.org

Association Typographique Internationale (ATypI)
Secretariat and Conference Office
10 Ridgeway Road
Redhill, Surrey
RH1 6PH UK
TEL +44 (0)1737-780-150
FAX +44 (0)1737-780-160
atypi@sharonirving.co.uk
http://www.atypi.org

Graphic Artists Guild, Inc.
90 John Street, Suite 403
New York, NY 10038-3202 USA
TEL 1-800-500-2672
TEL 212-791-3400
FAX 212-791-0333
info@gag.org
http://www.gag.org

The Society of Typographic Aficionados (SOTA)
PO Box 770, Dept. S
Buffalo, NY 14213 USA
TEL 716-885-4490
FAX 716-885-4482
info@typesociety.org
http://www.typesociety.org

Type Directors Club
60 East 42nd Street, Suite 721
New York, NY 10165-0721 USA
TEL 212-983-6042
FAX 212-983-6043
director@tdc.org
http://www.tdc.org

TypeRight
typeright@typeright.org
http://www.typeright.org

Appendix H: **Bonus Fonts**

Altered Ego	Mac PS & TT, PC PS & TT	American Spirit ▧☀✹☆○
Astigmatic	Mac PS & TT, PC PS & TT	CHARMILLE AOE
Astigmatic	Mac PS & TT, PC PS & TT	LoveSick AOE
Astigmatic	Mac PS & TT, PC PS & TT	NIGHTMARE AOE
Astigmatic	Mac PS & TT, PC PS & TT	Scrawn AOE
Astigmatic	Mac PS & TT, PC PS & TT	Sunspots AOE
Astigmatic	Mac PS & TT, PC PS & TT	TRANSPONDER AOE
Chank	Mac TT & PC TT only	FRIDAYLUCK
Chank	Mac TT & PC TT only	Patching Compound
Chank	Mac TT & PC TT only	SNIPPLE
Font Diner	Mac PS & TT, PC TT only	Schmookums
Font Diner	Mac PS & TT, PC TT only	Black Widow
Font Diner	Mac PS & TT, PC TT only	Fontdinerdotcom & Fontdinerdotcom Sparkly
Font Diner	Mac PS & TT, PC TT only	Fontdinerdotcom Loungy
Font Diner	Mac PS & TT, PC TT only	BOWL-O-RAMA
Fountain	Mac PS & TT, PC PS & TT	Eric sans
Fountain	Mac PS & TT, PC PS & TT	Eric sans italic
GarageFonts	Mac PS & TT, PC PS & TT	Sinsation
IHOF	Mac PS & TT, PC PS & TT	P22 Typewriter
IHOF	Mac PS & TT, PC PS & TT	Crap three dee
LettError	Mac PS, PC PS & TT only	how 3 can b typ
LettError	Mac PS, PC PS & TT only	many mar ny fa new par
P22 type foundry	Mac PS & TT, PC PS & TT	P22 Sinel
Psy/Ops	Mac PS, PC TT only	Faceplate Sans A Gauge
Psy/Ops	Mac PS, PC TT only	Faceplate Sans C Gauge
SynFonts	Mac PS & TT, PC TT only	Atomic Suck
SynFonts	Mac PS & TT, PC TT only	Stunned Leather Jackets
Test Pilot Collective	Mac PS, PC TT only	SCREWTOP REGULAR
Test Pilot Collective	Mac PS, PC TT only	SCREWTOP NEGATIVE
Typebox	Mac PS & TT, PC PS & TT	TX Manifesto
Typeco	Mac PS , PC TT only	Cypher7
Typodermic	Mac PS & TT, PC TT only	STRENUOUS 3D

The 33 indie fonts listed here are included on an unlocked Bonus Fonts CD-ROM located in a sealed package in the back of this book. The fonts are licensed from each contributing foundry for use solely by the owner of this book, and may only be used in accordance with the terms set forth in the respective End User License Agreements (EULA). Any further re-distribution or transfer of the license to use this software is strictly prohibited. Please consult the individual "read me" files and/or EULA files located in each foundry's directory.

By breaking the sealed package containing this CD-ROM, you are agreeing to be bound by the terms of the license agreement and limited warranty set forth by each foundry. If you do not agree to the terms of said agreements, please do not use these fonts.

Macintosh and Windows versions are included or available in PostScript and TrueType formats. Not all foundries may provide fonts in all formats/platforms on this CD-ROM.

P-Type Publications is not responsible for errors, omissions or technical problems inherent in the font software or in its accompanying documentation. Please contact the individual foundries for more information on licensing, upgrades or support.

Index

Legal Information

Acknowledgments

We'd like to express our appreciation to our friends and colleagues who assisted in the creation of *Indie Fonts*. Their support, hard work, and grace under pressure were essential to the production of this book.

Special thanks to our Project Manager, Carima El-Behairy, for taking care of business.

Many thanks to Jimy Chambers, Timothy J. Conroy, Allan Haley, Jonathan Jones, Barbara Peerson, and Natalie Swiatek.

Lastly, we'd like to acknowledge the efforts of the type designers we know, and those we have yet to meet. Your dedication to the art is admirable; please continue your good works.

The Editors

Colophon

This book was designed by James Grieshaber.

The text face is *Alisal,* designed by Matthew Carter from Carter & Cone.

The headlines and labeling are set in various weights of *Faceplate,* designed by Rod Cavazos from Psy/Ops.

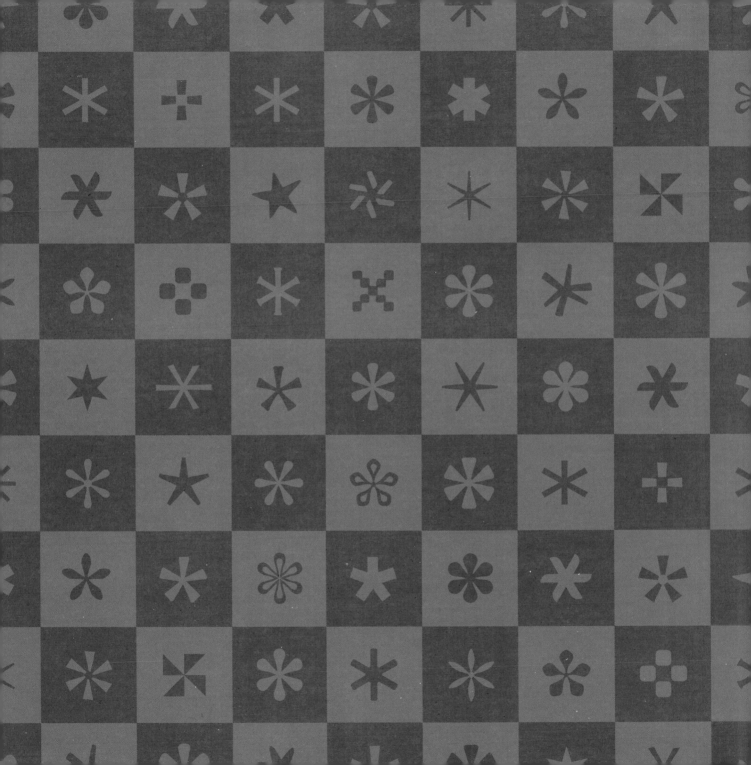